After the Czars and Commissars

After the Czars and Commissars

Journalism in Authoritarian Post-Soviet Central Asia

Edited by Eric Freedman and Richard Shafer

Michigan State University Press • East Lansing

☺ The paper used in this publication meets the minimum requirements of ANSI/NISO Z39.48-1992 (R 1997) (Permanence of Paper).

Michigan State University Press
East Lansing, Michigan 48823-5245
www.msupress.msu.edu

Printed and bound in the United States of America.

17   16   15   14   13   12   11   1   2   3   4   5   6   7   8   9   10

LIBRARY OF CONGRESS CATALOGING-IN-PUBLICATION DATA
After the czars and commissars : journalism in authoritarian post-Soviet Central Asia /
edited by Eric Freedman and Richard Shafer.
p. cm.—(Eurasian political economy and public policy studies series)
Includes bibliographical references.
ISBN 978-1-61186-005-4 (pbk. : alk. paper) 1. Journalism—Asia, Central. 2. Journalism—
Political aspects—Asia, Central. 3. Press and politics—Asia, Central. 4. Government and the
press—Asia, Central. 5. Freedom of the press—Asia, Central. 6. Mass media—Censorship—
Asia, Central. 7. Online journalism—Asia, Central. 8. Cyberspace—Government policy—Asia,
Central. 9. Reporters and reporting—Asia, Central. 10. Post-communism—Asia, Central. I.
Freedman, Eric. II. Shafer, Richard.
PN5449.C6A38 2011
079'.58—dc22
2010052157

COVER ART: Passers-by peruse newspapers on display in a park in Bishkek, Kyrgyzstan.
Photograph by Eric Freedman.
Cover design by Erin Kirk New
Book design by Charlie Sharp, Sharp Designs, Lansing, Michigan

g green
  press
  INITIATIVE   Michigan State University Press is a member of the Green Press Initiative
and is committed to developing and encouraging ecologically responsible
publishing practices. For more information about the Green Press Initiative and the use of
recycled paper in book publishing, please visit www.greenpressinitiative.com.

Visit Michigan State University Press on the World Wide Web at www.msupress.msu.edu.

To our wives, Mary Ann and Jill, who have explored Central Asia with us, and to the committed journalists, journalism students, press rights defenders, and journalism educators who struggle to establish free and effective press systems in their young Central Asian nations.

Contents

Theoretical Foundations for Researching the Roles of the Press in Today's Central Asia

Eric Freedman

Why should any man be allowed to buy a printing press and disseminate pernicious opinions calculated to embarrass the government?

—Vladimir Lenin, chairman, Council of People's Commissars, 1920

From the onset of Bolshevism through the era of postcommunist authoritarianism in Central Asia, a continuum of constraints has restricted the media. Lenin's candid acknowledgment that press freedom and public access to information could threaten his young regime was followed by Josef Stalin's acknowledgment of the power of a controlled press to sustain the Communist Party and its government. More recently, Turkmenistan president Gurbanguly Berdymukhammedov's made a bold—but patently false—assertion that "there was never in Turkmenistan any pressure on the press" (Krastev 2007), despite the government's reputation as one of the world's most repressitarian regimes. The techniques and mechanisms used to control the press during seven decades of communist rule—"total media control," as Krasnoboka characterizes it (2010, 320)—clearly have not fallen into disuse during two decades of independence. Rather, the new regimes have honed and refined those techniques and mechanisms to address new models of nationalism and new technologies.

Since the early 1960s, researchers in communication-related disciplines have investigated and theorized about the mass media's role in national development processes; their goals included designing and directing effective media systems to further development in underdeveloped nations and societies. However, mass media research since 1991 has largely ignored the five former Soviet republics in Central Asia—Kazakhstan, Kyrgyzstan, Tajikistan, Turkmenistan, and Uzbekistan—primarily due to the region's perceived remoteness and because it was off limits to most Western scholars during the Soviet period. Krasnoboka points out, "Despite the crucial role media played in the domestic and international affairs of the Soviet Union, international analysis of the Soviet media system was limited" (Krasnoboka 2010, 318). In addition, the Soviet Union obstructed critical media research by its own intellectuals. As a result, most critical scholars of Central Asian media are based in North America and Europe, and their studies are narrow and recent.

Kamalipour (2007, 24) says: "The Soviet theory assigned the media a role as collective agitator, propagandist and educator in the building of communism . . . The main principle was subordination of the media to the Communist Party—the only legitimate voice and agent of the working class." Although diversity existed within the Soviet press system, especially late in the Soviet era, the party at all levels directed journalistic practices, news selection, construction of opinion, and adherence to mandatory central planning. Journalists were told that to present information that failed to reinforce the state and party was to serve as an agent of reactionaries. Co-editor Richard Shafer's chapter, "Soviet Foundations of the Post-Independence Press in Central Asia," documents the integration of Marxism-Leninism with journalism professionalism and journalistic values.

The Soviet system hindered emergence of an above-ground post-independence press that could advance social change and economic development from a nationalist or local perspective. Thus the five Central Asian press systems are adapted from the Soviet model that was imposed during seventy years of communist dominance. The primary difference is the elimination of adherence to Marxist-Leninist ideology. For reporters and editors who worked in the Soviet press system, mandatory allegiance to the Communist Party was replaced with demands that they serve as agents of newly engineered and crudely fabricated nationalist ideologies and altered national histories directed to glorifying incumbent leaders.

With that background, this book is the first to gather and synthesize the research and analysis of mass media scholars from and beyond Central Asia to comprehensively explore overarching questions such as: What happens when concepts of press independence collide with concepts of authoritarianism and nationalism? What happens when Western ideas of "democratic journalism" clash with local and regional cultural, religious, social, and traditional values? How do journalists in Central Asia determine what stories to cover, how to cover them, and, as importantly, what stories not to cover? How does the lack of a non-state economic foundation cripple sustainability of independent news outlets?

Since most modern nations that gained independence from European and Japanese colonizers did so more than two decades before the Soviet Union imploded, media scholars have had a significantly longer period to analyze how press systems in other regions furthered or obstructed development. In examining the post-Soviet media scene, this book lays a research-grounded foundation for speculating about the future of the press in the region. Thus the collective authors are pioneers in analyzing contemporary Central Asian mass media and in constructing theories regarding the role of the press there. They do so through five interconnected themes: "Under the Commissars," "National Perspectives," "Trans-Regional Perspectives," "Journalism Education and Professionalism," and "New Media, New Frontiers."

Press Freedom and Democracy: Theoretical Underpinnings

There was early optimism that the demise of communist rule and the Soviet empire would lead to a rapid transition toward democracy—including press freedom. Such optimism failed to become reality (Ro'i 2004). Today these five countries form a political stage with few democratic institutions and weak, crippled civil society. Their leaders have used and continue to use a variety of techniques to legitimize repressitarian rule, including direct and proxy control of the press. Other methods include suppression of individual and collective rights—political, religious, and speech—exercise of the coercive power of the state, maintenance of extensive bureaucracies in the Soviet tradition, and strong centralized regulation of the economy (Matveeva 2009). Outright censorship, economic control of mass media outlets, and expectations that the media will propagate official ideology persist. So do policies that reinforce the duty of journalists as principal servants of regimes and the official ideology they construct. Wholly missing is a tradition of journalistic objectivity—a concept anathema to the Soviet thinking that guided Central Asian journalism for so long.

The interrelationship between press freedom and democratic governance is long established. In 1831, when "the press" meant newspapers, an aristocratic young French political thinker named Alexis de Tocqueville traveled with a companion for nine months across the United States. Based on his travels, observations, and interviews, Tocqueville wrote a study of the young country's institutions and people, *Democracy in America*. In it, he observed that the press makes political life circulate in all sections of this vast territory. Its eye, always open, constantly lays bare the secret springs of politics and forces public men to come in turn to appear before the court of opinion. It rallies interests around certain doctrines and formulates the creeds of the parties; through it they speak to each other without seeing each other and understand each other without being put into contact. When a large number of organs of the press come to advance along the same track, their influence becomes almost irresistible in the long term, and public opinion, struck always from the same side, ends by yielding under their blows. (2000, 178)

Interestingly, Tocqueville found himself in a country of ethnically and religiously diverse peoples, unlike his own France but much like Central Asia now. He wrote, for instance, of its "innumerable multitude of sects" (2000, 278). Thus the study of ethnic media reported in Olivier Ferrando's chapter on the Ferghana Valley, "Ethnic Minorities and the Media in Central Asia," would have resonated with that long-ago visitor to the United States.

Freedom of the press remains crucial to participatory government. The experiences of Eastern and Central Europe in the first decade after the fall of the Berlin Wall show how, as Rubin puts it, "the evolution of print and electronic media has been central to the larger process of political and cultural restructuring. Struggles for independent journalism are at once both symbolic of democratic aspirations and central to the building of the post-communist governments" (1999, 60).

Here is how Altschull explains that interdependence: With the basic assumption of democracy that the people rule, "the decisions made by the people in the voting booths are based on the information made available to them. That information is provided primarily by the news media. Hence, the news media are indispensable to the survival of democracy . . . Hence, for a society to be free, the flow of information to the citizens must come from news media that are free" (1995, 5). Therefore, citizens in democracies expect access to their choice of print and broadcast media—and in these times, online and other forms of new media—for accurate and objective political information (McNair 2000). They also expect journalists to remain relatively independent of their governments and to feel free to report to their publics. Under that concept a circle inexorably links the right of citizens to receive information with the right of journalists to freely report information. Authoritarian regimes reject that concept, preferring instead to "control and manipulate their media to serve better the goals of the state" (Hachten and Scotton 2007, xxi).

In this context, the press fulfills multiple roles and should not be regarded as a mere uncritical conduit for information. Acting as agents of the public in a public sphere, journalists serve as identifiers of their audiences; interrogators of news sources; seekers of a diversity of viewpoints and facts; sounding boards for divergent opinions; interpreters of what they see, hear, and read; commentators on those interpretations; facilitators of access to information held by governments, businesses, nongovernmental organizations (NGOs), and other repositories; and societally sanctioned (although not always popular) cynics, skeptics, and critics. Perhaps the power of the press to serve as an agent of political change and transformation toward democracy is most clear when its activities help topple an authoritarian regime and move that country closer to democracy, as occurred in Ukraine's 2004–05 Orange Revolution, in which widespread public protests led to the nullification of fraudulent elections and the reelection defeat of autocratic Prime Minister Viktor Yanukovych (Kartoshkina, Shafer, and Freedman 2007).

That is not to say that the Ukraine experience and any expectations it created are transferrable to Central Asia, given significant historic, cultural, demographic, and geographic differences between the Central Asian republics and most other ex-constituents of the Soviet Union. Unlike the Baltic countries of Latvia, Lithuania, and Estonia, for example, Central Asia has never bordered on any democratic nation; thus the Baltic republics had comparatively easier access to nearby independent media, as well as contact through cross-border trade and family visits. Writing about postcommunist transitions in Eastern and Central Europe, Mills (1999, 124) notes that speaking broadly, the degree of media change in that region coincided with the "degree of isolation before the collapse of communism." The westernmost countries, such as Czechoslovakia, Hungary, and Poland, made the most progress toward democratic media and press-supportive economic and political institutions, while more isolated newly independent states, including Albania, Romania, and those in Central Asia, lagged.

More important than geography, the five multiethnic Central Asia republics never had a sustained independent existence before 1991, unlike the Caucasus nations of Armenia, Azerbaijan, and Georgia, or Ukraine, Belarus, and the Baltic states. The closest the region came was after World War I with a brief (1917–23) non-Soviet–type democratic experience for some peoples of Central Asia. Those pre-Soviet autonomous governments and states were unable to build a nonauthoritarian political culture. That is because the Soviets after 1925 successfully wiped out memories of these short-lived entities from the minds of later generations of Central Asians, who underwent drastic national identity development in the new Soviet republics.

Therefore, the leaders of the nascent regimes in Central Asia swiftly transformed the mass media from tools to build the Communist Party to tools to build national identity and a sense of statehood. As an illustration, Tajikistan president Emomali Rakhmonov once sent a Tajik Press Day message to a gathering of journalists, saying, "We are grateful to you for your high sense of responsibility and worthy contribution in building civil society" (Khamadov 2002, 1).

Kahlid writes:

> They have all acted to "nationalize" their states—that is, to make the states ostensibly the instruments of the will of the nation, the nation being the ethnonational group from which each country takes its name. Each state presents itself as the result of centuries-long striving of its nation to unite and gain political independence, a process that was rudely interrupted by Russian conquest and then the continuation, ostensibly, of Russian rule under the Soviet guise. (2007, 130)

That pattern certainly is not unique to Central Asia and has proven a challenge in other postcolonial realms, including Africa, where post-independence leaders in the 1960s and 1970s demanded that journalists help build the new nations and unite diverse ethnic groups. In Central Asia the ability of rulers to use the mass media to "sell" national pride and identity has reinforced their ability to retain power with little or no fear of ouster through free and fair elections as happened elsewhere in the post-Soviet Eastern bloc (Bunce and Wolchik 2009). They also wield the domestic press as what Stalin would have considered a sharp, strong weapon to rebuff foreign critiques of their human rights policies, deeply flawed elections, and corruption, as occurred in Uzbekistan after the 2005 violence in Andijan, when authorities brutally suppressed protestors, causing at least 187 deaths, and possibly several thousand. Angered by adverse media coverage of the government's handling of the situation, the regime cracked down further on press rights, and some journalists went into self-imposed exile. "Delegitimisation of Western criticism has found a cultural resonance because it reflects shared beliefs of sovereignty and fatigue with being lectured by outsiders" (Matveeva 2009, 1119).

Noting that the objectivity concept long asserted in Western journalism has itself changed substantially in recent years, Waisbord cautions, "Given their persistent troubles to match prevailing expectations, it seems harder than in the past to submit Anglo-American journalism in toto as the virtuous model to be followed elsewhere" (2007, 116). We concur that no single "Western" model of a free press exists and certainly would not argue that any one model could be or should be viewed as a template. To the contrary, we believe that any viable and sustainable national press system must take into account political, cultural, economic, and historic realities and traditions; even so, we believe that a viable and sustainable national press system should adhere to fundamental journalistic values of fairness, balance, accuracy, and professional ethics.

There is no consensus among scholars on how to classify press systems. The long-popular but now antiquated Cold War–era quadpartite model of Siebert and his colleagues (1963) used four press theories: authoritarian, libertarian, communist, and social responsibility. More recently, some scholars such as McKenzie (2006) have placed media systems into six philosophies: authoritarian, libertarian, communist, social responsibility, developmental, and democratic-participant. For Central Asian media specifically, Juraev (2002) devised a tripartite analysis: "authoritarian-democratic" in Kazakhstan and Kyrgyzstan, with their authoritarian regimes that show some signs of press freedom; "post-conflict" in Tajikistan, where self-censorship is motivated in part by the desire to avert another internal conflict or civil war; and "total control" in Uzbekistan and Turkmenistan.

When it comes to press systems that, at least partly, incorporate the concept that governments should not interfere with how news is collected and disseminated, the categorizations from Hachten and Scotton (2007) are illustrative. Variables include the presence or absence of government financial support; of a sense of media "social responsibility" where public service may outweigh profits; of state economic intervention in ownership and management; and of democratic participation, where the media exists principally for the public good and must provide access to individuals and minority groups. Yet all of these categorizations rest on a foundational belief that a "marketplace of ideas" will strengthen the polity by empowering citizens to make informed decisions about policies and leaders and to participate meaningfully and knowledgeably in their own governance.

The idea of an objective press in any of these formats sharply contrasts with Marxism-Leninism—the predecessor and, in many ways, still the shaper of Central Asia's ongoing authoritarianism—and its view of the press as an activist agent of the Communist Party and later of the state. In 1901, a decade and a half before the Bolshevik Revolution, Lenin wrote: "A newspaper is not only a collective propagandist and a collective agitator: It is also a collective organizer ... With the aid of the newspaper, and through it, a permanent organization will naturally take shape that will . . . train its members to follow political events carefully, appraise their significance and their effect on the various strata of the population, and develop effective means for the revolutionary party to influence those events" (Altschull 1995, 211). With this pronouncement of Lenin's interpretation of the mission and duty of the press, we can see the actual impact of media systems that devoted seventy years as "collective propagandist" for the Communist Party and twenty more as "collective propagandist" for the post-Soviet autocrats. Today, Central Asia is hostile terrain for independent media and for other essential institutions of democratic and transparent governance, including human rights and press rights defenders and advocacy groups. Those who endeavor to practice journalism as an ethical profession in the region do so at great personal peril. The absence of press freedom impairs citizens' informed participation in public affairs; blocks progress toward democratization; shields autocratic rulers and their allies from criticism while reinforcing their tenure; allows corruption, nepotism, and favoritism to prosper; and impedes economic development and economic gains for the vast majority of the population in a strategic region. Meanwhile, international broadcasters attempt to fill some of the informational gap through the airwaves and Internet, as described in Navbahor Imamova's chapter, "International Broadcasting to Uzbekistan: Does It Still Matter?"

The State of the Media in Central Asia

Despite undisguised and extensive press controls in Central Asia, all five nations tout a commitment to press freedom and the ideal of an informed society. This charade makes sense in international diplomatic and economic arenas because of the influence of external media watchdog agencies and pressures from economically powerful governments that champion human rights, civil society, and democratic institutions in former communist nations.

Possible consequences of negative scores from media watch organizations include jeopardizing foreign aid and development loans from wealthy nations and multinational development agencies. Democratic-sounding provisions in Central Asian national constitutions have largely been negated or countered by additions and amendments that render such guarantees impotent. In addition, officials at local and national levels simply ignore such provisions. For example, Article 29 of the constitution of Uzbekistan (2009) promises:

> Everyone shall be guaranteed freedom of thought, speech and convictions. Everyone shall have the right to seek, obtain and disseminate any information, except that which is directed against the existing constitutional system and in some other instances specified by law.
>
> Freedom of opinion and its expression may be restricted by law if any state or other secret is involved.

Yet Uzbekistan ranks among the worst in the world for press freedom. For instance, in 2010 photojournalist and documentary filmmaker Umida Akhmedova was convicted of libel and insulting the Uzbek people for publishing photographs of village life and producing a documentary about premarital sex. The same year, police in Andijan jailed independent journalist Aleksei Volosevich for three days and seized his film and audio recorder because he filmed refugees fleeing from ethnic violence in nearby Kyrgyzstan.

Such incidents are by no means limited to Uzbekistan. Also in 2010, correspondent Igor Larra of the independent weekly *Svoboda Slova* (Freedom of Speech) was assaulted while covering a strike by employees of the national oil producer KazMunayGas. And in Kyrgyzstan, judges suspended three newspapers, *Forum*, *Achyk Sayasat* (Open Politics), and *Nazar* (Viewpoint).

Thus reality proves that constitutional promises of democracy, including an independent press—a keystone for civil society—remain unfulfilled in any of the five Central Asian countries since the Soviet Union imploded in 1991. National systems of authoritarian rule have succeeded communist authoritarianism, while instruments of democratization, including independent and opposition media, have been controlled, suppressed, punished, and, in many instances, outlawed. Rulers of these republics may claim that their ultimate aim is to establish democracy, and their constitutions purport to guarantee press freedom, free speech, and other democratic rights, but the gap between theory and practice is huge.

Nowhere is the stillborn nature of democracy-building in Central Asia clearer than in the state of press constraints, despite the promotion by foreign NGOs and multinational agencies of independent media as part of the broad development of civil society. "A trusted, respected, and independent mass media system is a major indicator of a country's development of democracy and civil society" (Freedman 2009, 844). And authoritarian regimes understand this, as evidenced by what Puddington (2007, 125) calls their "pushback" against press rights defenders and advocates. Human rights organizations consistently rate these countries among the most repressive regimes on the globe, whether the measure is of freedom broadly—as do the Freedom House (2010a) *Freedom in the World* reports—or specifically of the press, as do the Freedom House (2009) *Freedom of the Press* reports table 1). Other organizations making similar assessments of the media environment in Central Asia include the International Research and Exchanges Board and Reporters sans Frontieres (Reporters without Borders).

Longitudinal studies in *Nations in Transit* (Freedom House 2010b) track non-media variables related to democratization, national and local democratic governance, civil society, judicial framework and independence, electoral processes,

TABLE 1. FREEDOM INDICES FOR CENTRAL ASIA REPUBLICS

	TAJIKISTAN	UZBEKISTAN	KYRGYZSTAN	TURKMENISTAN	KAZAKHSTAN
Indicators					
Overall Freedom Index*	Not free	Not free	Not free	Not free	Not free
Press Freedom*	Not free	Not free	Not free	Not free	Not free
Variables					
Muslim population†	90%	88%	75%	89%	47%
Russian population†	1.10%	5.50%	12.50%	4%	30%
GDP per capita*	$1,870	$2,660	$2,150	$6,130	$9,720
Internet penetration rate‡	9.30%	16.80%	39.80%	1.60%	34.30%

SOURCE: *Freedom House, 2010; †U.S. Central Intelligence Agency, 2010; ‡Internet World Stats, 2010.

and corruption, as well as the presence of independent media. In 2010, for example, the organization found slightly improved media conditions in Tajikistan but deteriorating conditions in Kyrgyzstan and Kazakhstan; the situation remained abysmally unchanged in Uzbekistan and Turkmenistan (table 2). The media aspect of the ratings is based on legal protections for press freedom; protection of journalists from victimization; state opposition to onerous defamation laws and excessive legal penalties; editorial independence; diverse selection of sources of information; the degree of private ownership and lack of excessive ownership concentration; financial viability of private media; private control of newspaper distribution; viable professional organizations for journalists; and access to a diversity of opinions on the Internet without government controls.

Yet it is not enough to look solely at press rights or, more generally, at human

TABLE 2. MEDIA INDEPENDENCE RATINGS IN CENTRAL ASIA, 1999–2000 THROUGH 2010

	1999–2000	2001	2002	2003	2004	2005	2006	2007	2008	2009	2010
Kazakhstan	5.5	6	6	6.25	6.5	6.5	6.75	6.75	6.75	6.5	6.75
Kyrgyzstan	5	5	5.75	6	6	5.75	5.75	5.75	6	6.25	6.5
Tajikistan	5.75	5.5	5.75	5.75	5.75	6	6.25	6.25	6	6	5.75
Turkmenistan	7	7	7	7	7	7	7	7	7	7	7
Uzbekistan	6.5	6.75	6.75	6.75	6.75	6.75	7	7	7	7	7

Scale of 1 to 7, with 1 representing the highest and 7 the lowest level of democratic progress
SOURCE: Freedom House, Nations in Transit, 2010.

rights. "Democratic journalism, no matter its specifics, is not viable as long as states are unable to meet some of its key obligations" (Waisbord 2007, 116). Thus it is also essential to consider other metrics of instability in the region. They include state cohesion and performance, as measured in the Fund for Peace and *Foreign Policy* Failed States Index (2010) and corruption, as gauged in Transparency International's Corruption Perceptions Index (2009). The Failed States Index places Uzbekistan in the least sustainable, or "Alert," category. The other four republics are classified in the "Warning" category, the second-most at risk, based on twelve social, economic, and political indicators. One such indicator is "suspension or arbitrary application of the rule of law and widespread violation of human rights, including harassment of the press." With New Zealand ranked at 1 and Somalia ranked 180 (at the bottom), the Corruption Perceptions Index places Kazakhstan at 120, Tajikistan at 158, Kyrgyzstan at 162, Turkmenistan at 168, and Uzbekistan at 174.

Prospects for achieving a free, economically sustainable, ethically conscious, and publicly credible press remain dim for the foreseeable future. Even moments of hope have proven transitory. For example, an anticipated and hoped-for surge of participatory government and media freedom in Kyrgyzstan after the 2005 Tulip Revolution fizzled and died as the new regime of Kurmanbek Bakiyev recreated the pervasive corruption, favoritism, autocracy, and distaste for dissent that marked the ousted regime of Askar Akayev. Bakiyev, in turn, was ousted in an April 2010 coup, but it is too soon to gauge the new leadership's commitment to press freedom.

The intersection of regimes, professional journalists, and university-level journalism educators is at the heart of several chapters of this book. Olivia Allison's "Loyalty in the New Authoritarian Model: Journalistic Rights and Duties in Central Asian Media Law" asks whether the principle of loyalty remains central in media law and its enforcement and assesses the role of loyalty in official restraints on the media. Co-editor Eric Freedman's chapter, "Journalists at Risk: The Human Impact of Press Constraints," goes beyond the formalities of statutes and constitutions to spotlight high-profile cases of assassination, assault, disappearance, self-exile, and arrest. In addition to often-insurmountable forms of overt censorship, journalists who remain well-intentioned, ethical, and professionally committed routinely experience unavoidable pressures to engage in self-censorship, as illustrated by Peter Gross and Timothy Kenny in "Journalistic Self-Censorship and the Tajik Press in the Context of Central Asia." Also on point are studies by Gregory Pitts—"Professionalism among Journalists in Kyrgyzstan," which considers how journalists regard their own careers—and by Maureen J. Nemecek, Stan Ketterer, Galiya Ibrayeva, and Stanislav Los—"Journalism Education and Professional Training in Kazakhstan: From the Soviet Era to Independence," which puts the preparation of aspiring journalists into a national historical context.

In addition, journalists in the region are susceptible to multiple forms of harassment, persuasive threats, and actual harm. Other forces of less direct censorship include job insecurity, financial sanctions, intimidation through tax audits, bribery, license revocation, imprisonment, exile, and even assassination, for writing and reporting the facts. With such consequences for professional and socially responsible journalistic practices, it is little surprise that journalists have found it difficult to transition from the reactionary and defensive practices necessary for survival under a Soviet press system that rewarded loyalty and conformity while punishing creativity and objectively adversarial forms of reporting.

Yet another obstacle to press freedom is the way regimes use the threat of terrorism—real or hyped—to shape media coverage and public opinion, as laid out in the chapter "Hizb ut-Tahrir in Kyrgyzstan as Presented in *Vecherniy Bishkek*: A Radical Islamist Organization through the Eyes of Kyrgyz Journalists" by Irina Wolf.

New technologies offer opportunities for expanded press influence, yet also provide mechanisms for additional governmental controls. "Blogging Down the Dictator? The Kyrgyz Revolution and Samizdat Web Sites" by Svetlana V. Kulikova and David D. Perlmutter fits the first category in its discussion of the role an advocacy blog played in the run-up to the Tulip Revolution. Two other chapters, however, focus on authoritarian measures that rein in the ability of the Internet to provide access to independent voices: "The Future of Internet Media in Uzbekistan: Transformation from State Censorship to Monitoring of Information Space since Independence" by Zhanna Hördegen and "Internet Libel Law and Freedom of Expression in Tajikistan" by Kristine Kohlmeier and Navruz Nekbakhtshoev.

The condition of the media environment is even direr in Turkmenistan than elsewhere in the region. Luca Anceschi's chapter, "Reinforcing Authoritarianism through Media Control: The Case of Post-Soviet Turkmenistan," which delves into a press system without any pretense of independence before and after the 2006 death of President-for-Life Saparmurat Niyazov. Even if mass media in Central Asia were free from censorship and other forms of direct and indirect control over content, they lack commercial or other forms of sustained economic support. In her chapter, "Oligarchs and Ownership: The Role of Financial-Industrial Groups in Controlling Kazakhstan's 'Independent' Media," Barbara Junisbai illustrates new and creative methods of economic control that help to ensure established elites can manipulate the media to maintain their own wealth and power in the region's most affluent country.

Conclusion

Even in this broad an examination of Central Asia's media scene since independence, there are limitations on the amount of material that a single volume can cover. As such, there are topics we had no space to include, such as the economics of private and state media, the impact of Russian and other foreign ownership of mass media outlets, privatization of state-owned media, the applicability of ethics codes and ethical standards, successes and failures of foreign media-support NGOs, and comparisons between press systems in Central Asia and other postcommunist states, such as those in the Caucasus and Eastern and Central Europe.

Our aim is to provide readers with insights, knowledge, and context to better understand the complexities of the press—and of governance, nation building and national identity, and public policies—in a strategically important but remote and little-known region of the globe. Both common and country-specific obstacles exist that confront journalists and their news outlets, NGOs, opposition political groups, human and press rights defenders, government reform advocates, journalism educators and trainers, and multinational institutions in Central Asia. Many such obstacles are mirrored by situations in other parts of the world where comparatively young countries continue to wrestle with ways to move forward from their authoritarian and colonial pasts.

Why does all this matter? For Central Asians, of course, the answer is evident: because their press—through interaction with other formal and informal societal institutions—can serve as either an agent of change or an impediment to change. The press can play those roles for better or for worse, depending on individual perspective. Beyond these five countries in our increasingly globalized world, severe restraints on transparent, open, and participatory governance and active discouragement of a fully informed citizenry carry broad implications for security, poverty alleviation, political extremism, employment and migration, environmental and public health safeguards, trade and transportation, energy, personal and political rights, and technological evolution in other countries and regions, both neighboring and distant.

In October 1917 Vladimir Lenin signed the Decree on the Press that authorized "temporary and extraordinary measures to stop the flow of dirt and slander." Then amid the Bolshevik Revolution, little could he predict not only that communism would fail, but also that parallel "temporary and extraordinary measures" would survive so far from Moscow or St. Petersburg two decades after its fall.

REFERENCES

Altschull, J. Herbert. 1995. *Agents of Power: The Media and Public Policy.* White Plains, NY: Longman.

Bunce, Valerie J., and Sharon L. Wolchik. 2009. "Postcommunist Ambiguities." *Journal of Democracy* 10(3): 93–107.

Constitution of Uzbekistan. 2009. Governmental Portal of the Republic of Uzbekistan. Www.gov.uz/en/constitution.

Freedman, Eric. 2009. "When a Democratic Revolution Isn't Democratic or Revolutionary." *Journalism* 10(6): 843–61.

Freedom House. 2009. *Freedom of the Press.* Http://freedomhouse.org/template. cfm?page=251&year=2009.

———. 2010a. *Freedom in the World.* Http://www.freedomhouse.org/template.cfm?page= 363&year=2010.

———. 20010b. *Nations in Transit 2010.* Www.freedomhouse.org/template.cfm?page=551.

Fund for Peace and *Foreign Policy.* 2010. "Failed States Index 2010." Www.fundforpeace.org/ web/index.php?option=com_content&task=view&id=452&Itemid=900.

Hachten, William A., and James F. Scotton. 2007. *The World News Prism: Global Information in a Satellite Age,* 7th ed. Malden, MA: Blackwell.

Juraev, Alisher. 2002. "The Uzbek Mass Media Model: Analysis, Opinions, Problems." *Central Asia and the Caucasus* 13(1): 130–38.

Kamalipour, Yahya R. 2007. *Global Communication,* 2nd ed. Belmont, CA: Thompson Wadsworth.

Kartoshkina, Yuliya, Richard Shafer, and Eric Freedman. 2007. "The Ukrainian Press as an Agent of Social Change through the Soviet Era, Independence, and the Orange Revolution." *Communication and Social Change* 1: 4–21.

Khalid, Adeeb. 2007. *Islam after Communism: Religion and Politics in Central Asia.* Berkeley: University of California Press.

Khamadov, Sulton. 2002. "90 Years of History: Tajik Press Now and Then." *Media Insight Central Asia* 24. Www.cimera.org/files/camel/en/24e/MICA24E-Khamadov.pdf.

Krasnoboka, Natalya. 2010. "Between the Rejected Past and an Uncertain Future: Russian Media Studies at a Crossroads." In *Communication Yearbook 34,* ed. Charles T. Salmon. New York: Routledge, 317–345.

Krastev, Nikola. 2007. "Turkmenistan: President Says Press, NGOs Operate Freely." Radio Free Europe/Radio Liberty. 24 September. Www.rferl.org/content/article/1078780.html.

Matveeva, Anna. 2009. "Legitimising Central Asian Authoritarianism: Political Manipulation and Symbolic Power." *Europe-Asia Studies* 61(7): 1095–121.

McKenzie, Robert. 2006. *Comparing Media from Around the World.* Boston: Pearson.

McNair, Brian. 2000. *Journalism and Democracy: An Evaluation of the Political Public Sphere.* London: Routledge.

Mills, Dean. 1999. "Post-1989 Journalism in the Absence of Democratic Traditions." In *Eastern European Journalism: Before, During and after Communism,*" ed. Jerome Aumente, Peter Gross, Ray Hiebert, Owen V. Johnson, and Dean Mills, 123–45. Cresskill, NJ: Hampton Press.

Puddington, Arch. 2007. "The Pushback against Democracy." *Journal of Democracy* 18(2): 125–37.

Ro'i, Yaacov. 2004. *Democracy and Pluralism in Muslim Eurasia.* New York: Frank Cass.

Rubin, Joel. 1999. "Transitions: A Regional Summary." *Media Studies Journal* 13(3): 60–69.

Siebert, Frederick S., Theodore Peterson, and Wilbur Schramm. 1963. *Four Theories of the Press.* Urbana: University of Illinois Press.

Tocqueville, Alexis de. 2000. *Democracy in America,* vol. 1, part 2, ed. Henry C. Mansfield and Delba Winthrop. Chicago: University of Chicago Press.

Transparency International. 2009. "Corruption Perceptions Index." Www.transparency.org/policy_research/surveys_indices/cpi/2009.

Waisbord, Silvio. 2007. "Democratic Journalism and 'Statelessness.'" *Political Communication* 24:115–29.

PART 1

Under the Commissars

Soviet Foundations of the Post-Independence Press in Central Asia

Richard Shafer

T hroughout the Soviet Union, the press was assigned the role of propagandist, collective agitator, and educator, to build the Communist Party and to further Marxist-Leninist ideology. The guiding principle was the media's subordination to the party, the single voice and agent of the working class. Although the press did not favor free expression, it did push for a positive role for itself in society and acted as an agent of international propaganda for the Soviet system and for the USSR as a nation.

The region known as Central Asia today was for centuries referred to as Turkestan. Before effective Russian colonization and control beginning in the 1860s, it was a vast amorphous territory, comprised of khanates and puppet regimes, with ambiguous borders, unreliable tribal loyalties, multiethnic feuds, and foreign power grabs. In his memoir of Turkestan under the Bolsheviks in 1918–19, British secret agent F. M. Bailey (1946, 64) characterized the writers of major newspaper articles as "ignorant men with little knowledge of history or geography. The writer would take a few facts from an out-of-date book of reference, cut out what did not suit his argument, distort the rest so that it did, and add a few rhetorical expressions and slogans." Bailey also described a newspaper that dared criticize the new commissars, saying, "It was immediately repressed and possession of a copy was severely punished. Needless to say the paper which optimistically had been numbered 'one' never got beyond the first copy" (65).

Certainly, the concept of censorship in Central Asia predated the imposition of communism there. Khalid notes that there were no printing presses in the khanates at the time of the Russian conquest between 1864 and 1876, but that a local print trade sprung up during the era of imperial Russian rule, including an official organ launched in 1870 and printed in Arabic, *Turkistan Wilayatining Gazeti* (Turkestan Gazette). Under the czars, Khalid writes, "The Russian authorities had the political power to control the output of the presses through licensing and censorship, and the general poverty of the agrarian economy inhibited the investment needed to operate a printing press" (1994, 188). And ownership of printing presses rested mainly in the hands of Russians—not Central Asians— because they were more likely to have the financial resources and the political connections necessary to operate legally.

An historical analysis of the evolution of the early Soviet press discloses resistance among many professional journalists to serving as government agents for planned social change. That role ran counter to an international professional ethic advocating that journalists be merely observers and recorders, casting aside ideologies and political biases in favor of fair, balanced, and accurate reporting. Whether resistance to near-total control over journalists failed or succeeded is difficult to ascertain because of the paucity of objective studies of the Soviet press and because of the heavy press controls, arrests, and censorship that reached their height in the Stalinist purges of the late 1930s.

Although the structures of the Soviet system and the communist ideology that was its foundation have been dismantled or diminished since independence, these structures are not wholly erased in the now-separate republics of the former USSR (Freedman and Shafer 2003). Components, especially interpretive and persuasive reporting practices, survive and have been adapted to nation rebuilding, creation of national identities, and governmental controls. Plausibly, one principal reason such practices linger is that the pre-independence model includes some practical applications, conventions, and functions that remain useful to the press systems of post-Soviet societies that have yet to make a full transition to being commercially supported and committed to Western news values and the ideal of "objective," fact-based reporting.

Efforts to Replace the Soviet Press System with the Western-Based Model

Western governmental agencies, international organizations, development foundations, and donor organizations regard "democratic journalism" as a tool for liberalizing authoritarian Central Asian regimes and for helping to contain and combat religious fundamentalism and anti-Western elements in the region and elsewhere in the former Soviet Union. Democratic journalism has become synonymous with Western-style journalism and is viewed as dedicated to extending democracy and free market economics worldwide. Since the Soviet Union collapsed in 1991, democratic journalism has been exported to its former republics in the form of seminars and workshops that generally emphasize traditional U.S. news values such as impact, conflict, novelty, prominence, proximity, and timeliness. These news values are often touted as alternatives to those based on Soviet-era conventions, policies, and ideology under a system in which journalism training was directed at preparing professionals for propaganda-oriented careers and membership in the Communist Party.

The two key questions then become: How did seven decades of Soviet journalism philosophy and practice form the foundation for contemporary Central Asian journalism philosophy and practice? And how does that foundation continue to conflict with widespread adoption of independent journalism in which professionals owe their duty to readers, viewers, and listeners rather than to the state?

Western trainers in Central Asian and other postcommunist nations rarely consider the relevance of preexisting, Soviet-shaped news values and conventions. At the same time, these trainers heavily advocate for the uncritical adoption of Western journalism conventions, such as those inherent in the "inverted pyramid" style of reporting and writing. Training periods are often limited to a few days or weeks. Thus, alternative theories and reporting methods, such as those related to development communication or public journalism, are given little attention, even if elements of those alternative journalistic models may be useful to the press in Central Asia.

Democratic journalism trainers are involved in conveying practical content such as skills related to interviewing, generating story ideas, lead writing, source identification, and using quotes. They are also instructed in effective transitions, attribution of information, balancing sources, alternative lead styles, editing techniques, and other skills that are standard in U.S. and Western European media writing and reporting courses and textbooks.

According to Miller (2002), "The notion seems to be that these occupational practices embody qualities like objectivity, facticity, and disinterestedness, that add up to professionalism, which itself contributes to a watchdog relationship to state institutions that, in the end, produces a knowledgeable citizenry able to govern itself." Thus democratic journalism seminars and workshops in Central Asia have been primarily concerned with news gathering and reporting based on the journalistic conventions of mainstream and commercial newspapers and broadcasters in the United States. Of course, variations of these conventions are found in the presses of other democratic countries, such as the United Kingdom, Canada, Australia, the Philippines, India, and Japan, and in emerging democracies elsewhere in Asia, South America, Europe, and Africa. The United States government and American- and Western European–funded foundations are the largest sponsors of such trainings in Central Asia.

Although all journalists gather and process information for their audiences, the Soviet model in place from about 1922 to 1991 provided greater license for journalists to be opinionated and interpretive in news stories—as long as their opinions and interpretation did not deviate from official interpretations of Marxist-Leninist theory or contradict policies dictated by the party. Often journalists' advanced educations gave them the self-confidence and sense of authority to interpret complex political, international, economic, and social events and policies to citizen audiences that had only recently emerged from a state of peasantry, war, civil war, and autocratic domination under the czars.

Marxist-Leninist leaders envisioned an interventionist approach for the press, regarding it as a catalyst for revolution and creation of party solidarity. Lenin wrote in 1902 how a single national newspaper, staffed by "professional writers, professional correspondents, an army of Social Democratic reporters who establish contacts everywhere," could be an instrument of the "class struggle" that could unify the underground movement (Ruud 1981, 380–81). Lenin saw the newspaper's role as concentrating all elements of dissatisfaction and protest to make the proletarian revolutionary movement grow. After the Bolsheviks won power, they used the press to support their regime and counterbalance the bourgeois press (Tolstikova 2004). For example, two days after the Council of People's Commissars took control, it adopted a resolution empowering itself to shut down papers that sought to sow disorder or advocate resistance (Johnson 1999). And Lenin in 1917 signed the Decree on the Press that promised "full freedom within the limits of responsibility before the court" but imposed "temporary and extraordinary measures to stop the flow of dirt and slander" (Richter 1995).

Despite that merger of party and press, Mueller (1998) argues that the accepted image of the early Soviet press is too narrowly conceived. Although propaganda was its primary function, that was not its sole function. The press also had important nonideological objectives arising from expectations that it would disseminate news and information, educate the masses, and challenge corruption and nepotism in emerging state and party bureaucracies. Journalists were not to be propagandists, but rather a cadre of professionals simultaneously committed ideologically to the party and professionally competent. Mueller says:

It is generally believed that the Soviet press was an integral part of the Bolshevik Party's propaganda machine and that Soviet journalists were propagandists for the Bolshevik Party/state. This view first arose in the 1930s but was not articulated fully until the Cold War, when Western scholars assumed that Soviet newspapers and journalists had always possessed the attributes that they identified with the Stalinist and post-Stalinist period. Although recently several scholars have explored important aspects of the history of the pre-Stalinist press, media researchers have generally avoided engaging in reconsidering the dominant Western conceptualization and critique of the Soviet press, or challenged the fundamental but narrow assumption that equates Soviet newspapers with propaganda and Soviet journalists with propagandists (1998, 1). Only a minority Soviet-era journalists served as dedicated Party propagandists and ideologues after the initial Bolshevik period.

Immediately after the Russian Revolution, there were both a shortage of skilled journalists and widespread professional incompetence, especially in provincial areas and far-flung parts of the empire. The Central Committee of the Communist Party became concerned with developing journalists-communists capable of simultaneously communicating with audiences and acting as dedicated ideologues. In reality, such professionals were rare. Devoted loyalists often lacked professional skills. Press corps leaders usually shared the party's conviction that class identity closely related to allegiance to the Bolshevik leadership. The dilemma was that these press corps leaders also were determined to employ competent professionals to raise the quality of their newspapers. It became apparent, however, that noncommunists, the educated, and journalists from privileged backgrounds generally proved most competent.

Mueller details continuous conflict between governmental expectations that journalists conform to the party line and serve as propagandists and the reality that skilled journalists were least likely to accept such a role. Throughout the 1920s, major newspapers employed many staff who were not party members and who came from privileged and intellectual backgrounds. In 1924 the Soviet press department studied rank-and-file journalists to determine the level of party membership and found that only 41 percent of the 1,270 surveyed belonged to the Communist Party. A 1925 survey found that of the 16,752 members of the journalists' labor association, only 19 percent reported being party members or candidates; only 36 percent of respondents said they were from the proletariat or peasantry, indicating that the government had failed to attract or develop the kind of ideal journalist-communist professionals it sought.

According to Andronaus, Lenin's pronouncement about the press that was the most quoted by Soviet-era journalism educators and instilled in young journalists was:

> In contradistinction to bourgeois customs, to the profit-making, commercialized bourgeois press, to bourgeoisie literary careerism and individualism, "aristocratic anarchism" and drive for profit, the socialist proletariat must put forward the principle of Party literature, must develop this principle, and put it into practice as fully and completely as possible. What is this principle of Party literature? . . . Literature cannot be a means of enriching individuals or groups: it cannot, in fact, be an individual undertaking, independent of the common cause of the proletariat. Down with non-partisan writers! . . . Literature must become part of the common cause with the proletariat . . . Literature must become a component of organized, planned and integrated Social-Democratic Party work" (qtd. in Andronaus 1993, 40–41).

Andronaus adds that "journalism students in the Soviet Union could recite this quotation almost by heart, so often was it repeated in different courses. What they were not told was that by 'party literature' Lenin originally meant only party publications" (41).

The Soviets tried to formalize socialist journalism education and empower a cadre of journalists emerging from the working and peasant classes. This was a difficult endeavor because journalism is essentially an intellectual activity. The "flagship" of journalism education and professionalization efforts was the State Institute of Journalism, or GIZh, founded in 1921. GIZh combined technical and professional education; the professional aspect emphasized theoretical foundations of propaganda creation and dissemination.

There was a constant struggle within GIZh between accepting ideologically sound students and admitting competent ones. In 1921, 71 percent of incoming students were party- or Komosomol-affiliated (Komosomol was the Young Communist League); by 1923, more than 90 percent were. The proportion of incoming students with backgrounds in the intelligentsia dropped from 80 percent in 1921 to 51 percent in 1923, indicating an increased emphasis on enrolling students with approved class and political identities (Mueller 1998, 6). In 1924 GIZh announced that 72 percent of fifty-one incoming students had worker origins, but enrollments had dropped from eighty-one to fifty-one students in 1923, suggesting that the institute tried to maintain higher standards by admitting fewer students. By 1927, journalism applicants needed at least three years' experience as physical laborers or work experience in industry or agriculture. By the late 1920s, a press corps dominated by non-proletarians and non-peasants predominated; only editors had to belong to the party.

Lenoe (2004) says that the mobilization of journalists during a campaign to encourage frugality and lessen consumption among the mass of Soviet citizens involved sending reporters into factories with the mission to help organize production. The rhetoric of this campaign was the agitational rhetoric of the Russian Civil War (1918–1921), heavy with military metaphors and exhortations to action. In combining new forms of journalism such as socialist competition with the militant rhetoric of the civil war, Lenoe says, journalists were aimed not just at organizing factory workers but also at encouraging factory-level activism by equating increases in industrial production to victories achieved in the great battles of the Russian Revolution.

The organizers of this new form of interventionist journalism called themselves *massoviki,* or "mass activists," and their work *massovast,* or "mass work." Lenoe adds, "The language of the shock campaign, with its command-form headlines, military metaphors, grandiose superlatives, and vocabulary of urban revolt and class war, was a complex amalgam of elements that had entered the speech and writing of Boleshevik activists over a twenty- to thirty-year period" (2004, 37–38).

The "green eyeshade" (practical journalism) versus the "chi squared" (communication theory) debate, which continues within Western journalism programs, was evident at the end of the decade, as indicated by the proceedings of a 1925 GIZh forum. GIZh Professor and newspaper editor Aleksandr Kurs, for instance, argued that because information is the essence of a newspaper, reporting should be the emphasis of training. Another GIZh professor, Levidov, bravely used the forum to criticize the poor quality of Soviet journalism, urging students to master the "universal techniques" of newspaper journalism. Some Soviet journalism educators even advocated sending students abroad to study. Such faculty, however, were sharply criticized for upholding the bourgeois press as a model to emulate.

In April 1930, GIZh administrators and faculty could still debate and advocate the emphasis on practical journalism education over a theoretical and ideological one. Kurs called for curriculum changes to have instructors specialize in teaching a single subject. He further called for a student 'newspaper laboratory' and an emphasis on the importance of information as the foundation of all newspapers, both bourgeois and communist. Kurs argued that information was essential to Russia's press, saying the Soviet newspaper organizes, agitates, propagandises, teaches, educates, and recasts a person on the basis of information. Kurs went on to become an acclaimed screen writer but was executed in 1937 during the Stalinist purges (Mueller 1998, 11–13).

Hopkins (1970) explains how American press theory holds that journalists are obliged to stand somewhere between citizens and their government—serving in the "watchdog" function. From that perspective, he says, it was hypocritical for Soviet journalists to speak of their commitment to the people while disseminating endless government statements and interpretations of events, with little or no candid critical analysis from the journalists themselves. Either the press was a publicist for government, or it was a voice of the people. The Soviet retort was that its press system harmonized with Marxist-Leninist ideology and that government and party were one—meaning the press drew its power from the people. If a state-owned press organ opposes the government, it must also, simultaneously, oppose the people, an obviously illogical position.

In addition to the professional press, worker-peasant correspondents known as *rabsel'kor* were charged with facilitating communication from the masses to the central government. The Moscow Institute of Journalism set up a program to encourage the rabsel'kor; within two years it was reorganized into a college offering a three-year course. Still, it was far more ideological and political than practical or professional. Although students took courses in editing, publishing, and literary criticism, the objective was to produce partisan journalists. In 1930, small weekly or biweekly *raion* (county) newspapers were launched to use these worker-peasant correspondents who contributed essays and polemics; by 1924, forty thousand wall newspapers extended the central party's influence into distant communities. With regard to one of the most radical approaches to directly using the press for national development, Hopkins (1970, 64–65) says:

> A series of party resolutions organized the rabsel'kor into an assault force against bureaucracy, inefficiency, and law violations. The "shock correspondent" . . . was born. Raids were organized, whereby huge teams of worker-peasant correspondents conducted minute investigations of a given factory or collective farm and reported whatever flaws they unearthed. As before, the mass local press played a dual role. From one view, it was in fact an independent check on party policies, on economic performance and management.

Although Soviet news-gathering and -dissemination conventions were often extreme from a Western perspective, they may have had value as an interventionist model along the lines of public journalism, an alternative model espoused today by some American journalists and news organizations in recent years.

Community-level journalists were charged with leading and extolling campaigns to investigate corruption, reveal factory inefficiencies, and rally agricultural and industrial workers to raise production and meet centrally established quotas. If the subsequent economic development of the Soviet Union and its emergence as a world power are valid indicators, then such press policies arguably had merit.

In critiquing the Soviet press system, Hopkins says that in the constant evolution and interaction of Soviet social institutions, the press tended to assume assorted political responsibilities and duties that constituted the primary journalistic values its journalists adhered to—just as American press theory describes the duties and performance of American journalists in the context of American political and economic conditions. Hopkins cites a common Soviet reference book for journalists as listing the following values or virtues that were an ideal for Soviet journalists: (1) party orientation (*partiinost*), interpreted as conscious acceptance that the press is a politically partisan institution and thus expresses party philosophy and goals; (2) high level of ideology (*vysokaya ideinost*), suggesting that the press should be spiritually reinforced with Marxism-Leninism ideology; (3) truthfulness (*pravdinost*), an obligation to transmit information truthfully; (4) popular orientation (*narodnost*), reminding journalists of their responsibilities to the masses and simultaneously about the people's access to the state-owned press; (5) mass character (*massovost*), maintaining not only that the press serves the masses but also functions among them; and (6) criticism and self-criticism (*kritika* and *samokritika*), calling on the mass media to criticize faults and failures of the party, government, and their agencies, as well as to criticize its own shortcomings (1970, 34).

Hopkins acknowledges some positive aspects of the Soviet press as a tool for national development, saying, "The press has been instrumental in altering public attitudes toward farming and manufacturing methods, industrial management, distribution, work, and economic planning, to name a few of the areas radically affected as the Soviet Union developed an industrial, urban, planned society" (1970, 38). In other words, this form of interventionist press served as a powerful modernization tool that contributed to the development of society and raised the Soviet Union far above other developing nations as measured by multiple demographic and economic indicators.

Press campaigns for nationalism and a mass Soviet identity certainly played a critical role in reducing ethnic and religious discord. With the recent exceptions of predominantly Muslim Chechnya in the Russian Federation and Nagorno-Karabakh, a territory disputed by predominantly Orthodox Armenia and predominantly Muslim Azerbaijan, such conflicts remain relatively few in the majority-Muslim nations that were once part of the Soviet Union. This is not to say that Soviet methods of religious repression were humane or devoid of violence, but that the most brutal methods of repression, mostly during the Russian Revolution and civil war of the early 1920s, were tempered with policies and strategies for empowerment of religious and ethnic minorities that relied on the press and skilled journalists as propaganda tools.

Before the Bolshevik Revolution, the czarist government's treatment of Muslim minorities, for instance, might be favorably compared to U.S. government treatment of Native Americans during the same historical period; Russia did not engage in the kind of widespread genocidal warfare in its frontier territories to the east and south that America did on its own western frontier in the nineteenth century. However, it is undeniable that the czarist and Soviet governments engaged in mass arrests, confiscations, executions, and internal deportations directed at certain groups of ethnic minorities, particularly Jews under the czars, and at Germans throughout the first half of the twentieth century. And in comparison with other colonial powers, the Soviets were generally progressive in their determination to integrate cultural minorities, with exceptions such as ethnic Germans in the west and Koreans in the east. Particularly in Central Asia they extended a degree of self-determination, independence, economic opportunity, education, and general well-being under colonial rule.

Altschull (1995, 195) points out that although the collapse of the Soviet Union and the central Communist Party was widely heralded, especially in the market societies of the West, it was premature to consign to the grave the ideology that created and built the foundation of the USSR. He adds, "Eulogies have been pronounced over many ideologies throughout history, including conservatism and liberalism but they have nevertheless survived."

In Central Asia and throughout the former Soviet Union, a diminishing but significant number of journalists who were educated in high-status and competitive journalism programs, schools, and institutes have retained the knowledge—both theoretical and practical—they acquired. For instance, Soviet-trained journalists who were taught the ideal of serving the working class and helping to bring about an economic and social utopia through the use of the mass media they served are likely to be disappointed and intellectually dissatisfied by producing the sensational and often shallow content that newly independent and commercial media in developing countries often market today.

The Soviets' socialist approach included a concentrated effort at economic and social equality and general attainment of Second World status for those subjugated by the Russian empire. That approach contrasted greatly with colonial policies of the French, Italians, and British in the Middle East; the Indian sub-continent; and North Africa, where subjugation and exploitation were dominant polices. It also helps to explain the adoption of socialist ideology by nationalist liberation movements throughout the Third World after World War II.

Such integration was an expectation and charge of the press, and the results are evident, although other means were draconian, such as imprisonment and execution of religious and nationalist leaders who resisted communism, state-imposed atheism, and Russian occupation. Still, since recent ethnic and religious conflicts in other nations are clearly obstacles to development and national unity, a model that contributes to reduction or elimination of such conflicts—no matter how draconian in other respects—cannot be wholly faulted.

Of course, the Soviet model evolved over time as well, especially with the building of the momentum that led to the USSR's implosion. The late 1980s brought in what some scholars called a golden age for the press, and perestroika ushered in a radical reform of the political system, triggering major changes in state and society and a dramatic shift toward pluralism and a market-oriented economy in Central Asia and elsewhere in the former Soviet Union (Zassoursky 2005; Kulikova and Ibraeva 2002; Richter 1995). Central Asian journalists benefited from those policies as well, but in the waning years of Soviet control, political leaders in Central Asia "were especially angry with the new journalism, which they perceived as a threat to their power," according to Brown, referring in particular to media exposure of corruption. Not surprisingly, the increased openness and move toward greater press freedoms under prime minister Mikhail Gorbechev's policies of perestroika and glasnost did not last in the region: four years after independence, Brown noted that the influence of glasnost in Central Asia had largely disappeared. He called it the "natural death" of a Moscow-centered policy that never developed roots in the Central Asian republics seeking to build their own national press systems after independence (Brown 1995, 250).

Conclusion

Altschull contends that the Marxist-Leninist theoretical underpinnings of Soviet journalism education and practice were not as pervasive as Westerners might think. He says:

Journalism schools throughout the Soviet empire made a point of teaching "Marxist journalism." Whatever that phrase meant, the idea that "Marxist journalism"

> began with Marx was a central element of Soviet press doctrine. Yet this is not a valid idea; it is folklore that was politically useful in the Soviet Union just as the folklore of an adversary press is politically useful in the United States. In truth, Marx is as difficult to pin down as Jefferson, who can be found on all sides of the issue of press freedom at different periods of his life. (1995, 196)

There is a long history and established global constituency for Western styles of journalism based on an objective presentation of news and information. Because interventionist models such as that of the Soviets clearly depart from Western conventions, they share credibility problems that can dissuade the very journalists who are expected to establish their validity and sustainability. Since the most qualified and experienced professional journalists often are the most highly committed to traditional reporting methods and to the ideology and philosophy behind them, they must be shown sound justification for changing deeply embedded philosophies and practices. Fundamental to the Western modes is the concept that journalists share power with government and that, as part of the power structure, they are not obligated to change a system they belong to, or to directly challenge it and call for structural changes.

Thus a major challenge for the aging pre-independence journalists of Central Asia and for the new generation entering the profession is how to develop, evolve, and sustain composite press system models. That challenge is complex. Such models, which will differ from country to country, cannot ignore either the region's Soviet foundation or a commitment to globally accepted journalistic principles of fairness, balance, accuracy, and ethics. These new composite models cannot ignore the societal pressure on the press to help construct national identity and a sense of statehood. Nor can these evolving press systems ignore the realities of authoritarian regimes that sharply restrict press rights, cultural and religious traditions and expectations, insufficient market support to sustain truly independent media, and pressures from powerful extra-governmental players such as organized crime, dominant and opposition political parties, and domestic and foreign business and industry interests. Finally, both current and prospective journalists need better education and training in analytical thinking, practical skills, and understanding of the roles of the press in emerging democracies if they are to function professionally in these new systems. Elements of communitarian journalism, a reformed Marxist-inspired model, for instance, are most likely to appeal to journalists in underdeveloped countries working under authoritarian conditions and attempting to further social change and development within the constraints under which they work (de Beer and Merrill 2004).

Taken together, this challenge with its regional and country-specific realities mean it is impossible and undesirable to wholly ignore the seventy-year foundation of Soviet-style journalism pedagogy and practice. It is hardly surprising that after seven decades of Soviet rule state-controlled media, permeated with a pro-regime propaganda mission, will retain a significant and probably dominant place on Central Asia's mass media stage, at least for the foreseeable future.

REFERENCES

Altschull, J. Herbert. 1995. *Agents of Power: The Media and Public Policy.* White Plains, NY: Longman.

Androunas, Elena. 1993. *Soviet Media in Transition: Structural and Economic Alternatives.* Westport, CT: Praeger.

Bailey, F. M. 1946. *Mission to Tashkent.* London: Jonathan Cape.

Brown, Jeff L. 1995. "Mass Media in Transition in Central Asia." *International Communication Gazette* 54(3): 249–65.

de Beer, Arnold S., and John C. Merrill. 2004. *Global Journalism: Topical Issues and Media Systems,* 4th ed. Boston: Pearson.

Freedman, Eric, and Richard Shafer. 2003. "How Media Censorship and Enduring Soviet Press Practices Obstruct Nation-Building in Central Asia." *Journal of Development Communication* 14(2): 57–62.

Hopkins, Mark W. 1970. *Mass Media in the Soviet Union.* New York: Pegasus.

Johnson, Owen V. 1999. "The Roots of Journalism in Central and Eastern Europe." In *Eastern European Journalism: Before, During and After Communism,* ed. Jerome Aumente, Peter Gross, Ray Hiebert, Owen V. Johnson, and Dean Mills, 5–40. Cresskill, NJ: Hampton Press.

Khalid, Adeeb. 1994. "Printing, Publishing, and Reform in Tsarist Central Asia." *International Journal of Middle East Studies* 26(2): 187–200.

Kulikova, Svetlana V., and Gulnara Ibraeva. 2002. *The Historical Development and Current Situation of the Mass Media in Kyrgyzstan.* Geneva: Cimera.

Lenoe, Matthew E. 2004. *Closer to the Masses: Stalinist Culture, Social Revolution, and Soviet Newspapers.* Cambridge: Harvard University Press.

Miller, James. 2002. Research Report 2002, IREX Short-Term Travel Grants Program. Http://www.irex.org/programs/stg/research/02/millerj.pdf.

Mueller, J. (1998). "Staffing Newspapers and Training Journalists in Early Soviet Russia." *Journal of Social History* 31(4): 11–13.

Mueller, Julie Kay. 1998. "Staffing Newspapers and Training Journalists in Early Soviet

Russia." *Journal of Social History* 31(4): 851–73.

Richter, Andrei G. 1995. "The Russian Press after Perestroika." *Canadian Journal of Communication* 20(2): 7–23.

Ruud, Charles A. 1981. "The Printing Press as an Agent of Political Change in Early Twentieth-Century Russia." *Russian Review* 40(4): 378–95.

Tolstikova, Natasha. 2004. "*Rabonitsa:* The Paradoxical Success of a Soviet Women's Magazine." *Journalism History* 30(3): 131–40.

Zassoursky, Ivan. 2005. *Media and Power in Post-Soviet Russia.* Armonk, NY: M. E. Sharpe.

PART 2

National Perspectives

Oligarchs and Ownership: The Role of Financial-Industrial Groups in Controlling Kazakhstan's "Independent" Media

Barbara Junisbai

Kazakhstan is known for its authoritarian political system and the absence of guarantees protecting citizens' fundamental rights, including freedom of speech and freedom of the press. Under the rule of president Nursultan Nazarbaev, who has been in power since 1989,[1] a variety of mechanisms—formal and informal, legal and de facto—has been used to control the media and to limit political contestation. Web sites posting critical political views are routinely blocked, opposition newspapers are closed or denied access to printing presses, and journalists are subject to criminal investigations and even physical violence. Journalists engage in self-censorship, and the range of issues covered by the media is circumscribed.[2]

Within this generally repressive environment, however, unexpected bouts of criticism have punctuated Kazakhstan's normally pliant media coverage. Surprisingly, politically sensitive topics have at times been actively discussed and debated in the nongovernment press and on national television. Such a discussion occurred in 2007 in connection with a scandal involving Rakhat Aliev, then son-in-law to Nazarbaev and one of the richest people in Kazakhstan (Omarova 2007a). In late May 2007 the Astana television station devoted two evening prime-time hours to the former chair of Nurbank, a major Kazakhstani bank jointly owned by Aliev and the president's oldest daughter, Dariga Nazarbaeva. The ex–bank official alleged that Aliev had kidnapped and tortured him and two others as part of a business-related conflict. That same night, Commercial Television of Kazakhstan (KTK), owned by Aliev and his wife, Nazarbaeva, was taken off the air. The Aliev-owned weekly paper *Karavan* was also shut down. In response, the International Press Institute issued a statement condemning *Karavan's* temporary closure, calling it government censorship of the independent press. This was ironic, given that prior to these events, *Karavan* was closely associated with Nazarbaev's ruling coalition.

In important ways, the 2007 exposé of Aliev challenged media conventions in Kazakhstan.[3] In the past, those criticizing the president's family members in print had been hit with libel suits and, predictably, lost. In this instance, however, outrageous and potentially slanderous claims were made on national television against a key member of the president's family. Curiously, the station that aired the piece faced no negative consequences for its actions.

Research Question

Given Kazakhstan's entrenched authoritarianism, the astonishing national coverage of a scandal directly involving a member of the president's family (and indirectly involving the president) presents an empirical puzzle. Media owners, journalists, editors, and station managers all understand that coverage of politically sensitive topics inevitably will be met with serious penalties, such as loss of employment, lawsuits, physical punishment, and fines, among others. In this repressive environment, then, why and under what conditions have Kazakhstani media been permitted to cover topics that are widely understood as taboo and strictly off-limits to journalists? Answering this question helps us understand not only the dynamics behind media coverage in Kazakhstan but also government-media relations in similar post-Soviet countries—including Russia, Ukraine, Azerbaijan, and Kyrgyzstan—where oligarchs have emerged as the dominant economic and political actors.[4]

RESEARCH METHOD AND CHAPTER ORGANIZATION

Based on data collected by the author during fieldwork from December 2006 to June 2007, the media's uncharacteristic coverage of politically sensitive issues and events appears driven in large part by conflict within Kazakhstan's elite.[5] This elite is divided into financial-industrial groups, each of which competes with other financial-industrial groups for preferential access to lucrative political and economic goods, including the president's favor. A key weapon in their struggle is the mass media (Satpaev 2006).[6]

To explore the role of financial-industrial groups in Kazakhstan's nongovernment media, this chapter combines historical and case study approaches. First, the chapter traces the transformation of media ownership since the early 1990s in the context of an economy that has become dominated by financial-industrial groups. Next, it compares two instances of atypically critical media coverage, highlighting the ways that competing financial-industrial groups have used the media to influence politics and public opinion. The chapter concludes by considering some of the broader implications of media ownership by financial-industrial groups, in particular, how the actions of financial-industrial groups affect politics. It also examines policy implications of this pattern of media ownership for international donors working under conditions similar to those in Kazakhstan, where oligarchs are closely associated with print and electronic media outlets.

Findings

This section addresses the central question: why and when have Kazakhstan's media risked covering politically taboo subjects, which under normal circumstances would have them shut down? By way of response, this section presents a brief history of media ownership in the country, reviewing the initial period of media independence (1991–96) and the process by which financial-industrial groups eventually pushed out small private media companies (1997–2000) and came to dominate media ownership (2000-present). Finally, it cites two case studies in which normally behind-the-scenes conflicts among financial-industrial groups publicly surfaced and gained extensive press coverage. The first is the Democratic Choice of Kazakhstan (DCK) opposition movement, which signaled a major political crisis in 2001–02, and the second is the 2007 scandal involving former presidential son-in-law Rakhat Aliev.

A BRIEF EXPERIMENT WITH INDEPENDENT MEDIA

As in many post-Soviet states, Kazakhstan's era of relative media freedom was short-lived, ending in 1997. In 1990, one year before the fall of the Soviet Union, the first nongovernment television stations, Efir and KTK, had already appeared (Katsiev 1999). Then, two years after Kazakhstan gained independence, the Ministry of Information began granting licenses to small television and radio companies at minimal cost. All two hundred companies that applied were approved, gaining access to the airwaves and viewers' television screens (Human Rights Watch 1999). Although the country's image as a liberal polity during these early years was marred by retaliation against individual media outlets for including stories considered too critical of the government, a number of those working in television and radio recall the idealism of this period. One journalist describes the early years as follows: "We considered ourselves fortunate to have a democratic president, not like the presidents of Turkmenistan or Uzbekistan. We honestly believed that Nazarbaev would support free speech."[7]

The situation radically changed in 1997 when the government held its first auction—or, more formally, tender—to reallocate private television and radio frequencies. Especially in comparison with 1993, the cost of obtaining rights to electronic media became prohibitively expensive, and the majority of television and radio companies lost their licenses (Human Rights Watch 1998; International Press Institute 1998; Zhovtis 1999). Some argue that the tender was meant to silence those who continued to criticize Nazarbaev (Duvanov 2007). Others point to the president's desire to rein in the media in the preelection period, given that his chances of reelection were not yet secure (International Eurasian Institute for Economic and Political Research 1998). The former owner of the privately owned Totem television and radio company, Rozlana Taukina, explains that the tender was a convenient way for the president's daughter Dariga to get rid of competitors to her recently acquired media holdings. Taukina angrily recalls the loss of her company:

> My business was taken away, not because it had gone bankrupt, but because Dariga Nazarbaeva wanted to close us and get our advertisers. After that how could I not be an opponent of this regime, which has no normal democratic law? They held a tender and in one day closed the station. If only they had given me at least three months, so I could earn money to repay the advertising debts! Tell me, how could I be indifferent and praise the regime after such treatment? I understood that this is a completely unfair regime. How could you close a prospering company? How could they remove 150 people from their jobs? . . . They punished me doubly, including financial punishment, because I had to pay off all of the debts [the station had incurred] from my own pocket.[8]

Indeed, after the 1997 tender, Nazarbaeva and Aliev were widely known as the main players behind Kazakhstan's mass media (Dylevskaya 2001). In 1998 the two purchased the popular nongovernment newspapers *Novoe Pokolenie* and *Karavan*.[9] In addition to running the government-owned Khabar television and radio company, the couple also quickly gained ownership or control over the Kazakhstan Today news agency; the television stations KTK, NTK, and ORT-Kazakhstan; and a number of radio stations, including Europa-Plus Kazakhstan,

Hit-FM, Russian Radio, and Radio Retro. Not only did Nazarbaeva and Aliev own a significant share of the media market, but they also jointly engaged in the banking, natural resource, and sugar processing sectors. In other words, the two had formed a formidable financial-industrial group. As this chapter will show, the Aliev-Nazarbaeva group was just one of many such groups to form and prosper during this period.

THE ERA OF FINANCIAL-INDUSTRIAL GROUPS

In the last decade or so, financial-industrial groups with close ties to the president have purchased or gained control over much of the country's print and electronic media. Led by wealthy business and political elites and akin to oligarchs, financial-industrial groups head, control, or own industrial, financial, retail, media, and other businesses (Ashimbaev 2007; Khlyupin 1998; Kjænet, Satpaev, and Torjesen 2008; Satpaev 2006).[10] For the most part, the media avoid subjects that could get them in trouble with government officials or with the financial-industrial groups that finance them. However, when it has served the interests of their owners and the president, mainstream coverage has expanded to include subjects that are normally restricted to the small opposition press.

In contrast to the period prior to the 1997 tender, when a large number of small private companies competed in the broadcast markets, the subsequent period witnessed a concentration of ownership in the hands of oligarchs. By 2000, nongovernment stations and newspapers all over the country were closely associated with one or another financial-industrial group. This pattern of ownership continues (Dave 2007), as table 1 shows.

Table 1 lists the most commonly cited financial-industrial groups, the individual businesses in which they are involved, and the media with which they are associated.[11] This is not an exhaustive list, but rather a snapshot in time of the generally agreed-upon key players.[12] Before turning to interpretation of the data, it is important to note that it is not always clear which group or individual stands behind a given media outlet. As one journalist explains the situation, "It is obvious that the majority of large networks now belongs to different financial-industrial groups, but the details of specific ownership are not public information."[13]

Table 1 is divided into two groups: the inner circle and the second tier.[14] Those in the president's inner circle have exclusive access to the country's lucrative energy and metals industries, as the list of enterprises in the second column shows. The inner circle is comprised of the financial-industrial groups closest to the president, such as that led by Nurtai Abykayev, his close friend,

TABLE 1. SNAPSHOT OF KAZAKHSTAN'S MOST-CITED FINANCIAL-INDUSTRIAL GROUPS, 2007

NAME	ASSOCIATED WITH THE FOLLOWING BUSINESSES/ENTERPRISES	ASSOCIATED WITH THE FOLLOWING MEDIA
INNER CIRCLE		
Abykayev, Nurtai	Said to be associated with the Ispat-karmet steel producer, Kazakhmys light metals extraction company, and Petroleum Kazakhstan.	Said to control most government media
Aliev, Rakhat/ Nazarbaeva, Dariga*	Nurbank, Sakharnyi Tsentr sugar company, Neftyanoi Tsentr oil company, Mobil gas stations, series of oil refineries. Since summer 2007 the Aliev-Nazarbaeva financial-industrial group has lost all of its media holdings, but Nazarbaeva maintains a majority share in Nurbank.	Novoe Pokolenie and Karavan newspapers; NTK, KTK, ORT-Kazakhstan and Khabar television stations; Europa-Plus, Hit-FM, Russian Radio, and Radio Retro radio stations; Kazakhstan Today news agency; Alma Media; TV-Media
Kim, Vladimir/ Ni, Vladimir†	Series of light metal mining companies, including Kazakhmys Corporation, Zhezkazgansvetmet Corporation, and East Kazakhstan Copper-Chemical Plant. Kim was on Forbes magazine's list of billionaires two years in a row (2006 and 2007) and in 2007 was the wealthiest person in Kazakhstan, then worth an estimated $5.5 billion.	Vremya newspaper; according to Aliev, the Kim-Ni financial-industrial groups took over the Aliev-Nazarbaeva nongovernment media outlets
Kulibaev, Timur‡	Narodnyi Bank; series of oil-related companies, from extraction, processing, to transport, including Kaztranzoil Holding Company, Kaztranzgas, Mangystau-munaigaz, oil processing plants in Shymkent and Pavlodar; Bakhus alcohol and water bottling company; regional airline companies. The combined official wealth of Dinara Kulibaeva and Timur Kulibaev in 2007 was estimated at about $4 billion.	NTV-Kazakhstan television channel, Izvestiya-Kazakhstan, Kontinent magazine, Komsomol'skaya Pravda newspaper; Radio NS
EURASIA GROUP Mashkevich, Aleksandr/ Shodiev, Patokh/ Ibragimov, Alidzhan	Eurasian Natural Resources Corporation (ENRC); Aluminum Kazakhstan; said to control Kazakhstan's metals, energy, and coal markets; owns a series of metal and coal mines and power stations; Kazakh Mineral Resource Corporation; Eurasian Bank. Controlled the Agrarian and Civic Parties until their merger with the presidential Otan Party in 2007. According to Forbes, all three men were worth a little under $2 billion each in 2007.	Ekspress-K newspaper, Irbis television station (which won rights to radio stations in eight cities as a result of the 2007 media tender)

Utemuratov, Bulat§	Shareholder in Turan Alem Bank and Narodnyi Bank, former shareholder in ATF Bank, Kazzink (zinc mining), Kazfosfat (phosphates). Forbes estimated Utemuratov's net worth at $1 billion in 2008.	Said to be a former major shareholder in television Channel 31 and owner of a series of television stations, radio stations, and newspapers, including the newspaper Megapolis and the opposition news Web site Navigator

Ablyazov, Mukhtar	President, Astana Holding (1993–97); president, Kazakhstan Electricity Grid Operating Company (1997–98); minister of energy, industry, and trade (1998–99); chair, board of directors, Kazakhstan Airlines (2001); chair, board of directors, Temirbank (2001–02); chair, board of directors, Turan Alem Bank (2005–09). In 2009, charged with money laundering, fraud, and organizing a criminal group; Turan Alem Bank nationalized; Ablyazov currently in exile.	Said to have financed the Respublika and Vremya PO opposition newspaper; before 2002 owned Channel 31 and was associated with Tan TV
Atamkulov, Erlan	Rakhat Kazakh-Austrian conglomerate of 29 companies, including a hotel construction company, vodka production, Arabian race-horse breeding, and insurance companies (1992–2002); president, Kazakhstan Temir Zholy (2002–07); member, board of directors, Kedentransservis company (2007–08). Member, Otan Party's political council (2007–08).	None
Baiseitov, Bakhytbek	Forbes estimated net worth in 2009 at $1 billion; founder of and major shareholder in Centercredit Bank; president, Association of Banks of Kazakhstan; president, Atameken financial investment group; chair, board of directors, CenterInvest investment company. Member, Otan and Nur Otan political parties.	None
Batalov, Raimbek	Raimbek Group (grocery products, juices, milk processing, spirits, bottled water); chairs the Forum of Entrepreneurs; member, Atameken union; member, President's Council of Entrepreneurs; Nur Otan Party member and Mazhilis deputy (2007–).	None
Seisembaev, Margulan	President, chair of board of directors, Seimar Al'yans Financial Corporation (and earlier related businesses); chair, advisory council, Al'yans Bank. Member, Otan presidential party (2004).	None

| Subkhanberdin, Nurzhan** | Heads Kazkommertsbank conglomerate, which includes one of Kazakhstan's top banks, Kazkommertsbank, and a series of daughter companies. Said to have worked closely with the Ak Zhol Party, headed by political elite Alikhan Baimenov. Subkhanberdin's wealth in 2007 was estimated at $1.5 billion. | None |

*Until 2001, Aliev was considered the president's right hand and a potential successor. Aliev's influence declined after 2001, the result of a confrontation with the Ablyazov FPG and evidence that Aliev was plotting against the president and had posted compromising material about the president and his family on the Internet.

†Utemuratov is sometimes listed as a member of the inner circle. As a result of the financial crisis, as of 2008 Kim is no longer included among the world's billionaires.

‡According to Kharlamov (2005), Kulibaev united with the Kazkommerts FPG in 2000 and the Utemuratov FPG in 2005–06 and worked closely with the Ablyazov FPG. Other elites said to have been associated with the Kulibaev FPG are Nurlan Kapparov, Ulan Ksembaev, and Karim Masimov.

§Utemuratov is sometimes listed as a member of the second tier.

**Kharlamov (2005) categorizes the Kulibaev and Subkhanberdin FPGs as one entity, explaining that they united in 2000. Epitsentr (2005) places Subkhanberdin in the inner circle.

SOURCES: Author's interviews; Adilov 2003; Aliev 2000; Ashimbaev 2008; Dzhanibekov 2004; Epitsentr evraziiskii tsentr politicheskikh issledovanii i agentsvo sotsial'nykh tekhnologii 2005; Institut aktual'nykh politicheskikh issledovanii 1999; Kharlamov 2005; *Profil'* 2007; Satov 2007; Satpaev 2006; Yuritsyn 2007.

former speaker of parliament, and former ambassador to the Russian Federation; the leaders of the Eurasia Group (owner of the Eurasian Natural Resources Corporation, or ENRC), Aleksandr Mashkevich, Patokh Shodiev, and Alidzhan Ibragimov; the heads of Kazakhmys Corporation (a major producer of copper and other metals), Vladimir Kim and Vladimir Ni; and another presidential son-in-law, Timur Kulibaev. Until mid-2007 the inner circle also included the Aliev and Nazarbaeva financial-industrial group.

A number of other financial-industrial groups make up the second tier.[15] While permitted to engage in business and amass great wealth, they have been denied entry into the most lucrative sectors of the economy. None of those in the second tier have holdings in the metals or energy sectors. Instead, second-tier financial-industrial groups engage in the banking, construction, and food-processing industries, all of which have earned them huge profits. At the same time, these earnings pale in comparison to those associated with the exploitation of Kazakhstan's natural resources.

The third column in table 1 points to another key difference between financial-industrial groups in the inner circle and those in the second tier. Groups in the inner circle have acquired control over a large number of newspapers, television channels, and radio stations. While two or three financial-industrial groups in the second tier are also associated with print and electronic media, their holdings are minimal in comparison with those in the inner circle. This suggests that among the wealthiest and most influential groups, only those closest to the president are allowed access both to lucrative sectors of the economy and to the nation's nongovernment media.

The results of the January 2007 tender for frequencies also point to a concentration of media holdings among the financial-industrial groups in the president's inner circle. During the tender, 120 applicants competed for rights to about fifteen radio frequencies throughout the country.[16] Only three companies—the Irbis television group, the Astana channel, and Ria-Arna—received them (Golyshkin 2007; Makimbai and Taukina 2007). According to some of those interviewed for this study, the financial-industrial groups that own these three companies are known for their loyalty and close ties to Nazarbaev.[17] Although as of the writing of this chapter it is unclear which financial-industrial groups stand behind Astana and Ria-Arna, the owners of Irbis are widely considered to be the Eurasia Group, located in the president's inner circle.[18]

What explains the dominance of financial-industrial groups in media ownership? Print and electronic media are desirable not necessarily because of their profitability, but because of their potential as instruments for influencing public opinion and attacking rival elites in a legitimate and seemingly neutral form. According to the editor of one opposition newspaper: "The information business in our country is barely profitable. The dividends that their owners hope to earn from their media holdings are political, rather than economic."[19] Thus, many political and business elites have been eager to purchase print and electronic media, although revenues were and remain either small or nonexistent.[20] Given the exorbitant cost of participating in the 1997 electronic media tender and in subsequent ones, financial-industrial groups are the only players well positioned to enter the media market. And only those armed with surplus capital can withstand the losses incurred from supporting unprofitable stations.

CASE STUDIES: THE DCK OPPOSITION MOVEMENT (2001–02) AND RAKHATGATE (2007)

For the most part, financial-industrial groups use their media holdings to wage public relations campaigns against their competitors. Articles and editorials that are critical of rivals have often appeared, for example, in the pages of the nongovernment newspapers *Megapolis*, *Vremya*, and *Ekspress-K* (Omarova 2002, 2007b). The use of media not only to criticize rival financial-industrial groups but also to question the system of rule built by Nazarbaev, however, has happened only two or three times in Kazakhstan's short history as an independent state.[21]

The most serious attempts that elites have made to use the media as weapons in their political struggles took place in 2001 and 2007.

Understandably, the division of financial-industrial groups into two tiers, and, correspondingly, into two groups with unequal access to economic resources, has created tension between financial-industrial groups located in the president's inner circle and those outside of it. This tension erupted in political crisis during 2001–02 (Sysoev 2001). In November 2001 twenty high-ranking government officials and members of the business establishment formed the DCK opposition movement,[22] which was catalyzed by an escalating business conflict between Aliev and key second-tier financial-industrial groups. Mukhtar Ablyazov (see table 1), at the time one of the richest people in Kazakhstan, owned the increasingly profitable Turan Alem Bank, which was a competitor to Nurbank, controlled by the Aliev-Nazarbaeva group. When Aliev demanded a majority share in Turan Alem, Ablyazov refused.

Ablyazov was not the only financial-industrial group leader who came into conflict with Aliev and other financial-industrial groups in the inner circle. Just a few weeks before the DCK went public with its political demands, nineteen oligarchs, including owners of the country's largest banks, signed an open letter to the president complaining that their businesses were under threat from security organs that Aliev headed at the time (Serdalina 2001). Other financial-industrial groups, like that led by Bulat Abilov, who then owned a highly successful corporation and sat in parliament, felt that the two-tiered system had locked them out of the most lucrative sectors of the economy.[23]

The elites who came up against the two-tiered system began using their media outlets and others sympathetic to them to spread their political views and raise their public profile.[24] In fall 2001, Channel 31 aired a program documenting the life and political career of the governor of Pavlodar region, Galymzhan Zhakiyanov, who within a few months would emerge as one of the DCK's leaders.[25] Unusual in Kazakhstan, the program resembled an extended advertisement endorsing a presidential candidate, although no elections were scheduled. This was just one example of DCK members' attempts to increase their profile among ordinary citizens and create a positive public image in the process.[26]

As the conflict reached a head, it became evident that Nazarbaev had decided to support Aliev and the status quo over the DCK's demands to level the economic playing field and limit the privileges allotted to the inner circle.[27] In response, regional television stations like Rika TV in Aktobe, Irbis in Pavlodar, and Tan in Almaty, which before late 2001 had not aired opposition political views, suddenly became sharply critical. The stations began broadcasting programs calling for the acceleration of unrealized democratic reforms that the president had promised for a number of years.[28] DCK leaders were, in effect, attempting to use their media outlets not only against rival financial-industrial groups but also as a campaign to win public support for their larger political agenda. The criticism they aired ranged from the domination of financial-industrial groups close to the president over natural resources to government policy privileging the interests of a select few over the public good. In other words, the interests of the second-tier financial-industrial groups that had united under the DCK banner were associated with the public good, while the privileged status of the inner circle was framed as narrow interests in conflict with national ones.

In the end, it proved easy for the government to deprive the DCK of the media holdings that its leaders had quietly purchased in the period leading up to the movement's establishment. Undisclosed "hooligans" shot at Tan translation cables, putting the station temporarily out of commission.[29] The station later lost its license for violating the law on languages, which requires that 50 percent of broadcasting must be in Kazakh. The Irbis station, closely associated with Zhakiyanov, was taken over by the Eurasia Group; other stations were sold at the last minute to protect them from being shut down, becoming government property, or falling to rival financial-industrial groups. Without access to the electronic media, the DCK lost its main instrument for reaching a wider audience of potential supporters. Combined, these examples show how quickly the resources built up by elites can be lost, should they be used in a way that the president finds threatening to the status quo.

Five years after the sudden emergence and heavy-handed repression of the DCK, Kazakhstan's nongovernment media once again served as a venue for rival financial-industrial groups to attack one another. This time, however, the media were used not by second-tier groups to discredit those in the inner circle, but by ones within the inner circle against the leader of another group close to the president. Working with the president, inner-circle financial-industrial groups targeted their media against Rakhat Aliev, who had become a thorn in the president's side. Critically, by 2007 Aliev had alienated most of Kazakhstan's political and business elites—both in the inner circle and second tier—by strong-arm tactics to force others to cede their business holdings and by his naked ambition to become the next president (Sopranin 2007).

As is often the case with stories involving Kazakhstan's first family, the scandal surrounding Aliev and his former colleagues at Nurbank, which became known as Rakhatgate, was first reported in the opposition press.[30] At this early point in the scandal, the response to the allegations against Aliev was predictable.

Nurbank's attorney filed court papers against the editors for spreading rumors that harmed the bank's reputation.[31] The chain of events appeared to follow the typical pattern: coverage of topics that could potentially hurt the president's reputation or that implicated the president's family members in wrong-doing more often than not end with media outlets in court and their newspapers heavily fined or closed down.

Yet the papers that broke the Rakhatgate story did not suffer the usual fate. Instead, by summer 2007 the story incriminating Aliev in kidnapping, torture, and possible murder was freely and widely covered.[32] By this time Aliev was in exile in Vienna, Austria. Nazarbaev had stripped him of all official titles, Dariga Nazarbaeva had divorced him, and the Ministry of Internal Affairs had opened a criminal case and issued an international warrant for his arrest. It was no longer dangerous to print or broadcast material critical of Aliev, who had fallen out of presidential favor. Airing interviews with Aliev, however, remained problematic; opposition newspapers and Internet sites that did so were shut down or could not be directly accessed within Kazakhstan.

To explain this unusual turn of events, we return to the role of financial-industrial groups in politics and mass media. First, most groups were in conflict with Aliev for various reasons. Second, the president appears to have been behind the public campaign against Aliev, which was carried out by print and electronic media owned by groups in the president's inner circle. According to a series of unofficial telephone conversations between group leaders close to the president, which were wiretapped and released on the Internet, Nazarbaev authorized the two-hour showing on the Astana channel of a former Nurbank official who spoke in detail of being tortured by Aliev and his bodyguards.[33] In a separate telephone conversation between Nazarbaev's close ally, Vladimir Ni, and the editor in chief of the *Vremya* newspaper, the two men were recorded discussing plans to provide negative coverage of Aliev as part of the information war against him.

As was the case with the DCK in 2001–02, Aliev proved no match for the stockpile of weapons used to silence those who dared use the media in a manner that conflicted with the interests of the president. On the night that KTK was withdrawn from the air, Aliev had planned on giving a live press conference from Vienna to disseminate his version of Rakhatgate to the public, criticize Nazarbaev's authoritarian regime, and call for democratic reforms. To keep Aliev from doing so, KTK and *Karavan* were closed, and access to Aliev's other media holdings was cut off.[34] After Aliev's fall from grace, control over the media holdings that were formerly associated with the Aliev-Nazarbaeva financial-industrial group was given to the Kim-Ni financial-industrial group (Panfilova 2007) or, in the case of Khabar, to the presidential administration. In political exile far from Kazakhstan, the threat represented by Aliev—who is said to have stored up massive amounts of compromising materials implicating the president and key government officials in corruption and other illegal activity—also seems to have subsided. In June 2007 an official from the presidential administration was appointed to head KTK, and the court-ordered prohibition of the printing and sale of *Karavan* was lifted on condition that the paper refrain from publishing any information related to the ongoing investigation of Nurbank.

Conclusion and Discussion

Under a façade of media independence, financial-industrial group control over nongovernment media appears to serve as another government tool to curb freedom of speech and limit political contestation.[35] While avoiding direct monopolization of the media, thus outwardly meeting certain democratic standards, the government now remains in a position to ensure media conformity and regulate the information that citizens receive.[36] Group leaders openly professed their loyalty to Nazarbaev, and some have been his close allies since Soviet times or early independence. Because of such close ties, the media that they control generally toe the official Nur-Otan party line.[37] In addition, the two serious attempts by Kazakhstan's financial-industrial groups to use their media holdings to further their own interests in a manner that threatened the political status quo were, in the end, quickly suppressed and the threats they represented defused. Combined, these factors suggest that financial-industrial groups' management of the media is a sound strategy for ensuring political control.

However, domination of print and electronic media by financial-industrial groups may have negative political consequences for authoritarian rulers like Nazarbaev. Despite outward appearances of unity behind the head of state, financial-industrial groups are far from united or monolithic.[38] Competition among them to influence decision making and to gain access to key economic resources often pits groups in the inner circle against one another. Under such circumstances, the media have become weapons in this intra-elite struggle and are used to critique and leak negative information about rivals, sway public opinion, and influence policy in their favor.

To maintain the appearance of unity and to avoid appearing weak or vulnerable, President Nazarbaev attempts to minimize public manifestations of conflict within the elite surrounding him—as do authoritarian rulers in personalist regimes the world over.[39] By making their disputes public on the pages of their newspapers and on viewers' television screens, financial-industrial groups impede the president's ability to create an image of elite consolidation. When the discord and grievances of those closest to the president are publicly aired, it suggests that he may lack full control over his subordinates or the financial-industrial groups surrounding him.[40]

Furthermore, while the media outlets headed by financial-industrial groups have thus far lined up in support of Nazarbaev, their loyalty could quickly and sharply change under the right circumstances. Precedents for this kind of sudden about-face can be found in both Kyrgyzstan and Ukraine. In Kyrgyzstan a former ally of then-president Askar Akayev showed live footage of the anti-Akayev protests of March 2005 on his national television channel and provided a platform for opposition leaders to publicly and harshly criticize the president.[41] During Ukraine's Orange Revolution, oligarchs who had supported and been supported by former president Leonid Kuchma similarly used their media holdings, including national television, to successfully challenge the results of the 2004 presidential elections (Way 2005). As in Kyrgyzstan and Ukraine, outward expressions of support in Kazakhstan for the president belie financial-industrial groups' opportunism simmering beneath the surface.[42] One Kazakhstani journalist summarized the potential unfolding of events as follows: "The closer to the end of Nazarbaev's rule, the more the elite want to be prepared for that end and try to get into or take over power. Among the largest financial-industrial group, elites are preparing their platforms, buying up media groups, and even providing some support money to the opposition. For the time being, of course, they are acting as though they support the president, but what will come later is unclear."[43]

Kazakhstan's pattern of media ownership also raises a critical question for international donors working to promote independent media in authoritarian regimes: what are the prospects for development of independent media and widely accessible sources of alternative information in Kazakhstan?[44] Donor organizations have been working under the assumption that nongovernment media in Kazakhstan are independent media. Most nongovernment media, however, are not independent; rather, they are highly dependent on the financial-industrial groups that keep them operating. As such, the media are used by those who back them for their own ends. At times this results in mainstream media coverage that brings the country's normally inaccessible "corridor politics" (*kuluarnaya politika*) into the open. For the most part, however, because nongovernment media are financed by the very elites who benefit from the current political and economic rules of the game, these nominally independent outlets are unlikely to fundamentally challenge the status quo.

How, then, can international donor organizations encourage freedom of speech in countries like Kazakhstan, where oligarchs dominate nongovernment media? Recognizing that nongovernment media are not equivalent to independent media would assist donors in reformulating their approaches to better target their democracy-promotion programs. One of the problems some donors have faced in the past is that after helping their local private media partners build their facilities and expertise, these outlets were bought or taken over by financial-industrial groups or local government officials.[45]

Rather than working with particular partner outlets, it makes sense to expand programs that target *collective* journalistic activities. For example, expanded training for journalists, editors, and station managers in international codes of ethics and professionalism could go a long way in encouraging greater account-ability among media outlets backed by financial-industrial groups. Continuing financial support for local media watchdogs could also ensure systematized documentation of censorship and pressure on the nongovernment media. In addition, expanded funding for U.S. government–sponsored news sources, such as Radio Free Europe/Radio Liberty (RFE/RL), to increase its Russian-language programming could provide more journalists with an alternative outlet for their reports and citizens with an alternative source of information. Currently, the RFE/RL station, Radio Azattyq, broadcasts primarily in Kazakh. While the mission of RFE/RL is to broadcast in national languages rather than in Russian, greater Russian-language content of RFE/RL radio programming could broaden its audience. Many urban residents—including ethnic Kazakhs—are fluent in Russian and do not rely on Kazakh as their main language of communication.

Given the Kazakhstani government's decision to forego serious steps toward political liberalization, donor efforts to encourage fully independent media have not been welcomed. However, targeted programs like the ones outlined above could make a small but significant impact in the longer run. Experimentation in Kazakhstan could, in turn, inform donor activities in other authoritarian political systems in which elite business interests are similarly tied to print and electronic media outlets. Ultimately, however, it is domestic politics—especially intra-elite relations and relations between financial-industrial groups and President Nazarbaev—that will drive media developments.

NOTES

Research for this chapter was supported in part by the Title VIII Research Scholar Program, funded by the U.S. State Department, Program for Research and Training on Eastern Europe and the Independent States of the Former Soviet Union and administered by American Councils for International Education: ACTR/ACCELS. The opinions expressed are the author's and do not necessarily express the views of the State Department or American Councils.

1. Under Soviet rule, Nazarbaev served as first secretary of the Kazakh Communist Party from 1989 to 1991. He has been president of independent Kazakhstan since 1991.

2. As the head of a national nongovernment radio and television company noted, "In Kazakhstan, we don't have official censors. They aren't needed because we censor ourselves to keep from getting in trouble." (Quoted by former official at the U.S. Agency for International Development/Central Asia Regional Mission, personal communication with the author, January 2008.)

3. The criminal code stipulates prison sentences for "impugning the honor and dignity of the President of the republic" and for slandering public officials. See Law No. 167 of 16 July 1997 of the Republic of Kazakhstan, The Criminal Code of the Republic of Kazakhstan, articles 318, 319, and 320, http://www.legislationline.org/download/action/download/id/1681/file/ca1cfb8a67f8a1c2ffe8de6554a3.htm/preview.

4. Oligarchs are "wealthy, politically influential individuals, [many of whom have] . . . gained their wealth through access to cheap privatization, state monopolies, or budgetary resources" (Way 2005, 136).

5. The author conducted qualitative, in-depth fieldwork in Kazakhstan, interviewing seventy-five Kazakhstani political and economic elites, scholars, political observers, members of the political opposition, and NGO leaders in the capital, Astana, and the country's financial center, Almaty. Other source materials include official and opposition newspapers in Russian and Kazakh, secondary analyses published in Russian and English, and public information on the Internet.

6. The comments of the former Minister of Information and Culture, Yermukhamet Yertysbaev (2006–2008), highlight the dynamic under way: "The situation [i.e., the lack of media accountability] is deepening due to the association of a number of well known media with financial-industrial groups, which use them as ideological weapons [to further] their corporate interests [instead of] national interests" (Tarakov 2007).

7. Interview with anonymous Kazakhstani journalist, Almaty, March 15, 2007.

8. Interview with Rozlana Taukina, director of the media NGO Zhurnalisty v Bede (Journalists in Trouble), Almaty, March 6, 2007.

9. Aliev and Nazarbaeva reportedly used dubious or strong-arm tactics to force the previous owners of these papers into selling.

10. Political elites are defined as those who indirectly or directly play a regular and substantial part in national political outcomes, including political, government, and economic actors (Higley and Burton 1989; Mosca 1939; Pareto 1935, 1966; Putnam 1976).

11. The data are based on publicly available sources and interviews with journalists, political observers, politicians, and scholars in Kazakhstan during spring 2007.

12. Sources consulted include other elites in the inner circle; however, they were not included here due to a lack of information about their business activities. These include the president's nephew, Kairat Saltybaldy; former prime minister, former mayor of Almaty, and current mayor of Astana, Imangali Tasmagambetov; and former Minister of Foreign Affairs and current secretary of the National Security Council, Marat Tazhin (see also Adilov 2007).

13. Interview with anonymous journalist, Almaty, April 5, 2007.

14. This division follows the categorization used in most of the written works, both Kazakhstani and Russian, on Kazakhstan's financial-industrial groups.

15. The composition of the second tier has changed over time. Some groups that were formerly in the second tier have since lost their positions as the result of public political conflict with members of the inner circle. These include Bulat Abilov and Galymzhan Zhakiyanov, who until 2001 were among the financial-industrial group leaders. Zhakiyanov once owned a local television station in Pavlodar oblast (province) called Irbis, which the Eurasia Group took over.

16. Interview with the director of Internews Kazakhstan, Oleg Katsiev, Almaty, May 17, 2007.

17. Interviews with anonymous journalists, Almaty, February 4, 2007, February 13, 2007, April 10, 2007, and May 7, 2007.

18. Irbis received the rights to seven radio stations throughout Kazakhstan: in Pavlodar (its original location), Kyzylorda, Almaty, Ust-Kameogorsk, Kokshetau, Kostanay, and Astana. According to one source, Irbis won rights to almost half of the radio frequencies "because [the leader of the Eurasia Group, Aleksandr] Mashkevich is one of those who the president can trust" (interview with anonymous journalist, May 7, 2007). The Ministry of Information and Culture justified the selection by explaining that Irbis is the only TV/radio company that produces 70 percent of its own programs and has both a sound business concept and the ability to attract future financing. A number of private broadcast companies, however, disagreed with the results of the tender, arguing that the process was non-transparent and violated Kazakhstan's legal norms (see National Broadcasters Association of Kazakhstan 2007).

19. Gulzhan Ergalieva, editor in chief, *Svoboda Slova* opposition newspaper, December 21, 2005, http://www.medialaw.kz/index.php?r=87&c=1651.

20. In an interview (May 17, 2007), Oleg Katsiev explained: "In the late 1990s and early 2000s the national and regional media outlets that were bought up by elites were simply not profitable. It's only just recently that big media companies can bring in profits, and even in these cases not all do."

21. Perhaps the first attempt to run a public campaign against President Nazarbaev was undertaken in 1998 by former prime minister Akezhan Kazhegeldin, the president's main political rival at the time. Kazhegeldin established the longest-running Kazakh-language opposition newspaper, *Dat*, and is said to have opened a series of Russian-language newspapers as part of his political campaign. These papers, however, came under formal and informal pressure and were quickly shut down. For a detailed account, see Suleimenov, Ashimbaev, and Andreev 2003. While Kazhegeldin has been in political exile for more than ten years, *Dat* has been issued under different names and subjected to fines, closures, and lawsuits. In 2007, *Dat* was called *Taszharghan* and was published in both Russian and Kazakh.

22. See *Obrashchenie Demvybora k Kazakhstantsam*, November 21, 2001, http://www.kub.info/print.php?sid=405. The DCK had five political demands: an independent judiciary; greater parliamentary powers; popular election of governors; liberalizing the media; and greater control over natural resource exploitation. The last two demands are closely related to the discussion in this chapter. Because those in the second tier were restricted from desired media outlets and kept out of the oil, gas, and metals industries, it made sense that these should be included in their demands, framed as key issues that would benefit Kazakhstan's citizens as a whole rather than their own self-interest.

23. In effect, they faced a glass ceiling that prevented them from realizing their business ambitions. In an interview (Almaty, December 19, 2006, emphasis added), Abilov recounted: "I had already reached the ceiling in business. We built a major shopping center [*torgovyi tsentr*, the equivalent of a mall] in Almaty and purchased a series of other businesses. And so what? It was not interesting to me anymore; I had already accomplished all of that. *Why couldn't I get into other big manufacturing projects, metal processing, the oil sector, or the gas sector? They let in their own, their relatives, those close to them, others who paid big bribes.* I ran into a ceiling in which they said to me, 'Boy, feel free to build another Ramstor [grocery store/shopping center chain in Kazakhstan]. Be content with what you have . . . We let you get this far; we didn't touch you. You should be happy with that.'"

24. Recounting this period, Oleg Katsiev explains: "It turned out that those who suddenly went into the opposition had their own small television companies, but no one knew

about it before. What does this mean? Perhaps it signifies that they were preparing for their protest in advance. They needed some mass media outlets, which would be useful in their efforts. The regional companies in Aktobe and in Pavlodar and others in the oblast centers were not profitable businesses at all, especially at that time. But they [the DCK founders] bought them anyway. This suggests that they were primarily needed to further their owners' interests" (interview with the author, Almaty, May 17, 2007).

25. Kazakhstan is divided into fourteen provinces (called *oblasts*), each governed by an *akim* (governor) directly appointed by the president.

26. Petr Svoik, a current NGO leader, cofounder of the Azamat opposition party in 1996, a former member of Kazakhstan's parliament, and former minister, explains that "the airing of this television program [on Zhakiyanov] was not an accident. At that time Channel 31 was controlled by—let's say was helped by—the opposition, and programs of this type were short, but they were done with public politics in mind" (interview, Almaty, January 31, 2007).

27. Although the president's press secretary announced that the president supported the DCK's political platform (*Kazakhstan Today*, November 21, 2001), in a speech on KTK, the president, standing next to Aliev, criticized the DCK founders for breaking the law and avoiding taxes (KTK, November 20, 2001).

28. Interview with Galymzhan Zhakiyanov, Almaty, February 28, 2007.

29. For details on attacks on the media during this period, see International Press Institute 2002, International Press Institute 2003, and Human Rights Watch 2003.

30. Coverage began in early February 2007 with a series of articles and interviews alleging that Aliev had kidnapped and tortured three former top managers of Nurbank, the bank in which he owned a majority share, to force them into a business deal with terms favorable to Aliev. See Ergalieva Gulzhan, "Nurbank—Otlichnyi Rezul'tat," *Svoboda Slova*, February 8, 2007; Rozlana Taukina, "Strasti Nurbanka," *Taszharghan* [formerly *Dat*], February 8, 2007; and Madi Yan, "Nastal Ochered . . . Bankirov," *Taszharghan*, February 8, 2007.

31. "Nurbank protiv Gazet 'Svoboda Slova,' 'Taszharghan,' i Internet-gazety," February 16, 2007, http://zonakz.net/articles/19839.

32. Rakhatgate was now being reported in the official press, as well as in the mainstream (i.e., non-opposition) nongovernment press. See Saken Zhuagulov, "Missiya Nevy-polnina," *Biznes i Vlast,'* May 25, 2007, and Irina Sevost'yanina, "MVD Vozbudilo Ugolovnoe Delo v Otnoshenii Posla Kazakhstana v Avstrii," *Panorama*, May 25, 2007.

33. Transcripts of the telephone recordings can be found at: http://www.kub.info/article.php?sid=19843. The Astana channel, which had been little known until then, was one of three stations to win radio frequencies in the January 2007 tender.

34. Interestingly, the heads of media outlets associated with Aliev attempted to use the channels that opposition leaders and journalists regularly use to spread the word and seek protection during particularly repressive periods. See Rozlana Taukina, "V Zashchitu Informatsionnogo Agenstva 'Kazakhstan Today,'" *ZonaKZ*, July 1, 2007, http://zonakz.net/articles/17969; "Offitsial'noe Zayavlenie Uchreditelei TOO 'Izdatel'skii Dom Alma-Media,'" *ZonaKZ*, July 7, 2007, http://zonakz.net/articles/18026; and "Press-riliz Kolletiva Redaktsii Gazeta 'Karavan,'" *ZonaKZ*, July 5, 2007, http://zonakz.net/articles/17995.

35. According to the Ministry of Culture and Information, in 2007 Kazakhstan had 212 nongovernment electronic and print outlets.

36. A similar strategy was adopted in neighboring Kyrgyzstan, where close allies of former President Kurmanbek Bakiyev gained ownership or control over independent and formerly oppositionist newspapers (interviews with political observers and independent journalists, Bishkek, fall 2007).

37. Nur-Otan is the presidential political party that emerged in 2007 when a series of pro-presidential parties merged with Nazarbaev's Otan party.

38. Interview with Dosym Satpaev, director of Gruppa Otsenki Riskov, Almaty, February 24, 2007.

39. As one political figure emphasized: "In our country politics are based on the principle that no political or economic conflicts should arise among those in formal and informal positions of power. The president has outlined the direction in which the country is to go, and there should be no discussion over it. The president tries hard to keep all conflict among the elite hidden from view, to make it appear as though everyone is in agreement and has reached a common consensus over the rules and outcome of the game. Although, of course, this is far from true" (interview with anonymous parliamentarian, Astana, February 18, 2007).

40. Dosym Satpaev argues that this is, in fact, the case. Highlighting the president's increasing difficulty in maintaining control over the country's financial-industrial groups, he comments: "When the president founded the political system at the beginning of the 1990s, he did not have the kinds of political problems that we have now, because at that time there were few competing pressure groups [another term commonly used for financial-industrial groups]. As the players grow in number and their interests come into conflict with one another, the president can no longer control their actions. Now he is only in the position to control the *effects* of their actions. This is an important change that we are now witnessing" (interview, Almaty, February 24, 2007).

41. Interviews with political observers and independent journalists, Bishkek, fall 2007.

42. According to Petr Svoik: "To say that elites who criticize the president from the

opposition are not loyal and all the others are loyal would be incorrect. *No one is loyal; they are all loyal to themselves*. . . A change in rule [under personalistic regimes like Kazakhstan's] is always unexpected, and elites know this. This is why in recent years (ten years ago this was not the case, because the president was younger and had many years ahead of him) all the elites are preparing for the president's departure. The main stimulus or vector along which elites are orienting themselves is to be prepared for some unexpected factor x when the president will be replaced" (interview with the author, Almaty, January 31, 2007).

43. Interviews with anonymous journalists, Almaty, May 8, 2007.

44. Innovative sources of information and alternative views certainly exist, all of which target local Kazakhstani audiences and post items critical of the president and the political system. These have included Internet sites like KUB (www.kub.info), Navigator (http://zonakz.net), and Radio Inkar (www.inkar.info), which has not been updated since 2008. Yet such alternatives face one hard truth: users are limited to those with Internet access, and, in the case of Radio Inkar, to those with reliable and relatively fast connection. Because the government monopolizes Internet service, it is extremely expensive—according to some estimates, one thousand times the cost of similar service in Western Europe.

45. Author's conversation with a former official at the USAID/Central Asia Regional Mission, January 2008.

REFERENCES

Adilov, Mukhamedzhan. 2003. "Kto Smel, Tot i S'el!" *Respublika*, November 21.

———. 2007. "Krasnye Flazhki dlya Novogo Prem'era: Versii, chto Preemnikom Stanet Srednii Zyat' Prezidenta, Esli Ne Oshibochny, to Prezhdevremenny." *Respublika*, January.

Ashimbaev, Daniyar. 2007. "Politicheskaya Systema: Reformy, Vybory, Kadry," *Kazakhstan*, 3.

———. 2008. *Kto Est' Kto v Kazakhstane*. Almaty: Credo.

Dave, Bhavna. 2007. *Kazakhstan: Nations in Transit*. Http://www.freedomhouse.hu/images/ fdh_galleries/NIT2007/nt-kazakhstan.pdf.

Duvanov, Sergei. 2007. "Gop-stop po Nazarbaevski." *Radio Inkar*, November 15. Http://inkar. info/index.php?id=1145.

Dylevskaya, Svetlana. 2001. "Khabarizatsiya vse strany?" *Internews Bulletin*, 116–17. Http:// old.internews.kz/rus/bulletin/116/page01.htm and http://old.internews.kz/rus/bul- letin/117/page01.htm.

Dzhanibekov, Erlan. 2004. "Gosudarstvo RK: Eto Ne Kazakhstantsy, a Transnatsional'nye Oligarkhi iz Grupp Tipa Evraziya, Trans Uorld' i t.d." *ZonaKZ*, June 17. Http://zonakz.

net/articles/6488.

Epitsentr Evraziiskii Tsentr Politicheskikh Issledovanii i Agentsvo Sotsial'nykh Tekhnologii. 2005. *Gruppy Vliyaniya vo Vlastno-politicheskoi Sisteme Respubliki Kazakhstan.* Http:// zonakz.net/articles/10280.

Golyshkin, Yaroslav. 2007. "Irbis Vyros: Pavlodarskii Telekanal Menyaet Status, Propisku i, Vozmozhno, Nazvanie." *Versiya,* January 22. Http://www.presscenter.kz/index. php?show=news&id=834.

Higley, John, and Michael G. Burton. 1989. "The Elite Variable in Democratic Transitions and Breakdowns." *American Sociological Review* 54(1):17–32.

Human Rights Watch. 1998. *World Report: Kazakhstan.* Http://www.hrw.org/legacy/worldreport/ Helsinki-16.htm#P773_184363.

———. 1999. *Kazakhstan: Freedom of the Media and Political Freedoms in the Prelude to the 1999 Elections.* Www.hrw.org/reports/1999/kazakhstan.

———. 2003. *World Report: Kazakhstan.* Http://hrw.org/wr2k3/europe8.html.

International Eurasian Institute for Economic and Political Research. 1998. *Freedom of Speech and Mass Media in Kazakhstan: A Survey of the Press in Kazakhstan and Russia* (abridged version). Http://iicas.org/english/publruss.htm.

International Press Institute. 1998. *World Press Freedom Review: Kazakhstan.* Vienna, Austria.

———. 2002. *World Press Freedom Review: Kazakhstan.* Vienna, Austria.

———. 2003. *World Press Freedom Review: Kazakhstan.* Vienna, Austria.

Katsiev, Oleg. 1999. "Prospects for Development of an Independent Media in Kazakhstan." In *Civil Society in Central Asia,* ed. M. Holt Ruffin and Daniel C. Waugh. Washington, DC: Center for Civil Society International.

Kharlov, Vasilii. 2005. "Papa Nazarbaev." *Nezivisimaya Gazeta,* April 26. Www.ng.ru/ ideas/2005-04-26/10_nazarbaev.html.

Khlyupin, Vitalii. 1998. *'Bol'shaya sem'ya' Nursultana Nazarbaeva: Politicheskaya Elita Sovremennogo Kazakhstana.* Moscow: Institut Aktual'nykh Politicheskikh Issledovanii.

Kjænet, Heidi, Dosym Satpaev, and Stina Torjesen. 2008. "Big Business and High-Level Politics in Kazakhstan: An Everlasting Symbiosis?" *China and Eurasia Quarterly* 6:95–107.

Makimbai, Bakytgul, and Rozlana Taukina. 2007. "Ya Imeyu Pravo na Svoe Mnenie, Dazhe esli Oshibochno . . ." *KUB.* Http://kub.info/print.php?sid=17243.

Mosca, Gaetano. 1939. *The Ruling Class.* New York: McGraw-Hill.

National Broadcasters Association of Kazakhstan. 2007. *Otkrytoe Pis'mo Prim'er-Ministru i General'nomu Prokuroru Respubliki Kazakhstan.* Www.zakon.kz/our/news/news.asp?id =30088527.

Omarova, Aigul. 2002. "I v Informatsionnykh Voinakh Sluchayutsya Peremiriya." *ZonaKZ,* September 23. Http://zonakz.net/articles/1491.

———. 2007a. Kak Eto Vse Nachinalos' i Prodolzhalos.' *KUB,* June 4. Http://www.kub.info/

print.php?sid=17884.

———. 2007b. Vse Tainoe Rano ili Pozdno Stanovitsya Yav'yu. *Radio Inkar,* November 28. Http://inkar.info/?id=1213.

Panfilova, Viktoria. "Rakhat Aliev—Interv'yu pered Arestom: Zyat' Prezidenta Nazarbaeva Schitaet Sebya Postradavshim iz-za Sobstvennykh Mediaaktivov." *Nezavisimaya Gazeta,* June 1, 2007. Www.ng.ru/cis/2007-06-01/6_aliev.html.

Pareto, Vilfredo. 1935. *The Mind and Society.* New York: Harcourt, Brace, and World.

———. 1966. *Vilfredo Pareto: Sociological Writings.* New York: Praeger.

Profil'. 2007. April 2 Http://www.profile.ru/items/? item=22527.

Putnam, Robert D. 1976. *The Comparative Study of Elites.* New Jersey: Prentice-Hall.

Satov, Ariel. 2007. "Nachalo Krutogo Puti." *KUB.* Www.kub.info/article.php? sid=19856.

Satpaev, Dosym. 2005. *An Analysis of the Internal Structure of Kazakhstan's Political Elite and an Assessment of Political Risk Levels.* Http://srch.slav.hokudai.ac.jp/coe21/publish/ n014_ses/11_satpaev.pdf.

———. 2006. "Poka SMI: Lish' Instrument v Rukakh FPG i vVasti." *S perom i shagoi,* 2. Www. internews. kz/index.php?itemid=2951.

Serdalina, Zhanar. 2001. "Biznes-elita Pozhalovalas' Prezidenty." *Komsomol'skaya Pravda,* November 1. Www.kub.info/article.php?sid=211.

Sopranin, Anton. 2007. "Rakhat Aliev Ochistit Dazhe Trudnovyvodimye Pyatna." *Pozitsiya,* December 7. Www.posit.kz/?lan=ru&id=100&pub=4377.

Suleimenov, Nurlan, Daniyar Ashimbaev, and Viktor Andreev. 2003. *Kazakhstan 90-kh: Pravitel'stvo Kazhegel'dina: Privatizatsiya, Korruptsiya i Bor'ba za Vlast'.* Almaty: Credo.

Sysoev, Gennadii. 2001. "Mezhdu Zyatem i Demokraticheskim Vyborom." *Kommersant,* November 20. Www.kub.info/article.php?sid=388.

Tarakov, Aleksandr. 2007. "Natsiya Dolzhna Deistvovat' kak Edinoe Tseloe." *Kazakhstanskaya Pravda,* November 16. Www.kazpravda.kz/index.php?uin=1151645457&chap ter=1195163423.

Way, Lucan A. 2005. "Kuchma's Failed Authoritarianism." *Journal of Democracy* 16:131–45.

Yuritsyn, Vladislav. 2007. "Boi Milliardnogo Znacheniya. *ZonaKZ,* June 22. Www.zonakz. net/articles/18231.

Zhovtis, Evgenii. 1999. "Freedom of Association and the Question of its Realization in Kazakhstan." In *Civil Society in Central Asia,* ed. M. Holt Ruffin and Daniel C. Waugh. Washington, DC: Center for Civil Society International.

Reinforcing Authoritarianism through Media Control: The Case of Post-Soviet Turkmenistan

Luca Anceschi

Total control over national media featured prominently in the evolution of authoritarianism in post-Soviet Turkmenistan. Since its first edition in 2002, the annual Press Freedom Index from the Paris-based NGO Reporters sans Frontieres (RSF) has regularly ranked the Turkmenistani regime as one of the most serious offenders of press freedom internationally (RSF 2009). In the "List of Most Censored Countries," compiled by the Committee to Protect Journalists (CPJ) in 2006, the Turkmenistani state occupied third place, after North Korea and Myanmar (CPJ 2007), and the list of "10 Worst Countries to Be a Blogger" also includes Turkmenistan (CPJ 2009).

Despite his recurrent assurances during the 2007 electoral campaign, President Gurbanguly M. Berdymuhammedov's regime failed to relax its repressive stance toward the media.[1] As a consequence, Turkmenistani media remained "under tight state control" (Eurasianet 2007) after President-for-Life Saparmurat A. Niyazov's death.

Preliminary censorship aimed at silencing independent opinions and systematic repression of dissenting voices have been the main strategies through which the media landscape was transformed into a state monopoly. Brutal repression, however, was not the only salient facet of media politics in independent Turkmenistan, as the regime also used the national media to strengthen its power. Turkmenistan's media outlets in general, and its print media in particular, have been the preferred vehicles to promote the cult of personality of the national leadership. This strategy was predominantly used during the Niyazov era, when it emerged as one of the distinguishing features of the country's political landscape.

Therefore, a strong connection between the regime and the media represents a unifying thread in the evolution of Turkmenistani authoritarianism. Both Berdymuhammedov and Niyazov perceived media control as an indispensable tool for regime consolidation.

Statement of the Issue

This chapter provides a detailed analysis of the regime's media policy since independence. The chapter focuses on the significant contribution of the national media to the strengthening of authoritarianism, both before and after Niyazov's death.

The analysis revolves around the following key question: *In relation to matters of domestic consideration (i.e., regime consolidation), what role has the regime assigned to its media policy?* That media policy, the chapter argues, developed into two main prongs: repression and propaganda. The former helped maximize the regime's control over political life by silencing dissent and obliterating independent voices. The latter left an indelible mark on the political behavior of the population by promoting a window-dressing ideology designed to legitimize the regime. To different degrees and through different approaches, both facets of media policy helped the regime achieve an identical objective: consolidation of its own powers.

Western scholars have so far failed to illuminate the strong connections between media politics and regime consolidation in post-Soviet Turkmenistan. The literature has mostly been limited to considering media repression as evidence of the wholesale abuse of human rights or to describing the personality cults surrounding the Turkmenistani leaders in general terms. This chapter fills that void by placing the government's media policy in the broader context and processes of regime consolidation.

Methodology

The division of Turkmenistan's media policy into two prongs is crucial to the purposes of this study, and its importance strongly influenced the selection of the sources upon which the argument rests.

This analysis is based on primary sources (official documents from the government) and secondary sources (reports from international and nongovernmental organizations, plus analytical and scholarly articles). The latter are useful to describe the strategy through which the regime created a state monopoly over the media. Primary sources in turn are used to portray the regime's response to international criticism of its media policy. The analysis of the role played by the print media in the propaganda system relies entirely on primary sources: the complete collection of the regime's official mouthpiece, the Russian-language daily newspaper *Neytral'nyi Turkmenistan,* which, until 14 December 1995, was known by the Soviet-imposed name *Turkmenskaya Iskra.*

To present its central argument, this chapter uses a two-track analysis: a detailed description of the systemic repression of dissenting and independent voices on the one hand, and a comprehensive analysis of the role played by the print media in the propaganda system on the other. The first segment of the "Findings" section, "The Establishment of Media Monopoly in Post-Soviet Turkmenistan," describes the strategy through which the regime emerged as the sole actor in Turkmenistan's media landscape. The second segment, "The Role of Print Media in Turkmenistan's Propaganda System," examines the role of *Turkmenskaya Iskra/Neytral'nyi Turkmenistan* in fostering the ideology promoted by the two presidents who ruled Turkmenistan after the collapse of the Soviet Union.

Findings

THE ESTABLISHMENT OF MEDIA MONOPOLY
IN POST-SOVIET TURKMENISTAN

Since the demise of the Soviet Union, the Turkmenistani leadership successfully subjugated every aspect of politics to its own interests, and so consolidated its power position. The media was integral to this strategy. This section's main aim is to describe the regime's systematic media repression. The analysis focuses first on media legislation and then describes the country's media monopoly. After the examination of cases of brutal repression of Turkmenistani journalists, this section discusses the international criticism that followed those occurrences and the regime's responses to external pressures for media liberalization.

In relation to freedom of expression, the rights of the Turkmenistani people are nominally guaranteed by the constitution. According to Article 28 of the 2008 constitutional draft—which reprised the provisions of Article 26 of the 1992 constitution—the "[c]itizens of Turkmenistan have the right to freedom of conviction and the free expression of those convictions."[2] Strikingly, Article 28 is the only provision on freedom of expression in the constitution, which therefore fails to address important facets of media policy, notably those connected with the collection and dissemination of information. In line with what occurred with most principles enshrined in the constitution, the Niyazov and the Berdymuhammedov regimes failed to implement the provisions of Article 28.

So far as enactment of legislation, the government has steadfastly refused to regulate the national media landscape in any significant way. Creation and maintenance of a legislative vacuum became a crucial factor in the establishment of a regime's monopoly over the country's media system. Throughout the post-Soviet era, the government failed to develop "any substantial media legislation acceptable in the democratic family of [Organization for Security and Cooperation in Europe] participating States" (OSCE 2002, 96). Numerous aspects of its media landscape are still regulated by the Soviet-era law "[c]oncerning the press and other sources of mass media in the Turkmen SSR."

With virtually no independent print, broadcast, or electronic media, all media outlets are subject to the regime's control.[3] According to the OSCE (2002, 86–95), the regime enjoyed monopolistic control vis-à-vis media registration, media financing, and publishing facilities. At the same time, the regime dictated the editorial lines of each media outlet. Lack of legislative tools and the establishment of hegemonic control over the different facets of media politics ultimately allowed the Niyazov regime to transform the media landscape into a monopoly. As shown later in this chapter, repression did not relax in the Berdymuhammedov era.

Presenting a quantitative image of Turkmenistan's principal print and broadcast media is challenging. Figure 1 attempts to do so with reliable data in the public record (OSCE 2002, 92–93; Atayeva 2002, 1).

The Niyazov regime had an appalling record of violating press freedom. Instances of oppression of journalists occurred frequently throughout his years in power. Radio Free Europe/Radio Liberty's (RFE/RL) Turkmen service was intentionally targeted. For example, in September 2003, Saparmurat Ovezberdiev, a prominent journalist for the service, was held in custody for three days, during which he was tortured by the police (RSF 2003). In March 2004 two other members of the team, Rakhim Esenov and Ashyrguly Bayryev, were similarly mistreated, while Mukhamed Berdyev, Moscow's correspondent for RFE/RL Turkmen service, was severely beaten in his apartment in the Russian capital (RSF 2005).

In June 2006, police arrested three journalists (Annakurban Amanklychev, Sapardurdy Khadjiyev, and RFE/RL's Ogulsapar Muradova), who assisted a crew from France 2 TV in making a documentary titled *Turkmenistan: Welcome*

FIGURE 1. TURKMENISTAN: PRINCIPAL PRINT AND BROADCAST MEDIA

Print Media

NATIONAL PERIODICALS

Neytral'nyi Turkmenistan (daily: 23,110 copies)

Turkmenistan (daily: 23,000 copies)

REGIONAL PERIODICALS

Ashgabat (three times a week: 15,000 copies)

Vatan (three times a week: 15,000 copies)

SPECIAL–INTEREST PERIODICALS

Esger (once a week: 7,000 copies *circa*)

Adalat (once a week: 7,000 copies *circa*)

Mugalymlar (fortnightly: 10,670 copies)

Turkmen Duniyasy (fortnightly: 6,200 copies)

Gurbansoltan-Edzhe (monthly magazine: 2,000 copies)

Lukman (quarterly: 1,000 copies)

News Agencies

Turkmen Dowlet Habarlar Gullugy (TDH)

Television

Three state television stations: *TMT-1, TMT-2, TMT-3*

SOURCES: OSCE 2002; Atayeva 2002.

to Niyazovland. The three journalists, who were also involved in human rights advocacy, were tortured, unfairly tried, and condemned to six (Muradova) and seven (Amanklychev and Khadjiyev) years of imprisonment on charges of illegal possession of ammunition. A large wave of international criticism followed their imprisonment (RFE/RL 2006a; RFE/RL 2006b). On 14 September 2006, media throughout the world reported Muradova's death, which was regarded outside Turkmenistan as a political assassination. International organizations, a large number of foreign governments, and human rights groups demanded an independent investigation of the circumstances that led to Muradova's death, but the regime did not respond to such pressures.

In the Niyazov era, the regime faced many other calls for liberalization of the national media landscape. International organizations, both governmental (such as United Nations 2003; OSCE 2002, 102–04) and nongovernmental (such as RSF and CPJ), repeatedly called for a relaxation in the oppressive control over the media. The regime ignored and did not comply with such demands.

From the outset, Berdymuhammedov seemed preoccupied with projecting an image of discontinuity with Niyazov's ruling methods. In the view of the new regime, the intention to liberalize the media landscape—which the Turkmenistani president repeatedly flagged in early 2007—could potentially contribute to refreshing the government's image. Nonetheless, practical measures did not follow Berdymuhammedov's professed commitment to liberalize media outlets, and electronic media in particular (RFE/RL 2007a). Throughout 2007 fifteen Internet cafés opened across the country (Open Society Institute 2007, 2008b), although, as CPJ (2009) later reported, such outlets were "guarded by soldiers, [their] connections were uneven, [and] the[ir] hourly fee was prohibitively high." In mid-2008 the large majority of those cafés closed, mainly due to *Turkmentelecom*'s failure to provide the "adequate transmission speed" (OSI 2008b). On 12 October 2007, users were finally allowed to post comments on the pages of the government's official Web site. However, after the post of a number of comments criticizing Berdymuhammedov and his government, this feature quickly disappeared from the site (RFE/RL 2007b).

The issue of media liberalization was also raised during Berdymuhammedov's first official visit to the United States, in September 2007. After his address to the United Nations General Assembly, he spoke at Columbia University. In addressing questions regarding the media situation in Turkmenistan, Berdymuhammedov categorically denied state pressure on the press (Krastev 2007). Such paradoxical assertions are in line with the strategy devised by the prior regime to respond to external pressures on political liberalization in a manner that often entailed the rhetorical portrayal of the regime to domestic and international audiences as a staunch human rights supporter.

The Berdymuhammedov regime has continued to pay lip service to promotion of media freedom: in September 2010, official sources announced the publication of *Rysgal*, speedily presented as the first privately owned newspaper to appear in the country as reported by the State News Agency of Turkmenistan, or TDH (2010). Nevertheless, this newspaper—devoted almost entirely to business news—does not represent a genuinely independent voice, as its publisher; the Union of Industrialists and Entrepreneurs, is for all intents and purposes a state-controlled organization (Fitzpatrick 2010).

Rhetorical statements notwithstanding, with increasing regularity the post-Niyazov regime continued to violate the freedom of the media. As of July 2010, Amanklychev and Khadjiyev remained in a high-security prison in western Turkmenistan (RSF 2009), and Berdymuhammedov did not institute a commission to investigate Muradova's death, despite mounting international demands (RSF 2008).

Furthermore, the Berdymuhammedov regime did not cease its harassment of journalists and media operators. In late June 2008 Sazak Durdymuradov, an unpaid contributor to the RFE/RL Turkmen service, was severely beaten, tortured, and held for two weeks in a psychiatric clinic in the Lebap *velayat* (region). During his abduction, he reportedly refused to sign "a letter pledging never again to take part in an RFE/RL broadcast" (Synovitz 2008). Following a flood of international criticism (Saidazimova 2008b), Durdymuradov was released on 4 July (RFE/RL 2008).[4]

The immediate aftermath of the parliamentary election of December 2008 also witnessed a further regime crackdown on media operators. Two correspondents of the RFE/RL Turkmen service, Dovletmurat Yazguliev and Osman Hallyev, came under extensive pressure from authorities as a result of their affiliation with the service (Najibullah 2009).

In April 2009 Berdymuhammedov removed Annamurad Poladov—the most prominent censor of the Niyazov era—as chief editor of *Turkmenistan*, the principal Turkmen-language newspaper. In spite of the symbolic value that a number of internal and external observers attached to that action (OSI 2009), it did not lead to a relaxation of media conditions.

THE ROLE OF PRINT MEDIA IN TURKMENISTAN'S PROPAGANDA SYSTEM

Throughout the post-Soviet era, *Turkmenskaya Iskra/Neytral'nyi Turkmenistan* has been a principal actor in establishing the cult of Niyazov's personality. The regime viewed this cult as an essential tool to modify the public's political behavior, meaning the level of compliance that the population showed toward the sets of rules imposed by the regime. Substantial modification of the population's political behavior, in the elite's view, was equivalent to regime consolidation, and it can be reasonably inferred that the print media were an important instrument in achieving that objective.

To develop this argument, this section presents the findings of a two-pronged analysis. To begin with, it describes in details the symbols and slogans featured in the official newspaper to promote Niyazov's personality cult.[5] At the same time, it addresses the issue of continuity and change to identify different phases in which the newspaper placed different emphases on glorifying Niyazov.

In the first two years of the post-independence era, *Turkmenskaya Iskra* continued to play a role analogous to that of the late Soviet era. Strikingly, no substantial change of format and content appeared on the pages of the *Iskra* immediately after the collapse of the Soviet Union. Detailed reports of Niyazov's numerous decrees, complex—and untrustworthy—data on agricultural production, and complete biographical records of elite appointees to political positions appeared on the pages of the daily between 1992 and 1993, just as they had in the late Gorbachev years.[6]

In early 1992 there were two salient differences between the Soviet and the post-Soviet editions of the *Iskra*. On the one hand, the editorial team of the official newspaper quickly abandoned its ideological mission (i.e., promotion of Marxism-Leninism as the official state ideology). On the other hand, the newspaper devoted significant space (including a large number of front-page photographs) to the government's international activities as a way of emphasizing the international implications of the recently acquired independence (*Turkmenskaya Iskra* 1992a, 1992b, 1992c). No evidence of the regime's intent to establish a cult of personality has emerged from the analysis of the collection of *Turkmenskaya Iskra* in the biennium 1992–93. Thus it might be reasonably concluded that in the early post-Soviet era the regime was more focused on expanding its control over the processes of state building and policymaking (Anceschi 2008, 33–36).

Once the emerging regime had increased its powers vis-à-vis crucial political mechanisms and, perhaps more significantly, the country's key polities, establishment of a massive propaganda machine became a key objective. The official newspaper formed an active part of official propaganda. The earliest steps toward creating Niyazov's personality cult came in late 1993, immediately after the celebration of Independence Day, 26 October. Throughout November and December, the front page of *Turkmenskaya Iskra* regularly presented large photographs of citizens marching behind banners featuring one of the most famous slogans of Turkmenistan's propaganda: *Khalk, Vatan, Turkmenbashi*[7] (People, Homeland, Turkmenbashi).

Thereafter, roles and functions of the *Iskra* were revolutionized: glorification of the president, of his policies, his achievements, and, eventually, his ancestry became regular features in official newspapers. As a consequence, both format and content of *Turkmenskaya Iskra* had to adapt to the new targets the regime set for official propaganda.

As for format, a number of important conclusions can be drawn by observing the alternation of symbols in the frontispiece of the *Iskra* between early 1992 and late 1995.

In early 1992 all Soviet symbols disappeared from the title section of *Turkmenskaya Iskra* (see figure 2). As independent political institutions were yet to be

Figure 2. *Turkmenskaya Iskra,* frontispiece, 15 July 1992

Figure 3. *Turkmenskaya Iskra,* frontispiece, 10 September 1992

Figure 4. *Turkmenskaya Iskra,* frontispiece, 13 April 1994

Figure 5. *Turkmenskaya Iskra,* frontispiece, 1 February 1995

Figure 6. *Turkmenskaya Iskra,* frontispiece, 15 March 1999

established by the government, the newspaper could not act as an official organ of any of them. Therefore, the *Iskra*'s frontispiece in early post-independence days was characterized by a simple appearance: no symbol was included and the entire title section was occupied by the newspaper's name and information on the frequency of publication (*ezhednevaya gazeta*).

As the regime steadily progressed in creating independent political institutions, the *Iskra* became the official mouthpiece of the government and parliament (*Organ Pravitel'stva i Medzhlisa Turkmenistana*). At the same time, Turkmenistan's coat of arms was introduced in the bottom left section of the frontispiece (see figure 3).

During 1993–94 two new items were featured in the title section of the newspaper. The national flag joined the coat of arms on the left side of the frontispiece, and the new top section included a quote from one of the works of Magtymguly, chosen by the regime as Turkmenistan's national poet.[8] From 1993 onward, a large picture of Niyazov appeared virtually every day on the front page (see figure 4).

During 1995 another significant element was added to the title section of *Turkmenskaya Iskra*. The complete text of the "sacred oath"—regularly recited during public occasions in the Niyazov era—was featured on the far left section of the frontispiece (see figure 5). As Kuru remarked, one of the most significant rhetorical elements introduced by the oath is the glorification of the president (2002, 78).

After the redenomination of December 1995, the entire title section of *Neytral'nyi Turkmenistan* underwent substantial changes (see figure 6). National poet Magtymguly's quote disappeared, while the oath, flag, and coat of arms kept their places in the left section. At the same time, two new items were included in the frontispiece: (1) a slogan ("Our Motherland Turkmenistan is the world's first neutral country [whose neutrality is] recognized by the United Nations"), which was meant to remind the public about what the regime always considered one of its main achievements; and (2) the identification of Niyazov as the founder (*uchreditel'*) of *Neytral'nyi Turkmenistan*. Changes in the format of the frontispiece of *Turkmenskaya Iskra/Neytral'nyi Turkmenistan* reflected different phases in the nation-building process. To highlight this connection, we divide these symbols into three subcategories:

1. symbols associated with pre-Soviet narratives (Magtymguly's quote);
2. symbols associated with post-independence narratives (coat of arms, national flag, reference to "positive neutrality");

3. symbols associated with the glorification of the regime and its leader (sacred oath, identification of Niyazov as the newspaper's founder).

In the early post-Soviet era, nation builders engaged in a process of national revival aimed at rediscovering the ancestral origins of the population (Durdyev 1991). To that end, official propaganda identified a number of "symbols of past glories" (Akbarzadeh 1999, 275) and historical figures as central elements of Turkmenistan's nationalistic narratives (Kuru 2002, 75). Poet Magtymguly was perhaps the most powerful of these symbols, which might help to explain the inclusion of one verse of his poems in the *Iskra*'s title section.

From 1994 onward, national revival lost relevance within the nation-building process. The progressive "fusion between state and regime" (Cummings and Ochs 2002, 117) forced Turkmenistani nation builders to reshape the scopes and targets of their strategies. To this end, national narratives essentially became regime narratives and began to focus exclusively on post-independence symbols. The national coat of arms, the national flag, and "positive neutrality," even before its official adoption, were recurring elements in this second phase of nation building; all were represented in the *Iskra*'s title section. Soon afterward, the focus of this campaign shifted, and glorification of the regime was replaced by glorification of its leader.

With the increasing personalization of authoritarianism, the president's figure acquired central significance in relation to regime narratives. As Niyazov "fused nationalism with loyalty to his person" (Akbarzadeh 1999, 275), nation builders began to associate all national symbols with his persona. Relevant examples are the decision to celebrate Flag Day—a main national holiday—on Niyazov's birthday, 19 February, and adoption of the text of the "sacred oath," which established that loyalty to the president was equivalent to loyalty to the motherland. Turkmenistan's official newspaper had to adapt to this new setting. The conceptualization of the frontispiece of *Neytral'nyi Turkmenistan*—which predominantly included symbols from the second and third subcategories—mirrored the regime's deliberate intention to establish a cult of personality for Niyazov.

In light of this evidence, the reasonable conclusion is that shifts in the targets of the nation-building process between 1992 and 1995 revolutionized the role played by *Turkmenskaya Iskra/Neytral'nyi Turkmenistan* in relation to indoctrination of the population. A brief analysis of the contents of articles and editorials in the post-1995 editions of *Neytral'nyi Turkmenistan* lends further weight to this proposition.

To glorify the personality of the president, the official press launched a massive campaign aimed at (mis)informing the population about the regime's new policies. That campaign entailed idealization of the agency of the policies—usually entirely attributed to the president—and misrepresentation of policy successes. Simply put, glorifying the leader who supposedly shaped the policy inevitably led to idealization of the policy itself.

As the government of post-Soviet Turkmenistan engaged in economic reforms, often within pompously named frameworks (*Novoe Selo* [New Village], *10 let blagopoluchiya, spokoistviya, edinstva, stabil'nosti* [Ten years of prosperity, tranquility, unity, and stability]), the official press did not hesitate to publish lengthy descriptions of these programs. In doing so, the *Iskra* (1) underlined the central role played by Niyazov in designing these programs; (2) raised the regime's degree of innovation in economic reforms; and (3) overemphasized the scarce success those reforms experienced. In relation to foreign policy, *Turkmenskaya Iskra/Neytral'nyi Turkmenistan* deliberately presented Niyazov as the sole driving force behind the conceptualization and operationalization of the Doctrine of Positive Neutrality, even before official adoption of the doctrine itself (Anceschi 2008, 55). During 1994 every message of congratulations received by the government on the occasion of national holidays was accompanied by the slogan *Politika Turkmenbashi: otsenka liderov mirovogo soobshchestva* (The politics of Turkmenbashi: opinions from the leaders of the international community). Ultimately, this press campaign was intended to promote the internationalization of Niyazov's figure.

Slogans and images also played a significant role in promoting the cult of Niyazov's personality. Throughout 1994 the slogan *Slovo Prezidenta—zakon* (The word of the president is the law) appeared frequently on the pages of the *Iskra*. Most recently, the slogan *Khalk, Vatan, Turkmenbashi* was featured with regularity on the second page of *Neytral'nyi Turkmenistan*.[9] After 2000, when full-color editions of *Neytral'nyi Turkmenistan* began to be published,[10] the slogan *XXI Vek–Zolotoi vek turkmenskogo naroda* (The twenty-first century is the golden age of the Turkmen nation) was a regular feature on the front page.[11]

As glorification of Niyazov entailed idealization of his achievements, the editors of *Neytral'nyi Turkmenistan* could not exclude the president's literary works from their propagandistic mission. From 2000 onward, a slogan (*Rukhnama–nash dukhovnyi svetoch* [Rukhnama is our spiritual illumination]) dedicated to the *Rukhnama*[12] was featured on many front pages,[13] and excerpts from the book were quoted in the newspaper. As for images, the president's figure became a standard item in *Neytral'nyi Turkmenistan*. Although at least one large photograph appeared on the front page every day, the editors did not hesitate to use other opportunities to reproduce his picture.[14]

Until Niyazov's death, promotion of his personality cult maintained a central place in *Neytral'nyi Turkmenistan*'s propaganda mission. With the accession to power of Berdymuhammedov, Turkmenistani authoritarianism became less personalistic, and, therefore, glorification of the leader was not a top priority for the new regime, which had to consolidate its power position vis-à-vis the domestic political landscape.

An analysis of issues of *Neytral'nyi Turkmenistan* published in the post-Niyazov era confirmed what a number of international experts suggested (Saidazimova 2008a): the new regime was progressively dismantling the cult of Niyazov's personality. As the official daily newspaper ceased to refer to the late president through his self-bestowed title of Turkmenbashi, references to the *Rukhnama* became sporadic, and the importance of his role in relation to the agency of Turkmenistan's post-Soviet policies drastically declined.[15] Crucially, at the end of September 2009 there was insufficient evidence to suggest that, at least on the pages of *Neytral'nyi Turkmenistan*, the cult of personality of the new leader had replaced that of his predecessor.[16]

Nevertheless, it may be suggested that even after Niyazov's death, the modification of the political behavior of the population has continued to occupy a central role in the media policy of the regime. During a meeting of the Cabinet of Ministers in January 2008, Berdymuhammedov stressed that "cultural and mass media workers, who were called upon to propagate the ideology of the epoch of new revival, serve as a powerful factor of moral and aesthetic development of the Turkmen nation" (OSI 2008a). In doing so, he assigned a clear ideological mission to media. Ultimately, this evidence establishes a direct link with propaganda strategies implemented by the prior regime.

To complete the analysis of the interplay between the personality cult fostered by the official press and matters of domestic consideration, this study addresses another critical issue that, like much of the chapter itself, establishes a clear connection between media policy and regime maintenance. As explained earlier, since 1992 the regime has identified the media—print media especially—as the most efficient vehicle for establishing and promoting a cult of the national leadership. This strategy differs strikingly from analogous choices by other Central Asian regimes. In general terms, the region's other post-Soviet dictatorships opted to use the media to foster a sense of statehood and nationhood within an authoritarian framework.

What is the rationale behind such a salient difference in the media policies implemented by the Turkmenistani regime and those of the elites in neighboring countries? The answer, this chapter argues, lies in the particular essence of Turkmenistani authoritarianism, which, especially in the Niyazov era, consummated its evolution toward extreme forms of nondemocratic rule. Western writing on Turkmenistan (Anceschi 2008, 51–53; Kiepenheuer-Drechsler 2006, 137; Bohr 2003, 17; Cummings and Ochs 2002, 116–17) suggested that the Niyazov regime, unlike its regional counterparts, pursued a number of elements that connected Turkmenistani authoritarianism to the sultanistic category of nondemocratic governance, as described by Chehabi and Linz (1998a, 7).

Sultanistic regimes do not aim at modifying the political culture of their citizens; instead, they incline to foster an ideology that "is more likely to be mere window dressing, [and] elaborated after the onset of the ruler's regime to justify it" (Chehabi and Linz 1998b, 14). To these ends, the media—as integral components of the official propaganda machine—of a regime that shows sultanistic characteristics, as Niyazov's Turkmenistan did, had to contribute to the establishment of the leader's personality cult. Glorification of the leader must be considered the keystone of the window-dressing ideology discussed earlier in this chapter. Print media—*Turkmenskaya Iskra/Neytral'nyi Turkmenistan* in particular—largely conformed to that role during the Niyazov era.

Conversely, as other post-Soviet Central Asian regimes did not show sultanistic or neo-patrimonialistic tendencies, establishment and promotion of personality cults for their leaders were not objectives pursed by Uzbekistani, Kazakhstani, Kyrgyzstani, and Tajikistani nation builders. Therefore, their propaganda machines and media policies were concerned more with "traditional" forms of nation building, focused on promoting new perceptions of statehood and nationhood rather than glorifying their dictators.

Conclusion

This chapter has established that the media policy implemented in Turkmenistan, before and after Niyazov's death has significantly consolidated the power of the regime. Niyazov articulated that media policy through two prongs: repression and propaganda. His successor, Berdymuhammedov, did not substantially change that policy.

Failure to regulate the media landscape; strict controls over the content of print, broadcast, and electronic media—only an estimated 1.6 percent of the population has access to the Internet (Internet World Statistics 2010)—and brutal suppression of dissenting voices constituted the main elements of the first prong. Turkmenistan's media landscape now remains rigidly state controlled, with the government as the only editor, broadcaster, and publisher recognized by law.

Multilateral organizations, foreign governments, and NGOs have frequently expressed concern about systematic abuses of press freedom. As this chapter has demonstrated, the regime's response to external demands for media liberalization has been articulated in two prongs: heightened repression at home and systematic refusal to comply with demands for remediation.

This chapter has also explored the relationship between nation building and media policy. In the view of the Turkmenistani leadership, propaganda has been a substantial element in the process of regime consolidation and enhanced the public's compliance with rules promoted by Niyazov and his associates. Because media played an essential part in that process, it is reasonable to conclude that the regime perceived *Turkmenskaya Iskra/Neytral'nyi Turkmenistan* as essential to strengthening its power position.

With his unrestricted powers, Niyazov could implement both prongs of this national media policy. And although Berdymuhammedov has not shown clear plans to establish his own cult of personality, the image of monopoly is still appropriate to describe the post-Niyazov media landscape, as the regime continues to enforce rigid central control over print, broadcast, and electronic media.

NOTES

1. Berdymuhammedov was nominated Turkmenistan's interim leader immediately after President Saparmurat Niyazov's death on 21 December 2006. His election as president was formalized in the largely fraudulent vote of 12 February 2007.
2. For the full text of the 2008 Turkmen Constitution, see www.turkmenistan.gov. tm/_ru/laws/?laws=o1dw. For the full text of the 1992 Turkmen Constitution, see *Turkmenskaya Iskra*, 19 May 1992, 1–3.
3. Turkish-owned international newspaper *Zaman Turkmenistan* is the exception.
4. The harassment of Durdymuradov occurred during the first round of the European Union-Turkmenistani Human Rights Dialogue, an annual initiative promoted under the umbrella of the EU New Strategy for Central Asia. Interestingly, there is no trace of any EU criticism for Turkmenistan's media policy in the final communiqué of the dialogue.

5. Mills (2005, 225–27) also advanced interesting conclusions on this point.

6. See, for instance, biographies of members of Turkmenistan's first post-independence Cabinet of Ministers, as appeared in *Turkmenskaya Iskra*, 27 June 1992, 1–2.

7. This was the (self-appointed) honorific title (literally meaning Head of all Turkmens) with which the late president Niyazov chose to be addressed. A crucial element in the official narratives fostered by the regime, the word Turkmenbashi became an ubiquitous nationalist landmark in Niyazov's Turkmenistan. Many streets in central Ashgabat and at least one etrap (province) per velayat were renamed after the late president; in 1993, the Caspian Sea port (and capital of the Balkan velayat) of Krasnovodsk became known as Turkmenbashi.

8. *Zdes' bratstvo—obichai i druzhba—zakon* (Here brotherhood is the custom and friendship law).

9. See *Neytral'nyi Turkmenistan*'s editions of 26 April 2000, 15 November 2000, and 19 July 2002.

10. The shift to full-color editions was completed on 19 February 2000, which was Niyazov's birthday and Flag Day.

11. Neytral'nyi Turkmenistan, 21 April 2001.

12. Niyazov's first book, *Rukhnama: Reflections on the Spiritual Value of the Turkmen*, was mandatory reading in mosques, schools, and universities. It contains his opinions on Islam, culture, history, and the nation.

13. *Neytral'nyi Turkmenistan*, 4 May 2001.

14. See, for instance, the detailed description of Turkmenistan's *manat*, whose *verso* reproduced Niyazov's profile (*Neytral'nyi Turkmenistan*, 22 December 1999, 1.)

15. See the revised treatment of the policy of Positive Neutrality as it appeared on the pages of *Neytral'nyi Turkmenistan* in December 2007.

16. Horák (2009) nevertheless pointed out that a few events—including the opening of the Gurbanguly-Hajj Mosque in Mary—suggest that the regime accelerated establishment of the cult of Berdymuhammedov's personality in 2009.

REFERENCES

Akbarzadeh, Shahram. 1999. "National Identity and Political Legitimacy in Turkmenistan." *Nationalities Papers* 27(2): 271–91.

Anceschi, Luca. 2008. *Turkmenistan's Foreign Policy: Positive Neutrality and the Consolidation of the Turkmen Regime*. New York: Routledge.

Atayeva, Nazik. 2002. "Mass Media Freedom in Turkmenistan: Only a Mirage." *Media Insight Central Asia* 23:1–3.

Bohr, Annette. 2003. "Independent Turkmenistan: From Post-communism to Sultanism." In *Oil, Transition and Security in Central Asia,* ed. Sally N. Cummings. New York: Routledge.

Chehabi, Houchang E., and Juan J. Linz. 1998a. "A Theory of Sultanism I: A Type of Nondemocratic Rule." In *Sultanistic Regimes,* ed. H. E. Chehabi and J. J. Linz. Baltimore: Johns Hopkins University Press.

———. 1998b. "A Theory of Sultanism II: Genesis and Demise of Sultanism." In *Sultanistic Regimes,* ed. H. E. Chehabi and J. J. Linz. Baltimore: Johns Hopkins University Press.

Committee to Protect Journalists. 2009. "10 Worst Countries to Be a Blogger." Http://cpj.org/reports/2009/04/10-worst-countries-to-be-a-blogger.php.

———. 2007. "North Korea Tops CPJ List of `10 Most Censored Countries.'" Www.cpj.org/censored/censored_06.html#null.

Cummings, Sally N., and Michael Ochs. 2002. "Turkmenistan: Saparmurat Niyazov's Inglorious Isolation." In *Power and change in Central Asia,* ed. Sally N. Cummings. New York: Routledge.

Durdyev, Marat. 1991. *Turkmeny: Poiski predkov turkmenskogo naroda i ego istoricheskoi prarodiny.* Ashgabat, Turkmenistan: Kharp.

EurasiaNet. 2007. Turkmenistan: The government retains its iron grip on mass media. *Eurasianet,* 7 May. WWW.eurasianet.org/departments/insight/articles/eavo50707.shtml.

Fitzpatrick, http://www.eurasianet.org/taxonomy/term/2818. Catherine A. 2010. "More—And Less—Than Meets the Eye for First Private Newspaper in Turkmenistan." *Sifting the Karakum—INdependent News from Turkmenistan,* 22 September. WWW.eurasianet.org/node/61996.

Horák, Slavomír. 2009. "Turkmen Elite Reshuffles." *Central Asia-Caucasus Analyst.* 17 June.

Internet World Stats. 2010. Www.internetworldstats.com.

Kiepenheuer-Drechsler, Barbara. 2006. "Trapped in Permanent Neutrality: Looking behind the Symbolic Production of the Turkmen Nation." *Central Asian Survey* 25(1–2): 129–41.

Krastev, Nikola. 2007. "Turkmenistan: President Says Press, NGOs Operate Freely." RFE/RL, 23 September. Www.rferl.org/featuresarticle/2007/09/96cbe108-ba4b-4b35-ba75-6b2d4064ae97.html.

Kuru, Ahmet T. 2002. "Between the State and Cultural Zones: Nation Building in Turkmenistan." *Central Asian Survey* 21(1): 71–90.

Mills, Courtney. 2005. "Turkmenbashy: The Propagation of Personal Rule in Contemporary Turkmenistan." PhD diss. School of International Relations, University of St. Andrews.

Najibullah, Farangis. 2009. "A `Black Week' for Central Asian Media Freedom." RFE/RL, 13 January. Http://www.rferl.org/content/A_Black_Week_For_Central_Asian_Media_Freedom/1369600.html.

Organization for Security and Cooperation in Europe 2002. "*Situation of Media in Central Asia: Kazakhstan, Kyrgyzstan, Tajikistan, Turkmenistan, and Uzbekistan.* Vienna: OSCE representative on freedom of the media.

Open Society Institute. 2007. "Internet Cafés Link Turkmenistan to Outside World, but at a Price." *OSI Turkmenistan Project Weekly Report*, 16–22 February.

———. 2008a. "Turkmen Leader Assigns Media Ideological Role, Urges Accuracy." *OSI Turkmenistan Project Weekly Report*, Vol. 4, 19–25 January.

———. 2008b. "Internet Cafés Closed, Blocked in Turkmenistan: Human Rights Group." *OSI Turkmenistan Project Weekly Report*, Vol. 20, 9–15 May.

———. 2009. "Turkmen President Sacks Niyazov-era Media Censor." *OSI Turkmenistan Project Weekly Report*, Vol. 15, 11–16 April.

Radio Free Europe/Radio Liberty 2006a. "RSF Demands Release of Turkmen Journalist, Activists." 23 August. Www.rferl.org/featuresarticle/2006/8/DD3403CC-59AF-4BDE-859F-4380AD684C6D.html.

———. 2006b. "OSCE, France Criticizes Turkmenistan Sentences." 28 August. Www.rferl. org/featuresarticle/2006/8/D9D6A4B2-23A8-4B89-AD50-B853B6E45999.html.

———. 2007a. "Turkmen Acting President Hints at Reforms." *RFE/RL Newsline*, 11(2), 2 January.

———. 2007b. "Turkmen State Website Removes Readers' Comments Feature." *RFE/RL Newsline*, 11(191), 16 October.

———. 2008. "RFE/RL Turkmen Contributor Released from Detention. 5 July. Www.rferl. org/content/RFERL_Turkmen_Contributor_Released_From_Detention_/1181825.html.

Reporters sans Frontieres. 2003. *Turkmenistan 2003 Annual Report*. Www.rsf.org/article. php3?id_article=6542.

———. 2005. *Turkmenistan 2005 Annual Report*. Www.rsf.org/article.php3?id_article=13451.

———. 2008. *Turkmenistan 2008 Annual Report*. Www.rsf.org/article.php3?id_article=25584.

———. 2009. *Worldwide Freedom of the Press Index*. 2009. Http://en.rsf.org/press-freedom-index-2009,1001.html.

———. 2009. "Details of Jail where Two Journalists Have Been Held for Past Two and a Half Years." Www.rsf.org/Details-of-jail-where-two.html.

Saidazimova, Gulnoza. 2008a. Turkmenistan: Take Down the Portraits! Niyazov's Personality Cult Being Dismantled." RFE/RL, 27 February. Http://rferl.org/featuresarticle/2008/2/46828B63-1D30-4C53-A031-8061105193A3.html.

———. 2008b. 'Freed Turkmen Teacher Vows to Keep Working for RFE/RL." RFE/RL, 8 July. Www.rferl.org/content/Freed_Turkmen_Teacher_Durdymuradov/1182408.html.

Synovitz, Ron. 2008. "Rights Groups Press for Release of RFE/RL Turkmen Contributor." RFE/RL,, 2 July. Www.rferl.org/content/Rights_Groups_Press_For_Release_of_RFERL_Turkmen_Contributor/1181202.html.

TDH 2010. "Rysgal--Private Newspaper of Turkmen Business." Www.turkmenistan.gov.tm/_en/?idr=7&id=100919a, 19 September.

Turkmenskaya Iskra. 1992a. "Ustanovleni diplomaticheskie otnosheniya mezhdu

Turkmenistanon i Turtsiei." 2 March.

———. 1992b. "Kitai priznal Turkmenistan i obeshchal okazyvat nam podderzhku na mezhdunarodnoi arene." 10 January.

———. 1992c. "Turkmenistan-Rossiya: vstrecha na vysshem urovne." 4 August.

United Nations. 2003. *Situation of Human Rights in Turkmenistan.* UN Doc E/CN.4/2003/34/ Rev.1, 16 April.

Hizb ut-Tahrir in Kyrgyzstan as Presented in *Vecherniy Bishkek:* A Radical Islamist Organization through the Eyes of Kyrgyz Journalists

Irina Wolf

For ordinary people, knowledge about any radical clandestine organization usually comes from the mass media rather than from direct interaction. In theory, given the space and resource limitations of print media, it is expected that newspapers create reduced but not distorted pictures of events or social phenomena. In practice, the media intentionally create images that would be in line with state policies—if owned or heavily influenced by the government—or with any other force standing behind the media. The importance of some issues is manipulated by garnering prominent, high-priority coverage aimed at making readers not only think about them but also think about them in a specified way.

This study analyzes coverage of the Hizb ut-Tahrir organization in *Vecherniy Bishkek,* a Kyrgyz national daily newspaper, during 2001–05. The aim is to establish how much and what kinds of information readers received during that key period; how coverage of the group changed over time; and to what extent the terms and information journalists used to describe Hizb ut-Tahrir reflected their personal or editorial attitudes, as well as state policies. Finally, it attempts to determine whether *Vecherniy Bishkek* was successful in creating a reduced but not distorted picture of the organization.

The study period begins in the year of the war in Afghanistan launched by international allies in response to 11 September 2001 terrorist attacks in the United States, which consequently placed 'war on terrorism' high on the Kyrgyz political agenda. It ends in the year of Kyrgyzstan's Tulip Revolution, when regimes changed and there was a historical momentum for the Kyrgyz press system to become independent of direct state control. After assuming power, however, the new regime that promised democratization, transparency, and loosening of controls over the press instead tightened constraints until its own overthrow in April 2010. Journalists still confront the threat of libel suits, assaults, and other sanctions for reporting that angers public officials, their allies, and their associates. Fair and accurate coverage of controversial issues, including corruption cases, ethnic clashes, terrorism and religious extremism, remains largely difficult. As the nongovernmental organization International Media Support (IMS), based in Denmark, observes, "Nobody can guarantee that an article published in a paper or TV/radio programme on religious extremism would not have negative consequences for a journalist" (2008, 71).

Hizb ut-Tahrir al-Islami (Party of Islamic Liberation) was founded in the Middle East in 1952 and reached Central Asia in the second half of the 1990s. The core of its ideology is to reestablish a caliphate and apply Islamic law in all spheres of life. An important factor that dictates against Hizb ut-Tahrir being labeled "terrorist" is the absence of historical records showing Hizb ut-Tahrir's involvement in terrorist activities or military actions. However, after the organization's 2002 call to kill Jews, its professed rejection of violence has been heavily debated (Whine 2006, 105). It is banned in Jordan, Syria, Egypt, Iraq, Germany, Denmark, and all Central Asian states, but not in the United States. It legally maintains headquarters and Web site hosting in Great Britain.[1]

While early reports on Hizb ut-Tahrir's activities in Kyrgyzstan stressed their prevalence in the Kyrgyz southern provinces and overwhelmingly ethnic Uzbek membership of the organization (International Crisis Group 2003; Karagiannis 2005; Grebenschikov 2002), the more recent studies indicate that Hizb ut-Tahrir continuously gains support in the northern part of Kyrgyzstan and among the ethnic Kyrgyz population (McGlinchey 2009).[2] In 2008 the head of the Kyrgyz State Agency on Religious Affairs claimed there were fifteen thousand Hizb ut-Tahrir activists in Kyrgyzstan; the International Crisis Group (ICG) estimated the party's membership in Kyrgyzstan in 2009 to be as much as seven thousand to eight thousand, of whom some eight hundred to two thousand could be women (ICG 2009, 6). Under Kyrgyz law, members caught distributing literature with extremist content are usually charged with instigation of religious and ethnic tensions and fined or sentenced to two to five years of imprisonment; in practice, "any evidence linking a person to the Hizb ut-Tahrir—party literature, reports by neighbors, or an anonymous tip—are grounds for police action" (ICG 2009, 7). ICG believes the government tended to label many of these incidents as the work of "Islamic extremists" rather than acknowledging the growth of organized crime linked to drug trafficking (2003, 38), and said government entities often used the Hizb ut-Tahrir "threat" to broaden their own powers (2002, 12). While the government used arrests as a way of combating extremism, members claimed that propaganda in prisons was one of their most effective ways of recruitment.

The first occasional reports referring to Hizb ut-Tahrir appeared in the Kyrgyz press in 1997–98 in relation to the initial arrests of people disseminating party leaflets. More regular and detailed reporting on the group appeared only after 11 September 2001. Perhaps the Kyrgyz government overlooked or ignored the problem of religious extremism before that date, but after that, it appeared that Hizb ut-Tahrir was both a serious threat as well as an available rationale to justify political decisions, government activities, and errors.[3] The law "On combating extremist activity" of 17 August 2005 prohibits mass media activities that spread extremist materials or publish materials on behalf of extremist organizations.[4] Reportedly, Kyrgyz regional administrations tried to prevent press coverage of Hizb ut-Tahrir to avoid accusations of violating that and other laws related to media and extremism (Marat 2005, 3). In Kyrgyzstan "newspapers and television channels have no balanced approach to the forbidden movement. The media persistently repeat the cliché that Hizb ut-Tahrir's members are terrorists and extremists who wish to destroy the existing regime and establish an Islamic state in Central Asia and this is all the authorities want to talk about" (Grebenschikov 2002, 2).

Coverage of Hizb ut-Tahrir in early 2000s was controversial in other Central Asian countries as well. In Tajikistan, for example, "any information related to this movement [Hizb ut-Tahrir] is published under the heading 'Crimes' and only with the reference to the law enforcement press service" (Mansurova 2002, 2). In Uzbekistan "there are no reports whatsoever about the activities of the Hizb-ut-Tahrir radical Islamic party; no accounts of the party's members brought to trial; no accounts about protests staged in Ferghana province by wives and mothers of those arrested for links with informal religious organizations" (Tokhakhojayeva 2002, 1).There is little evidence that the situation changed after the study period. Thus, the IMS and the Kyrgyz Public Association "Journalists" monitored coverage of political extremism and terrorism in twenty-two print, broadcast, and online news outlets in Bishkek and Osh from 1 October to 30 November 2007. Their study found that the vast majority of 209 news reports—161 of them—were neutral in tone, 38 were negative, and 10 were positive. While most of those stories were about arrests and confiscation of Hizb ut-Tahrir materials, analytical articles and reports directly related to extremism and terrorism were rare (International Media Support 2008, 69).

Of about one thousand officially registered news outlets in Kyrgyzstan, only fifty newspapers and magazines are regularly printed, many of them private but not independent (Freedom House 2008, 2009). *Vecherniy Bishkek* is one of a few newspapers in Kyrgyzstan that provide qualitative political information on a regular basis. Published in Russian since 1974, it has the highest circulation in the country: eight thousand copies daily from Monday to Thursday and sixty-two thousand on Friday (www.vb.kg). It is the only national newspaper that maintains electronic archives dating back to 1998. From May 2001 to August 2005, the newspaper was loyal to the government of then-president Askar Akayev, whose son-in-law, Adil Toigonbaev, owned a controlling interest. Shortly after the change of government on 24 March 2005, Aleksandr Kim, its previous owner, demanded a return of his ownership, insisting that Toigonbaev had unlawfully appropriated shares of *Vecherniy Bishkek* in 2001. The new regime allowed restoration of Kim's ownership, and the newspaper again became loyal to the government, under Kurmanbek Bakiyev, who succeeded the ousted Akayev (AKIpress 2005).

Since *Vecherniy Bishkek* published considerably more articles about Hizb ut-Tahrir than any other quality newspapers,[5] it was expected that it would create a reduced but not distorted picture of the organization. One reason why it failed to do so could be the general trend among journalists to write critically and often negatively about topical issues, including Hizb ut-Tahrir, to increase their newspaper's popularity. Another reason, however, could be that covering any positive aspect about an officially banned, clandestine group went against the official stand on Hizb ut-Tahrir, and journalists feared accusations of supporting a religious extremist organization. Finally, the personal and professional backgrounds of journalists, as well as their attitudes to religious matters in general and to Hizb ut-Tahrir in particular, played a crucial role in their coverage. Since this study focused on the country's largest-circulation newspaper during a five-year period, its findings reflect ongoing journalism practices in Kyrgyzstan on the whole.

Research Questions and Methodology

Since this study is exploratory in nature, it addresses general questions about the quantity and quality of information that readers of *Vecherniy Bishkek* received about Hizb ut-Tahrir in 2001–05; changes of coverage of Hizb ut-Tahrir during that period; and the extent to which the terms and information that journalists used to describe Hizb ut-Tahrir reflected their personal and/or editorial attitudes, as well as state policies regarding the organization.

To answer these research questions I first conducted a quantitative media content analysis of 215 articles published in Vecherniy Bishkek from 1 January 2001 until 31 December 2005, in which the name Hizb ut-Tahrir appeared, and then conducted in-depth interviews with four *Vecherniy Bishkek* journalists, who reported extensively about Hizb ut-Tahrir during that period. The qualitative analysis of certain articles was not systematic and was used solely to illustrate some quantitative findings.

The methodology for the quantitative part of the study was based on the following steps and principles for media content analysis: (1) literature review; (2) definition of messages and/or variables studied; (3) sampling data to make the population representative; (4) identification of units of analysis; (5) creation of categories in which units of analysis could be assigned; (6) coding data in accordance with those categories; (7) testing the reliability of the coding system; and (8) tabulation, analysis, and interpretation of results (Neuendorf 2002; Stacks and Hocking 1992, 252–53; Stempel and Westley 1981, 119–29). The study examined the universe of articles; the unit of analysis was an article. The coding book included the independent variables "year" and "author" and dependent variables "content" and "tone." The inter-coder reliability sample consisted of every tenth article. Simple percent agreement for "content" and "tone" variables was 93.2 percent.

The variable "Year" was coded in five categories corresponding to the five years of the research time frame. The variable "author" first contained surnames of journalists who were later assigned to five categories: Erlan Satybekov, Shuhrat Abbasov, Ravshan Umarov, Urii Kuzmihyh, and "Others," which included articles without bylines.[6] The "content" variable first contained thematic descriptions of articles that were later grouped into three categories: (1) "arrests," short crime stories about arrests of Hizb ut-Tahrir members; (2) "informative," articles often containing some descriptive information about the organization and its activities in the region and abroad; and (3) "irrelevant," articles that contained passing references to Hizb ut-Tahrir and were mainly not informative about the organization. The "tone" variable was coded in three categories that represented sets of terms and information used in relation to Hizb ut-Tahrir: (1) neutral; (2) negative; and (3) very negative. "Neutral" articles usually contained little or no descriptive terms or information related to Hizb ut-Tahrir; they usually referred to it as a religious or political organization aimed at building a caliphate. "Negative" articles contained such references as "prohibited organization," "clandestine organization," "spreading leaflets of an anti-constitutional content," and "government is concerned (or alarmed) because of Hizb ut-Tahrir activities." "Very negative" articles contained such references to the organization as "religious extremists," "terrorists," "radicals," "religious fanatics," or "threat to the state and/or people." There was no "positive" category, because no article fit the criterion: a positive attitude toward the organization that could have been expressed by mentioning that members help each other address such problems as unemployment, religious education, funerals, and medical care.

In-depth interviews of four *Vecherniy Bishkek* journalists took place to explain the quantitative findings and to explore the issue of self-censorship of journalists and their views about the newspaper's coverage. These journalists—Erlan Satybekov, deputy editor in chief; Urii Kuzminyh, who covered crime; and Shuhrat Abbasov and Ravshan Umarov, both based in Osh, the southern oblast of Kyrgyzstan—were of interest not only because they wrote almost half of the articles but because they also belong to different ethnic groups in Kyrgyzstan—Kyrgyz, Russian, and Uzbek respectively—which could reveal personal biases in their coverage. Personal contacts with journalists allowed the author to determine several factors, including professional backgrounds, degrees of religious observance, personal views on ways to combat religious extremism, and perceptions about the "neutral" dissemination of information.

Findings

What were the quantity and type of information the newspaper provided its readers?

QUANTITY OF INFORMATION

During 2001–05 *Vecherniy Bishkek* published 215 articles containing references to Hizb ut-Tahrir. The number grew drastically from 10 in 2001 to 48 in 2002 and stayed virtually the same until 2005 at approximately 52 per year. To compare, in 2006 it published 70 such articles; in 2007, 40; and in 2008, 55. Thus, the number of articles with at least one reference to Hizb ut-Tahrir grew in 2006 and returned to the previous level in 2008. During the exceptional year 2001, 9 of 10 articles appeared after 11 September, the day of major terrorist attacks in the United States. Perhaps no journalist at *Vecherniy Bishkek* was interested in writing detailed stories about the organization before the attacks, or perhaps the problem of religious extremism was not yet on the Kyrgyz government's agenda.

Forty-nine articles (22.8 percent) were about arrests of members; 109 (50.7 percent) were informative; and 57 (26.5 percent) were mainly irrelevant. Of 109 informative articles, 58 (53 percent) primarily focused on describing activities of Hizb ut-Tahrir in Central Asia; 30 (17.8 percent) provided general information about the organization; and 21 (12.5 percent), apart from providing relevant information on Hizb ut-Tahrir, focused on how to combat the organization.

During an interview, Satybekov said he felt that *Vecherniy Bishkek* kept readers well informed about the organization's ideology, objectives, and origin; much detailed information about Hizb ut-Tahrir has been provided by *Vecherniy Bishkek* and can be reiterated for readers about six times a year through interviews with knowledgeable people. He claimed that frequent references to Hizb ut-Tahrir and too many articles on the topic would be counterproductive. If people got used to reading a lot about Hizb ut-Tahrir, they would either skip such articles or accept the organization as part of everyday life. The popularity of the newspaper would, consequently, decrease. Finally, Satybekov noted that all the mass media informed the public about Hizb ut-Tahrir, and knowledge about the organization depended not on the quantity of relevant articles but on their quality.

Thus it was established quantitatively that *Vecherniy Bishkek* often published information about arrests of members and that the Hizb ut-Tahrir name was often used even when articles were irrelevant to the organization. The study did not find qualitatively on which occasions and for which purpose Hizb ut-Tahrir was referred to: Was it mentioned only to attract reader attention? Was it an inevitable part of the covered news? Were there some issues about Hizb ut-Tahrir journalists hesitated to cover?

TYPE OF INFORMATION

Although the number of "informative" articles was high, *Vecherniy Bishkek* published only ten articles during 2001–05 that provided exhaustive information about the organization, including historical information on its origins, ideology, and objectives, types of activities, reasons for its ban in parts of the world, location of its headquarters, and/or its position on violence and various forms of governance. The remaining articles were a mixture of use of its name and a description of the organization with various degrees of relevance to the focal points of those articles.

The assumption that the content of relevant articles would be closely connected to particular political events was supported by the qualitative analysis and interviews with journalists. Abbasov said Hizb ut-Tahrir became a scapegoat during times of instability in the region and on political occasions. Umarov also expressed such a view and explained the growing number of references to Hizb ut-Tahrir during political events as the organization took advantage of opportunities to spread its propaganda. Indeed, the majority of relevant articles in 2001 appeared in September, after the attacks and shortly before U.S.-led military operations began in Afghanistan and Iraq. In 2002 the majority of relevant articles appeared in March, the month of peaceful protests in the Aksy region of southern Kyrgyzstan that resulted in the killing of civilians. Most articles in 2002 appeared in September, following: a murder attempt on Misir Ashyrkulov, at that time secretary of the Kyrgyz Security Council; the injury of a Hizb ut-Tahrir member by the militia in Jalalabad, which led to protests by area residents; and discovery of weapons allegedly belonging to Hizb ut-Tahrir in the area. In 2003 the majority of articles appeared in November and referred to terrorist attacks in Istanbul and the Kyrgyz Supreme Court's ban on the group. In 2004 most relevant articles appeared in April, following terrorist attacks in Tashkent and Bukhara, Uzbekistan, and in November, the month of local administration elections. Most 2005 articles appeared in July, the month of presidential elections.

Thus it appears that Hizb ut-Tahrir was mentioned not only in the context of domestic events that were presumably of high importance to local readers but also in connection with events abroad. In these articles Hizb ut-Tahrir was framed as a negative factor that either explained or contributed to negative coverage of the events without being a central part of the news covered.

The assumption that journalists would not write about some controversial issues—like the ethnicity of members and the organization's possession of arms—was also qualitatively supported. Thus, no article directly mentioned that the majority of members in Kyrgyzstan were Uzbeks, although articles occasionally referred to the fact that confiscated leaflets were published in Uzbek. Similarly, a number of articles mentioned both the discovery of weapons and Hizb ut-Tahrir but did not directly accuse the group of possessing arms. Such references were carefully crafted so that readers could themselves infer that the weapons belonged to Hizb ut-Tahrir. Being fully aware of these tendencies, Abbasov and Umarov—ethnic Uzbeks themselves—explained that highlighting the Uzbek ethnicity of members could escalate conflict between Kyrgyz and Uzbeks, leading to violence; however, possession of arms could not be alleged, since it was not proved by law enforcement agencies. Finally, they noted that some journalists from the north of the country lacked in-depth knowledge about the organization, and "sometimes are too harsh" in their references to Hizb ut-Tahrir, meaning they were too critical of or exaggerated its threat.

MEDIA AND EXTREMISTS: GIVING THE FLOOR
OR HEARING THE OTHER SIDE?

Satybekov wrote six of the ten articles with exhaustive information about Hizb ut-Tahrir. They included two interviews with members, one interview with a religious scholar, and a three-article series titled "Servants of Death." Satybekov explained that interviews with members allow people "to hear the voice on the other side, and at the same time to increase the popularity of the newspaper." Satybekov did not disclose whether he knew about the then-new law that prohibited the mass media from providing a forum for extremists or publishing their material. He stated, "This law, just like any other law in Kyrgyzstan, doesn't function, and it will not function for many years to come because of the very low law culture in Kyrgyzstan." Abbasov, Umarov, and Kuzminyh said they were unaware of that law. An open question is whether interviews with members of Hizb ut-Tahrir published in *Vecherniy Bishkek* could be classified as material published on behalf of extremists, which otherwise would have clandestinely spread through leaflets.

Qualitative analysis of interviews of members in *Vecherniy Bishkek* supports the assertion that the newspaper has, in fact, given a platform to the organization. Thus, an interview with Rahimjan Charikov, an imprisoned member of Hizb ut-Tahir, published on 26 September 2001, reported on the group's views on the 11 September terrorist attacks, the relation of Uzbekistan president Islam Karimov to Turkish independence leader Mustafa Kemal Ataturk, and terrorist attacks in Uzbekistan in 1999.[7] An interview with Diler Djumabaev, an entrepreneur and Hizb ut-Tahrir's Kyrgyz press attaché, published after the presidential elections in Kyrgyzstan on 22 July 2005, discussed the group's assessment of the election; the March 2005 change in government; killings of civilians in Andijan, Uzbekistan, on 13 May 2005; the American airbase in Kyrgyzstan; and bombings in London in July 2005.[8] In 2006 and 2007 the newspaper published two additional interviews with members that covered Hizb ut-Tahrir's relations with and attitudes toward the Islamic Movement of Uzbekistan and the organization's strategy of cooperation with the mass media in Kyrgyzstan (Urumbaev 2006, 2007). It appears that people in Kyrgyzstan could read in *Vecherniy Bishkek* what they otherwise could learn from prohibited leaflets without being arrested for possessing such leaflets.

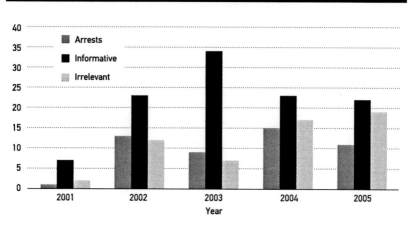

What were the content and tone of the newspaper's coverage over time?

CONTENT AND TONE OVER TIME

The number of articles about arrests grew significantly from 1 in 2001 to 13 in 2002 and stayed virtually the same from 2002 to 2005. The number of "informative" articles grew drastically from 7 in 2001 to 34 in 2003 and decreased to 22 in 2005. The number of "irrelevant" articles fluctuated over the years, from 2 in 2001 to 19 in 2005, but there was a tendency for the number of such articles to grow from 2004 onward. The relation between variables "content" and "year" was not statistically significant $X^2(8, N=215) = 13.02$, $p > 0.05$. For a graphic presentation of the data, see figure 1.

The number of "neutral" articles steadily grew from 0 in 2001 to 11 in 2005. The number of "negative" articles also steadily grew from 1 in 2001 to 20 in 2005. The number of "very negative" articles fluctuated, with 9 articles in 2001, 40 in 2002, 37 in 2003, 40 in 2004, and 21 in 2005. The relation between variables "tone" and "year" was statistically significant $X^2(8, N=215) = 32.445$, $p < 0.01$ with the tone of the articles becoming more neutral over time. For a graphic presentation of the data, see figure 2.

The cross-tabulation of "content," "tone," and "year" variables revealed that in 2001 70 percent of "informative" articles were "very negative" in tone; in 2002, 78.3 percent were "very negative"; in 2003, 76.55 percent of "informative" articles were "very negative"; in 2004, 87 percent were "very negative"; and in 2005, 36.4

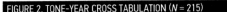

FIGURE 2. TONE-YEAR CROSS TABULATION (*N* = 215)

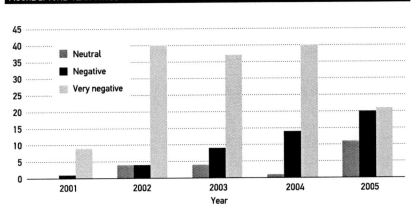

percent were "very negative" in tone. The assumption attributing the growing number of articles about arrests to the fact that articles became more neutral over time was not supported. Such articles were usually terse crime stories about arrests but providing little or no information about the organization's goals, activities, and ideology. Articles on arrests were never neutral in tone except in 2005, when articles with a neutral tone were observed regardless of topic. The study assumed that such a change in coverage could be attributed to the changes of government and *Vecherniy Bishkek* ownership in 2005. This assumption was tested qualitatively.

HIZB UT-TAHRIR AND *VECHERNIY BISHKEK*: CHANGE OF COVERAGE FOLLOWED BY POLITICAL CHANGES?

The four interviewees asserted that changes in government in March 2005 and in the newspaper's directorship in August 2005 influenced neither the content nor the tone of references to Hizb ut-Tahrir. However, the quantitative analysis showed that coverage in 2005 was more balanced and that the number of articles written in a "neutral tone" had increased drastically. The qualitative analysis showed that after the opposition seized power, *Vecherniy Bishkek* stopped referring to the former opposition as having contacts with and supporting Hizb ut-Tahrir. Thus, the political changes indeed influenced how the newspaper covered the controversial issue.

To what extent did the terms and information used by journalists to describe Hizb ut-Tahrir reflect their personal and/or editorial attitudes, as well as government policies?

THE JOURNALISTS

Of the articles analyzed, Satybekov wrote 39 (18.1 percent); Abbasov wrote 20; (9.3 percent); Umarov wrote 23 (10.7 percent); Kuzminyh wrote 13 (6.0 percent); and 31 other journalists wrote 73 (34.0 percent). Forty-seven (21.9 percent) of the articles were unattributed.

The fact that the articles were written mainly by four interviewed journalists had a practical explanation. Satybekov joined *Vecherniy Bishkek* in 2001, and his colleagues consider him an expert on Muslim extremism. He has an undergraduate degree in journalism, has lectured in the United States on religious extremism and terrorism in Central Asia, and has traveled to Israel and other countries to learn more about religious extremism. Reporting on religious extremism in general and on Hizb ut-Tahrir in particular was part of his specialization. Umarov and Abbasov joined the newspaper in 2000. They reported on Hizb ut-Tahrir as part of their assignment to cover events in the southern part of the country. These three journalists said they covered Hizb ut-Tahrir by choice and were never assigned by their editor in chief to submit additional articles about the organization. Kuzminyh joined the newspaper in 1995 and since then he has written crime stories based on reports of law-enforcement bodies as part of his everyday job.

TONE OF ARTICLES

Of the 215 articles, 20 (9.3 percent) contained neutral references to Hizb ut-Tahrir, 48 (22.3 percent) had negative references, and 127 (68.4 percent) were very negative.

In an interview, Satybekov estimated that 90 percent of references to Hizb ut-Tahrir in *Vecherniy Bishkek* were negative. He attributed that assumption mainly to the fact that the organization is banned and its objectives conflict with the Kyrgyz constitution. Of his 32 articles about Hizb ut-Tahrir in the five years studied, Satybekov referred to the group very negatively 82.1 percent of the time. He explained that his attitude toward the organization had changed over time. As an atheist since childhood, he claimed to regard all religious organizations negatively, including Hizb ut-Tahrir; to him, any religion presents a misleading view of the world. Trying to understand religious organizations that differenti- ate themselves from mainstream Islam and Orthodox Christianity, he saw a confrontation between official Muslim clergy and Hizb ut-Tahrir as competition for followers. He viewed the reason why people join Hizb ut-Tahrir, apart from trying to survive in difficult economic and social situations, as trying to fulfill their spiritual needs and learn more about Islam. Hizb ut-Tahrir theologians, he said, were knowledgeable people who could explain complicated issues in simple words to ordinary people; official Muslim clergy found it difficult to accept that more people were joining the organization, and the clergy failed to reverse this trend.

Kuzminyh reported that he stayed neutral while covering the group. He saw his job as reporting information from law enforcement agencies without adding analytical information, thus avoiding personal criticism of the organization.

According to Abbasov, articles about Hizb ut-Tahrir in *Vecherniy Bishkek* were neutral because the newspaper didn't blame the organization for anything. He was convinced that he stayed neutral and that his tone of reference about the group did not change over time. However, 65 percent of Abbasov's stories were very negative in tone.

Umarov believed the portrayal of Hizb ut-Tahrir in his newspaper reflected reality: "*Vecherniy Bishkek* provides combined information of four parties: law enforcement agencies, Hizb ut-Tahrir, local clergy, and the local population. References to Hizb ut-Tahrir are close to being neutral, but stay a bit negative because of the critical nature of analytical articles. After all, this organization is officially banned in the territory of the Kyrgyz Republic and cannot be portrayed positively." Umarov's stories, however, included the second-highest percentage of very negative references to Hizb ut-Tahrir (73.9 percent).

Nevertheless, Satybekov and Umarov acknowledged that there were some positive aspects about the group that could have been covered. They said, for example, that it is known in southern Kyrgyzstan for charitable activities such as organizing big meals for the local population. Members can also count on financial support from the organization in case of emergency or medical need. They said that such information could not, however, appear in *Vecherniy Bishkek* because, as Umarov explained, "The end goals of this organization are well known," and as Satybekov said, "*Vecherniy Bishkek* doesn't do promotion of the Hizb ut-Tahrir organization."

COMBATING EXTREMISM WITH HELP OF MEDIA: MYTH OR REALITY?

The findings show that only 21 (12.5 percent) articles contained information about or discussed ways to combat Hizb ut-Tahrir. While civil society leaders and scholars contend that the mass media should be used to combat religious extremism through positive reporting on religious tolerance and exposure of the real objectives of such organizations, the journalists interviewed held a different view.

Kuzminyh stated that his job is only to report what happened and where; the "why" and "how" questions fall outside his competence. Satybekov explained: "Our country is not the one where mass media can be seen as a fourth pillar of the state. I don't believe mass media's role is combating religious extremism." Asserting that Hizb ut-Tahrir should be combated with forceful measures, Satybekov said he is a proponent of dictatorship, since it brings "law and order."

Abbasov said the government, not the mass media, should resolve the issue: "This group has a right to think whatever they want, and we just inform the public about their ideas and objectives. It is up to people to follow them or not." Abbasov said he believes that to combat Hizb ut-Tahrir the state should combine "harsh" and "soft" measures.

Umarov stated that "mass media, and *Vecherniy Bishkek* in particular, can only conduct explanatory work in its pages and provide objective information about the organization so that people are fully informed and updated on the issue." He added that Hizb ut-Tahrir cannot be combated with harsh measures; instead, the state and clergy should conduct explanatory discussions and activities to help people understand the falsity of its ideas.

Conclusion and Recommendations

Since virtually no quantitative and qualitative research has been conducted on the portrayal of religious extremist organizations in newspapers in Central Asia, this study attempted to fill that gap. The aim was to assess how Hizb ut-Tahrir was covered in *Vecherniy Bishkek* during 2001–05 and how much the personal views and positions of its journalists were reflected in their coverage of the controversial organization.

It appears that Hizb ut-Tahrir started drawing attention of Kyrgyz media only after terrorist attacks in the United States in September 2001. Since 2002, this group was mentioned in about fifty articles per year. However, only half of those articles provided some information about this group, a quarter contained no more than information about arrests of members and/or sympathizers, and another quarter made only passing reference to the group. The overwhelming majority of articles were written in very negative tones—that is, referring to its members as religious extremists, terrorists, radicals, or religious fanatics.

No positive aspect of its activities, like charitable or employment activities, was covered. Even the number of articles referring to it in neutral terms—a Muslim religious political organization aimed at building a caliphate, for instance—was small. The growing number of articles with the neutral references over the years can be attributed to changes in the government and the newspaper's directorship rather than to the growth of the number of short crime stories about arrests.

It appears that the professional backgrounds of journalists and their views on religion and ways to combat religious extremism had the major influence on their coverage. Thus, Satybekov—an expert on Muslim extremism and a nonbeliever—wrote the most negative stories, perhaps intending to convey the negative nature of the group. Umarov and Abbasov—the ethnic Uzbeks reporting from the southern region of Kyrgyzstan, where Islam has a stronger influence than in the north of the country—also felt negatively about the group, but as a result of their personal experiences in a conflict-prone area and denunciation of radical Islam. Kuzminyh—an ethnic Russian and non-Muslim—was the most neutral about Hizb ut-Tahrir. He saw coverage of this organization as part of his routine job of writing crime stories based on reports from law-enforcement agencies.

The government's role in setting the agenda for this private—yet not independent—newspaper to cover the banned organization in very negative terms should not be underestimated. Relying on official sources of information and opinions of often-unidentified "experts," journalists reported in a way that was aligned with the general state policies; that reporting lacked in-depth analysis and cross-checking of information. The search for sensationalistic news, big headlines, and "shocking" facts also contributed to giving a floor to extremists who wanted to spread their ideas, not clandestinely through leaflets but through the largest national newspaper. While attempting to "hearing the voices on the other side," journalists failed, to pose questions that might discredit the organization.

The journalists interviewed did not acknowledge the media's potential to contribute to combating religious extremism; they felt that was a task for law enforcement officials, not for privately owned, profit-oriented media. In this regard training journalists on coverage of controversial issues, including religious extremism and terrorism, would make them better aware of reporting techniques aimed at de-escalation of existing or potential conflicts and would empower them in the constructive conflict coverage.

NOTES

1. For more detailed information on Hizb ut-Tahrir, see Baran 2004 and International Crisis Group reports 2002, 2003, and 2009.

2. Grebenschikov (2002) explained the larger proportion of ethnic Uzbeks sympathizing with Hizb ut-Tahrir than of ethnic Kyrgyz by the fact that Kyrgyzstan was unable to provide the population in the south with print media, textbooks at school, and other channels from which ethnic Uzbeks could generate information in their language. In the early 2000s, the informational vacuum that could not be filled by Kyrgyz officials was filled by Hizb ut-Tahrir leaflets, which contained information on urgent political, social, and economic developments in the region and the world.

3. For example, the government imposed a moratorium on meetings and demonstrations in September 2002 shortly after a Hizb ut-Tahrir member was injured by the militia in Jalal-Abad; the incident led to protests of the village inhabitants and discovery of weapons allegedly belonging to Hizb ut-Tahrir in the surrounding area. Also, the shooting of a prominent imam in August 2006 by the Kyrgyz National Security Service was first explained by the fact that the victim was in a car with extremists and was possibly also a member of the organization. Later, to pacify protestors in the south of Kyrgyzstan, it was said that the imam had been hijacked by extremists and shot by mistake. See AKIpress 2006.

4. See Jogorku Kenesh 2005, articles 8, 11, 17.

5. During 2001–05 *Vecherniy Bishkek* published 215 articles referring to Hizb ut-Tahrir at least once; *MSN*, a private national newspaper with the second-highest circulation after *Vicherniy Bishkek*, published 114 articles referring to Hizb ut-Tahrir (www.msn. kg); *Slovo Kyrgyzstana*, a state-owned newspaper that maintains electronic archives dating back only to 2004, published 30 relevant articles in 2004–05 (www.sk.kg). *MSN* and *Slovo Kyrgyzstana* published two and three times per week respectively.

6. Shuhrat Abbasov and Ravshan Umarov are pseudonyms used to protect their identities.

7. Excerpts of the interview with Charikov: "America should blame itself. It provokes terrorism, because leading the West, it wants to suppress Islam." "Turkish activist Mustafa Kemal Ataturk destroyed it [a caliphate] by splitting it into a multitude of small states. He did it under the influence of the West . . . Why should we be amazed? Mustafa Kemal was a representative of a Jewish tribe Yahudi, as well as, by the way, is the current Uzbek president, Islam Karimov." "On 16 February 1999, Islam Karimov organized a great provocation: murder attempt . . . on himself, with the help of special services, to accuse true Muslims, including Hizb ut-Tahrir of organizing bombings. After that he started arresting everybody who was in disagreement with the government. It is politics!" (qtd. in Satybekov 2001).

8. Excerpts of the interview with Djumabaev: "If a mob of people could take over power [in Kyrgyzstan on 24 March 2005] in a couple of hours, we could have done it even faster." "We inform the population what *sharia* [Islamic law] says about elections—election of those who rule without Koran and *hadis* [narratives about the words and deeds of the prophet Muhammad] is a sin—and to go to vote or not to go is a private affair of each individual." "It was tough for us during Akayev's rule; now it is even worse. As an entrepreneur, I opened the TV studio Ong that couldn't function even for three days. There is an ideological struggle going on." "[The Andijan events] were organized by the Uzbek special services. Three or four months ago they offered 820 million U.S. dollars to the interested forces to overthrow Karimov's regime. They offered Hizb ut-Tahrir to lead this activity. We refused [because] there will be another Karimov, but the regime would not change." "Yuldashev is blamed for having been a Hizb ut-Tahrir member. Why doesn't Uzbekistan slander other activist who occupies high post in official religious structures and at the same time a post of *nakib* [assistant to a leader of Hizb ut-Tahrir at the district level] in our organization." "They [the USA] and their allies set up a base here in order to kill our brothers in Afghanistan. How can we silently observe it?" "If England starts pressing Hizb, it means that democracy is on the verge of collapse. Democracy has its own principles: freedom of personality, speech, religion, et cetera. If they renounce these principles, it means that it was curtains for their ideology" (qtd. in Satybekov and Oibek 2005).

REFERENCES

Abbasov, Shuhrat [pseudonym]. Phone interview, 4 May 2006.

Akipress. 2005. "Sud pervoi instantzii vernul Aleksandru Kimu sobstvennost" (Lowest court restored ownership of Aleksandr Kim). Http://news.akipress.org/news/21564.

———. 2006. SNB: "Imam mecheti Karasuu, vozmojno, ne prichasten k IDU, a byl vzjat boevikami v zalojniki" (SNB: Imam of Karasuu mosque, perhaps, had no connections to IDU but was hijacked by militants). Http://kg.akipress.org/news/30317.

Baran, Zeyno. 2004. *Hizb ut-Tahrir: Islam's political insurgency*. Washington, DC: Nixon Center. Www.nixoncenter.org/Monographs/HizbutahrirIslamsPoliticalInsurgency.pdf.

"Ekstremism i nasilie" (Extremism and violence). 2004. *Vecherniy Bishkek* 127(8554).

Freedom House. 2009. *Freedom of the Press: Kyrgyzstan*. Www.freedomhouse.org/inc/content/pubs/pfs/inc_country_detail.cfm?country=7641&year=2009&pf.

———. 2009. *Freedom of the Press: Kyrgyzstan*. Www.freedomhouse.org/inc/content/pubs/pfs/inc_country_detail.cfm?country=7427&year=2008&pf.

Grebenschikov, Igor. 2002. "The Hizb ut-Tahrir through the eyes of Kyrgyz journalists." *Media*

Insight Central Asia, 22. Www.cimera.org/files/camel/en/22e/MICA22E-Grebenshikov.pdf.

International Crisis Group. 2002. *The IMU and the Hizb-ut-Tahrir: Implications of the Afghanistan campaign.* ICG Asia Briefing Paper No. 11, 30 January. Osh/Brussels: International Crisis Group.

———. 2003. *Radical Islam in Central Asia: Responding to Hizb ut-Tahrir.* ICG Asia Report No. 58, 3 June. Osh/Brussels: International Crisis Group.

———. 2009. *Women and radicalisation in Kyrgyzstan.* Crisis Group Asia Report No. 176, 3 September. Osh/Brussels: International Crisis Group.

International Media Support. 2008. *Political extremism, terrorism, and media in Central Asia.* Research report, 15 February, Bishkek/Copenhagen: International Media Support.

Jogorku Kenesh. 2005. Zakon KR No. 150 "O protivodeistksoi dejatelnosti" (Law of the Kyrgyz Republic No. 150 "On combating extremist activities"). 17 August.

Karagiannis, Emmanuel. 2005. "Political Islam and social movement theory: The case of Hizb ut-Tahrir in Kyrgyzstan." *Religion, State, and Society* 33(2): 137–49.

Kuzminyh, Urii. 2006. Personal interview, Bishkek, 8 May 8.

Mansurova, Gulchehra. 2002. "The Absence of Debate on Islam in the Tajik Media." *Media Insight Central Asia* 22. Www.cimera.org/files/camel/en/22e/MICA22E-Mansurova1.pdf.

Marat, Zulfia. 2005. "Zakon Kyrgyzskoi Respubliki O protivodeistvii ekstremistskoi deyatelnosti (izvlecheniya) s kommentariyami" (Law of the Kyrgyz Republic on combating extremist activities [extractions] and commentaries). In *Zakonadatelstvo I praktika mass-media: Kirgisien* (Legislation and practice of mass media: Kyrgyzstan) 1(10). Www.medialaw.ru/publications/zip/national/new/kg/10.htm#3.

McGlinchey, Eric. 2009. "Islamic revivalism and state failure in Kyrgyzstan." *Problems of Post-Communism* 56(3) (May/June 2009): 16–28.

Neuendorf, Kimberly. 2002. *The Content Analysis Guidebook.* London: Sage.

Satybekov, Erlan. 2001. "Chelovek so stekljannymi glazami" (Person with glass eyes). *Vecherniy Bishkek,* 185 (7857).

———. 2006. Personal interview, Bishkek, 4 May.

Satybekov, Erlan, and Hamidov Oibek. 2005. "Hizb ut-Tahrir: s glazu na glaz" (Hizb ut-Tahrir: privately). *Vecherniy Bishkek,* 138 (8812).

Stacks, W. Don, and John E. Hocking. 1992. *Essentials of communication research.* New York: Harper Collins.

Stempel, Guido H., III, and Bruce H. Westley. 1981. *Research methods in mass communication.* Englewood Cliffs, NJ: Prentice-Hall.

Tokhakhojayeva, Marfua. 2002. "A review of Islam and the media in Uzbekistan." *Media Insight Central Asia* 22. Http://www.cimera.org/files/camel/en/22e/MICA22E-Tokhtakhojayeva.pdf.

Urumbaev, Mahamdjan. 2006. "Hizbutchiki nam ne poputchiki" (Members of Hizb ut-Tahrir are not our fellow-travellers). *Vecherniy Bishkek,* 15(9099) September: 175.

———. 2007. "Tak li krut Hizbut?" (Is Hizbut so tough?). *Vecherniy Bishkek* 13(9220) March: 48.

Umarov, Ravshan (pseudonym). 2006. Phone interview, 8 May.

Whine, Michael. 2006. *Is Hizb ut-Tahrir changing strategy or tactics?* Hudson Institute, Center for Eurasian Policy, Occasional Research Paper No. 1. Www.thecst.org.uk/docs/EurasianPaper_Aug42006.pdf.

The Future of Internet Media in Uzbekistan: Transformation from State Censorship to Monitoring of Information Space since Independence

Zhanna Hördegen

The Internet remains an underused means of expression for the majority of citizens in Uzbekistan (United Nations Development Programme 2007; Guard 2004, 203). Connectivity is not the main obstacle, because it has kept improving since the state monopoly on access was abandoned in 2002.[1] The government also demonstrates strong commitments to develop the infrastructure of modern technologies.[2] Still, amid subsequent liberalization of Internet services, access and use remain a challenging task due to the state's control of the medium. As the OpenNet Initiative reports, the Uzbek government maintains the most extensive and pervasive state-mandated filtering system in Central Asia (Deibert et al. 2008, 409–15). Web sites of international and domestic human rights organizations, as well as sites of opposition-in-exile political parties—banned for purportedly promoting the ideas of religious fundamentalism and separatism—are permanently filtered and blocked.[3] In addition, Web sites of independent electronic mass media, both domestic and foreign, account for the most frequently silenced Internet content (Khodjaev 2006, 145–47).[4]

Against this background, Uzbekistan has been labeled an "enemy of the Internet."[5] Such a "hostile" response to the medium reinvigorates the debate over the significance of a state's coercive power to control the flow of information within its territory and, thereby, to design its own version of how open the Internet should be (Goldsmith and Wu 2006, 179–84). According to some commentators, however, no national governments in Central Asia have asserted Internet control to the same degree as their control over the press (Guard 2006, 135). Yet that assessment does not hold true for Uzbekistan for at least three reasons. First, the regulatory framework no longer distinguishes between Internet and traditional print forms of content distribution. The laws specifically applicable to print and broadcasting media apply to Web sites, which are assigned the country code top-level domain names (ccTLD) and thus exist under Uzbekistan's top-level domain space.[6] The legal framework requires these sites to officially register as mass media. In so doing, that framework resembles the perspective of Soviet-era law where "every microcomputer or word processor connected to a printer [was] a potential printing press" (Graham 1984, 130). Web sites of "foreign states," as far as they "distribute their products" in Uzbekistan, are regulated under the mass media legislation, too. Both domestic and "foreign" sites are subject to the whole panoply of content-based restrictions of Uzbek law. Still, in light of the jurisdictional complication of such regulation, the government resorts to filtering and blocking "foreign" sites as the most efficient method of restraint. Secondly, the government controls the allocation and administration of the ccTLDs to the extent that both a ccTLD registry and administrator are effective points of governmental control of the Internet.

The third reason, and the one that this chapter sets to explore, is the legal regulation of access to information on the grounds of information security of the individual, society, and the state. This regulatory response to the advent of the Internet in Central Asia is often only superficially mentioned in writings on state policies about Internet control (Ibraimov 2006, 108; Khodjaev 2006, 143; Nougmanov 2007, 128–33; Deibert 2008, 314, 319, 387, 412). The notion of information security originally developed in the Commonwealth of Independent States and, therefore, bears strong similarities across Central Asia and the Russian Federation (Kozhamberdiyeva 2008, 118–21).[7] China joined these states in their commitment to international information security.[8] Still, Uzbekistan's information security rules and their practical implementation are distinct. To recognize that distinctiveness requires looking beyond legal rules and at the nonlegal context in which they operate. Thus this chapter highlights the basic ideas propagated by the Uzbek national ideology known as the "idea of national independence" upon the legislative development of information security rules in particular and the exercise of freedom of speech on Internet media in general.[9] It then argues that information security–justified restrictions on speech further legitimize the alarming institutionalization of systematic governmental control over the mass media evident since independence. First, it provides an overview of the scope of protection given to the freedoms of speech, information, and mass media under the constitution.

Constitutional Guarantees and Limits of Free Speech

CONSTITUTIONAL GUARANTEES

Under the constitution, Uzbekistan is a democratic republic,[10] and Article 29 guarantees everyone freedom of thought, speech, and convictions. Moreover, it guarantees the right to seek, receive, and disseminate any information that is not directed against the existing constitutional order or otherwise restricted under statute. Article 29 permits restrictions upon "freedom of opinion and its expression" if provided by statute to protect state and other secrets.[11]

Freedoms of speech and information are normatively categorized as personal rights under the constitution. In contrast to political rights, personal rights aim to secure the autonomy of individuals, but not necessarily the individuals' "active inclusion into the life of the country, a process in which conditions are created for strengthening a link between a person and society, a citizen and the state" (Tadjikhanov 1997, 37–38). This is a subtle but important contrast in justifying the underpinning rights. It implies that framers of the constitution construed free speech guarantees primarily as an aspect of individual intellectual self-development and fulfillment (Barendt 2006, 13–18). Their role was to protect citizen participation in political discourse; development of a free and democratic society seems less appreciated (Barendt 2006, 18–21; Nowak 2006, 460). The lack of interpretation of the scope of constitutional protection of free speech by the constitutional court or of open access to existing jurisprudence of the country's supreme court adds uncertainty about whether the constitution equally protects nonpolitical speech and political expression.[12] Still, freedom of speech is interpreted as the liberty to speak openly on sociopolitical and public issues and to actively engage in the political process and debate, individually or in association with others (Yakubov 2001, 191). The validity of their argument is weakened by legislative practice, however.

The constitution guarantees freedom of the mass media. Article 67 declares that the mass media is "free and has to act in accordance with the statute." In addition, the mass media bear responsibility in a prescribed manner for the trustworthiness of information.[13] For writers and journalists, guarantees of a free mass media underline a constitution's "deeply democratic character" (Kerzhner 2001, 333–34). It is an especially valuable observation in light of the background of the 1977 USSR constitution, which was the highest law in the Uzbek Soviet Socialist Republic until independence (Elst 2005, 45–47). However, because free media is a manifestation of democratic freedoms, an objective purpose of this constitutional guarantee is largely eroded by the legal formulation of Article 67 itself. First, this provision guarantees the mass media no more protection against state interference in the scope of freedom than they enjoy under statutes; they are free only to the extent to which they are unrestricted. An amended statute on the mass media provides a particularly striking confirmation: it no longer reaffirms constitutional protection but makes it the mass media's duty to act in accordance with that statute and other legislative acts.[14] Second, mass media responsibility for the trustworthiness of information it circulates is worrisome because, as this chapter demonstrates, it introduces a potential legal tool to stifle a broad range of legitimate speech. This requirement seems to pose no infringement of press freedom, but serves as an important legal factor that precludes dissemination of information "known to be false or not otherwise objective" (Kerzhner 2001, 338). Freedom of free speech for the mass media can become meaningless when there are weak constitutional guarantees against state interference.

Article 67 makes censorship impermissible, but the constitutional court has not yet resolved questions about the scope or conditions of the censorship ban. It remains unclear whether this rule covers only a "classical" form of censorship or any prior restraint on publications.[15] Or would government control over information after its distribution be tantamount to censorship and therefore unconstitutional? For instance, would filtering and denying access to private Web sites by administrative bodies fall under the censorship ban? This chapter explains the importance of that distinction in the scope of the censorship ban.

LEGITIMATE OBJECTIVES OF HUMAN RIGHTS RESTRICTIONS

Under Articles 29 and 67, government interference with the exercise of freedoms of speech, information, and the mass media is legitimate only if a statute adopted by parliament provides for it. In turn, Article 20 sets forth constitutionally legitimate purposes that statutes affecting individual's rights and freedoms in general must strive toward. Government may restrict the exercise of constitutional rights if justified to protect the lawful interests, rights, and freedoms of others, society, and the state.[16] However, a balancing decision may become a challenging task under Article 16, which requires that no single constitutional provision be interpreted to prejudice other state rights or state interests.[17] Read together, Articles 16 and 20 suggest that a collision between state interests and citizens' rights would pose a potential constitutional problem for the courts.

It is difficult to set ultimate limits on the scope of state interests, especially when the constitution does not define them. The same holds true of "lawful interests of society" or public interests. Thus government's discretion to restrict human rights may be broad, unless limited by the state's constitutional goals. Articles

2, 7, 13, 14, and 55 of the constitution declare that the state must: (1) express the will of the people and serve the people's interests; (2) develop democracy based on "general humanistic principles that place supreme value in the person, human life, freedom, honour, dignity, and other inalienable rights"; (3) function according to the principles of social justice and the rule of law in the interests of the welfare of a person and society; and (4) protect the environment. Taking these state goals into account, circumvention of the tension between state interests and constitutional rights may be reconciled if there is an independent and active judiciary. As Internet restrictions exemplify, the legislative goals of protection of public and state interests undermine the very substance of free speech in the country's current political and institutional reality.

Information Security Restrictions on Free Speech and the Regulation of the Internet

INFORMATION SECURITY OF THE INDIVIDUAL, SOCIETY, AND THE STATE DEFINED

The law "On principles and guarantees of freedom of information" restricts the exercise of freedom of information to maintain "information security of an individual, society, and the state."[18] That statute has been widely criticized for establishing a legal regime that restricts dissemination of information irrespective of the media, rather than providing effective protection of freedom of information against government interference.[19] Under Article 11 it is legitimate to protect information and, for that reason, to interfere with the exercise of freedom of information to: (1) prevent threats to information security; (2) maintain confidentiality of information and prevent leakage, stealing, or loss of information; and (3) prevent distortion and falsification of information. The concept of information security does not encompass actions that "violate the rules of use of information" and are subject to administrative and criminal penalties.[20] Information security means a "state of security of the interests of an individual, society, and state in the information sphere" (Article 3).

What follows here is a brief summary of the three-dimensional interests listed in Articles 13, 14, and 15.

Individuals' information security protects their interest in "open access to information and protection of private life." It also protects an author's interests in publishing under a pseudonym and the rights of an informant who in disclosing information to the press wishes to remain anonymous. Information security of society, in turn, protects the public interest in development of a "democratic civil society and free press." All of these interests are legitimately protectable. Still, it is debatable whether the concept of information security is a correct legal mechanism to realize these interests. In fact, people's interest in protecting their private life is guaranteed by the scope of the right to privacy, rules on confidentiality of personal data, and privacy of personal communications. Also, constitutional guarantees of free speech, information, and the press may already cover their interests in open access to information, anonymous dissemination and disclosure of information, and democratic development through public discourse in associations or through independent media.

The concept of information security is corrupted by contradictions, however. Interests in open access to information, democratic civic discourse, and press freedom become undermined by a set of interests labeled "information security." Freedom of information may be limited to the purposes of protecting an individual and society against such threats as "unlawful informational-psychological influences" and "manipulation of the public consciousness through information." Furthermore, information is said to undermine information security of society if it "deforms national self-consciousness," "disconnects society from its historical and national traditions and customs," "destabilize[s] the social and political situation," and "infringe[s] upon the interethnic consent and consent among different religious confessions." Finally, information security of society is maintained when the spiritual, cultural, and historical values of society and the scientific and technical potential of the state are "preserved and developed." Doubtless, these restrictions target particular viewpoints or content.

In turn, information security of the state is also a multidimensional concept. First, it protects "state information resources from unsanctioned access." What may be interpreted as a security of the crucial state information infrastructure is indeed a legitimate state interest to protect, especially in light of the volatility of computer networks storing that information to external attacks and manipulation.[21] From this perspective, information security of the state may be seen as a part of what is widely known as "computer security" or "network security." The concept in Uzbekistan goes further, however. In its second dimension, the state information security is a part of national security, so threats against territorial integrity and state secrets automatically become threats to information security. Thus, it is a state task to maintain information security on the basis of a unified state policy in the information sphere, irrespective of the media used.[22] Finally, speech prohibited under the Criminal Code is a threat to the state information security.[23]

The three-prong dimensions of information security interests add legal complexity to counterbalancing these interests and free expression rights. This broad notion is not free from internal controversies either. The scope of information security embodies interests that are formulated in inherently imprecise language that makes it difficult for individuals to predict the conduct of those interests. However, if we move from the sphere of legal rules to the nonlegal context in which these rules operate—namely, a national ideology of independence of Uzbekistan—we may appreciate why the information security of the individual and society are defined in such open-ended language.

NATIONAL IDEOLOGY OF INDEPENDENCE AND ITS RESPONSE
TO THE FREE FLOW OF INFORMATION

The national ideology of independence is a "constantly evolving" system of moral values and beliefs to which the "entire population, all political parties, groups and movements" have an interest in adhering (Karimov 2000; Shetinina 2003, 42, 44, 46–47, 69, 71). As elsewhere in Central Asia, state leaders developed moral virtues with support from political philosophers; their aim was to provide legitimacy to the existing social and political order (Marat 2008). To serve that aim, the ideology uses both positive and negative legitimation.[24] The positive legitimation is based essentially on the residual political promises of economic progress.[25] The negative legitimation concentrates on threats of "open or hidden ideological influence," "pressure," "aggression," and even "dictatorship" on Uzbek society (Shetinina 2003, 23–24, 27). These threats emerge as a result of information exchange and a concurrent information explosion as far as the quantity of information individuals receive in the modern information society.[26] The Internet is seen to have a particularly deleterious effect as a means for the influx of "alien ideologies and destructive ideas" and "the struggle for minds and moods of the people," especially youth (Karimov 2005). The idea of national independence is also meant to counterbalance the ideas of terrorism and Islamic extremism, including the idea of creating the Islamic caliphate (Shermatova 2001, 219; Shetinina 2003, 41). Ideologists claim, therefore, that only a "truly humanistic" ideology serves people as a basis for their perception of the world and has formative influences upon the development of the "ideological immunity" or "sustainable public consciousness" (Shetinina 2003, 4; Karimov 2003, 7–8).

The national ideology is often referred to as an ideology of the "revival of spirituality," as it actively encourages the individuals' adherence to selected moral values to benefit the whole society.[27] These moral values are rooted in the centuries-old "spiritual heritage" of Uzbek people. It is expressed in symbolic Uzbek cultural images (Adams 2004, 97; Jones Luong 2002, 135), the philosophical musings of a fourteenth-century national hero, Amir Timur, and misrepresentations of Uzbek history, including in the Soviet period (Shetinina 2003, 41; Djumaev 2001, 330–31). By paying "extremely little attention . . . to the values of modernity," the ideology seeks to engender almost unconditional fidelity to national traditions by means of a "monolithic discourse of [Uzbek] nationalism" (Abdullaev 2005, 267–68; Adams 2004, 95, 97) and to downplay identities of ethnic minorities and religion (Marat 2008, 17, 89). The ideology persuades individuals to "harmoniously combine"—read "subordinate"—individual interests to those of society and the state (Shetinina 2003, 29, 49). In particular, individuals are expected to advance their interests to fulfill such collective goods as social stability, solidarity, and economic progress (Shetinina 2003, 57, compare Shlapentokh, 1986, 19). There is little doubt, therefore, about the national leadership's deliberate approach of interpreting individuals' rights in favor of specific collective interests of society through ideological and cultural predispositions. In doing so, the ideology disrespects the principle of individual autonomy that human rights are based upon.

So far the government has been fairly successful in developing an extensive mechanism of overt propagation of the idea of national independence to maintain its effectiveness.[28] State-controlled mass media and educational and other public institutions perform a propaganda role.[29] Still, the de facto hegemony of the national ideology is objectionable from the constitutional law perspective on two points. First, it contradicts the constitutional ban against imposition of a single state ideology (Article 12). This provision also declares that public life develops itself on the basis of pluralism of political institutions, ideologies, and opinions. Scholars undermine these constitutional purposes and objectives, however, by declaring that the constitution advances the goal of creating the ideology of national independence (Tadjikhanov 2001a, 70; Saidov, Tadjikhanov, and Odilkoriyev 2002, 428).

Second, the ideology lacks institutional legitimacy in a democratic Uzbekistan.[30] Ideologists justify their system of values as a practical realization of democracy and justice: they see it as a catalyst and a means to realize public interests that are, in fact, largely shaped by the ideology itself (Shetinina 2003, 39, 44). Legal scholars echo this worrisome approach; they eventually declare, although not explain, the dichotomy between spiritual and democratic freedoms and their coexistence under the constitution (Tadjikhanov 2001b, 71, 74). They acknowledge no difficulty in reconciling democratic freedoms based on constitutional principles of democracy, human rights, and the rule of law, with a monolithic societal system of moral virtues based on the "ideology of spirituality." In this light the officially imposed national ideology takes on critical dimensions in blurring the difference between the legal and ideological-moral orders as promoted by the government. Taking into account the fact that the official national ideology was conceptualized many years after the constitution entered into force, such interpretation is another eloquent example of a contemporary and overwhelming trend by scholars to keep the constitutional law doctrine congruent with current political postulates.[31] A relation between constitutional law and politics always exists. It seems, however, that the constitutional virtues of separation of powers, rule of law, democratic governance, and human rights are sacrificed to maintain that relationship in Uzbekistan.

EFFECTS OF INFORMATION SECURITY UPON FREE SPEECH

The legal content of information security restrictions on speech is similar to the politics propagated by the national ideology of independence. These restrictions may have a significant harmful effect on speech and access to information on the Internet because they are best understood as policies to control the dissemination of information that has the potential to undermine the "constructed legitimacy" of the state's political authority (Kertcher and Margalit 2005, 28–30). Crucial policy strategies for maintaining this legitimacy are "unifying myths" (Kertcher and Margalit 2005, 12, compare Shlapentokh 1986, 25). By fostering adherence to consolidating myths or state-imposed moral virtues, the national ideology negates the fundamental concept of pluralism of opinions and dissent.

The aim of maintaining the ideology-based state of security of the individual, society, and the state underlies the policy goals in regulating an information sphere—the activities through which information, irrespective of content and means of dissemination, is "created, processed, and consumed" by people.[32] The obligation to maintain the three-dimensional information security rests primarily with state bodies.[33] In particular, the state must "establish a system of counter-measures to prevent expansion of information that undermines information security of society" or, to put it plainly, that directly or indirectly influence public opinion beyond the "tolerable limits" of speech.[34] From this perspective, information security may be seen as both the legal and institutional counterbalancing response to globalization and media globalization—a response that varies among governments and greatly depends on what free speech entails for them (Price 2002, 245–46). To appreciate the extent to which the measures to maintain information security are developed in Uzbekistan, this chapter highlights the roles played by state bodies and private actors. It demonstrates that these measures may contribute, in the long run, to the creation of an isolated, country-bound "sphere of ideas," where open access to diverse Internet content is deemed a threat to the individual, society, and the state.[35]

STATE POLICY MEASURES TO MAINTAIN INFORMATION SECURITY: STATE CENSORSHIP OR MONITORING OF THE "INFORMATION SPHERE"?

To maintain information security, the state primarily targets the Internet for its distinct role "in the struggle for minds and mindsets of people."[36] It does so through two types of measures: (1) controlling public dissemination of ideas by designing specific Internet access infrastructures; and (2) controlling content within Uzbekistan's domain space. The former type of measure includes operation of two state-regulated intra-Uzbek information networks or intranets, UzSciNet and ZiyoNet; a search engine, at the national level; and content-filtering software for private use as developed by a provider that is not independent of the government (Kozhamberdiyeva 2008, 128–30). ZiyoNet intranet, for instance, provides Internet access in all public institutions, but is designed primarily for secondary and higher education institutions. Mindful of the role of the educational system in the ideological propaganda, ZiyoNet provides the country's youth with strictly filtered content that conforms to the idea of national independence, state interests, and domestic laws.[37] Thus the younger generation is not exposed to a wider variety of views and information than the state says is necessary for the self-development and fulfillment of its citizens.

To understand how content-based control of Uzbekistan's Internet domain space operates, one must be aware of the problem of institutionalized censorship of speech that persists despite the constitutional ban. It is wrong to think that administrative censorship effectively ceased to exist after the State Committee of the Republic of Uzbekistan for the Press—informally referred to as Uzlit for its functional similarity to the Main Directorate for Safeguarding State Secrets in the Press of the USSR (Glavlit)—was reconstructed into the Uzbek Agency for the Press and Information (UzAPI) in 2002.[38] This new specialized administrative body was indeed "categorically prohibited to carry out censorship, editorial functions, make prohibitions [eventually, upon distribution of publications] and other forms of illegitimate interference into the activity of the mass media."[39] Still, its administrative order strictly regulates publishing so no publication or issue of a newspaper is disseminated without UzAPI approving "control copies."[40] Arguably, this body also has the authority to "instruct" printing houses to destroy publications whose distribution is declared "inexpedient."[41] That said Internet publishing may be an option to avoid administrative censorship.

However, government monitoring "mass communications," as discussed next, makes that option fairly impossible.

From a historical perspective, the government's monitoring resembles a monitoring scheme proposed by a head of the Soviet Glavlit as necessary to prevent "the demise of a system of protection of state secrets" or the system of political censorship in the USSR, which was on the verge of its collapse.[42] Upon its establishment, UzAPI was assigned the task to "monitor compliance of publishers, the mass media, television and radio broadcasters and other participants of a domestic information market with laws in the field of information" from the moment of their official registration till the dissemination of issues.[43] To effectively perform this function, a UzAPI Center for Monitoring of the Mass Media and Licensing was restructured into a Center for Monitoring of Mass Communications Sphere (CMMCS)[44] under the Agency for Communications and Information (UzACI)—a state body with the duty to provide for information security on the telecommunications networks, post, TV and radio, and information systems, including Information and Communication Technologies (ICTs).[45] Simple comparison of their names demonstrates the straightforward extension of monitoring from the mass media to all "mass communications." The latter term is much broader and encompasses all possible means of expression, including the Internet.[46]

Government monitoring is permanent and systematic.[47] It follows three procedural stages: (1) collection and compilation of information products that are generated and disseminated within the "national information space"; (2) content analysis for their conformity with the legal framework for production and dissemination of mass communications, protection of information security, prevention of "destructive negative information-psychological influence upon the public conscience of citizens," and preserving "national and cultural traditions"; and (3) drafting motivated conclusions, preventive warnings, and recommendations if it determines that violations of laws and administrative orders affecting the exercise of free speech and mass media freedom have occurred.[48] The function of preventive warnings is particularly important as such warnings inform individuals and legal entities about their wrongdoings. In principle the CMMCS has the duty to communicate warnings to these addressees no later than five days after the end of monitoring to enable them to take "urgent actions to avoid further violations and prevent possible negative consequences." The CMMCS, however, reserves the right to communicate its warnings only in "exceptional," but unspecified, cases. No limits are set on the center's discretion to decide when and if ever it informs individuals about their alleged violations of the regulatory framework. Simultaneously with warnings, the CMMCS has the duty to prepare separate opinions or motivated conclusions about the same alleged violations and communicate them to state bodies for them to implement necessary measures.

Such content-based control of the media also functions flawlessly with respect to Web sites with independent content that provide for civic discourse on Uzbek reality.[49] Accordingly, owners of sites registered in Uzbek domain space may find their online resources closed from one day to another without written notice of purported violations and without the opportunity to take corrective action. Taking either motivated conclusions or opinions of the CMMCS as the basis for its actions, the administrator of the Uzbek domain space UZINFOCOM—which is a body of the UzACI—may use its authority to order a particular ccTLD registry to close down sites.[50] A ccTLD registry, usually a private provider of Internet services, has technical capacity to cancel domain name registrations and, thus, make sites inaccessible. This, in turn, prevents site owners from deleting any purportedly illegal information if they choose. It remains to be seen whether officially registered sites will face similar obstacles.

Monitoring the national information space is inherently flawed in many respects. First, the immense intensity of infringements of free expression rights is provided for under administrative orders that lack statutory grounds other than those of information security restrictions and the requirement of trustworthiness of information.[51] However, these restrictions are not democratically legitimized because the government has decided what to encapsulate into the legislative norms adopted by the parliament in violation of the principle of separation of powers. The constitutional and legislative requirement of trustworthiness also fails the test of international human rights standards because it targets a person's viewpoint.[52] Second, state monitoring of mass communications impairs constitutional guarantees because it serves the goal of legitimizing and delegitimizing the dissemination of media content to the same degree as censorship. It seems that the constitutional ban on censorship—narrowly defined by legislators as a prior restraint—does not protect against various forms of political control of the media and its content after publication. Finally, a non-transparent state monitoring of Uzbekistan's information space denies justice to individuals. The regulation neither explicitly envisages the mechanism of appeal of the CMMCS administrative decisions nor mentions domestic courts as state bodies—recipients of information about alleged violations in a legal framework. Also, Web site owners may be prevented from pursuing claims in court because the administrative regulation does not impose a duty on the monitoring body to officially inform them about the matter and reasons for closing a site or the state bodies that effectively shut them down.

The effective reach of a state system of Internet control would not be altogether possible without collaboration by domestic providers of Internet access and host services. Faced with the prospect of business license revocation and liabilities, these private actors cooperate with state authorities in surveillance and monitoring of computer networks and servers for the flow of content (Kozhamberdiyeva 2008, 130–32). Other "internet providers," such as individuals or legal entities that provide public access points like Internet cafés, also must monitor access and cooperate with state bodies.[53] These methods of privatized censorship are highly contested under international law (Tambini, Leonardi, and Marsden 2008, 267–86), but seem to raise no questions of legality in Uzbekistan.

Conclusion

Long after the Uzbek constitution proclaimed guarantees of freedoms of speech, information, and freedom of mass media, the Internet is generally viewed as a "last resort of pluralism" of opinions.[54] This chapter demonstrates that it is hardly possible for the Internet to survive as an open and pluralistic source in Uzbekistan's physical and domain space under current regulation of the Internet media based predominantly on administrative rules. Openness on the Internet is severely undermined by ideological and, thus, above all, political pressures. Politics, instrumentally transformed into law, recognize that an individual, society, and the state have interests to be secure in the information sphere. As a result, vaguely defined threats against their information security have to be responded to by government measures; for effective implementation, the state simultaneously relies on its own apparatus and private actors.

Measures directed particularly against Internet media shed new light on the long-standing practice of a permanent and systematic control of the mass media. This practice is legitimized by a state function of monitoring conformity of individuals with the domestic regulatory framework for the exercise of free speech irrespective of its form and means of expression. Despite the constitutional ban on censorship, the monitoring function illustrates that the process of legalization and institutionalization of state political censorship of mass communications is irrevocable. The monitoring function also explains the effectiveness of state control of Internet media. There is little doubt that the Uzbek reality has evolved not away from, but back toward, Soviet-era legal and ideological-political censorship.

It is one of the stark explanations of the overall and enduring narrowing of the independent mass media since independence.

The Internet is often seen as a source "of great hope for the future vitality of democracy" (Gore 2007, 6). But it is also seen as a technology of "Repression 2.0" that makes it easier for government to spread fear among users.[55] Authoritarian governments tend to move toward the second extreme (Deibert 1997, 164–69). Still, the Uzbek government generally claims that its information policy aims to ensure "proper and full observance" of constitutional principles of freedom of speech, information, and the press.[56] Yet this chapter shows how the government does not take its own claims seriously. Lawyers and the judiciary should subject legislated restrictions on speech to critical and independent assessment and review that includes consideration of Uzbekistan's international obligations for human rights.[57] Without critical debate on matters of public interest that are deemed an "informational threat" to a person, society, and the state, democracy cannot flourish and the Internet will fail to contribute toward its vitality in Uzbekistan.

NOTES

1. See Resolutsiia KM RU "O Sozdanii natsionalnoi seti peredachi dannikh e upori-adochenii dostupa k mirovym informatsionnym setiam" (Resolution of the Cabinet of Ministers "On the Establishment of the National Data Communication Network and Streamlining of Access to World Information Networks") No. 52 (5 February 1999) (not published in the official compilations of legal acts); Resolutsiia KM RU "O detsentralizasii dostupa k mezhdunarodnym komputernym setiam" (Resolution of the Cabinet of Ministers "On the Decentralization of Access to International Computer Networks") No. 352 (10 October 2002), *Sobranie zakonodatelstva RU* (2005) No. 34–36, 264. See also United Nations Development Programme (2001).

2. See Postanovlenie KM RU "O Merakh po dalneishemu razvitiu komputerizatsii i vnedreniu informatsionno-kommunikatsionnikh technologiy" (Resolution of the Cabinet of Ministers "On Measures for the Further Development of Computerization and Information and Communications Technologies") No. 200 (6 June 2002), Annex I, "Program for the development of computerization and information and communica-tions technologies for 2002–2010," *Sobranie zakonodatel'stva RU* (2006) No. 40, 396.

3. See Omar Sharifov 2004, "Obzor 30 saitov, posveschennikh Uzbekistanu" (Overview of 30 Web sites Reporting on Uzbekistan), 14 December (www.freeuz.org); P. Loshodkin, "Internet censorship in Uzbekistan is worsening," 9 August. (http://enews.ferghana. ru/article.php?id=1544) (listing Web sites of banned political parties at www.ezgulik.

org, www.muhammadsalih.info, www.uzbekistanerk.ru, www.birlik.net). Alsowww. shamelist.ru was set up to systematically report about Internet censorship in Central Asia. However, the most recent entries for Uzbekistan date back to 2006.

4. Independent news reporting stes blocked in 2007 and 2008 were www.uzngo.info (Bulletin of Civil Society in Uzbekistan);, www.ferghana.ru; www.uzmetronom.uz; www.informator.uz; www.uznews.net; and www.newsuz.com.

5. See Reporters sans Frontieres 2005, "The 15 Enemies of the Internet and Other Countries to Watch," Report presented to the World Summit on Information Society, 7 November 2005; Resolution of the European Parliament "On Freedom of Expression on the Internet," P6_TA(2006)0324 (6 July 2006), para. H.

6. A web site is an electronic form of mass media. Art. 4, Zakon RU "O sredstvakh massovoi informasii" (law "On mass media") No. 541-I (26 December 1997), as amended (15 January 2007), *Sobranie zakonodatel'stva RU* (2007) No. 3, 20. For web site registration requirements, see Postanovlenie KM RU "O vnesenii izmeneniy i dolneniy v polozhenie o poriadke gosudarstvennoi registratsii sredstv massovoi informatsii v Respublike Uzbekistan" (Resolution of the Cabinet of Ministers "On changes and amendments to the resolution on the state registration of the mass media in the Republic of Uzbekistan") No. 68 (2 April 2007), *Sobranie zakonodatel'stva RU* (2007) No. 14, 141.

7. See, however, Deibert et al. (2008, 180), arguing that Central Asian countries have adapted Russia's 2000 doctrine on information security to fit their own regulation of the Internet and "national information space".

8. Bishkek Declaration of the Meeting of the Council of Heads of State of the Shanghai Cooperation Organization, 16 August 2007. See Annex to the letter dated 17 October 2007 from the Permanent Representative of Tajikistan to the United Nations addressed to the Secretary-General, U.N. Doc. A/62/492-S/2007/616, 19 October 2007.

9. The definition of ideology is used here to reflect "the system of ideas, theories, values and norm, ideals and directives for action of a certain social class . . . that help to strengthen the destruction of . . . actual social relations." See Shlapentokh (1986, 1).

10. See art. 1, Konstitutsiia Respubliki Uzbekistan (Consitution of the Republic of Uzbekistan), 8 December 1992, *Sobranie zakonodatel'stva RU* (2007) No.15, 152.

11. Human Rights Committee, "Concluding Observations: Uzbekistan," U.N. Doc. CCPR/CO/71/UZB (26 April 2001), para. 18 (stating that the national legislation on state secrets is too broad to be consistent with freedom of expression).

12. No data is available on cases in which individuals have claimed a violation of their free speech rights and on the relevant judicial interpretation and application of laws by the Uzbek supreme court.

13. The mass media must "check out" the trustworthiness of information it is going

to bring to the public view. They share the responsibility for the trustworthiness of information together with a source of information. See art. 11, Zakon RU "O Garantiyakh i svobode dostupa k informatsii" (law "On guarantees and freedom of access to information"), No. 400-I, 24 April 1997, *Vedomosti Oliy Mazhlisa RU* (1997) No. 4–5, 108. See also art. 5, law "On mass media," which establishes the responsibility for the objectivity of the disseminated information.

14. Art. 5.

15. Art. 7 defines censorship as "the right to demand prior approval of the communications and materials, as well as to demand alterations introduced to text or to withdraw communication and materials in full intended for print (broadcast)."

16. Compare to art. 39, USSR Constitution of 1977: "Enjoyment by citizens of their rights and freedoms must not be to the detriment of the interests of society or the state, or infringe the rights of other citizens."

17. As rights, in principle, are conferred upon individuals or legal persons, the scope of "state rights" when applied within the national legal order in contrast to the international one, is unclear and not explicitly recognized under the constitution.

18. Zakon RU "O printsipakh e garantiiakh svobody informatsii" (law "On principles and guarantees for freedom of information") No. 439-II (12 December 2002), *Vedomosti Oliy Majlisa RU* (2003) No.1, 2.

19. For a general analysis, see article 19 Global Campaign for Free Expression, "Memorandum on the Law of the Republic of Uzbekistan 'On Principles and Guarantees for Freedom of Information,'" December 2002, www.article19.org/pdfs/analysis/ uzbekistan-law-on-freedom-of-information-june-.pdf. See also Banisar (2005, 135 and 144).

20. Breach of the latter two paragraphs of art.11of Freedom of Information Law are prohibited by art. 155, Administrative Code, *Sobranie zakonodatel'stva RU* (2007) No. 39, 400; and art. 174, Criminal Code, No. 2012-XII (22 September 1994), *Vedomosti Verkhovnogo Soveta RU* (1995) No. I. The sanction under art. 174 was amended by Law No. 254-II (29 Augist 2001), *Vedomosti Oliy Majlisa RU* (2001) No. 9–10, 165.

21. State online information resources may fall victim to computer attacks. See "Cyberattack on Estonia stirs fear of 'virtual war,'" *International Herald Tribune*, A 4, 19–20 May 2007.

22. Zakon RU "Ob utverzhdenii kontseptsii natsional'noi bezopasnosti Respubliki Uzbekistan" (law "On establishment of the concept of national security of the Republic of Uzbekistan"), No. 467-I (29 August 1997), *Vedomosti Oliy Majlisa* (1997) No. 11–12, 295.

23. In Uzbekistan, criminal prosecution is used extensively to silence political expression. See, e.g., Ambeyi Ligabo, "Summary of Cases Transmitted to Governments and Replies Received," Addendum to the Report of the Special Rapporteur, E/CN.4/2005/64/Add.1

(29 March 2005), paras. 972–90.

24. The dichotomy between positive and negative legitimizion is introduced and elaborated in Shlapentokh (1986, 10 and 14–16).

25. Goals such as "political stability," "prosperity of the motherland," "peace and state of calmness in the country," and "well-being of the people" are to be reached at an uncertain future time. State ideology is expected to serve the population as a "torch brightening the way to the progress" and to be centered on the postulate that "Uzbekistan is a country with a great future" in justifying its hegemony. See Shetinina (2003, 50–54). For critical evaluation of ideological values, see Abdullaev (2005, 269).

26. See Karimov (2003, 7), Shetinina (2003, 22–23) (mentioning the notion of information society only once, with no specific details clarifying the statement).

27. See Shodiev Narzulla, Natsionalnaia idea: kak eto videtsia v Uzbekistane (National idea: As it is seen in Uzbekistan). *Trud.* 23 June, http://choe.tfi.uz/p10.html. ("In a unity of cultural wealth and national idea, spirituality is primal. Spirituality is a moral and ethical being that leads the nation to progress. The national idea in the destiny of the nation is, first of all, the spiritual phenomenon.") See Shetinina (2003, 54–55), Karimov (1998, 9, 19, 49).

28. With respect to its function and complexity, the ideology has a certain degree of resemblance to the Soviet official ideology but without its role and magnitude. See Abdullaev (2005, 277).

29. On the role of the educational system, see Rasporiazhenie Presidenta RU "O sozdanii e vnedrenii v sistemu obrazovaniia Respubliki uchebnikh programm po predmety "Ideia natsionalnoi nezavisimosti: osnovnie poniatiia e principi"" (Order of the President of the Republic of Uzbekistan "On the Creation and Introduction of the Subject 'Idea of National Independence: Basic Concepts and Principles' in the Curriculum of the Educational System of the Republic") (18 January 2001) (unpublished), http://www.press-service.uz. On the role of state authorities, see Ukaz Presidenta RU "O podderzhke Respublikanskogo Soveta Dukhovnosti e Prosviaschenia" (Edict of the President of the Republic of Uzbekistan "On the Support of the Republican Council for Spirituality and Enlightenment" (3 September 1999), *Vedomosti Oliy Majlisa RU* (1999) No. 9, 242 (for example, art. 4 establishes that a deputy prime minister of the Republic of Uzbekistan is to be appointed to a management position of the Council on Spirituality and Enlightenment). Senators of the parliament are also expected to work on the "spirituality and spiritual immunity of the youth." See Press Service of the Senate of the Oliy Mazhlis of the Republic of Uzbekistan, "Press Release on the 7th Plenary Session of the Senate" (26 August 2006), www.gov.uz/ru/content.scm?contentId=22318. On the propaganda role of cultural elites, see Adams (2004,

116–17). The National Center on Human Rights, National Society of Philosophers are called upon to propagate the ideas of the ideology. See Shetinina (2003, 69–70).

30. See, however, Marat (2008, 88–93).

31. It became the practice to quote Karimov's public speeches and publications in academic articles on constitutional law and human rights. The commentary on the constitution of Uzbekistan is no exception. Being a mechanical engineer and economist by education, the president is called "the greatest" academic of law. See Urazaev (2001, 25).

32. See law "On the guarantees and principles of freedom of information," arts. 3, 12.

33. Art. 12, requires private actors, including citizens, entities of citizen self-governance (i.e., *mahallas*), public associations, and other nongovernmental, noncommercial organizations, to have their "place and role" to play in maintaining information security. It is difficult to discern if this provision creates any specific legal obligations for those private actors, and if so, what those obligations are.

34. Art. 14.

35. See *Pravda Vostoka*, 2 September 2005, as cited in Kimmage (2005): "In order to understand and properly acknowledge the significance of the idea of national independence, one must take into account particular patterns in the sphere of ideas. Otherwise, various extremes are possible. We find evidence of this in the real experience of certain post-Soviet countries."

36. As recognized in the list of state reforms in the field of further "democratization of the activities of the mass media. See Postanovlenie Prezidenta RU "O Programme po realizatsii tselei e zadach democratizatsii obnovlenia obshchestva, reformirovania e modenizatsii strani" (Resolution of the President of the Republic of Uzbekistan "On the Programme on the Realization of the Aims and Tasks of Democratization and Renewal of Society, The State Reforms and Modernization"), (10 March 2005), *Sobranie zakonodatel'stva RU* (2005) 71, No. 45, 337.

37. Art. 2, Postanovlenie Presidenta RU O sozdanii obshestvennoi obrazovatelnoi informazionnoi seti Respubliki Uzbekistan (Decree of the President of the Republic of Uzbekistan "On the Establishment of the Public Educational and Informational Network of the Republic of Uzbekistan") (28 September 2005), *Sobranie zakonodatel'stva RU* (2005) No. 40, 305.

38. See art. 1, Ukaz Presidenta RU "O sovershenstvovanii upravlenia v oblasti pechati i informatsii" (Edict of the President "On the Improvement of the Management in the Field of the Press and Information") (3 July 2002), *Vedomosti Oliy Majlisa RU* (2002) No. 6–7, 119.

39. Art. 4.

40. Prikaz General'nogo Directora Uzbekskogo Agenstva Pechati i Informatsii

"Ob Utverzhdenii pravil pechatania izdaniy" No. 29 (15 March 2006), *Sobranie zakonodatel'stva RU* (2006) No. 15, 130.

41. Arts. 49–52.

42. Letter of the Head of GUOT B. A. Boldiyrev to USSR President Gorbachev on reestablishment of an organ to control compliance with the Law on Press and Other Mass Media at the highest level of the USSR, 30 May 1991. See text in Goriaeva (1997, 397–99).

43. Art. 2.

44. Postanovlenie Kabineta Ministrov RU "O merakh po sovershenstvovaniu strukturi upravlenia v sfere massovikh kommunikatsiy" (Resolution of the Cabinet of Ministers of the Republic of Uzbekistan "On Measures for the Further Improvement of the Management Structure in the Sphere of Mass Communications"), No. 555 (24 November 2004), *Sobranie zakonodatel'stva RU* (2004) No. 47, 486.

45. Postanovlenie Kabineta Ministrov RU "O merakh po sovershenstvovaniu deiatelnosti Uzbekskogo Agenstva sviazi i informatizatsii" (Resolution of the Cabinet of Ministers of the Republic of Uzbekistan "On Measures for the Further Improvement of the Activity of the Agency for Communications and Information of Uzbekistan"), No. 215 (7 May 2004), *Sobranie zakonodatel'stva RU* (2004) No. 19, 220. See the structure of the UzACI at www.aci.uz/en/Structure/Venture.

46. A "sphere of mass communications" implies the activity of legal and private persons for "creation, development, processing, retransmission, broadcasting and storage of radio- and television programs, other public information with the use of ICTs (space and satellite communications, data transmission network and Internet and others), and computer games" and "production, dissemination and storage of print publications, book products [i.e., books, brochures, and booklets], audiovisual media, and phonograms designed for the mass use (audio- and videocassettes, video-, CDs and others)." See art. 3, Postanovlenie Kabineta Ministrov RU "O merakh po sovershenstvovaniu monitoringa za sobludeniem zakonodatelstva v sfere massovikh kommunikatsii" (Resolution of the Cabinet of Ministers of the Republic of Uzbekistan "On Further Improvement of the Monitoring of Compliance with the Legislation on the Mass Communications"), No. 132 (28 June 2007), *Sobranie zakonodatel'stva RU* (2007) No. 25–26, 265.

47. Arts. 2, 5, 13, Annex I, Resolution No. 132.

48. Art. 13, Resolution No. 132; art. 1, Resolution No. 555.

49. Informator.Uz at www.informator.uz was closed down in this manner. See "Pochemu zakrito nezavisimoe SMI Uzbekistana—Informator.Uz?" ("Why the independent mass media of Uzbekistan, Informator.Uz, is closed?"), U-FORUM blog of the UZINFOCOM, first entry 20 September 2007. Www.uforum.uz/showthread.php?t=2565.

50. Ibid.

51. Preamble, art. 1, Resolution No. 555.

52. See HRC, "Annual General Assembly Report," U.N. Doc. A/50/40 (3 October 1995), para. 89; HRC, "Concluding Observations: Armenia," U.N. Doc. CCPR/C/79/Add.100 (19 November 1998), para. 20.

53. See Polozhenie "O poriadke predostavlenia dostupa k seti Internet v obschestvennikh punktakh pol'zovania" (Regulations "On Adoption of the Terms of Provision of Access to the Internet Network in Public Points of Use"), promulgated by Order of the Uzbek Agency for Comunications and Information No. 216 (23 July 2004), *Sobranie zakonodatelstva RU* (2004) No. 30, 350.

54. See Almaty Declaration on Pluralism in the Media and the Internet, 14 October 2005, OSCE FOM.GAL/15/05 (28 October 2005).

55. Adam Kushner, Repression 2.0. *Newsweek* (14 April 2008), 27–29.

56. See letter dated 26 June 2006 from the Permanent Representative of Uzbekistan to the United Nations, addressed to the secretary-general, U.N. Doc. A/60/914 (30 June 2006), paras. d and m (denying as unfounded allegations of an intolerance of any kind of dissent expressed in the independent media).

57. Uzbekistan became a State Party to the International Covenant on Civil and Political Rights on 28 December 1995 without reservations. Art. 19 ICCPR protects the right to freedom of expression.

REFERENCES

Abdullaev, Evgeniy. 2005. Uzbekistan: Between traditionalism and westernization. In *Central Asia at the end of the transition,* ed. Boris Rumer, 267–96. Armonk: M. E. Sharpe.

Adams, Laura. 2004. Cultural elites in Uzbekistan: Ideological production and the state. In *The transformation of Central Asia: States and societies from Soviet rule to independence,* ed. Pauline Jones Luong, 93–119. Ithaca, NY: Cornell University Press.

Banisar, David. 2005. Freedom of information: Global practices and implementation in Central Asia. In *Twenty-first century challenges for the media in Central Asia: Dealing with libel and freedom of information,* ed. OSCE Representative on Freedom of the Media, 127–46. Vienna: OSCE Representative on Freedom of the Media.

Barendt, Eric. 2005. *Freedom of speech,* 2nd ed. Oxford: Oxford University Press.

Deibert, Ronald J. 1997. *Parchment, printing, and hypermedia: Communications in world order transformation.* New York: Columbia University Press.

Deibert, Ronald J., John G. Palfrey, Rafal Rohozinski, and Jonathan Zittrain, eds. 2008. *Access denied: The practice and policy of global Internet filtering.* Cambridge, MA: MIT Press.

Djumaev, Aleksander. 2001. Nation-building, culture, and problems of ethno-cultural identity in Central Asia: The case of Uzbekistan. In *Can liberal pluralism be exported? Western political theory and ethnic relations in Eastern Europe,* ed. Will Kymlicka and Magda Opalski, 320–45. Oxford: Oxford University Press.

Elst, Michiel. 2005. *Copyright, freedom of speech, and cultural policy in the Russian Federation.* Boston: Martinus Nijhoff.

Goldsmith, Jack, and Tim Wu. 2006. *Who controls the Internet? Illusions of a borderless world.* Oxford: Oxford University Press.

Gore, Al. 2007. *The assault on reason.* New York: Penguin.

Goriaeva, Tatiana. 1997. *Istoria Sovetskoi politicheskoi tsenzuri: Dokimenti e kommentarii (History of Soviet political censorship: Documents and commentary).* Series "Culture and Power from Stalin to Gorbachev: Research Studies." Moscow: Russian Political Encyclopedia.

Graham, Loren. 1984. *Science and computers in Soviet society.* In *The Soviet Union in the 1980s,* special issue of *Proceedings of the Academy of Political Science* 35 (3), ed. E. Hoffmann, 124–34. New York.

Guard, Colin. 2004. The Internet access and training program in Central Asia. In *The media freedom Internet cookbook,* eds. Christian Möller and Arnaud Amouroux. Vienna: OSCE Representative on Freedom of the Media: 203–09.

———. 2006. Observations on Internet freedom and development in eleven countries of Eurasia. In *Pluralism in the media and the Internet.* Seventh Central Asia Media Conference, Almaty, 13–14 October 2005, ed. OSCE Representative on Freedom of the Media, 133–35. Vienna: OSCE Representative on Freedom of the Media.

Hördegen, Zhanna. 2008. Freedom of expression on the Internet: A case study of Uzbekistan. *Review of Central and East European Law* 33(1): 95–134.

Ibraimov, Bakyt. 2006. Media pluralism in Kyrgyzstan: Before and after the revolution. In *Pluralism in the media and the Internet.* Seventh Central Asia Media Conference, Almaty, 13–14 October 2005, ed. OSCE Representative on Freedom of the Media, 103–10. Vienna: OSCE Representative on Freedom of the Media.

Karimov, Islam. 1998. *Spravedlivost, interesi rodini e naroda—previshe vsego (Justice, Interests of the Motherland and People—Above All).* Tashkent: Uzbekiston.

———. 2000. Natsinonalnaia ideologia—osnova buduuschego (National Ideology—the Basis for the Future). Official Speech, 6 April. Http://www.press-service.uz.

———. 2003. Introduction. In *Ideia natsionalnoi nezavisimosti: osnovnie poniatiia e prinsipi (Idea of national independence: The main notions and principles),* ed. N. Shetinina, 7–10. Tashkent: Uzbekiston.

———. 2005. "Nasha osnovnaia zel'—demokratizasiia and obnovlenie obschestva, provedenie reform e modernizasiia strani" (Our Main Aim—Democratization and the Renewal of Society, Reformation and Modernization of the Country). Address to Oliy Mazhlis,

28 January 2005. Http://www.press-service.uz/rus/rechi/r01282005.htm.

Kertcher, Zack, and Ainat N. Margalit, 2005. Challenges to authority, burden of legitimisation: The printing press and the Internet. *International Journal of Communications Law and Policy* 10 (Autumn): 1–30.

Kerzhner, M. J. 2001, Kommentariy k statie 67. In *Komentariy k Konstitutsii Respubliki Uzbekistan* (*Commentary on Uzbek Constitution*), ed. Shavkat Z. Urazaev, 333–39. Tashkent: Uzbekiston.

Khodjaev, Alo. 2006. The Internet media in Uzbekistan. In *Pluralism in the media and the Internet*. Seventh Central Asia Media Conference, Almaty, 13–14 October 2005, ed. OSCE Representative on Freedom of the Media, 143–48. Vienna: OSCE Representative on Freedom of the Media.

Kimmage, Daniel. 2005. Uzbekistan: Andijon and the "information war," Radio Free Europe/ Radio Liberty., 9 September. Www.rferl.org/content/article/1061210.html.

Liu, Morgan Y. 2003. Detours from utopia on the silk road: Ethical dilemmas of neoliberal triumphalism. *Central Eurasian Studies Review* 2(2): 2–11.

Luong, Pauline Jones. 2002. *Institutional change and political continuity in post-Soviet Central Asia: Power, perceptions and pacts.* Cambridge: Cambridge University Press.

Marat, Erica. 2008. National ideology and state-building in Kyrgyzstan and Tajikistan. Silk Road Paper. Central Asia-Caucasus Institute and Silk Road Studies Program, January.

Niazova, Umida. 2005. Amir Timur—velikii democrat? (Amir Timur—a Great Democrat?). *Oasis* 17(17). Http://www.ca-oasis.info.

Nougmanov, Rachid. 2007. Internet governance in Kazakhstan. In *Governing the Internet: Freedom and regulation in the OSCE Region*, eds. Christian Möller and Arnaud Amouroux, 119–32. Vienna: OSCE Representative on Freedom of the Media.

Nowak, Manfred. 2005. UN covenant on civil and political rights: CCPR commentary. Kehl am Rhein, Germany: N. P. Engel..

Price, Monroe, E. 2002. *Media and sovereignty: The global information revolution and its challenge to state power.* Cambridge, MA: MIT Press.

Saidov, Akmal, U. T. Tadjikhanov, and Kh. Odilkoriyev. 2002. *Osnovi gosudarstva e prava: Uchebnik* (*The basics of the state and law: A textbook*). Tashkent: Sharq.

Shermatova, Sanobar. 2001. Islamskii factor v rukakh politicheskoi eliti (The islamic factor in the hands of a political elite). In *Islam na postsovetskom prostranstve: vzgliad iznutri* (*Islam in the post-Soviet newly independent states: The view from within*), eds. Aleksei Malashenko and Martha Olcott Brill, 205–31. Moscow: Moskow Carnegi Centre.

Shetinina, N. ed. 2003. *Ideia natsionalnoi nezavisimosti: osnovnie poniatiia e prinsipi* (*Idea of national independence: The main notions and principles*). Tashkent: Uzbekiston.

Shlapentokh, Vladimir. 1986. *Soviet public opinion and ideology: Mythology and pragmatism in interaction.* New York: Praeger.

Sunstein, Cass R. 2003. *Why societies need dissent*. Cambridge: Harvard University Press.

Tadjikhanov, B. U. 1997. *Konstitutsia e prava cheloveka: uchebnoe posobie (Constitution and human rights: study material)*. Serii "Democratizatsia e prava cheloveka" ("Democratic development and human rights" Series), Zhalilov Sh. I. Tashkent: Publishing House "Mireconomici e prava."

Tadjikhanov, U. T. 2001a. Kommentariy k statie 12. In *Komentariy k Konstitutsii Respubliki Uzbekistan (Commentary on Uzbek Constitution)*, ed. Shavkat Z. Urazaev, 68–70. Tashkent: Uzbekiston.

———. 2001b. Kommentariy k statie 15. In *Komentariy k Konstitutsii Respubliki Uzbekistan (Commentary on Uzbek Constitution)*, ed. Shavkat Z. Urazaev, 73–74. Tashkent: Uzbekiston:.

Tambini, Damian, Danilo Leonardi and Chris Marsden. 2008. *Codifying cyberspace: Communications self-regulation in the age of Internet convergence*. New York: Routledge.

United Nations Development Programme. 2007. E-readiness assessment of Uzbekistan. Final report .27 July.

———. 2001. ICT in Uzbekistan (2002–2007) at glance. Http://ru.ictp.uz/downloads/wsis_report_brief_2007_eng.pdf.

Urazaev, Shavkat Z. 2001. Introduction. In *Komentariy k Konstitutsii Respubliki Uzbekistan (Commentary on Uzbek Constitution)*, ed. Shavkat Z. Urazaev, 7–35. Tashkent: Uzbekiston.

Yakubov, A. 2001. Kommentariy k statie 29. In *Komentariy k Konstitutsii Respubliki Uzbekistan (Commentary on Uzbek Constitution)*, ed. Shavkat Z. Urazaev, 190–201. Tashkent: Uzbekiston.

Journalistic Self-Censorship and the Tajik Press in the Context of Central Asia

Peter Gross and Timothy Kenny

The press and other mass media in the Republic of Tajikistan shall enjoy freedom. Each citizen of the Republic of Tajikistan shall have the right to freely express convictions and hold opinions, to impart them in any form through the press and other mass media. No censorship of the mass information shall be allowed.

—The Law of the Republic of Tajikistan on the Press and
Other Mass Media, Article 2—Freedom of the Press

Tajikistan's constitution and press law have officially ended censorship. Despite such legal directives, however, the government and power elites continue to control the media—directly and indirectly—and to frame a constricting press atmosphere that forces media owners, editors, and reporters into "politically correct" editorial choices. A list of the government's overt acts of censorship is long. Major opposition newspapers have been closed, foreign broadcasting has been banned from the airwaves, and the Communications Ministry has demanded that Tajikistan's Internet service provider "filter and block access to Websites on the Internet that aim to undermine the state's policies in the sphere of information."[1] High taxes dangle like a governmental sword of Damocles over the heads of media owners, severely limiting their independence. Journalists who anger the government are jailed, often under secretive media regulations that were passed in May 2005.[2] The end result of Tajikistan's systematic censorship is unsurprising: writers and editors limit their reporting to avoid harassment, intimidation, firing, or worse.

In his acclaimed *The Future of Freedom*, Zakaria wrote, "At the very least, without a government capable of protecting property rights and human rights, press freedoms and business contracts, antitrust laws and consumer demands, a society will not get the rule of law but the rule of the strong."[5] Tajik society, clearly laboring under the rule of the strong, provides a concrete example of Zakaria's insights.

Statement of the Issue

Censorship and self-censorship are two of seven paralyzing problems faced by the Tajik media *and* society. And if it is unclear where censorship ends and the seamless flow of self-censorship begins, other factors that restrict press freedom are easier to discern: (1) no independent news distribution; (2) poor financial market conditions; (3) high taxes; and (4) an unprofessional journalism that is (5) unwilling to produce stories based on fact and supported by truth. Arguably, some of these impediments may be resolved over time if the yoke of self-censorship is lifted from the neck of Tajik journalism. But self-censorship lies at the core of the country's central press problems, fully emergent as the product of a culture that puts a premium on familial ties, friendships, and personal contacts. Self-censorship is circumscribed by a political system controlled by president Emomali Rakhmonov and his People's Democratic Party of Tajikistan and undermined by unsupportive economic conditions promulgated by a quasi-feudal financial system.

Planting the seeds of democracy in such an arid sociopolitical and cultural landscape presents problems replicated throughout Central Asia. In societies in which governments are loath to end the censorship of print, broadcast, and Internet media—and politicians are more than happy to capitalize on traditions and extant cultures that quash initiative and foster self-censorship—establishing independent media and journalistic freedom has proven a daunting challenge.

This chapter examines journalistic censorship and self-censorship in Tajikistan, placing both within the context of their presence across Central Asia, especially Kazakhstan and Kyrgyzstan.

Methodology

This chapter is based primarily on sixty-one interviews with Central Asian journalists, journalism educators and students, politicians, lawyers, researchers, and other media experts, principally in Tajikistan, Kyrgyzstan, and Kazakhstan. The authors also spoke directly with U.S.-funded nonprofit foundation executives working in the region, diplomats from American embassies, USAID (U.S. Agency for International Development) employees, and the directors and employees of nongovernmental foundations in Central Asia. Interviewees were selected on the basis of their journalistic insight, regional knowledge, and professional reputation. All author interviews were conducted in person. In a few instances, follow-up information was provided by e-mail. The majority of interviews were conducted in English; a dozen or so interviews were conducted in Russian, using a translator. The authors conducted interviews in Almaty, Bishkek, and Dushanbe, Tajikistan, in June and July 2007 and in November 2007. Interviewees were, in general, open and responsive in outlining the problematic roles that censorship and self-censorship play across Central Asian journalism; they acknowledged the difficulties that loom if the use of both is not sharply diminished. The authors also conducted traditional academic research, supplementing information gathered directly through their interviews in Central Asia.

Findings

NEITHER A LEADER NOR A FOLLOWER: CENSORSHIP AND SELF-CENSORSHIP

Outright censorship is an historic reality that has been eliminated legally in Tajikistan's post-Soviet period, or so it is meant to appear. Self-censorship, on the other hand, lies beyond the boundaries of legal restriction, endemic and fully functioning within journalism's social code, uninhibited by cultural stigma or taboo. Censorship and self-censorship spring from the same cultural genes that are fueled by common political, economic, and social values. Both methods of information restriction punish news consumers as well as news producers, eliminating facts and opinions that stand outside the narrow confines of the politically and socially allowable.

President Rakhmonov called for a new press policy of patriotic journalism in 2007, asserting that the mass media was "expected to raise patriotism with the public."[4] Furthermore, he said journalists are obliged in their stories to call the president "worthy" and "reliable" whenever he is mentioned.[5] Attacking the president, his party and its members, or friends is taboo for political, cultural, and legal reasons. Article 137 of the Tajikistan Criminal Code "forbids public criticism of the president" and sets a penalty of up to five years in prison; other sections of the code make it a crime to insult another's dignity.[6]

Five elements in the postcommunist evolution of Tajik society have reignited self-censorship and made it "one of the main obstacles to a free press," according to the New York–based Committee to Protect Journalists (CPJ):[7] (1) the 1992–97 civil war; (2) the repressive atmosphere created by the ruling elite; (3) defamation laws; (4) the broadcast licensing process; and (5) a history of newspaper, television, and radio station closures.

The civil war saw at least twenty-nine Tajik journalists murdered, acts of violence that produced an unremitting caution in reporters who weighed each word in every story and watched each TV standup carefully in their minds' eye to decide what to publicly unveil and what to withhold.[8]

Rashid Ghani, an independent political researcher, believes that after the civil war journalists made censorship their own, not because they feared the authorities but because they feared repeating the situation when society split into factions.[9] Ghani's comments echo those of journalists across Central Asia, who consistently decline to identify government's constricting role in shaping the region's press or journalism's reliance on self-censorship for survival. His remarks also fail to fully explain the constraints that undermine journalism today. Fear of authority is clearly one of two social elements at the heart of the country's postcommunist self-censorship. The second is forced patriotism, imposed on journalists by government-mandated expectations.

Although the outright murder of journalists in Tajikistan has ended since its peak during the five-year-long civil war, harassment remains, as documented by CPJ and the Paris-based Reporters sans Frontieres (Reporters without Borders). Scores of newspapers were closed after 2005, partly explaining the absence of a single daily newspaper in the country from 1992 until August 2010, when *Imruz News* (News Today) debuted. Meanwhile, television and radio stations, including cable stations, have been shut down or denied frequencies. "The process of broadcast media licensing is not carried out within the provisions of the current law," reports the International Research and Exchanges Board (IREX): "Licenses are issued by the Licensing Commission under the State Committee for Television and Radio Broadcasting, which also oversees state-run broadcasting. The presiding commissioner is the Chairman of the State Committee for Television and Radio Broadcasting, and most members are government officials."[10]

Journalists, like many other citizens, continue to cope with personal financial pressures in the poorest country of the Commonwealth of Independent States and one of the poorest in the world, with a per capita gross domestic product of $1,900 and an average life expectancy of sixty-five years.[11] In addition to low pay and social pressure, journalists work under a press law that is clearly dangerous to press freedom and that has grown increasingly hostile to freedom of expression since its enactment in 1990. The scope of criminal defamation laws has been expanded by subsequent amendments. The international outcry was pointed and immediate when the upper house of Tajikistan's parliament (the National Council) amended articles in the penal code that were aimed at broadening the defamation laws to include Internet publications.

Joel Simon, executive director of CPJ, called on Rakhmonov to veto the amendments: "They would effectively criminalize critical reporting and commentary on Internet news sites. We ask Tajik authorities to decriminalize defamation altogether. Journalists should not be imprisoned for their work."[12] Miklos Haraszti, then the representative on media freedom for the Organization for Security and Cooperation in Europe (OSCE), said, "Whether published on the Internet or in any other media, only explicit incitement to violence or discrimination should be criminalized; the rest of the verbal offenses should belong to civil courts."[13] As Mukhtor Bokizoda, director of the Tajik press freedom Foundation for the Commemoration and Protection of Journalists, said, "Tajik officials tend to interpret any criticism of themselves as libel and sue the critics."[14] Despite such international and domestic condemnation of the proposal, Rakhmonov signed both offending articles (135 and 136) into the criminal code on August 23, 2007.

Articles 135 ("slander contained in public speeches") and 136 ("insult contained in public speeches") add to the chilling effect that has sidelined the media and made them irrelevant to the political and economic development of society. Article 144 ("illegal collection and distribution of private information") also contributes to the widening government suppression of journalism.

The IREX 2010 Media Sustainability Index for Europe and Eurasia ranks Tajikistan's freedom of speech near the bottom among postcommunist nations, listed at fifteenth among the twenty-one nations surveyed.[15] Journalists recognize the problem and acknowledge its severity, even if no easy solutions come to mind. The "biggest problem in Tajik journalism" is self-censorship, says Umed Babakhanov of Asia Plus Media, one of a handful of media entrepreneurs in Dushanbe. "We try to be critical of government policies but in a diplomatic way, not in a sharp or hard way."[16]

Tajikistan's media outlets include thirty to sixty weekly newspapers, three government-owned national television stations (Tajik, Soghd, and Khatlon), twenty-two small privately owned local/regional stations, and ten radio stations. Its widespread self-censorship does not, however, make it unique. An Open Society Justice Initiative report on indirect restrictions of freedom of expression throughout the world contends that "indirect pressures combine a semblance of legality with clearly unlawful methods and goals of improperly influencing media content and other forms of political expression."[17] The report identifies three major forms of indirect pressure on the media: (1) abuse of public funds and monopolies;[18] (2) abuse of regulatory and inspection powers;[19] and (3) extra-legal pressures.[20] These forms of "soft censorship" are present to one degree or another in Tajikistan; to them can be added the weight of familial and friendship ties, the social glue that encourages journalism to maintain society's status quo.

The consequences of such media conditions become clear when editors and reporters describe what they do: "Everyone practices self-censorship—media owners, editors, and journalists," says Akbarali Sattorov, general manager of the Charhi Gardun Media Group and president of the Tajik Journalism Union. "A phone call will draw your attention to what you can and cannot write about."[21] For those who have to be educated in exercising a degree of self censorship, Babakhanov says that the "tax inspector is used to dampen independence." Media laws that are allegedly protective of a free press "don't work if we cross a virtual red line; officials don't respect their own laws."

Other means of maintaining journalistic self-censorship—in a country where 97 percent of newspapers are unprofitable—include selective apportionment of government advertising and subsidies, denial of access to state printing facilities, payments to reporters for "services," and inspections over labor issues, taxes, and other regulatory matters. Bribery and influence peddling remain part of the repertoire of government pressure employed to retain the deeply entrenched culture of self-censorship for profit and self-protection.

Direct restriction of access to information sources is also frequently used to censor journalists. Article 28 of the Law on Information specifies the following procedure for accessing official documents: "A letter of inquiry is sent and an official answer (both written and oral) should be given within no more than 30 days. It is quite difficult to be granted an interview with a government official of any rank. An official must address the inquiry to their direct boss who, in turn, passes it on to their chief. Consequently, a simple clerk or press-secretary must receive permission for an interview from the head of a local administration." Only the powerful define journalism's roles and responsibilities, heightening the sense that self-censorship—as opposed to censorship, which is officially rejected by a regime that claims to be a nominal democracy—is an integral part of those roles and responsibilities.

PUTTING TAJIK SELF-CENSORSHIP INTO A REGIONAL CONTEXT

"The forbidden ground (for journalists) is internal and foreign policy, oil profits, local politics, and bribery in government," says Kazakhstani journalist Alyona Alyoshina.[22] "Every journalist should know what he can do and what he can't. Sometimes reporters are able to tell the truth, sometimes they aren't. It usually depends on what kind of information you're going to write." Alyoshina was speaking of journalism in Kazakhstan but just as easily could have been talking about Central Asia in general. Asked about the state of the profession in their countries, regional journalists commonly complain about the local press, often pointing fingers at the inadequacies of its practitioners or uneducated audiences. Government intimidation, direct censorship, and self-censorship are rarely, if ever, mentioned as problematic.

Nayil Ishmukhametov, editor in chief of *Interfax Kazakhstan*, echoed sentiments heard widely in weeks of interviewing in Central Asia. "The first problem is the journalists themselves. There is a lack of good professionalism in Kazakhstan. The problem is the education of journalists. There are no skilled teachers. The second problem is their worldview. They don't know enough in general. Newspapers still have a partly Soviet mentality. Media is still in transition from Soviet times."[23] This same safe ground—generalized complaints about colleagues' work, the lack of education, or the audiences they serve—allows journalists to publicly criticize their profession while exhibiting a common form of self-censorship that remains acceptable to politicians, government officials, and colleagues alike.

Antonina Blindina is the editor of two weekly newspapers in Kyrgyzstan: *For You*, which she started six years ago, and the *Chui News*, the official newspaper of the Chui oblast. Her office is just off the entryway to a rabbit warren of low-ceilinged rooms that house the newspapers' editorial space. Across the hall, four reporters write stories on desktop computers that appear to be fairly new and were provided by USAID funds. "During the Soviet era," Blindina says, "journalism was more professional. There were high requirements to study journalism and demanding editors with high standards. One of the requirements was to be honest and follow a code of ethics. Journalism was valued. Today it is very unprofessional. The young journalists can't write. One problem is that too many university journalism teachers and professors are not professionals."[24]

Alan Kubatiev, at the time a faculty member at the American University of Central Asia in Bishkek, adds this perspective: "Soviet journalists were very effective in many aspects. Soviet journalists had the ability to influence human lives and correct social and political mistakes. Journalism today is more informative, but service is one-third, one-third is social criticism, and one-third is information. Information does not mean real information, however. They could be invented stories that contain some truth, but only some."[25]

There are pragmatic reasons why self-censorship flourishes throughout Central Asia. The yoke of legal restrictions that range from libel suits to tax audits to alleged violations of broadcast law has strangled the profession. Journalists also must consider government intimidation and the fear of physical violence. Those who stray too far from the dictates of self-censorship face potential loss of government financial support or other income derived from related work, such as public relations.[26] Finally, strictures of clan and culture, significant societal barriers to practicing Western-style journalism, have proven difficult for local practitioners to overcome. Such worries provide self-censorship with a fertile ground for widespread growth. The upshot is that few news outlets can realistically employ Western-style reporting methods. Cultural, political, and financial restrictions—as well as the fear of physical violence—have short-circuited Western attempts to produce a fact-based journalism in a region where journalism operates under limitations that vary in quantity but not in kind.

Not surprisingly, the problems that beset journalism practitioners also impair journalism education. Kazakhstan and Kyrgyzstan boast some sound, well-attended university journalism education programs based on Western models. But inadequacies in development of a bona fide independent media in both countries have sharply affected the study of journalism. Educators and professionals alike say journalism students, practitioners, and news consumers find it increasingly difficult to untangle what is fast becoming an unrestricted mix of marketing, public relations, and journalism in the profession. At Almaty's well-regarded Kazakhstan Institute of Management, Economics, and Strategic Research (KIMEP), journalism graduates and undergraduate students increasingly shun jobs in journalism, opting instead for public relations. PR pays better, there are more jobs available, and, perhaps most importantly, it is a safer profession today. "The most talented of journalists are moving into PR," notes Gulnara Assanbayeva, a KIMEP senior lecturer in journalism. "They're well paid, paid much better than in the local marketplace of journalism." A similar waning of interest in the practice of journalism can be found among graduates of the American University of Central Asia, the largest and best-known journalism program in Kyrgyzstan, say both students and teachers.[27]

From the newsroom to the classroom, self-controlling behavior—and government strictures against an open, information-based journalism—has forced the profession of journalism and journalism education to follow a well-trod path away from behavior that is culturally difficult and toward that which is politically and economically viable. Research since the 1930s has examined how personal values affect social behavior, finding in general that "values may be conceptualized . . . as global beliefs (about desirable end-states or modes of behavior) that underlie attitudinal processes."[28] Connor and Becker note, "Behavior, finally, is the manifestation of one's fundamental values and corresponding attitudes."[29] The social behavior of Central Asian journalists seems as much a product of clan and culture as citizens of any other place. "Blau noted that individuals behave within cultures according to prevailing values, and found that such values had structured effects, i.e., social controls on behavior independent of what the individual believes."[30]

Uzbekistan and Turkmenistan: Worst of the Worst

In Uzbekistan, government press restrictions remain heavy-handed, with cabinet-level officials keeping tabs on Web use, supported by the physical presence of police officers at Internet cafés.[31] In its 2010 press freedom assessment, Freedom House lists Uzbekistan and Turkmenistan "among the 10 most repressive media environments" in the world.[32]

In Turkmenistan, President Gurbanguly Berdymukhammedov sanctioned more Internet cafés in 2007, providing an apparent glimmer of openness for Turkmen citizens. But in a country with an 11 P.M. public curfew in Ashgabat, the capital, government-run Internet outlets are carefully monitored via Turkmen telecom, the country's telecommunications agency.[33] Costing about two dollars an hour to use, the cafés remain largely ignored by ordinary citizens, and Turkmenistan's press ranks among "the world's worst-rated countries," rubbing shoulders with Burma, Cuba, Libya, and North Korea.[34]

The West has attempted to invigorate the region's press with the basics of a journalism system charged to present verifiable facts and attributed information. To lay the problem of self-censorship on the doorstep of the West would be unfair. European and American governments, foundations, and multinational organizations have worked since 1991 to facilitate a valid, viable press. Hundreds of millions of dollars have been spent since then to develop independent media, much of it to promote Western journalism's values in formerly communist countries. Although there has been success in bringing Western-oriented media systems to Central and Eastern Europe, similar efforts have proven ineffective in Central Asia.[35]

The U.S. State Department and USAID have spent at least $760 million to foster independent media around the world since 1989, a good deal of that in Eastern Europe and Central Asia; European organizations have spent even more. Europe's governments have provided an estimated $7 billion for media development over the last nineteen years, a figure that excludes spending in the millions by European nonprofits like the Reuters Foundation. George Soros's Open Society Institute (OSI) conservatively estimates it has spent $35 million annually since 1991—approximately $630 million—principally in Central and Eastern Europe and Central Asia.[36] Add U.S. government media spending to that of OSI, and the total rises to approximately $1.35 billion since 1991.

KAZAKHSTAN AND KYRGYZSTAN: BEST OF THE WORST?

Journalistic professionalism in Kazakhstan is commonly seen as worse than in the first five years of independence, said Kairat Zhantikin, executive director of Internews in Central Asia. The media "was more free and independent, and the government control was not as strict as it is now. Most young journalists don't know the difference between journalism and public relations."[37] The press in Kazakhstan and Kyrgyzstan—currently the only Central Asian nations that might have a chance someday at legitimate news gathering—largely shuns Western journalism's traditional Fourth Estate watchdog role. With few exceptions, journalists in both countries tend to focus on stories about local and international celebrities, the sensational, and the political, avoiding controversy that could cause personal or professional trouble. Even-handedness in reporting and telling both sides of a story—or more accurately, all sides—are uncommon in Kyrgyzstan media. Clashes between ethnic Uzbeks and Kyrgyz in the southern provinces of Jalal-Abad and Osh in June 2010 left 350 people dead and forced 400,000 from their homes—and provide the most recent examples of a Kyrgyz journalism lacking in factual fairness.[38] Kyrgyz news stories about the unrest frequently fell back on nationalistic rhetoric and stereotype about ethnic Uzbeks; media reports largely failed to offer coverage that included the voices of ethnic Uzbeks.[39]

The 2010 IREX Media Sustainability Index ranks Kyrgyzstan eighth out of 21 countries surveyed in Europe and Eurasia; Kyrgyzstan is included in the "near sustainability" category along with Bosnia-Herzegovina, Croatia, Kosovo, and five others. Kazakhstan ranked seventeenth, appearing in its "unsustainable" category, one category below Kyrgyzstan.[40]

In Kazakhstan, media outlets are often subtly ordered to cover certain stories. "They need to get money from somewhere," Zhantikin says. "And getting it from the government, per se, is not considered bad." Mariya Rasner, deputy regional director for Internews in Central Asia, adds: "Everyone is still following orders. It's still puppet theater here. Money is the ruling king. A lot of people are doing it (journalism) for money. They don't care what they do. I'm not even sure if they stop and ask is this the right way or the wrong way. They're making money."[41] The chance for personal financial gain remains widespread among journalists in Kazakhstan and Kyrgyzstan and helps account for the continued growth of self-censorship. "Hidden advertising," "envelope journalism," and other forms of under-the-table payments for complimentary coverage abound on television and in print. "The values of consumerism are being interjected into our society now," notes KIMEP's Assanbayeva: "There are no borders or ethics. We're building not a civil society, but a consumer society. These values are promoted in the newspapers and other mass media. Media do a big promotion for the oligarchs. Journalists often have their own media business and use their media personalities to do business."[42]

More than in any other Central Asian nation, the merger of public relations and journalism has come full circle in Kazakhstan. PR firms not only tailor their clients' messages for television but also commonly help produce them. Channel 31, a TV station described as the country's most independent, provides a typical example of how the system works. A PR firm that wants air time tells the advertising department to produce a story promoting the agency's client. The ad department then talks to the top editor, who assigns a reporter to the story. The PR company often has specific guidelines for how such stories are to be produced, as well as the final say about content. One firm is said to have paid more than seven thousand dollars for a piece that ran one and a half minutes in summer 2007. Not uncommonly, PR employees sit with editors and help edit the final version of the client's piece, which is aired without disclosure that it was paid for privately.[43]

Commingling of self-censorship and public relations works a bit differently in Kyrgyzstan, varying in specific detail, but not in principle. The country was once hailed as the bastion of Central Asian press freedom and the best bet for becoming a true democracy. Such views have been altered over the years by the political and social reality on the ground, however. For example, voting in 2007 parliamentary elections appears to have been tampered with, leaving the opposition in political limbo. Plans to convert the state-run National Broadcasting Corporation into a public-service broadcaster were scrapped. Legislation that parliament passed in 2008 nullified reform efforts aimed at making the system state-funded but more independent.[44] Kyias S. Moldokasymov, president of the national broadcasting service, hinted as much in an interview, saying, "Media has a huge effect on people and can be positive or negative, depending on how the media does its job. If they report negatively on things, there won't be stability in society. That is vital. We follow the state policies. And for the state, the most important thing is for people to live in stability."[45]

Kyrgyz President Rosa Otunbayeva, who came into office following the April 2010 ouster of former President Kurmanbek Bakiyev, noted in a 2007 interview with the authors that journalism in Kyrgyzstan "doesn't play a serious, crucial role in the organization of this society. We are at the same stage. We are in eternal transition. We stick in this eternal transition. We want to join the modern world, but the press does not help us to join to the recognized world. The press does not have the capacity to help us do that. It has no such experience. It's not a good time for media in Kyrgyzstan. It's all the time a very fragmented media."[46]

Journalism in Kyrgyzstan remains hindered by ownership restrictions, all-but-mandatory political affiliations, and off-the-book payments for "news." Omurbek D. Sataev, director of press services for Gazprom Oil/Asia, in Bishkek, explained the differences between journalism in the two countries this way: "In Kazakhstan, business runs journalism. In Kyrgyzstan, politics runs journalism."[47]

What frequently passes for news in Kyrgyzstan is based on notions that stem from an oral tradition, born in Turkic languages and known as "the long ear." It is the spread of gossip, rumor, and innuendo, passed orally from one person to another, each perhaps embellishing the facts, using his or her own literary license. Turkic cultures across the region—in Kazakhstan and Uzbekistan as well—work in a similar fashion, providing contemporary regional journalism with an uphill battle that pits modern media forms against centuries of common practice.[48] It is a "rumor-based society," according to Kimberly Verkuilen, former head of the Bishkek office for the American Councils for International Education. "People believe rumors as much as they believe what they hear on television . . . People are used to *not* believing in an independent media source."

Ruslan Myatiyev is a journalism graduate of the American University of Central Asia who earned a master's degree in an OSCE program. He speaks fluent English, attended community college in New York, and worked in Washington, D.C., as a Scripps-Howard intern. He was also employed as an editor for the Kyrgyz Internet news agency 24.kg. Myatiyev believes journalism's low pay and lack of prestige have propelled many of his contemporaries into public relations. "They think—and they are right—that journalism in Kyrgyzstan is not rewarding," he said. "By this I mean writing stories or making news packages is dedicating time and effort, but time and effort are not valued by media organizations. Media in Kyrgyzstan are tools to fight with political rivals, but not to inform."[49]

Conclusions and Implications

In Tajikistan, self-censorship serves as an important social mechanism that allows journalism to seemingly function while simultaneously avoiding the pursuit of gathering potentially controversial news and information. Without self-censorship, however, ordinary professionals could not survive in an industry that is watched so closely by government, controlled so tightly by legal restrictions, and brought so quickly to heel by financial and political powerbrokers. Unwritten but well-known rules dictate what reporters and editors can write or broadcast. Such unwritten rules are widely observed. Those who fail to do so pay a price:

- In September 2008, Tajikistan's Interior Ministry issued an arrest warrant for exiled journalist Dodojon Atovullo, charging him with "public calls to violent change in the constitutional regime" and the "public insult" of President Rakhmonov. Atovullo's "crime" was telling journalists in Moscow that Tajikistan was in dire economic straits and that another civil war was possible. Tajik prosecutors labeled him an "information terrorist."[50]
- Radio Free Europe/Radio Liberty correspondent Abdumumin Sherkhonov, editor of the newspaper *Pazhvok*, was beaten in February 2009 by three men who identified themselves as from the Interior Ministry. He believes his professional work prompted the assault.[51]
- When Rakhmonov's brother-in-law Hasan Sadulloev, a wealthy and prominent banker, was reported missing in May 2008, the official media went silent on what otherwise would have been a major story. Rumor had it that Sadulloev was killed in a family fight over control of Orion Bank. Journalists did not dare to raise the issue with Rakhmonov or his government.[52]

Journalism in Tajikistan is not alone in its willingness to accede to self-censorship. Central Asia's journalism terrain remains uneven and restricted. Optimism over the prospect that fact-based journalism could take hold once brimmed over in the region. For the first few years after independence, hopes ran high that journalistic practices—at least in Kazakhstan, Kyrgyzstan, and Uzbekistan—might begin to reflect Western professional standards. Although journalists continued to mingle opinion with fact in their stories, change still seemed possible in the early 1990s.

Such optimism now flags badly. In addition to pragmatic self-interest and the chance for financial advancement, omnipresent self-censorship is also the product of clan and culture, which impose restrictions on journalists that are not easily altered. Social continuity—the connection felt by generations through custom and religious practices—helps keep autocracy alive and thriving. To move toward a consistent, fact-based journalism that is fair, thorough, and believable, widespread self-censorship must be replaced by a system that is allowed to operate outside contemporary constraints imposed by government and culture.

In Tajikistan, where this chapter began, journalism remains subservient to self-censorship, with prospects for press freedom exceedingly grim over the short term. Like neighboring Afghanistan, Turkmenistan, and Uzbekistan, Tajikistan looks more and more like a weak, foundering state teetering on the brink of social insolvency, its chances for a journalism that works dwindling faster than ever. But in the minds of some Tajiks there remains alive a memory of that brief, bright period between the end of communism and the beginning of the country's civil war, a time when journalists and the public glimpsed what press freedom might mean. That memory may yet germinate, producing a meaningful, even robust, effort to loosen political control over an overburdened media.

NOTES

1. Alexander Sadikov, "Tajikistan Blocks Access to Web Sites in the Run-up to Presidential Election," *Domestic Affairs, Media, Human Rights*, October 31, 2006, www.neweurasia. net/media-and-internet/tajikistan-blocks-access-to-web-sites-in-the-run-up-to-presidential-election.

2. Valentina Kasymbekova and Aziza Sharipova, "Tajikistan: Media Pressure Intensifies; Non-Government Media Subjected to Closures and Threats in Run-up to 2005 Elections," Institute for War and Peace Reporting, 21, http://iwpr.net/report-news/tajikistan-media-pressure-intensifies.

3. Fareed Zakaria, *The Future of Freedom: Illiberal Democracy at Home and Abroad* (New York: W. W. Norton 2003), 77.

4. Committee to Protect Journalists, "Attacks on the Press in 2007: Tajikistan," w.

5. Reporters sans Frontieres, "Tajikistan—Annual Report 2008,"http://arabia.reporters-sans-frontieres.org/article.php3?id_article=25644.

6. Sadikov, "Tajikistan Blocks Access."

7. Antoine Blau, "Tajikistan: Journalist-Rights Group Says Self-Censorship Stifling Media," Radio Free Europe Radio Liberty, May 28, 2002, www.rferl.org/content/Article/1099832.html.

8. Committee to Protect Journalists, "CPJ requests information on 29 murdered journalists," August 27, 2003, http://cpj.org/2003/08/cpj-requests-information-on-

29-murdered-journalist.php.

9. Blau, "Tajikistan."

10. International Research and Exchanges Board (IREX), "Tajikistan," *Media Sustainability Index (MSI)—Europe and Eurasia 2010*, www.irex.org/system/files/EE_MSI_2010_Intro_ES_Methodology.pdf.

11. Central Intelligence Agency, "Tajikistan," *The World Factbook*, 2010, www.cia.gov/library/publications/the-world-factbook/geos/ti.html.

12. Committee to Protect Journalists, "CPJ calls on Tajik president to veto Internet criminal defamation bill," July 26, 2007, http://cpj.org/2007/07/cpj-calls-on-tajik-president-to-veto-internet-crim.php.

13. Committee to Protect Journalists, "Attacks on the Press in 2007: Tajikistan,"http://cpj.org/2008/02/attacks-on-the-press-2007-tajikistan.php.

14. Committee to Protect Journalists, "CPJ calls on Tajik president."

15. IREX, "Tajikistan."

16. Umed Babakhanov interview with author Gross, Dushanbe, Tajikistan, December 8, 2007.

17. Open Society Justice Initiative, "The Growing Threat of Soft Censorship: A Paper on Indirect Restrictions on Freedom of Expression Worldwide," December 12, 2005, 3, www.soros.org/initiatives/justice/focus/foi/articles_publications/publications/threat_20051205/threat_20051205.pdf.

18. According to the report: "These range from abusive allocation of government advertising or subsidies to arbitrary denial of access to state printing facilities to direct cash payments to reporters for dubious or undeclared services. These are doubly pernicious, as taxpayer money and public wealth is used and bused to promote partisan or personal interests," 3.

19. The report states: "These forms of interference operate under the color of law or market rules: broadcast licensing processes are manipulated to benefit political allies or silence independent voices; critical media find themselves subjected to a barrage of selective and draining fiscal, labor or other regulatory inspections; and sometimes, they are taken over by government cronies as legitimate owners are bullies into handling over control. Media owners with non-media businesses subject to regulatory regimes are often made to understand that their other businesses can only prosper if their media are friendly to the government of the day," 3.

20. The report states: "At the most delinquent end of the spectrum, powerful officials and politicians use raw power and clearly illegal means to buy influence or muzzle dissent: they pressure private businesses to advertise or not advertise on certain media, interfere directly with editorial decision making (so-called 'telephone censorship'), or seek to bribe reporters and editors outright," 3.

21. Akbarali Sattorov interview with author Gross, Dushanbe, Tajikistan, December 7, 2007.

22. Alyona Alyoshina interview with author Kenny, Almaty, Kazakhstan, August 21, 2005.

23. Nayil Ishmukhametov interview with author Kenny, Almaty, Kazakhstan, June 18, 2007.

24. Antonina Blindina interview with author Kenny, Bishkek, Kyrgyzstan, June 25, 2007.

25. Alan Kubatiev interview with author Kenny, Bishkek, Kyrgyzstan, June 20, 2007.

26. IREX, "Tajikistan."

27. Ruslan Myatiyev interview with author Kenny, Bishkek, Kyrgyzstan, June 20, 2007; author Kenny interview with Gulnura Toralieva, journalism faculty, American University of Central Asia, Bishkek, via Skype. September 10, 2010.

28. Patrick E. Connor and Boris W. Becker, "Personal Value Systems and Decision-Making Styles of Public Managers," *Personal Public Management* 32(1) (2003): 156.

29. Ibid.

30. George Sylvie and J. Sonia Huang, "Value Systems and Decision-making Styles of Newspaper Front-line Editors," *Journalism and Mass Communication Quarterly* 85(1) (2008): 62.

31. Deirdre Tynan, "How the Uzbek Government Maintains a Choke-Hold over the Internet," Eurasianet.org. July 22, 2008, http://www.eurasianet.org/departments/insight/articles/eav072308.shtml.

32. Aili Piano and Arch Puddington, eds., "Restrictions on Press Freedom Intensify," Freedom House, 2010, www.freedomhouse.org/template.cfm?page=70&release=1177.

33. Turkmenistanis, who asked to remain anonymous, interviewed by author Kenny, Kyrgyzstan, July 2007.

34. Karen Deutsch Karlekar, "Press Freedom in 2007: A Year of Global Decline," Freedom House, www.freedomhouse.org/uploads/fop08/OverviewEssay2008.pdf.

35. See, for example, Karol Jakubowicz, *Rude Awakening: Social and Media Changes in Central and Eastern Europe* (Cresskill, NJ: Hampton Press, 2006); Peter Gross. *Entangled Evolutions: Media and Democratization in Eastern Europe* (Baltimore: Johns Hopkins University Press, 2002).

36. Ellen Hume's "Global Media Development Report: The Media Missionaries" said that the "Soros foundations spend at least $20 million annually on media development" (2004, 19) (www.ellenhume.com/articles/missionaries.html). But Gordana Jankovic, director of OSI's Network Media Program in London, said in a May 19, 2008, telephone interview that Hume's figure was "conservative." Jankovic put OSI spending on media development at $35 million to $40 million annually since 1991.

37. Kairat Zhantikin interview with author Kenny, Almaty, Kazakhstan, June 13, 2007.

38. Farangis Najibullah, "Is Kyrgyz Media Providing the Whole Picture?" Radio Free

Europe/Radio Liberty, July 31, 2010.Www.eurasianet.org/node/61648.

39. Ibid.

40. IREX, "Tajikistan."

41. Mariya Rasner interview with author Kenny, Almaty, Kazakhstan, June 13, 2007.

42. Gulnara Assanbayeva interview with author Kenny, Almaty, Kazakhstan, June 11–12, 2007.

43. Yulia Marchenko interview with author Kenny, Almaty, Kazakhstan, June 16, 2007; other Almaty-based journalists anonymously corroborated her account.

44. Committee to Protect Journalists, "KYRGYZSTAN: Broadcasting Bill Rolls Back Press Freedom," May 15, 2008, http://cpj.org/2008/05/kyrgyzstanbroadcasting-bill-rolls-back-press-freed.php,

45. Kyias S. Moldokasymov interview with author Kenny, Bishkek, Kyrgyzstan, June 22, 2007.

46. Rosa A. Otunbayeva interview, with author Kenny, Bishkek, Kyrgyzstan, June 26, 2007.

47. Omurbek D. Sataev interview, Bishkek, Kyrgyzstan, June 22, 2007.

48. Alan Kubatiev interview with author Kenny, Bishkek, Kyrgyzstan, June 20, 2007.

49. Ruslan Myatiyev interview with author Kenny by e-mail from Bishkek, Kyrgyzstan, February 18, 2008.

50. Committee to Protect Journalists, "Attacks on the Press in 2008," February 10, 2009, www.cpj.org/2009/02/attacks-on-the-press-in-2008.php,

51. Radio Free Europe/Radio Liberty, February 12, 2009. Www.rferl.org/content/journalists_in_trouble_Tajik_Correspondent_is_Summoned/1947652.html.

52. International Press Institute, "World Press Freedom Review 2008," February 9, 2009, www.freemedia.at/fileadmin/import/media/WPFR_2008_PDF.pdf.

PART 3

Trans-Regional Perspectives

Loyalty in the New Authoritarian Model: Journalistic Rights and Duties in Central Asian Media Law

Olivia Allison

A fter almost twenty years transitioning from a single-party press, Central Asia was still defined by a set of laws and behavioral patterns that restricted media pluralism, which stemmed from early the early 1990s. This chapter assesses how Central Asian media law has developed by analyzing both journalists' and governments' behaviors leading to the restrictive press environment. On one hand, governments overlooked the relatively wide freedoms guaranteed by post-Soviet media laws, gradually passing newer, more oppressive laws; they also targeted all enforcement measures at the most troublesome media outlets. On the other hand, by failing to comply with laws and professional ethical standards, journalists were also culpable.

These behaviors are rooted in the history of post-Soviet media law itself. Under the Soviet system based on a press committed to promoting information from the Communist Party, there was no specific law on the media; there was no need for one. The idea of drafting a media law became prominent under the party general secretary Mikhail Gorbachev in the late 1980s, when he inducted the principles of glasnost and perestroika (McNair 1991; Schmidt 1990). Prior to that, there had only been the Basic Law of 1906, which allowed for freedom of expression, "orally or in written form," but only "within the limits established by the law." According to reports at the time, the drafting of Gorbachev's law on the media began about 1986, lasting until it passed days after the Soviet Union collapsed. The law fundamentally changed the government's relationship with media from one based on party permission for information distribution—in which independent publishing was banned—to one in which the granting of registration gave a person or media organ the right of expression (McNair 1991). While that was a large step toward pluralism at the time, specific provisions of the law underscored a remaining principle of *partiinost*, or the concept that the media should be loyal to the party (and later, by extension, to the government) (Schmidt 1990): the 1991 law lays out not only journalists' rights (freedom of expression, access to information), but also their duties (registration, accreditation, acting responsibly) (Schmidt 1990). The juxtaposition acted to limit pluralism; if the journalists did not fulfill these duties, any rights could be revoked.

This expectation of loyalty on which the 1991 media law and all subsequent post-Soviet media laws are based, continued to limit pluralistic media development in Central Asia after independence. Loyalty was no longer defined by a journalist's position in the Communist Party, so *partiinost* is no longer an accurate term; loyalty was still required of journalists in practice—both through fulfillment of legal duties and through loyalty to the government. Because journalistic duties—which include the ill-defined duty of responsibility—form the basis of journalistic rights, disloyal media outlets received fewer rights than pro-governmental media. Indeed, the goal was not a vibrant press, but one that was uncritical of the regimes in their respective states. As Sigal writes, the laws and their enforcement were designed to "restrict access to those in power; not to allow a variety of opinion and information to reach the public, but to force those media without connections to power to operate in a *semi-legal state*, vulnerable to closure on the command of authorities and hesitant to speak out for fear of punishment" (2000; emphasis added). The formation of media laws designed to push critical voices into a "semi-legal state" is a unique feature—a legacy of the 1991 media law, on which subsequent laws rest—and forms the basis of this study.

Statement of the Problem

The focus of this chapter is how Central Asia's media laws and their enforcement developed from this 1991 law and whether the conditionality of journalistic rights hardened, as some researchers have argued, into a "reconstituted authoritarian model" (Walker 2007). Thus this study asked: In what ways do Central Asian media laws restrict journalistic rights? What journalistic behaviors trigger these restrictions, if any, and what governmental actions illustrate what the restrictions are and how they are imposed? The hypothesis is that media laws and their enforcement continued to be framed by the expectation of loyalty rooted in the 1991 law, meaning that enforcement and writing of laws remained targeted at controlling disloyal media rather than encouraging pluralism.

Sub-questions in this study concern the multiple types of media laws and restrictions in Central Asia. As the "Methodology" section explains, interviewees were asked about fifteen categories of media law.[1] This chapter does not address all of those interview categories; rather, it examines the seven that best answer the research question: media registration, frequency licensing, access to information, libel/defamation, finance/tax laws, censorship, and journalist behavior.[2] The research questions corresponding to these categories are:

1. How difficult is it to register media, and are official decisions made with a view to ensuring loyalty?
2. What type of broadcast frequency licensing procedure does the country use, and are official decisions made with a view to ensuring loyalty?
3. How is access to information guaranteed in law and in practice?
4. How do libel and defamation laws curb journalist expression?
5. What are the financial and tax requirements for media outlets, and are tax investigations conducted selectively?
6. What formal and informal censorship mechanisms exist?
7. In what ways do journalists defy the duties written into the laws? Does the government understand this defiance as disloyalty? How does this affect their rights?

Of course, the governments use other types of law to curb perceived disloyalty, including election, advertisings, journalist accreditation, Internet censorship, and language laws. In addition, governments use or allow physical attacks on offices and journalists, including murders, but such measures fall outside the scope of this chapter; although the threat of harassment is a prominent aspect of the retributive punishment on disloyal media, it is not enforced through legal mechanisms.

Methodology

This chapter is based on a study of press freedom in Central Asia between 2003 and 2005 that included hundreds of interviews and meetings with newspaper editors, TV and radio producers, other journalists, nongovernmental organizations (NGOs), governmental bodies, and press-freedom/human rights groups in Kazakhstan, Kyrgyzstan, Tajikistan, and Uzbekistan.[3] The study excluded Turkmenistan because of the practical difficulties of finding and interviewing opposition journalists and because its laws—authoritarian even by Central Asian standards—did not lend themselves to substantive analysis. Journalists from pro-governmental media outlets and trade unions were contacted, as well as oppositional or critical media outlets and journalist associations. Members of the international media based in Central Asia were included in the study. Given the nature of the topic, most of them requested anonymity in any published work. Diplomats, NGOs, and press-freedom groups that monitor lawsuits against, attacks on, and harassment toward media outlets were contacted for wider perspectives on the media environment.

Interviews were based on an overall list of about eighty questions in fifteen categories of media law and enforcement. Interviews usually lasted between one and two hours; most interviews were conducted individually to obtain more candid answers, although two group interviews took place when journalists requested them. Answers were compared, and the analysis in this chapter is based on multiple interviewees' responses: all statements were confirmed by more than one journalist.

Findings

The following analysis of laws, restrictions, and enforcement is broken into the seven categories listed previously: media registration, frequency licensing, access to information, libel/defamation, finance/tax laws, censorship, and journalist behavior.

MEDIA REGISTRATION

Registration is the first hurdle for media outlets, and while theoretically simple, it is often politically loaded. All media outlets, or "media of mass information"—defined in general as an informational source that produces materials under consistent titles—must register with the government, regardless of the form of ownership. Specific "mass media" are defined differently in each country, although newspapers, TV stations, magazines, almanacs, and bulletins are always included. Web sites, including blogs, are problematic for Central Asian parliamentarians, and all countries struggled with how to force registration of such nebulous entities; Uzbekistan defines even blogs as mass media (Institute for War and Peace Reporting 2007).[4] The intent of the registration process—like that of the licensing process—is to determine which outlets will be given the rights laid out in media laws. As such, it is an early method of disallowing disloyal journalists' expression.

The registration process varies by country; the appropriate ministry (usually the Ministry of Information or Justice) has between fifteen days and one month to approve or deny the request, depending on the country. In practice, registration bodies move slowly at best, and at worst, deliberately work against opposition and independent media. The registering body often takes much longer than the mandated period without explanation or accountability. Media experts blame some delays on incompetence—often a valid charge—but registration is frequently withheld for political reasons. Tajik opposition newspaper editor Ermurat Bapi, whose first newspaper *SolDat* was shut down in 2003 on tax-related grounds, unsuccessfully attempted six times in three years to register a new newspaper. Similarly in Kyrgyzstan, the opposition newspaper *Moya Stolitsa* (now *MSN*) was refused registration six times while Askar Akayev was president, and overall waited ten months for registration of a second paper. Chief editor Aleksandr Kim said his "refusals" occurred unofficially, in the form of total silence from the ministry, so he was unable to appeal (Kim 2003).[5]

In Uzbekistan, which required annual registration and licensing, journalists complained that the Committee for Print occasionally decided not to register media for a few months and claimed most applications were refused summarily. Although such decisions were not publicly announced, there were often long gaps when Uzbekistan registered no new outlets. According to Internews Tajikistan's lawyer, Farrukhsho Junaidov, the government started wielding this tool against the media in 2004–05, when the only newly registered newspaper had strong ties to the government (Junaidov 2004, 2005). Journalists working for foreign media outlets were also forced to register for accreditation, and Natalia Bushuyeva, a stringer from Germany's international broadcaster Deutsche Welle, was the first journalist prosecuted there for not having a journalism license (World Press Freedom Review 2007).

FREQUENCY LICENSING

Frequency licensing—issuing permits for airwaves to TV and radio stations—is likely considered with a media outlet's loyalty or disloyalty in mind. In general, two types of licenses are required for a new broadcast outlet: a broadcast license and a frequency permit. Frequencies are distributed either through a "tender"—a competition—or through an application process. Licensing laws are used throughout Central Asia to varying degrees to keep out disloyal—or critical—broadcast media.

Kazakhstan saw the most pronounced example of the use of these laws against independent media in the late 1990s. Exorbitant licensing fees imposed in 1997 had closed almost twenty stations by mid-1998, according to a report from the Organization for Security and Cooperation in Europe. Under the 1995 decree "On Licensing" and subsequent amendments, stations needed a frequency permit from the Ministry of Communications and had to compete for a broadcast license in a tender run by the Committee for Communication and Information, part of the same ministry. Internews Kazakhstan director Oleg Katsiev said broadcast licenses became extremely expensive after a 1997 sub-decree increased prices. Although a later decree decreased prices somewhat, costs remained relatively high.

The licensing process is too technical—requiring small but frequent changes unsuited to the parliamentary legislative process. Thus, it is the area of media law in Kazakhstan that is most controlled by ministerial decrees. The Ministry of Communications often used that fact to the government's advantage. In 1996, for example, it proclaimed in the "Decision of the Ministry of Transport and Communication" that all VHF frequencies would be used for governmental television stations only, but the decree was vague and contained no enforcement provision.[6] That decree went unnoticed for about a year, but in May 1997 most nongovernmental stations on VHF frequencies were shut off. Only a government-affiliated station, KTK, was allowed access to VHF and satellite channels (Benjamin N. Cardoza School of Law 1998). Since then, few new stations have appeared, and President Nursultan Nazarbaev and his family are believed to monopolize the broadcast media (Committee to Protect Journalists 2010b).

In Uzbekistan, although in theory it was not expensive to obtain a license, the interagency licensing agency had not given out new licenses for several months, and licenses are good for only one year. More significantly, private stations lacked resources to buy their own transmitters, so they rented the use of state-owned transmitters, allowing the state to intervene at any point. Licenses went first to government outlets and then to those with government ties (International Research and Exchanges Board 2008).

In Tajikistan the initial application involved high "official and unofficial" fees reaching up to three thousand dollars, according to Internews Tajikistan lawyer Junaidov. The licensing process was unfair, and the primary ways that stations obtained application approvals was either to know someone or to bribe the licensing committee. Asia Plus, a corporation with several media outlets, waited five years for its radio license; the station got that license only after

President Emomali Rakhmonov directly and publicly intervened. Another station, in Khorog, claimed in 2008 to have waited five years for the licensing commission to examine its application (International Research and Exchanges Board 2008). Official data indicates that there are about thirty TV and radio stations in the country, but the capital, Dushanbe, had no independent TV station; only state-run TV and radio stations (or those with personal links to the president) received licenses (International Research and Exchanges Board 2010).[7]

ACCESS TO INFORMATION

Media laws guaranteed theoretical access to information about governmental activities at various levels, but as with other rights, in practice it was contingent on media's fulfillment of their duty of loyalty. The laws usually gave citizens, including journalists, the right to search for, gather, and distribute information freely.[8] At first glance, such guarantees seem to authorize unlimited access to official information: They do not name specific information that is exempted, as other countries' laws do (for example in U.S. laws pertaining to freedom of information and open meetings). In theory, journalists could use that to their advantage—anything *could* be open (Myers 2004). In practice, however, the concept of "open documents" is arbitrary and susceptible to the whim of authorities. Journalists could also be prosecuted for revealing "secret" information and be punished if a court felt the journalist had jeopardized national security. Because authorities could classify most politically sensitive topics as "state secrets," regimes had almost unlimited discretion to punish journalists for releasing uncomfortable or embarrassing political or economic information, even if accurate.

Access-to-information laws did not consider journalists' need for timely information, with answers guaranteed in periods ranging from three days to a month.[9] Even with such long time allowances, few official organs responded to journalists' requests, because journalists rarely took the matter to court (Kaleeva 2006). Tajikistan's newspaper *ASIA-Plus* sought information from all ministries in Dushanbe; within a month only a few had responded, editor Marat Mamadshoev said. The newspaper printed the results of its experiment (Mamadshoev 2004).

If journalists face obstacles obtaining official and theoretically open gov-ernmental information, information on business activity is even more difficult to obtain because of rampant corruption.[10] Business information that should be open, like ownership, was not public. The phenomenon of business "holdings" distanced a business from its true owners. The presidents' relatives and friends owned many prominent businesses (Pannier 2008; Human Rights Watch 2008), but on paper these "holdings"—often several layers of holdings—owned each business. That made responsible, accurate, and fact-based business reporting virtually impossible. For instance, although it is widely accepted that Kazakhstan president Nazarbaev's daughter, Dariga Nazarbaeva, owns a plurality of the country's media, corporations that are registered through holdings and other third parties make the truth impossible to verify, even by the most dedicated journalist.[11] Thus, Central Asian laws draw an opaque curtain in front of business and political matters.

These limitations forced journalists in all four countries to publish information that cannot be cited or attributed to official sources. Consequently, journalists either obtained information through acquaintances working in official organs—meaning they could not divulge their sources' names—or they published rumors. One Uzbekistani journalist remarked: "Journalists don't get information by filing a formal request or by filing a written request, but by saying, 'How is your wife? How are your kids? Also, I need this one piece of information—can you help me?'"(anonymous 2004). Because controversial journalists are often denied access or not invited to official press conferences, they may miss even those facts that are officially announced. In such cases—and to obtain information—journalists sometimes look to colleagues. Aleksey Volosevich, an Uzbekistan journalist who had worked for the Web site Ferghana.ru, said that those who are accredited by the government and invited to press conferences "naturally divide up information with their colleagues—they give their film, documents—albeit with a delay of a few hours, as soon as they have produced their own materials" (2004). Thus, lacking documentation for their publications, journalists are vulnerable to libel and defamation suits. Indeed, often no official documentation exists. Because information was obtained unofficially, it further reinforced the principle of loyalty—the more loyal journalists were more likely to get better information.

LIBEL AND DEFAMATION

The most obvious areas in which loyalty was central in the enforcement of Central Asian media law are provisions concerning libel, defamation, slander, moral damages, and similar allegations. These countries' libel and defamation are still criminal offenses, so the laws do not adhere to international standards. Although it is rare for a journalist to receive a jail sentence for libel, it does occur.[12] For example, Samarkand-based journalist Shadi Mardiev was sentenced to prison for eleven years for defamation and extortion for a satirical TV broadcast in June 1998 (Freedom House 1998); he was released in 2002. Two Kyrgyzstan journalists were sentenced to imprisonment for libel but received amnesty in the early 2000s. In late 2009, criminal authorities in Uzbekistan charged photojournalist and filmmaker Umida Akhmedova with insulting and libeling the Uzbek people and its traditions through her photo album showing village life and her documentary about premarital sex (Ferghana.ru 2009).

There are multiple categories for libel, defamation, and slander, generally based on moral versus material damages. The vast majority of prosecuted cases involve nonmaterial, or moral, damages. Such laws provide that a claim for compensation for moral damages must meet three conditions: (1) the publication contains data and not opinions, beliefs, or evaluations; (2) the publication's material is false; and (3) the publication discredits the plaintiff's honor, dignity, or business reputation from a social or moral point of view.[13]

In theory, these conditions place a burden of proof on both parties: defendants—media outlets—must prove the information is true, while plaintiffs must prove their reputation was damaged. In practice, few plaintiffs, who are usually governmental officials, ever prove actual damage, because judges often do not require it (Adil Soz 2008, 2009),[14] but media outlets are always pressed to prove that the information they publish or broadcast is true, a difficult task in the informational vacuum that exists. Roger Myers, a U.S. media lawyer working for an American Bar Association project in Kazakhstan, said: "Whereas in the West, a plaintiff has to meet all these conditions . . . in Central Asia, many steps are skipped. The information is not really proven, and harm is assumed, and defendants find themselves immediately in the sentencing phase" (2004). Also, unlike in most Western countries, people have sued for moral harm on behalf of a vague "entity" (like the Kazakh nation or the Kyrgyz people). There is no statute of limitations, so libel cases can arise long after a story is published or aired.

Awards of compensation for moral damages often reached alarmingly high amounts, especially considering that newspapers earn meager if any profits and journalists earn abysmally low salaries.[15] Since the mid-2000s, fines against Kazakhstan's opposition press frequently reach between 50 and 70 million KZT (about $370,000–$466,000) (International Research and Exchanges Board 2010). Kyrgyzstan's politicians also ask for high fines in defamation suits. An often-named request for moral damages in Kyrgyzstan was 1 million *som* (about $20,000), although several politicians won 5-million-*som* awards (Orozbekova 2001).

Such suits were prevalent earlier in Kazakhstan and Kyrgyzstan, but there were no libel or defamation cases in Tajikistan until spring 2004, when Vahdat city mayor Ismoiljon Gulov demanded 30,000 *somoni* ($10,300) for compensation from *Neruyi Suhan* journalist Mustafo Rasulov and the editorial boards of *Tojikiston* and *Neruyi Suhan*. Judge Namoz Amirov demanded the same amount from the weekly newspaper *Vecherniy Dushanbe*. Such high sums indicate

Tajikistan's officials learned well from their neighbors. Three Tajikistani judges filed civil libel litigation against three independent weekly newspapers, seeking 5.5 million *somoni* (about $1.2 million) in damages, an amount high enough to bankrupt the papers (International Freedom of Expression eXchange 2010). A 2007 law criminalizes slander on the Internet (International Research and Exchanges Board 2008).

Authorities have hesitated to change their libel laws, because journalists do write defamatory articles. Kyrgyzstan's former president Akayev called for decriminalization of libel for almost ten years, but some parliamentary deputies asserted that "without that provision there would be anarchy [and] . . . politicians and public officials would be left unprotected from the lies printed by the media" (Mould 1998). Libel suits against outspoken journalists continued under President Kurmanbek Bakiyev's rule (British Broadcasting Corporation 2010).

FINANCIAL AND TAX CONTROLS

Like defamation laws, tax laws and their implementation prove the hypothesis that disloyal media can face prosecution for legal infractions. Businesses, including media everywhere except in Kazakhstan, were overtaxed, but on the other hand, tax evasion was rampant. Revenue taxes in Kyrgyzstan and Tajikistan were 30 percent, and both countries had a 20 percent value-added tax (VAT). (Tajikistan's VAT was introduced in 1996; a Kazakhstan presidential decree revoked the revenue and value-added taxes for media from 1995 to 2005, but that decree has not been renewed since 2005.) Other levies—like road taxes and municipal, city, and national taxes—chipped away at whatever money newspapers earned, which was usually nominal anyway.[16] Tajikistan editors claimed they paid a total of seventeen kinds of taxes, and Kyrgyzstan's editors claimed to pay only slightly fewer. Tajikistan's press freedom group NANSMIT (National Association of Independent Media of Tajikistan) said a newspaper's total taxes amount to more than half of its profit. Uzbekistan media outlets faced similarly high taxes.

Many, if not most, newspapers practiced tax evasion at some level. Tajikistan's tax situation caused newspapers to act against their own commercial interests, releasing circulation figures lower than they actually were to reduce their VAT.[17] Other newspapers simply did not pay their taxes. One source claimed that "the Tax Inspection discovered 800,000 *soms* ($17,000) of unpaid VAT taxes by the *Vecherniy Bishkek* newspaper" (Kasybekov 2000). Marat Mamadshoev, an *ASIA-Plus* editor, estimated that his country's newspapers pay 20 to 40 percent of the amount they should pay (2004). Other media outlets were untrained in accounting and miscalculated earnings, at times to such an extent that they did not know they were earning profits. They thus opened themselves to pressure from tax police eager to investigate businesses' accounts.

Tax investigators interfered in many businesses' activities, often arbitrarily asking to review their books. Mamadshoev said inspectors ignore tax-code violations for small bribes, unless instructed to act otherwise: "When the tax inspectors come in, they just close their eyes. If they have an order from above, they'll find something" (Mamadshoev 2004). Opposition newspaper *MSN*'s editor Kim described the situation succinctly: "How dependent [the media outlets] are on the government dictates how much of your taxes you can get out of" (2004). In the event of a politically motivated inspection, newspapers' best recourse is to be completely accurate in accounting, and even then harassment from inspectors could continue.

Another factor discouraging media outlets from earning profits is that grants were not usually taxable. However, that was irrelevant in Uzbekistan, where foreign investment in the media is prohibited, and international organizations like the National Democratic Institute, Soros Foundation/Open Society Institute, and Internews were punished or closed in the aftermath of the 2005 Andijan massacre in which Uzbekistani military forces fatally attacked protestors.

CENSORSHIP

In all four countries, censorship is nominally forbidden by constitutions and other laws. Only Uzbekistan had an official censor in its post-Soviet past; although the 1992 constitution outlawed censorship, Uzbekistan had an official prepublication censor, the organ "for the protection of state secrets." The position was abolished in May 2002, making editors' jobs more difficult (Khodjaev 2004): "When there was a censor, the editors slept," one Bukharan journalist said. "Now the editors themselves are responsible for knowing which information is forbidden." Furthermore, all reports related to the military required Ministry of Defense approval before broadcast or publication. That gave the ministry full control over materials pertaining to these issues, a gross extension of its previous powers (Ganiev 2004).

Even where censorship was not officially in place, press openness remained limited. Many unofficial censorship mechanisms exist: The government has turned off electricity or water. Journalists have faced violence, excessive tax inspections, information blockades, and demands for prepublication review. Government-owned or -affiliated printing houses have refused to print independent and opposition media. Conflicts among opposition newspapers in Kazakhstan and the printing press Vremya-Print are another example of that form of de facto censorship.

Police have confiscated print runs in several cities, signaling a full-out assault on these journalists (Adil Soz monitoring 2010, Adil Soz 2009).

Self- or internal censorship remains a more significant problem. Journalists admit they did not allow themselves to tackle controversial topics in most cases, claiming they felt threatened by their editors or local government bodies. Indeed, the degree to which self-censorship occurs determines the level of loyalty the government is likely to perceive—the more self-censorship, the more loyal the media outlet. Self-censorship and fear are so embedded in journalists' attitudes that they often refuse to report rights infringements to monitoring bodies for fear of repercussions.[18] Forbidden topics included corruption of the political and business elites and trials of opposition figures. In other cases, pressure stemmed from financial reliance on wealthy figures more than from direct political pressure.[19]

JOURNALIST BEHAVIOR

Journalists' legal duties include the ill-defined notion of responsibility, as well as practical duties such as registering and paying taxes already described. Journalists identify media laws with their authoritarian governments because the laws juxtapose their rights and duties, and the media is judged first on loyalty and then on other merits. Thus, many rejected the laws, the concept of legality, and legal knowledge as tools of the regimes that oppressed them. Interviewed journalists said that they believed that fulfilling any legal duty meant expressing loyalty to the regime. Thus, many manifested their "disloyalty" or opposition through technically illegal activities such as printing "state secrets." The results of this disloyalty and defiance were that media outlets became financially insolvent, and they produced materials that would not meet international ethical and professional standards. In most cases, not fulfilling journalistic "duties" was widespread, but only disloyal journalists were punished, thus underscoring the principle of loyalty in media law enforcement. Even simple oversights gave authorities tools for repression; for example, a Kazakhstan newspaper was fined heavily for not sending its "control copies"—copies they are required to provide to the national library and ministries.[20]

Other violations were more deliberate. This included the rampant tax evasion discussed previously, a reality of the abysmal economic situation that opposition media face. That tactic only aided the authorities, however, because charging a disloyal media outlet with hefty back taxes was a fast way to close it: it required no court battle and thus no lengthy process. Journalists' outputs were frequently libelous by Western standards; frequently unsupported by facts, they would not stand up in Western courts any more than they do in Central Asia.

However, disloyal media outlets that did act in those ways were more susceptible to punishment; even worse, such behavior weakened their attempts to expose official corruption. They had, in effect, contributed to the corruption that they complained about, while also eliminating their ability to criticize those who bribed them. Tajikistan journalist Jovid Mukim bemoaned the situation, saying: "If you want to write the truth, you have to be honest yourself. Right now, everyone takes bribes, so the government is happy. At any given point they can criticize or punish a newspaper because everyone is corrupt" (Mukim 2004).

Conclusions

The hypothesis that the relationship between journalists and government in post-Soviet Central Asia continues to be framed by loyalty was supported by the analysis of media registration, frequency licensing, access to information, libel/defamation, finance/tax laws, censorship, and journalist behavior. Restrictions on journalistic rights are, to a large degree, determined by the journalists' and media outlets' fulfillment of legal duties. A more important determinant of whether and what type of enforcement would occur was a media outlet's loyalty to the government. Where both pro-governmental and oppositional media outlets broke laws—for example, failing to pay taxes or writing libelous articles—it was the oppositional media outlets that were punished.

The broader issue, posed at the beginning of this chapter, of whether Central Asian governments had formed a "reconstituted authoritarian model" (Walker 2007). This authoritarian model defines journalists' key responsibility as loyalty to the regime. In support of this definition, laws and legal enforcement are designed primarily to restrict the variety of opinion and restrict press materials to those in power. This is indicated by the persistent attacks on critics of each country's regime, illustrating the systematic nature of Central Asian media control. The governments' goal in such cases was to neutralize critics—the most disloyal media—using all available tactics until the media outlet was unable to function.

The difficulties of the independent Kazakh newspaper *Respublika* (which has sister publications with similar names, including *Respublika-Delovoye Obozreniye* and more recently *Golos Respubliki*) demonstrate that strategy. Its offices were firebombed in 2002, it has faced myriad expensive libel claims, and it has been shut by court decisions (Lillis 2010). The newspaper was unable to find a printer after several presses refused it in September 2009, and so it began printing its materials on standard A4-sized paper. In April 2010 Kazakhtelecom's Internet provider blocked its website (Committee to Protect Journalists 2010a).

The newspaper re-opened after each difficulty, but its inability to print its materials has severely restricted its audience. Other regional newspapers facing similar onslaughts of court cases—including Tajikistan's *Ruzi Nav*, which was also unable to print its materials (Kimmage 2004)—have been forced to close. Kyrgyzstan's deputy ombudsman Sadyk Shar-Niyaz said the region's court cases were aimed not at punishment but at obliterating oppositional media: "Of course they want to close the newspaper. If they just wanted to punish them, there are many other ways they could do that" (Shar-Niyaz 2005).

NOTES

1. A full list of these questions is available in an earlier version of this chapter (Allison 2006).
2. These topics match the categories on which interviews were conducted.
3. These groups and people provided special assistance: the Kazakhstan, Tajikistan, and Uzbekistan offices of Internews Network; the Kyrgyzstan NGO Public Association "Journalists"; and International Center for Journalists press development trainers Jack Ronald and George Krimsky.
4. In Kazakhstan, Article 1 of the law "On the press and media" includes Web sites in its definition of media, but Web sites are not required to register. Kyrgyzstan's law does not address Web sites but requires informational agencies, which often produce Web sites, to register (Kyrgyzstan government 2007). In the Tajik law on TV/radio, Internet is included as a media outlet, but there is no mechanism set up for enforcement, and the Ministry of Justice has never registered a Web site as a media outlet. Uzbekistan's legislative situation regarding Internet is identical to Kyrgyzstan's.
5. *MSN* became far less oppositional in tone after the 2005 Tulip Revolution.
6. *Reshenie Ministerstva transporta i kommunikatsiy, Respubliki Kazakhstan* (Decision of Ministry of Transport and Communication, of the Republic of Kazakhstan), 26 June 1996. There are two basic kinds of frequencies: Very High Frequency (VHF) is stronger than Ultra-High Frequency (UHF). VHF signals are usually stronger than UHF signals and are more desirable for broadcast in Central Asia because of its mountainous terrain. Authorities have used all these issues—and numerous others—to disadvantage or silence certain stations.
7. In all four countries, retransmitted Russian programming is commonly believed to have extremely large audiences, and many local stations have almost no self-produced

programming. The exception is Kazakhstan, where only 50 percent of programming can be in Russian and retransmissions are limited to 20 percent of a station's airtime.

8. In Kazakhstan, Articles 18 and 20 of the media law and the law "for complaints against illegitimate actions of the state executive agencies and officials infringing rights of citizens" govern access to information. In Kyrgyzstan, the media law, the law "On the guarantees and freedom of access to information," the law "On informing," and the law "On the order concerning proposals, applications and complaints of citizens" govern this sphere. The Kyrgyzstan law "On mass media" oddly gives governmental bodies and official entities "the right" to fulfill journalists' requests without requiring governments to do so. However, governmental bodies and organizations are required to give socially important information to journalists. In Tajikistan, the print media law (Articles 5, 27, and 31), the constitution, the laws on information, and the law on TV and radio address access to information. Uzbekistan's law "On mass media" (Article 2) and its law "On principles and guarantees to freedom of information" address access to information.

9. The Kazakh law was the best in the region, requiring an answer within three days of receipt of the request (although it gives official bodies up to a month if the information requires "special inquiries"). The minimum time limit for official bodies in Kyrgyzstan was fifteen days, and in Tajikistan and Uzbekistan, official organs had a month to respond.

10. Transparency International's 2003 Corruption Perception Index rating gave Kazakhstan and Uzbekistan a score of 2.4, Kyrgyzstan 2.1, and Tajikistan a score of 1.8, on a scale of 10, where the lowest-ranking country (Bangladesh) received a 1.3.

11. These trends apply also to Kyrgyzstan (International Research and Exchanges Board 2004, 245).

12. That is not to say that jailing journalists is rare, however. Many journalists have been imprisoned for alleged offenses, ranging from Sergey Duvanov's jailing for "raping a minor" (Kazakhstan) to imprisonment for homosexuality (Uzbekistan). Mukhtor Boqizoda of Tajikistan's *Nerui Sukhan* received a two-year sentence in a correctional labor facility for stealing state property—electricity for his printing press (Committee to Project Journalists 2005).

13. Kazakhstan's law on libel has shifted this burden slightly, but it remains unclear how much it has been shifted in practice (Institute for War and Peace Reporting 2008).

14. This refers to demands for protection of honor, dignity, and business reputation, based on the publication of specific data, www.adilsoz.kz.

15. Journalists rarely make more than a couple of hundred dollars per month in Kazakhstan and often less than one hundred dollars per month in Kyrgyzstan and Tajikistan (Adil Soz 2003b).

16. Most Central Asian newspapers are financially unsuccessful for a variety of reasons.

17. Interviews in Dushanbe, Tajikistan, in March and April 2004 confirmed that under-reporting circulation was widespread. One journalist said up to half of the newspapers practiced the tax-reduction tactic.

18. Group interview conducted by the author, July 2004, Bukhara, Uzbekistan.

19. Many journalists expressed extreme dependence on their advertisers, especially in Kazakhstan, where economic development is far ahead of the rest of the region (Kozhakhmetov 2003; Krimsky 2002).

20. More examples and other types of punishment can be found in *Zakonodatel'stvo i Praktika Sredstv Massovoy Informatsii Kazakhstana* (Legislation and Practice of the Media of Mass Information of Kazakhstan), nos. 2(17)–20(35), February 2003–August 2004; see also *Mass-Media v Kazakhstane: Zakony, Konflikty, Pravonarusheniya* (Mass Media in Kazakhstan: Laws, Conflicts and Rights Violations), results of 2002, Almaty: Adil Soz (2003a).

REFERENCES

Adil Soz. 2003a. *Mass-media v Kazakhstane: Zakony, konflikty, pravonarusheniya* (Mass media in Kazakhstan: Laws, conflicts and rights violations). Results of 2002. Almaty: Adil Soz.

———. 2003b. *Zhurnalisty Kazakhstana: Popytka avtoportreta* (Journalists of Kazakhstan: An attempt at a self-portrait). Almaty, Kazakhstan.

———. 2008. *Freedom of Expression Situation in Kazakhstan, 2008*. Almaty, Kazakhstan. Www.adilsoz.kz/site.php?lan=english&id=67&pub=11.

———. 2009. *Freedom of Expression Situation in Kazakhstan in 2009*. Almaty, Kazakhstan. Www.adilsoz.kz/site.php?lan=english&id=67&pub=13.

Adil Soz monitoring. 2010. *Narusheniye prava na rasprostraneniye sretsv massovoy informatsii.* 8 February. Www.adilsoz.kz/site.php?lan=russian&id=999.

Allison, Olivia. 2006. "Selective Enforcement and Irresponsibility: Central Asia's Shrinking Space for Independent Media." *Central Asia Studies* 25(1–2): 93–114.

Anonymous. 2004. Interview by author, June. Tashkent, Uzbekistan.

British Broadcasting Corporation. 2010. "Wave of Brutal Attacks Shocks Kyrgyz journalists." 6 February. Http://news.bbc.co.uk/2/hi/8496660.stm.

Benjamin N. Cardozo School of Law. 1998. "Kazakhstan." *Post-Soviet Media Law and Policy Newsletter* 46 (15 May). Www.vii.org/monroe/issue46/fsu.html.

Committee to Protect Journalists. 2005. "Tajikistan: Editor of independent weekly sentenced to two years corrective labor." 25 August. Www.cpj.org/news/2005/Tajik25aug05na.html.

———. 2010a. "State-owned Internet provider blocks Kazakh news sites." 29 April. Http://

cpj.org/2010/04/state-owned-internet-provider-blocks-kazakh-news-s.php.

——. 2010b. "Disdaining press freedom, Kazakhstan undermines OSCE." 14 September. Http:// cpj.org/reports/2010/09/disdaining-press-freedom-kazakhstan-undermines-osc.php.

Ferghana.ru. (2009). "Uzbekistan: The Criminal Case Has Been Filed against the Photographer and Documentary Film Maker Umida Akhmedova." 17 December. Http://enews. ferghana.ru/article.php?id=2597.

Freedom House. 1998. *Freedom in the World.* Www.freedomhouse.org.

Ganiev, Shuhrat. 2004. Interview with author, June. Bukhara, Uzbekistan.

Human Rights Watch. 2008. "Kazakhstan: An Atmosphere of Quiet Repression." December.

Institute for War and Peace Reporting. 2007. "Internet hit by media law change." 30 January. Http://iwpr.net/report-news/internet-hit-media-law-change.

——. 2008. "Kazak reform bills offer little new." 21 November. Www.iwpr.net/tg/node/10517.

International Freedom of Expression eXchange. 2010. "Judges Seek Millions from Three Weeklies in Civil Libel Case." 3 February. Www.ifex.org/tajikistan/2010/02/04/ papers_defamation_charges.

International Research and Exchanges Board. 2002–10. Media sustainability index.

Junaidov, Farrukhsho. 2004–2005. Interview with author, 16 March 2004, 2 April 2004, 3 August 2005. Dushanbe, Tajikistan.

Kaleeva, Tamara. 2006. "Situation with freedom of speech in Kazakhstan for 2006: Analytical report." Adil Soz. Http://www.adilsoz.kz/site.php?lan=english&id=67&pub=7.

Kasybekov, U. 2000. "Press under the conditions of transitional economy in Kyrgyzstan." Mass Media of Central Asia: Today and Tomorrow conference. Osh, Kyrgyzstan: Central Asian Media Support project, Bulletin No. 1, February/March.

Khodjaev, Alo. 2004. Interview with author, July. Tashkent, Uzbekistan.

Kim, Aleksandr 2003–2004. Interviews by author, December 12, 2003, March 9, 2004. Bishkek, Kyrgyzstan.

Kimmage, Daniel. 2004. "Analysis: Tajik independent newspaper waiting for a new day." 19 November. Eurasianet.org. Www.eurasianet.org/departments/civilsociety/articles/ pp112104.shtml.

Kozhakhmetov, Bagdat. 2003. Interview with author, 14 November. Astana, Kazakhstan.

Krimsky, George. 2002. "Struggle and promise: The independent media of Central Asia." Almaty, Kazakhstan: Report to Central Asian Media Representative. U.S. Agency for International Development.

Kyrgyzstan Government. 2007. "Statement on the Licensing Commission and the procedure for the State Communications Agency's granting of licenses in the Kyrgyz Republic," No. 195-pr, 1 November. Www.gov.kg.

Lillis, Joanna. 2010. "Central Asia: Brutal Murder of Kyrgyz Journalist in Kazakhstan Points to Press Freedom Concerns." 27 January. Eurasianet.org. Www.eurasianet.

org/departments/insightb/articles/eav012810.shtml.

Mamadshoev, Marat. March 18, 2004; Aug. 3, 2005. Interview with author. Dushanbe, Tajikistan.

Mamaraimov, Abdumomun. 2004. Interview with author, 24 February. Jalalabad, Kyrgyzstan.

McNair, Brian. 1991. *Glasnost, perestroika and the Soviet media.* London: Routledge.

Mould, David H. 1998. "Television and Radio in Kyrgyzstan: Problems and prospects for development." Analysis conducted for the United States Agency for International Development) regional mission for Central Asia. Www.internews.ru/report/mould/index.html.

Mukim, Jovid. 2004. Interview with author, 21 March. Dushanbe, Tajikistan.

Myers, Roger. 2004. Interview with author, 1 July. Almaty, Kazakhstan.

Orozbekova, Cholpon. 2001. "Need money? Sue journalists." *Central Asian Media Electronic List.* Cimera 12. February. Http://wWww.cimera.org/files/camel/en/C12E-Orozbekova.pdf.

Pannier, Bruce. 2008. "New Kazakh media company bodes ill for independent press." Radio Free Europe/Radio Liberty. 12 July. Www.rferl.org/Content/New_Kazakh_Media_Company_Bodes_Ill_For_Independent_Press/1183277.html.

Schmidt, Albert J. 1990. *The Impact of Perestroika on Soviet Law.* The Hague: Martinus Nijhoff Publishers.

Shar-Niyaz, Sadyk. 2005. Interview with author, 18 August. Bishkek, Kyrgyzstan.

Sigal, Ivan. 2000. "Kazakhstan." *Communications Law in Transition* 1 (7).

Volosevich, Aleksey. 2004. E-mail correspondence with author, 5 April. Tashkent, Uzbekistan.

Walker, Christopher. 2007. "Muzzling the media: The return of censorship in the Commonwealth of Independent States." Freedom House. 15 June. Www.freedomhouse.org/uploads/press_release/muzzlingthemedia_15june07.pdf.

World Press Freedom Review. 2007. "Uzbekistan." International Press Institute. Www.freemedia.at/cms/ipi/freedom_detail.html?country=/KW0001/KW0005/KW0138/.

Zakonodatel'stvo i praktika sredstv massovoy informatsii Kazakhstana (Legislation and practice of the mass media Information of Kazakhstan). 2003–06. Internews Kazakhstan. Www.internews.kz.

Ethnic Minorities and the Media in Central Asia

Olivier Ferrando

The most captivating feature of Central Asia is undoubtedly its multiethnic and multilingual population. This mosaic of peoples and languages results from a rich precolonial history, as well as the legacy of the Russian and Soviet empires. The region was structured during the national-territorial demarcation that the Soviet authorities ordered in 1923 to lay the foundations of modern Central Asia (Haugen 2003). Five native peoples—Kazakhs, Uzbeks, Kyrgyz, Tajiks, and Turkmens—were promoted to the rank of ethnic groups, or "nationalities" in Soviet terminology, and given national republics. However, their intertwined settlements made the initial plan of five ethnically homogeneous entities clearly unattainable. Each republic comprised a large part of the nationality it was named for but also incorporated significant proportions of the four other groups, as well as a myriad of non-native nationalities.

In accordance with its ideology, the Soviet regime promoted all native dialects to the status of written national languages and codified them in Cyrillic. Lenin believed the press should also play the role of propagandist, agitator, and collective organizer.[1] The media that developed immediately after the establishment of the Soviet regime were conceived primarily as ideological tools to educate the masses (Aumente et al. 1999, 50). Because of their multiethnic character, Central Asian republics enjoyed an extremely rich press system, with newspapers published at national, provincial, and local levels in most existing native languages. The regime paid particular attention to using native languages in the communication sector, because language was instilled as the key feature of ethnic identity. The media turned out to be ethnic in form—the language of publication—but socialist in content. This ethnic press facilitated circulation of political messages to all ethnic groups, regardless of their language skills, and therefore contributed to the rapid spread of Soviet rule.

As long as Central Asian republics were separated by insignificant administrative boundaries within a strongly centralized federal system, all Soviet citizens enjoyed the same legal rights regardless of their residence. Following dissolution of the Soviet Union in 1991, however, the emergence of international frontiers between former sister republics left sizeable shares of native groups stranded across the border of their eponym kin state. Each republic became a sovereign nation-state with a multiethnic population comprising a titular nation and hosting more than a hundred other nationalities. The latter were reduced then to the status of ethnic minorities, including kin minorities from bordering states.[2] Table 1 shows the ethnic composition of Uzbekistan, Tajikistan, and Kyrgyzstan. On the eve of independence in 1989, Uzbeks represented the indisputable majority of Uzbekistan's population (71.4 percent) and accounted for nearly 25 percent of Tajikistan's and 13 percent of Kyrgyzstan's populations. Russians were present in the three republics, as well as significant Tajik and Kyrgyz minorities beyond the borders of their respective kin state.

The newly independent states inherited the Soviet media system. But the media experienced the same status changes as their respective audiences. The titular nations' media became the mainstream media, while those meant for ethnic minorities became minority media. "Minority media" should therefore be understood in terms of audience rather than content, regardless of whether they address mainstream or ethnic issues. As audiences remain targeted through their native languages, minority media are actually the ones published in a minority language. "Ethnic minority media" and "minority language media" are equally used.

After suggesting a typology of minority language media, this chapter explores the role they play in multiethnic Central Asian societies, and outlines the limits and perspectives of minority media.

Statement of the Issues

This chapter addresses the interaction between ethnicity and the mass media sphere through an unprecedented exploration of minority media in these multiethnic societies. The combination of ethnic and media studies reflects

TABLE 1. ETHNIC COMPOSITION OF UZBEKISTAN, TAJIKISTAN, AND KYRGYZSTAN, 1989–2005						
		UZBEKS	**TAJIKS**	**KYRGYZ**	**RUSSIANS**	**OTHERS**
Uzbekistan	1989*	71.4%	4.7%	0.9%	8.3%	14.7%
	2005 (est.)†	79.0%	4.5%	1.4%	3.9%	11.2%
Tajikistan	1989*	23.5%	62.3%	1.3%	7.6%	5.3%
	2000‡	26.1%**	69.1%**	1.1%	1.1%	2.6%
Kyrgyzstan	1989*	12.9%	0.8%	52.4%	21.5%	12.4%
	1999§	13.8%	0.9%	64.9%	12.5%	7.9%

SOURCES: *Goskomstat SSSR 1991–93; †Goskomstat RU 2005; ‡Goskomstat RT 2002; §Goskomstat KR 2000; **Because of the unreliability of official statistics, these data were replaced by the author's projections.

controversies about media representations of ethnicity in societies, in that the media perform a crucial role in the public perception of social relations and the play of cultural power (Cottle 2000a).

"Multiethnic" and "multicultural"' present fundamental questions and imminent disputes about the relationship between ethnic/cultural identity and civic identity, between specificity and universality, between exclusiveness and inclusiveness, and between essentialism and constructivism. We do not assume that these relations conflict or constitute an exclusive alternative to each other; rather, they are expected to complement each other.

Modern research tends to conceptualize ethnicity as a social construction, a matter of negotiated self-identity and "imagined communities." The widespread dissemination of newspapers led to a heightened awareness of the "steady, anonymous, simultaneous experience" of communities of readers (Anderson 1983). Mass media play a key role in this dynamic by defining, preserving, or weakening ethnic identities (Riggins 1992). Multiculturalism is not just a description of ethnic diversity, but also a political philosophy of how diverse ethnic identities coexist. One's identity as a member of dominant or minority ethnic communities is necessarily relevant to how one feels about society's negotiation of ethnic diversity (Husband 2000, 200).

In the Central Asian context, however, national identities were created and cemented by the Soviet policy of nationalities. Ethnicity was mostly viewed and experienced as a fixed identity feature. From a public policy perspective, minority media continue to reflect a model of ethnic pluralism with the emphasis on languages, the key element of a Soviet ethnic identity. Minority media navigate between specific aims, including language retention and community-based expectations on the one hand and universal appeals, market imperatives, and systems of patronage on the other. They contribute to the communication environment of ethnic minorities and their struggles for an "authentic" and/or pluralistic representation (Cottle 2000a, 3). It is thus necessary to analyze the content of both mainstream and minority media to understand how representations of ethnicity are reproduced, elaborated, and challenged within the media.[3]

In this chapter, we also assume that the Central Asian public sphere is experiencing a challengeable fragmentation of its media audiences along language lines. The "public sphere" is a communicative and institutional space where the state and the citizens enter into contact. If the media are expected to play a central role in facilitating this dialogue (Husband 1994), a public sphere that operates through parallel and exclusive communication systems, as in post-Soviet Central Asia, fails to promote exchange between the state and its minorities. Conversely, such a segmented media system fosters self-consciousness within ethnic communities and a partisan ethnic political participation within the state. As minorities talk only to and among themselves, little is expected from a shared public space between minority media and the state.

Finally, the legal framework illustrates the continuing dichotomy between form and content. In Soviet times the "right to information" did not refer to information content but to the language in which a citizen received information. It should therefore be similarly understood as the right of any citizen to access information in his or her native language. That right was first mentioned in the Language Act that each republic adopted in 1989. Those laws guaranteed all citizens the right to receive information and documents in the state language, as well as in the native language of nationalities living in compact settlements. That guarantee remained unchanged in most post-Soviet laws, with the exception of Uzbekistan.[4]

Methodology

To address minority media in such a large and complex region would be unrealistic without empirical focuses. This chapter concentrates on native minorities present before Russian colonization and the related mass arrival of non-native peoples. This focus is justified by the fact that language became a distinctive feature of native identities in Soviet Central Asia, while sparsely settled non-native nationalities in the region failed to keep their mother tongues alive and were mostly subjected to russification. Russian-language newspapers were overrepresented in the Central Asian public sphere and became tools to upgrade Russian proficiency among the local populace (Rogers 1987, 83).[5] The 1989 census shows that the

Russian language achieved significant infiltration in the region.[6] In addition, post-Soviet legal documents reveal that Russian still benefits from its status in all five countries.[7] In view of both the language practices and legal framework, Russian-language media cannot be reasonably considered "minority media" in the sense of this chapter. In each country, mainstream media exist in the state language and in Russian. The term "minority media" is therefore understood as media published neither in the state language nor in Russian.

In geographic terms, Central Asia covers a large territory divided among five countries. This study focuses on a more limited area, the Ferghana Valley, which presents an illustrative case study of Central Asian sociopolitical diversity. The valley covers significant parts of Uzbekistan, Tajikistan, and Kyrgyzstan and provides an opportunity to observe the states' recent evolution from a comparative perspective.[8] The valley also reflects the complexity of Central Asian ethnic composition. As a result of Soviet border demarcations, significant but compact Uzbek, Tajik, and Kyrgyz communities were stranded outside their nominal kin states. Uzbeks constitute sizeable minorities in Tajikistan's province of Sughd (31.3 percent), and Kyrgyzstan's provinces of Osh (31.8 percent) and Jalal-Abad (23.6 percent). In Uzbekistan, Tajiks account for 8.8 percent of Namangan province and 5.3 percent of Ferghana, as well as 6.9 percent of Kyrgyzstan's Batken province. Kyrgyz represent 4.1 percent of Andijan province residents.

Findings

The findings of this study were developed through interviews with newspaper publishers, editors, other journalists, nongovernmental organizations, state administrations, and human rights groups. The author conducted interviews in Russian in 2006 and 2007. The findings are also based on a content analysis of mainstream and minority newspapers and magazines. The author directly analyzed publications in Russian and worked with local translators to analyze material in Uzbek, Kyrgyz and Tajik.

A TYPOLOGY OF MINORITY MEDIA IN POST-SOVIET CENTRAL ASIA

Any attempt to classify minority media requires first identifying relevant criteria such as ownership, budget, print run, and content. This study assumes that the organizational structure of newspapers has a significant impact on content (Riggins 1992). Publishers, owners, and editors influence media outlets' performance with respect to sources of funding (public vs. private), sources of information

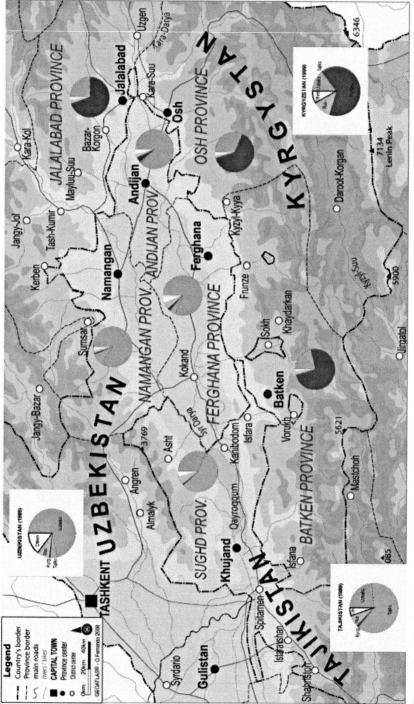

Figure 1. Physical and political map of the Ferghana Valley.

(self-production vs. translation of existing news), and editorial leaning (pro-governmental vs. independent or opposition). Owners of minority media can be the state, an ethnic association, or a private corporation (see table 2).

STATE-OWNED MINORITY MEDIA

Most Central Asian media are still state-owned and are continuations of former propagandistic newspapers. As in Soviet times, language is viewed as a means to convey a single content, be it communist propaganda then or nation-state discourse now. State-owned media serve the interest of their editors—state administrations—so their editorial leaning fully favors the authorities. In addition, they help authorities reach people who have not achieved functional bilingualism or fluency in the state language. However, the public holds little interest in reading government decisions and official chronicles, and the circulation of such newspapers has declined considerably; circulation does not exceed a few thousand copies each, with 75 percent of them secured by subscriptions for state administrations.[9]

At the national level, governmental bodies publish their own gazettes in mainstream and minority languages (see figure 2). Uzbekistan's Cabinet of Ministers edits *Uzbekiston Ovozi* (Voice of Uzbekistan) and *Khalk Suzi* (People's Word) in Uzbek; *Golos Uzbekistana* (Voice of Uzbekistan), *Narodnoe Slovo* (People's Word), and *Pravda Vostoka* (Truth of the East) in Russian; *Ovozi Tojik* (Tajik Voice) in Tajik; and *Nurli Jol* (Enlightened Road) in Kazakh. The Tajikistan government issues *Jumkhuriyat* (Republic) in Tajik, *Narodnaya Gazeta* (People's Newspaper) in Russian, and *Khalk Ovozi* (People's Voice) in Uzbek. In Kyrgyzstan, countrywide governmental newspapers exist only in Kyrgyz (for instance *Kyrgyz Tuusu*) and Russian (*Slovo Kyrgyzstana*).

At province, district, and municipality levels, state-owned media exist in minority languages or in multilingual editions in areas where ethnic minorities live compactly. In Uzbekistan, such local newspapers are published in Uzbek, Russian, Kazakh, Karakalpak, Turkmen, and Korean.[10] In Tajikistan, the official newspaper of the province of Sughd (formerly Leninabad) has been edited in three language versions since 1930: *Khakikati Leninobod* in Tajik, *Leninabadskaya Pravda* in Russian, and *Leninobod Khakikati* in Uzbek (Truth of Leninabad).[11]

MINORITY MEDIA EDITED BY ETHNIC ASSOCIATIONS

Ethnic associations known in Central Asia as ethnic/national cultural centers are community-based organizations that have developed since perestroika (1985–91) to give larger visibility to cultural identities and foster public recognition. The

TABLE 2. TYPOLOGY OF MINORITY MEDIA IN POST-SOVIET CENTRAL ASIA

	LANGUAGE	PUBLISHER	CIRCULATION	
Uzbekistan	Uzbekiston Ovozi	Uzbek	State	National
	Khalk Suzi	Uzbek	State	National
	Golos Uzbekistana	Russian	State	National
	Narodnoe Slovo	Russian	State	National
	Pravda Vostoka	Russian	State	National
	Ovozi Tojik	Tajik	State	National
	Nurli Jol	Kazakh	State	National
	Bukhoroi Sharif	Tajik	Cultural association	Provincial
	Oina	Tajik	Private	Provincial
	Bokhtar	Tajik	Private	Provincial
	Parvina	Tajik	Private	Provincial
	Bulbulcha Dono	Tajik	Private	Provincial
Tajikistan	Jumkhuriyat	Tajik	State	National
	Narodnaya Gazeta	Russian	State	National
	Khalk Ovozi	Uzbek	State	National
	Khakikati Leninobod	Tajik	State	Provincial
	Leninabadskaya Pravda	Russian	State	Provincial
	Leninobod Khakikati	Uzbek	State	Provincial
	Khak Suz	Uzbek	Cultural association	National
	Dustlik	Uzbek	Cultural association	Provincial
	Kadriyat	Uzbek	Cultural association	Provincial
	ASIA-Plus	Russian	Private	National
	Varorud	Tajik/Rus.	Private	Provincial
	Tong	Uzbek	Private	Provincial
	Sughd Yoghdusi	Uzbek	Private	Provincial
Kyrgyzstan	Kyrgyz Tuusu	Kyrgyz	State	National
	Slovo Kyrgyzstana	Russian	State	National
	Osh Shamy	Kyrg/Uzb/Rus	State	Provincial
	Diidor	Uzbek	Cultural association	Provincial
	Ittipak	Uyghur/Rus.	Cultural association	National
	Mezon	Uzbek	Private	Provincial
	Demos Times	Uzbek	Private	Provincial
	DDD	Kyrg/Uzb/Rus	Private	Provincial
	Fergana	Kyrg/Uzb/Rus	Private	Provincial

Ministry of Culture or local authorities award grants to associations to produce cultural programs, perform folklore during official celebrations, and edit bulletins and newspapers. Often an umbrella organization coordinates and funds the activities of ethnic associations, as does the International Cultural Center in Uzbekistan or the TODKS, Russian acronym for Tajik Society of Friendship and Cultural Relations in Tajikistan.[12]

In Uzbekistan, several newspapers were created along with Tajik cultural centers in the late 1980s. One is *Bukhoroi Sharif* (Glorious Bukhara), the first Tajik-language newspaper established in Uzbekistan in 1922 as a state-owned medium. It was closed in Soviet times and revived by the Tajik ethnic association of Bukhara to disseminate information about Bukharan Tajik culture.[13] The Uzbek Cultural Center launched two Uzbek-language newspapers in Uzbekistan: *Khak Suz* (Word of Truth) at the national level in 1991 and *Dustlik* (Friendship) in the province of Sughd in 1992.[14] In addition, the provincial branch of the Uzbek Society of Tajikistan has edited the provincial cultural newspaper *Kadriyat* in Uzbek since 1996.[15]

The Uzbek National Cultural Center (UNCC) has offices at national, provincial, and municipal levels in Kyrgyzstan. However, only the Jalal-Abad branch has been editing a cultural newspaper in Uzbek, *Diidor* (Appearance) since 1991.[16] The Uyghur Society of Kyrgyzstan launched the monthly newspaper *Ittipak* (Union) in 1994 in three languages, Russian, Cyrillic Uyghur, and Arabic Uyghur.[17]

PRIVATE MINORITY MEDIA

Private status is new in Central Asian media space. Private media are owned neither by a state administration nor a public association, but rather belong to individuals or private corporations. In Uzbekistan, private media were the first to enjoy freedom of expression, as did *Oina* (Mirror), a Samarkand-based Tajik newspaper that published articles on society and, especially, education. But since the late 1990s and stricter governmental control over their editorial leanings, all private media are registered; they generally focus on entertainment or commercial publications and avoid social or political issues. That is the case of the Tajik-language *Bokhtar* (West), circulating in the province of Surkhandaria; *Parvina* (Pleiades), dedicated to literature; and *Bulbulcha Dono* (Good Nightingale), published for the Tajik youth of Samarkand.[18]

In Tajikistan's Sughd province, the Uzbek-language *Tong* (Dawn) was launched in 2002 with financial support from the National Endowment for Democracy, a U.S.-based nonprofit organization seeking to strengthen democratic institutions. Its articles deal mainly with social, political, and economic issues and are written by correspondents from all the districts where Uzbeks live compactly. In 2006

Figure 2. In Uzbekistan, *Khalk Suzi* (*top left*) in Uzbek, *Pravda Vostoka* (*top center*) and *Narodnoe Slovo* (*top right*) in Russian, *Ovozi Tojik* (*bottom left*) in Tajik; in Tajikistan, *Khalk Ovozi* (*bottom right*) in Uzbek.

Tong launched *BƏB*, a newspaper dedicated to the Uzbek youth of Sughd with a print run of five thousand.[19] In 2008, Uzbek poet and business owner Tursunali Aliev launched the literary magazine *Sughd Yoghdusi* (Light of Sughd) in his native town of Proletar with a print run of one thousand.

Kyrgyzstan is home to the largest number of private media in the region. Minority media can be monolingual as is *Mezon* (Scale), the country's first Uzbek-language private newspaper, founded in Osh in 1996, and *Demos Times*, a weekly launched in Osh in 2000 by the private information agency Alliance Press. Media can also be multilingual, as is *DDD* (the initials for "friendship" in Kyrgyz, Uzbek, and Russian) in Osh or *Fergana*, a weekly launched in Jalal-Abad in 2000. But Kyrgyzstan's political arena and media sector are so well connected that most ethnic associations actually back charismatic Uzbek leaders, such as Kadyrjan Batyrov, head of the UNCC branch in Jalal-Abad, or Davran Sabirov, head of an Uzbek association in Osh. Both have a close link with minority media: Batyrov with the newspaper run by the UNCC branch and Sabirov with the private newspaper *Mezon* and the station *Mezon TV*. Both won parliamentary seats in 2005.

The interconnection among business, media, and politics requires a differentiation among the terms "private," "independent," and "opposition." Few privately owned newspapers and other media are truly independent because their owners dictate content and slant to a large degree. Private media outlets may turn out to be pro-government or pro-opposition, depending on their owners' political orientation, either backing or opposing the ruling party (Allison 2006, 94). The role of minority media, then, depends chiefly on the political and economic environment in which they operate.

The Role of Minority Media in Central Asian Multiethnic Societies

THE ETHNIC APPROACH: FROM CULTURAL SURVIVAL
TO MINORITIES' EMPOWERMENT

The Central Asian public sphere is fragmented along ethnic lines. Several factors perpetuate this fragmentation and promote cultural containment. First, language is a major contributor to the survival of a people as a distinct entity because it empowers them with a positive self-image and a unique linguistic identity (Riggins 1992, 283). By targeting their audience through language, minority media provide a significant ingredient toward cultural containment. The systematic use of the language of one ethnic group seems concerned not with the promotion of its cultural values but rather with mere retention of its native language, regardless of the content developed by the media. For instance, state-owned minority media have been designed in a top-to-bottom logic to circulate official statements in the native languages of their audience: the Tajik-language *Ovozi Tojik* in Uzbekistan, and the Uzbek-language *Khalk Suzi* in Tajikistan, among many others, greatly contribute to the linguistic survival of the ethnic minorities they target.

A second feature of cultural survival is establishment of a minority news agenda—the ranking of importance attached to pieces of information. In addition to native language retention, minority media affiliated with ethnic associations contain a majority of articles related to their ethnic group. For instance, *Kadriyat*, the newspaper of the Uzbek Society of Sughd province, usually devotes a quarter of its news space to Uzbek artists and folkloric festivities, such as handicrafts, folk dances, and traditional clothes. Most minority media face difficulties moving beyond folkloric conceptions of multiculturalism.[20] Minorities are deliberately portrayed in cultural ways through a superficial focus on traditions and individual success stories. Such stereotypical representations may actually reinforce culturally crystallized views of ethnic minorities as "other" rather than producing politically engaged and culturally challenging representations.

Minority media may also pursue a survival strategy through empowerment of their target ethnic groups. Empowerment is the reinforcement of a community threatened by various forms of cultural domination, including linguistic subversion, by a powerful majority group. Empowerment is an ethnic survival reaction in what Brubaker (1996) calls "nationalizing states" and is viewed as a strategy to avoid assimilation. Private minority media may act as agents of such empowerment. The Tajik-language provincial newspaper *Oina* was popular among Uzbekistan's Tajik minority, with a circulation of three thousand copies, one of the highest rates among private media at that time.[21] *Oina* was frequently critical and gave voice to the challenges faced by the Tajik minority until March 2001, when the provincial administration ordered its liquidation after an article exposed bad conditions of education in Tajik-language schools.[22]

Mass media affiliated with politicians or business owners can be used as instruments to create and sustain beliefs in collective goals or to demand change in some aspect of the social order (Riggins 1992, 12). The UNCC branch of Jalal-Abad, Kyrgyzstan, which publishes *Diidor*, is headed by Batyrov, a business owner and former member of parliament, whom fellow Uzbeks consider their patron because of his investments in his native city, Jalal-Abad.[23] Empowerment of the Uzbek minority thus results from multiple actions and cannot be imputed only to media outlets.

Minority media also have symbolic significance in the eyes of their target audiences. As far as ethnic associations and private media are concerned, the mere possession of these means of media production publicly validates a minority's modernity, thereby contributing to its empowerment. What better strategy exists to ensure minority survival than minorities' development of their own media, conveying their own point of view in their own language? Thus cultural traditions are not reduced to folklore, and languages evolve in a way that is adaptive to the requirements of modern societies.

THE CIVIC APPROACH: AN INTEGRATION IN THE MAINSTREAM SOCIETY

A multiethnic public sphere must reflect the diversity of society in a way that facilitates the autonomous expression of ethnic identity of both minority and majority groups (Husband 2000, 209) and promotes development of a common civic belonging across ethnic identities. If minority media provide information that fosters ethnic survival, they may also provide content that promotes their audience's adherence to common civic values. The first element in this development is publication of mainstream information. Focusing on the information published, it appears that most minority-language media provide information either originating from the state ideology or dealing with mainstream subjects. That is true for state-owned minority media, which consider language the major means of informing ethnic minorities about the dominant social values of their host society.

The official press of Sughd province, Tajikistan, is illustrative because its newspaper is published in three parallel versions and offers a unique opportunity to compare content. Each newspaper has its own editorial team, although most articles are a translation or mere adaptation of the same information. *Kadriyat*, published by the Uzbek Society of Sughd, reserves a quarter of its edition to feature Uzbek personalities, but the remaining six pages are used for mainstream information. Rather than mentioning events of interest to the Uzbek minority, the September 2006 issue, for instance, emphasized national civic celebrations.[24] The newspaper's layout features proverbs and phrases from literature. Interestingly, although these headings are in Uzbek, as is the whole newspaper, the classical authors quoted are predominantly Persanophone (Rudaki, Jomi, Shirozi). By using minority languages to publish mainstream information originating from the state with a pro-governmental or nationalistic stance, these minority media reveal a deliberate attempt to instill their audiences with dominant values. However, the impact of both state-owned and ethnic associations' minority media is limited by their low popularity and modest circulation.[25]

In Kyrgyzstan, violent clashes in 1990 between Kyrgyz and Uzbeks generated a general but unwritten taboo about coverage of interethnic issues, often motivated by the authorities' unwillingness to "agitate the people" (Organization for Security and Cooperation in Europe 2003, 90).[26] The trilingual newspaper *Osh Shamy* (Osh's Candle) was created by the city council in 1991 to support the rebuilding of strong ties among the city's ethnic communities Organization for Security and Cooperation in Europe 2003, 217). Local media's deliberately limited coverage of interethnic issues contributes to development of a unique public sphere where inhabitants are primarily considered citizens, regardless of ethnic origin. After adoption of a new constitution in 2006, the private newspaper *Mezon* published a special report on the subject. The article covered three pages (out of eight), including the front page; it contained a translation into Uzbek of the main constitutional provisions, as well as insightful analysis of the changes and their impact on the country's political life.[27] During the 2010 political upheaval in Kyrgyzstan when public discontent drove President Kurmanbek Bakiyev from office and voters considered a new constitution, the very question of whether to publish the draft version in Uzbek sparked controversy. After the interim government decided to publish it only in Kyrgyz and Russian, the editor-in-chief of *Diidor* unofficially translated the draft in Uzbek and published it.[28] The existence of such media may contribute to a significant sense of civic identity.

However, those examples show that it is uncertain whether minority media encourage audiences to retain ethnic values or whether they further integration of ethnic minorities into the surrounding dominant society, chiefly through promotion of common civic values. Rather than choosing between these two opposing tendencies, it is more realistic to assume that minority media fulfill both functions. They contribute to ethnic pluralism while also supporting civic consciousness. In their attempt to promote democracy in Central Asia, many international donors view private minority media as "agents of social intervention" (Shafer and Freedman 2007) in that they are expected to behave both as watchdogs guaranteeing cultural diversity and pluralism and as propagandistic tools contributing to the civic education of their audience by disseminating Western democratic values. By providing information in a specific language, minority media face competing demands. On the one hand, they generate news that speaks to the specific concerns of their target ethnic group; on the other hand, they promote democratization of society regardless of their target audience.

Limits and Perspectives of Central Asian Minority Media

The Central Asian minority press shows a certain vitality. In multiethnic societies, however, the media's ethnic specialization may lead to the "ghettoization" of minority newspapers and a marginalization of their audiences (Husband 1994, 16). Several facets of the limits and perspectives of minority media can be explored, including the education of journalists, sources of funding, and future prospects for cross-border media outlets.

THE EDUCATION OF MINORITY MEDIA JOURNALISTS

The legacy of Soviet journalism education is still apparent in Central Asia. Most university programs dedicated to journalism continue to apply "old-fashioned propagandistic techniques" (Aumente et al. 1999, 149–51). Since independence, many international donors and Western media organizations have provided an array of vocational training courses to build modern skills among the new generation of journalists.[29] Yet universities and international actors offer courses in a limited number of languages—the state language or Russian. Thus journalists for Uzbek-language media in Tajikistan and Kyrgyzstan and Tajik-language media in Uzbekistan have few or no such training opportunities in their native language, the one they use to write articles. The issue of language of education was resolved in Soviet times by the possibility for most nationalities to complete secondary school in their native language and then study further in their kin republic, where most subjects were taught in their native language.[30]

Since the collapse of the U.S.S.R., students' cross-border mobility has almost disappeared because of high travel costs and Uzbekistan's strict visa regime. Therefore, most minority journalists below thirty-five graduated in a language—the state language or Russian—that they do not use in their regular editorial work. Readers can easily notice discrepancies in language quality between, for instance, a newspaper edited in literary language in Uzbekistan and Uzbek minority media across the border, which are more colloquial. This gap has become critical for Uzbek print media since Uzbekistan switched from Cyrillic to Latin script; it now requires that all material in Uzbek be printed in the Latin alphabet. Neighboring countries hosting Uzbek minorities did not undertake such a reform of their state language. And for both financial and political reasons, they are unwilling to conduct an alphabet reform for a limited part of their population, a move that would contribute to a higher degree of cleavage within their multiethnic society.

MARKETPLACE AND FUNDING: MINORITY MEDIA'S INDEPENDENCE AT STAKE

While all newspapers were funded by the state in Soviet times, today only state-owned media enjoy such status and economic security. Newspapers affiliated with ethnic associations also rely on governmental subsidies that are indirectly channeled through the associations. This public funding molds a press that is chiefly conservative and accommodating and that surreptitiously reinforces integrationist drives. Private minority media have no other choice but to adhere to the general logic of the marketplace. The largest markets and profits in a multiethnic society are found in the dominant ethnic group, thereby inhibiting successful formation and growth of ethnic minority media. Those that have managed to secure a niche market, meanwhile, depend on external financial support. One major supporter is the international community, which provides grants to launch new independent media and support operating costs. In return, donors insist on the editors' commitment to promote pluralism and defend democracy.[31]

An even more problematic situation is patronage from business owners who consider the media instruments to promote their own political agendas. Besides partisan content, these private minority media must comply with the successes and difficulties of their patrons. In Kyrgyzstan, the Uzbek-language newspaper *Mezon*, which openly supported former parliament member Davran Sabirov during his campaigns, was forced to suspend its publication twice to respect the principle of neutrality.[32] Minority media have great difficulty maintaining a balance among various sources of funding, including the advertising market, and are hence subject to financial insecurity and recurrent instability.[33] Often a conflict between the sponsor and the editor, or the sponsor's mere withdrawal, bankrupts private minority media. That was so for the Tajik newspapers *Bokhtar* and *Parvina* in Uzbekistan and the Uzbek newspapers *Khak Suz* and *Dustlik* in Tajikistan.

COMMUNICATING ACROSS BORDERS: CURRENT ISSUES AND FUTURE PROSPECTS

Cross-border communication implicates the relationship between minority media and their kin state. Soviet borders were insignificant, so minority media circulated freely within their respective language group. Today each nation-state applies strict border controls. Retailers cannot import publications from neighboring countries without prior authorization. In July 2001 the Uzbek government seized and burned ten thousand brochures offered by Tajikistan to its kin minority, claiming that such material threatened the country's security.[34] The situation is different for broadcast media, because governments cannot technologically impose the same level of control; TV and radio programs are not stopped at the frontier and enjoy great popularity among minorities. Uzbekistan's TV channel *Yoshlar* and radio station *Sezam* are both received in the bordering districts of Tajikistan and Kyrgyzstan where Uzbek communities reside. Because of geographical and technical constraints, a significant share of border populations lack access to their host country's broadcasting system, and the airwaves of Tajikistan and Kyrgyzstan are overpowered by high-capacity Uzbekistani stations. The hegemonic circulation of Uzbek programs encouraged the Tajik government to promote TV and radio stations in its bordering areas and to fill the vacuum left by national airwaves.[35]

The progress of communication technologies has transformed the media environment, leading to new forms of production and circulation of minority media (Cottle 2000a). An example is the rapid development of information Web sites and electronic newspapers, either based in Central Asian countries or edited abroad.[36] Some information agencies target cross-border multiethnic regions with an emphasis on access to information in all native languages. International news organizations such as Radio Free Europe/Radio Liberty, Voice of America, and the British Broadcasting Corporation offer programming from a Western perspective in national languages, including Uzbek, Tajik, and Kyrgyz.[37] Since 2002 and more intensively after the violently suppressed uprising in Andijan in May 2005, the Uzbek government has closed most independent national and international media, and many Uzbek journalists resettled in bordering countries.[38]

Conclusion

This chapter shows that the main limitation of minority media lies in the structure of the public sphere. A highly differentiated public sphere—with minorities talking to and among themselves in their native language and a deaf mainstream culture—does not promote shared space and values. Finding crosscutting cleavages is a more creative solution than restricting mainstream and minority cultures and their respective media channels (Sreberny 2005). Rather than maintaining minority-language media in separate channels, public policies should promote a permeable interface between mainstream and minority media within their state boundaries.

A first model could be development of multilingual media that address issues regardless of the language of their audience. Some successful examples of multilingual private independent media already exist. The Tajik/Russian-language weekly *Varorud* was launched in Sughd province in 2002 with Organization for Security and Cooperation in Europe support and has captured a considerable audience among all ethnic groups. In southern Kyrgyzstan, *Fergana* started circulating in 2000 with a unique trilingual edition in Kyrgyz, Uzbek, and Russian. Radio Salam, a private station created in 2001 by the Kyrgyz NGO Foundation for Tolerance International in Batken province, continues to broadcast entertainment and music in most of the languages spoken in the Ferghana Valley. Despite limited provincial broadcasting, *Salam* gained popularity in bordering areas of Uzbekistan and Tajikistan.[39]

A second possibility is to accept the role of media in a neutral regional language, namely Russian. Currently, the Dushanbe-based Russian-language newspaper *ASIA-Plus* is the most popular private media in Tajikistan, The reason for its success is not ethnic—Tajikistan has an insignificant Russian minority—but the perception of the Russian language as a modern means of communication.[40]

This chapter illuminates the processes and practices by which media routinely grapple with institutional constraints and cultural obligations. But it should be acknowledged that there are methodological limits to this analysis of the structure and content of minority media because the study does not assess the social influence of minority media on audiences. Further research should focus on ethnographic and qualitative approaches to the study of audiences to assess their reception to processes of identity building.

NOTES

This chapter is the result of field research conducted from October 2006 to September 2008 in Uzbekistan, Tajikistan, and Kyrgyzstan. Research was funded by the French Ministry of Education and Research (2006), the French Ministry of Foreign Affairs (2008), and the French Institute for Central Asian Studies in Tashkent.

1. The press system experienced a rapid growth. In the 1960s, 63,000 journalists worked at 7,985 newspapers in 56 languages (Aumente et al. 1999, 51).

2. The terms "'host" and "kin" refer to the polities where a kin-minority resides (host state) and where the majority of its fellow ethnics live (kin state).

3. As Riggins shows, the emergence and evolution of ethnic media as a tool for minority empowerment or domination remain conditioned by a system of variables. Internal factors include the absolute and relative size of the ethnic minorities; their level of assimilation and integration; and their capacity to finance, administer, and handle their own media. We also consider the host state's political structure and prevailing ideology where the process of empowerment or domination is manifested and varies from assimilation to relative tolerance of diversity. Finally we pay attention to how international actors—particularly donors and media support organizations—influence the media space in Central Asia. The presence or absence of some of these variables commands a range of distinct strategies for development of minority media.

4. For instance, the Tajik law "On mass media" adopted 12 March 2002 declares that "the state guarantees to the citizens of the republic of Tajikistan the right to use their native language to receive and spread mass media information" (Article 3). The Uzbek parliament refined the 1989 provision in the new Language Act of 21 December 1995. Article 16 states that "television and radio programs shall be conducted in the state language, as well as in other languages," and Article 17 states that "publishing activity shall be conducted in the state language, and in other languages, as needed." The objectively verifiable criteria of "population compactness," included in 1989, was dropped in favor of a highly subjective "need," whose assessment mechanism was not determined by the law.

5. In 1967, Uzbekistan had 72 print media in Russian and 121 in Uzbek, while Russians

accounted for only 12.5 percent of the population. Kyrgyzstan had an almost equal number of newspapers—30 in Russian and 35 in Kyrgyz—although Russians represented less than a third of the population (Hopkins 1970, 198).

6. The russification process concerned most non-Russian Slavs (Ukrainians, Belorussians, and Poles), as well as the peoples who had been deported before and during the Great War: Germans, Koreans, Greeks, and Caucasians. Consequently, in 1989 in Uzbekistan, ethnic Russians accounted for 8.3 percent of the population, but the Russian language was mastered by 33.4 percent. In Tajikistan, the progression was even more visible, with 7.6 percent Russians but 36.4 percent Russian speakers. As for Kyrgyzstan where the proportion of ethnic Russians was 21.5 percent, declared Russian speakers made up 56.7 percent of the population (Goskomstat SSSR 1991–93).

7. In Kyrgyzstan, Russian enjoys the rank of "official language" (Article 5 of the constitution), while Kyrgyz is the state language. In Tajikistan and Uzbekistan, Russian was acknowledged as the "language of interethnic communication" in their respective Language Act of 1989 (Article 2). Tajikistan confirmed this status in its constitution of 1994 (Article 2), but Uzbekistan dropped it from its constitution of 1992 and in the revised Language Act of 1995.

8. Beside the mere geographical argument, Turkmenistan was excluded from the analysis chiefly because of the impossibility to conduct in-country field research. As for Kazakhstan, the issue of minority media needs to be addressed in a distinct way as for the three target countries, particularly because of the specific role played by both the Russian minority (37.8 percent vs. 39.7 percent of Kazakhs on the eve of independence) and the Russian language.

9. G. Mansurova, "The market economy and mass media in Tajikistan," and M. Hamidov, "Print media in Kyrgyzstan" (papers presented at the conference "The Mass Media of Central Asia: Today and Tomorrow," Tashkent, Uzbekistan, March 2000).

10. In particular, *Yangi Kun* (New Day) and *Markazii Osiyo Madaniyati* (Culture of Central Asia) are published in Kazakh, Kyrgyz, Tajik, Turkmen, Uzbek, and Russian.

11. Interestingly, despite the renaming of the province, the newspaper continued to be edited with its Soviet title. Local authorities eventually renamed it in 2008: *Khakikati Sughd* in Tajik *Sogdiiskaya Pravda* in Russian; and *Sughd Khakikati* in Uzbek ("Tajikistan: Gazety Khujanda otkazalis' ot svoikh sovetskikh nazvanii," *Novosti Tsentral'noi Azii*, Ferghana.ru information agency, 2 January 2008. Www.ferghana. ru/news.php?id=8100.)

12. Both umbrella organizations edit a quarterly magazine: *Garmoniya* (Harmony) in Uzbekistan and *Dusti* (Friendship) in Tajikistan. Both magazines gather articles and reports from their members and publish them exclusively in Russian with a clear view to foster inter-ethnic communication (interview with Maisara Kalonova, former

head of the TODKS, Dushanbe, Tajikistan, 13 September 2008).

13. Eventually the association had to stop editing the newspaper because of a lack a funds (interview with a Tajik activist from Bukhara, Samarkand, Uzbekistan, 28 August 2008).

14. Interview with Numonjon Fahriddinov, cofounder of the Uzbek Cultural Center of Tajikistan, Dushanbe, Tajikistan, 11 September 2008.

15. Interview with Jamshed Pirimov, chief editor of *Kadriyat*, Khujand, Tajikistan, 5 September 2008.

16. Interview with Ulughbek Abdusalamov, deputy president of the UNCC branch of Jalal-Abad province, Jalal-Abad, Kyrgyzstan, 11 December 2006.

17. Interview with Abdrahim Khapizov, journalist from *Ittipak*, Bishkek, Kyrgyzstan, 7 August 2008.

18. Interview with Asadullo Shukurov, poet and founder of *Bulbulcha Dono*, Samarkand, Uzbekistan, 29 August 2008.

19. Interview with Mirzohakim Kobilov, chief editor of *Tong*, Khujand, Tajikistan, 19 December 2006.

20. This feature is not specific to Central Asia or the former Soviet Union. As an example, the British Broadcasting Corporation faced a similar situation when developing ethnic minority programs (Cottle 2000b)

21. Interview with a Tajik editor, Tashkent, 1 December 2006.

22. Institute for War and Peace Reporting, "Outspoken Uzbek Editor Dismissed." *Report Central Asia* no. 62, 27 July 2001, http://iwpr.net/sq/node/9173.

23. For instance, Batyrov founded in Jalal-Abad a campus providing education from kindergarten through university (interview with Dilmurat Akhmedov, head of the University of Peoples' Friendship, Jalal-Abad, Kyrgyzstan, 9 December 2006).

24. For instance the September 2006 issue was dedicated mostly to the celebration of the Aryan civilization and the twenty-seven-hundredth anniversary of Kulov, the native city of the president. It also reported the World's Tajiks and Persanophones conference, founded and headed by the president.

25. For example, *Sughd Khakikati* has a run of 790 copies and *Kadriyat* 1,400 copies for an estimated six hundred thousand Uzbeks in Sughd province.

26. Reportedly, 171 civilians were killed during these short but brutal clashes between Uzbek and Kyrgyz residents of southern Kyrgyzstan, particularly in Osh and Urgent (Douglas Goodie, "An overview of the Ferghana Valley." *Perspectives on Central Asia* 1 [1996]).

27. *Mezon* 19 (213), 1 December 2006.

28. Human Rights Watch, *Where is the Justice? Interethnic Violence in Southern Kyrgyzstan and its Aftermath*, 16 August 2010.

29. International donors include UNICEF, Organization for Security and Cooperation in Europe, U.S. Agency for International Development, European Union, and the Soros Foundation. Western media organizations include the International Research and Exchanges Board, Internews, Cimera, and Institute for War and Peace Reporting.

30. In Soviet times, secondary education was provided in seven languages in Uzbekistan (Uzbek, Russian, Kazakh, Tajik, Kyrgyz, Turkmen, and Karakalpak), six languages in Tajikistan (Tajik, Russian, Uzbek, Kyrgyz, Turkmen, and Kazakh), and four languages in Kyrgyzstan (Kyrgyz, Russian, Uzbek, and Tajik) (USSR, *Vestnik statistiki* 12 [1991]). Central Asian journalists over thirty-five years old who worked for Uzbek-, Tajik-, or Kyrgyz-language newspapers usually graduated respectively from Tashkent, Dushanbe, or Bishkek state universities, regardless of their republic of residence.

31. Interview with Mirzohakim Kobilov, chief editor of *Tong*, Khujand, Tajikistan, 19 December 2006.

32. Satkanbaev, Kamil. "Trials and tribulations of an independent Uzbek newspaper," *Media Insight Central Asia* no. 22, January 2002.

33. Minority media have limited access to the advertising market because of low circulation, limited target audiences, and specific languages. Only cellular phone companies order advertisements, and, remarkably, their inserts are always published in Russian.

34. International Crisis Group, "Tajikistan: an uncertain peace," *Asia Report* no. 30. Osh, 2001, www.crisisgroup.org/~/media/Files/asia/central-asia/tajikistan/Tajikistan%20 An%20Uncertain%20Peace.ashx.

35. In 2001 the Sughd-based radio *Tiroz* was the first private station in post-Soviet Tajikistan. Its director acknowledged that the purpose of the station was to "protect the information space of northern Tajikistan against the ideological influence of neighboring countries" (qtd. in Nargis Zakirova, "Private Tajik radio station against 'ideological influence' of Uzbekistan," *Central-Asian-Media-Electronic-List* 19, September 2001). With such an emphasis on the airwaves, Sughd province now contains the majority of the country's broadcast media, with reportedly twelve TV channels and three radio stations.

36. In Tajikistan there is ASIA-Plus (www.asiaplus.tj in Russian and English) and Avesta (www.avesta.tj in Tajik, Russian, and English) and in Khujand, Varorud (www.varorud. org in Tajik, Russian, and English). In Kyrgyzstan, there is a plethora of news agencies, including CentrAsia (www.centrasia.ru in Russian), Akipress (www.akipress.com in Russian and English), 24kg (www.24.kg in Russian and English), Belyy Parakhod (www.parohod.kg in Russian), and *Bishkek-News* (www.nbt.kg/news/news.html in Russian). The best-known information Web sites or electronic newspapers edited or hosted abroad are Ferghana.ru (www.ferghana.ru in Russian, Uzbek, and English)

based in Moscow; EurasiaNet (www.eurasianet.org in Russian and English) based in New York; Oasis (www.ca-oasis.info in Russian) based in Moscow; and the Uzbek service of Radio Free Europe/Radio Liberty (www.ozodlik.org).

37. Navbahor Imamova, "International broadcasting to Central Asia: The voice of reason or opposition," *Central Eurasian Studies Review* 5, no. 2 (2006): 43–47.

38. On 13 May 200,5 the Uzbek government violently suppressed a protest in Andijan, leaving hundreds of civilians dead (International Crisis Group, "Uzbekistan: The Andijan uprising," *Asia Briefing*, 38, Bishkek, 2005) The Uzbek service of Radio Free Europe/Radio Liberty now operates from Tajikistan (interview with Radio Free Liberty/ Radio Liberty Uzbek service correspondent, Dushanbe, 20 November 2006).

39. Interview with Robert Abazbekov, Foundation Tolerance International representative in Batken, June 2001.

40. Central Asian languages have evolved considerably since independence. They were purified and modernized by the addition of new native words to replace borrowed Russian words. Also, Uzbekistan adopted a new alphabet. As a result, most interviewees acknowledged that they were imperfect readers of their literary native language and preferred newspapers in Russian. For this reason, Russian-language media remain popular, and Russian is overwhelmingly preferred both in print and broadcast.

REFERENCES

Allison, Olivia. 2006. "Selective enforcement and irresponsibility: Central Asia's shrinking space for independent media." *Central Asian Survey* 25(1–2): 93–114.

Anderson, Benedict. 1983. *Imagined communities: Reflections on the origins and spread of nationalism.* London: Verso.

Aumente, Jerome, Peter Gross, Ray Hiebert, Owen V. Johnson, and Dean Mills. 1999. *Eastern European journalism: Before, during and after communism.* Cresskill, NJ: Hampton Press.

Brubaker, Rogers W. 1996. *Nationalism reframed: Nationhood and the national question in the New Europe.* Cambridge: Cambridge University Press.

Cottle, Simon. 2000a. "Media research and ethnic minorities: Mapping the field." In *Ethnic minorities and the media: Changing cultural boundaries,* ed. Simon Cottle, 1–30. Philadelphia: Open University Press.

———. 2000b. "A rock and hard place: Making ethnic minority television." In *Ethnic minorities and the media: Changing cultural boundaries,* ed. Simon Cottle, 100–17. Philadelphia: Open University Press.

Ferrando, Olivier. 2008. "Manipulating the census: Ethnic minorities in the nationalizing states of Central Asia." *Nationalities Papers* 36(3): 489–520.

Goskomstat KR [National statistical committee of the Kyrgyz republic]. 2000. *Naselenie Kyrgystana: Itogi pervoy natsional'noy perepisi naseleniya Kyrgyzskoy Respubliki 1999 g. v tablitsakh (Population of Kyrgyzstan: Results of the first population census of the Kyrgyz republic of 1999 in tables)*. Publication II (1). Bishkek, Kyrgyzstan.

Goskomstat RT [State statistical committee of the republic of Tajikistan]. 2002. *The population of the Republic of Tajikistan 2000*. Dushanbe, Tajikistan.

Goskomstat RU [National committee on statistics of the republic of Uzbekistan]. 2005. *Naselenie Respubliki Uzbekistan na 1.1.2005 g. (Population of the republic of Uzbekistan on 1.1.2005)*. Tashkent, Uzbekistan.

Goskomstat SSSR [Central statistical department of the USSR]. 1991–93. *Itogi vsesoyuznoy perepisi naseleniya 1989 g. (Results of the 1989 Soviet population census)* (electronic version). Moscow.

Haugen, Arne. 2003. *The establishment of national republics in Soviet Central Asia*. New York: Palgrave MacMillan.

Hopkins, Mark W. 1970. *Mass media in the Soviet Union*. New York: Pegasus.

Husband, Charles. 2000. "Media and the public sphere in multiethnic societies." In *Ethnic minorities and the media: Changing cultural boundaries*, ed. Simon Cottle, 199–214. Philadelphia: Open University Press.

Husband, Charles, ed. 1994. *A richer vision: The development of ethnic minority media in Western democracies*. Paris: UNESCO Publishing.

Organization for Security and Cooperation in Europe. 2003. *Central Asia–In defense of the future: Media in multicultural and multilingual societies*. Vienna: Office of the Representative on Freedom of the Media.

Riggins, Stephen H., ed. 1992. *Ethnic minority media: An international perspective*. Newbury Park, CA: Sage.

Rogers, Rosemarie. 1987. "Language policy and language power: The case of Soviet publishing." *Language problems and language planning* 11(1): 82–103.

Shafer, Richard, and Eric Freedman. 2007. "Journalists as agents of social intervention: Three models." *Journal of Development Communication* 18(1): 16–28.

Sreberny, Annabelle. 2005. "'Not only, but also': Mixedness and media." *Journal of Ethnic and Migration Studies* 31(3): 443–59.

Journalists at Risk: The Human Impact
of Press Constraints

Eric Freedman

entral Asia has been physically and psychologically dangerous territory for journalists, both in the Soviet era and afterward. The reasons are many, including the authoritarian nature of its regimes; the lack of a tradition of independent media; inadequate education and training opportunities for journalists; pressure on journalists and their news organizations to nurture the development and public acceptance of national identity and statehood; and dependence on governments, political parties, oligarchs, business interests, and foreign donors for economic survival. Legal and extra-legal restraints also pose perils for journalists whose work is viewed as a threat or embarrassment to the ruling administration; organized crime; or influential business, social, or political elites. While many official constraints are imposed by central governments, local authorities sometimes impose their own as well, as occurred in Kyrgyzstan's Talas oblast, or region. Journalists there were required to provide their names, phone numbers, addresses, and political affiliations to the local National Security Committee (Radio Free Europe/Radio Liberty 2009).

The suppression of press rights, political freedom, and other human rights in the five republics has come under frequent criticism from media advocacy and watchdog groups, human rights organizations, international funders, foreign governments, and other monitoring entities. Most often those abuses are recounted in broad policy-oriented, politics-oriented, or law-oriented terms that give little sense of the human beings involved: journalists who risk physical assaults, imprisonment, harassment, loss of employment, libel suits, tax audits, even assassination, for practicing their profession. Importantly, not all such threats and attacks come from government and public officials. Whether those attacks are governmental or extra-governmental in origin, the assailants often operate with impunity. In other words, those responsible face little or no chance of prosecution and imprisonment by the regimes. At the same time, many journalists themselves engage—as a matter of timidity, caution, or reality—in self-censorship, meaning they avoid or tone down their coverage of sensitive topics to avoid repercussions (Walker 2007; Allison 2006; Lupis 2005b; Bakhriev 2003; Freedman and Shafer 2003a).

Statement of the Problem

Journalism can be deadly, as demonstrated by the October 2007 assassination of Alisher Saipov in Kyrgyzstan, reportedly by agents of the Uzbek government in retaliation for his coverage of human rights abuses in neighboring Uzbekistan. That type of attack serves as a potent deterrent to other journalists. Characterizing Saipov's murder as part of a wider campaign against journalists and civil society in Central Asia, Stern quotes an unidentified Osh journalist as saying: "In my soul, I'm afraid. They wanted to demonstratively frighten journalists. [They're saying,] 'Today it was Saipov—tomorrow it could be you'" (2008, 21). In fact, on a global level journalists are more likely to be murdered than to die in war (Simon 2007). More than a year after Saipov's murder, Radio Free Europe/ Radio Liberty's Uzbek service still was unable to find a freelance correspondent to replace him in Osh (Imamova, Freedman, and Shafer 2008). In 2008, the European Union and Uzbekistani government sponsored a conference in Tashkent on mass media liberalization. Foreign speakers asked their audience about the lack of news coverage of President Islam Karimov's abuse of power, the use of child labor to pick cotton, and the repression of fellow journalists. One young reporter quietly approached a speaker from the International Crisis Group, a Western NGO, to respond: "I must tell you the reason why they don't report these things. They cannot because they are scared of losing their jobs and what the National Security Service might do" (Stroehlein 2008).

Even for journalists who are not killed, the profession can be high-risk and high-stress, yet most receive little or no training or other preparation for its potential adverse effects on their mental health and emotional well-being. There is a growing body of research into the trauma journalists may suffer as a result of covering war, tragedy, disasters, and other violence or depredations.

For example, the nonprofit Dart Center for Journalism and Trauma operates internationally, conducting research into and training on such psychological and emotional impacts (Hight and Smyth 2003). Its work involves not only journalists but also health professionals and journalism educators, with the goal of "improving media coverage of trauma, conflict, and tragedy. The Center also addresses the consequences of such coverage for those working in journalism" (2008). Feinstein characterizes war correspondents as engaged in a "hazardous profession" (2006, 1) and details the psychological hazards of covering war, including domestic terrorism such as the 11 September 2001 attacks on the World Trade Center and Pentagon.

In June 2010, the president of Journalists in Danger, a press rights advocacy group based in Almaty, interviewed imprisoned Kazakh editor Ramazan Yesergepov. Yesergepov was serving a three-year sentence after he was convicted and his newspaper was closed for printing internal security service agency memoranda about the agency's efforts to influence a prosecutor and criminal court judge. In the interview, he described his treatment behind bars:

> As for my health, I try to keep myself in good shape. Of course, the conditions I was subjected to when I was held in pre-trial detention . . . for more than 11 months were torturous: I was sent tuberculosis patients as cell mates; I was denied medical help even when my blood pressure had hit critical readings. These conditions took a toll on my health but I became stronger in spirit.
>
> Here in the prison colony the conditions are better, but even here the medical facilities lack equipment, specialists, and medicine. (Ognianova 2010)

The psychological and emotional pressures journalists confront under repressitarian regimes such as those of Central Asia have been less studied. Journalists in the region pay what Lupis (2005a, 2005b) calls a "psychological cost . . . for practicing their profession," a cost measured in emotional stress, trauma, and a feeling of isolation, coupled with a lack of support that drives some of them to abandon their careers, some to yield to such pressures—even if it requires acting unprofessionally—and some to flee their homelands. He quotes an unnamed investigative journalist from Uzbekistan who described the atmosphere under which reporters work in that country:

> This threat does not have a precise face. It's around you but you cannot physically sense it . . . This threat is very silent. And it breaks you down slowly and heavily. And it has a habit to appear in an environment which looks peacefully. That's why

you may not see this threat from the very beginning. This threat can follow you for years but you can't see the borders of danger. You may realize the danger just after the border has passed. But even then, when you realize the threat, you are not able to ask relevant authorities to give you protection. Such a request may even increase the threat. (Lupis 2005b)

Research Question and Methodology

A number of human rights and press defender organizations, some based in Central Asia but most headquartered elsewhere, monitor media freedom conditions in the region. They include the Committee to Protect Journalists (United States); Reporters sans Frontieres (France); Freedom House (United States); Institute for War and Peace Reporting (United Kingdom); Human Rights Watch (United States); Amnesty International (United Kingdom); Center for Journalism in Extreme Situations (Russian Federation); International Research and Exchanges Board (United States); Adil Soz (International Foundation for Protection of Freedom of Speech) (Kazakhstan); Public Association "Journalists" (Kyrgyzstan); International Freedom of Expression eXchange (Canada); International Press Institute (Austria); International Helsinki Federation for Human Rights (Austria); Article 19 (United Kingdom); and International Center for Journalists (United States). There is also monitoring by foreign governmental and multinational agencies, including the U.S. State Department and the Organization for Cooperation and Security in Europe (OSCE) Representative on Freedom of the Media.

To better illuminate and humanize the dangers of working in such an environment, this chapter relates a series of accounts of the impact of press repression as told by Central Asian journalists and their press rights defenders. By focusing on individuals in serious, even fatal, peril, this chapter attempts to impart a better understanding of how governments in the region constrain the press and the broad impact of such constraints on print, broadcast, and Internet professionals. The intent is to flesh out statistical data and formal pronouncements about events such as arrests and prosecutions, libel suits, broadcast license delays, and registration denials, thus advancing public understanding of that media environment from the abstract to the concrete. As exemplars, the chapter draws from interviews, reports, and statements from journalists and entities that fight for their rights and advocate on their behalf.

Therefore the chapter poses this research question: how do journalists and their defenders describe the media environment in Central Asia that endangers journalists, thus personalizing press constraints in the region? The findings are drawn from advocacy organizations and first-person accounts by journalists of their experiences.

In the Words of Journalists

In recounting her nearly fatal experience while covering the brutal military suppression of public protests in Andijan, Uzbekistan, in May 2005, journalist Galima Bukharbaeva (2005) recalls:

> It was only after I had stopped running that I realized I could have been one of the men, women, and children falling around me. I reached for my backpack to take out my notebook only to find that a bullet from an AK-47 rifle had torn through it, punching a neat hole in the face of Che Guevara on the cover. My press card from the Institute for War & Peace Reporting was also shot through . . .
>
> Neither I nor the other five reporters and one photographer in Andijan that day could stay to count the casualties. Like many others much worse off than me, I became a refugee. The prosecutor in Tashkent has opened a case against me for working as a journalist without proper accreditation. It would be dangerous for me to return while the present government is in power. The authorities will want revenge for my reporting and testimony to the U.S. Congress about the Andijan killings.

Bukharbaeva was not the only reporter who fled Uzbekistan after the Andijan massacre. There was what Volosevich (2006) characterizes as "a journalistic exodus" of professionals who worked for independent and foreign news organizations. Some ended up in Europe, including five in Sweden. He quotes one of these self-exiles as saying, "We belong there, in Uzbekistan," and further writes:

> There is more to life than material well-being. They find life in Sweden boring. These men find problems of their native country interesting but that is not something they can discuss with the Swedes, particularly since they do not speak the Swedish language. They long for communications and the feeling that they are doing something worthwhile. Free journalism in Uzbekistan is something dangerous and thrilling. These men are like deep-water fish brought to the surface. No pressure, no struggle they are used to—and life becomes boring (2006).

The physical departure from one's homeland is not an escape from such trauma. Those who flee Central Asia, usually to the Russian Federation or the West, are burdened with severe emotional challenges once they arrive "in a strange country with a strange language and they are without friends or family and do not know if they will be granted political asylum or when they may be reunited with their families" (Lupis 2005b). To assist with the immediate problems of such transitions, the advocacy group Reporters sans Frontieres provides financial aid to threatened journalists forced into exile, offering assistance from the time they leave their home countries until they secure national or international protection elsewhere.

Shortly upon his release after four years in prison in Uzbekistan for broadcasting a radio show that satirized local officials in Samarkand, journalist Shadi Mardiev spoke at a World Press Freedom Day event in Tashkent hosted by the media-development NGO Internews. His remarks reflected a psychological dilemma among some journalists in post-Soviet Central Asia, a dilemma that pits a commitment to independent reporting and commentary against a patriotic commitment to their relatively new nations.

Mardiev told the audience, "All my life I worked for my country. I'm so sorry my country abandoned their son and a reporter." He distinguished between the autocratic president, whom he insisted was doing his best to build Uzbekistan, and other officials who thwart Karimov's policies. "Journalists are doing their best to go in line with the president's programs," he continued. "I'm so surprised that some authorities try to twist the president's policies and put slander on journalists. I was the victim of such a slander." At the end of his remarks, he read a poem written in prison, "What Can I Do?" that included these two sentences: "My youth was lived in a hurricane. My pencil was my everlasting friend" (Freedman 2002).

Accounts of Individual Journalists under Fire

This section of the chapter focuses on the experiences of several journalists as described by international press rights groups.

KAZAKHSTAN: ORALGAISHA OMARSHANOVA, DISAPPEARED ON 30 MARCH 2007

The Committee to Protect Journalists is deeply worried about the fate of investigative reporter Oralgaisha Omarshanova who has been missing since March 30. Colleagues believe Omarshanova's disappearance is related to her journalism for the Astana-based independent weekly *Zakon i Pravosudiye* (Law and Justice), whose anti-corruption department she directed, local press reports said . . .

At the time of her disappearance, Omarshanova, 39, who uses the pen name Oralgaisha Zhabagtaikyzy, was in Kazakhstan's financial capital, Almaty, on a business trip with several colleagues. The colleagues said they last saw Omarshanova on the afternoon of March 30 getting into a jeep, the Moscow-based news agency Regnum reported.

Four days before her disappearance, Omarshanova had published an article in *Zakon i Pravosudiye* about ethnic clashes between rival Chechen and Kazakh residents in the Almaty region villages of Kazatkom and Malovodnoye. The clashes, which took place on March 17 and 18 claimed at least five lives, according to local and international press reports. In her report, Omarshanova identified the instigators of the unrest and mentioned their alleged connection to the government and local businesses, the Almaty-based press freedom group Adil Soz reported.

In February, the paper published Omarshanova's investigative report, which exposed the dangerous working conditions of miners in the central city of Zhezkagan, according to international press reports.

At a press conference in Almaty on Wednesday, the journalist's brother, Zhanat Omarshanov, told reporters that in the weeks prior to her disappearance Omarshanova had received several death threats by telephone, warning her to stop her reporting, Regnum reported.

During the press conference, *Zakon i Pravosudiye* reporter Mukhit Iskakov said Omarshanova told him she had purchased a rifle to defend herself after receiving the threats, the U.S.-funded Radio Free Europe/Radio Liberty reported. The broadcaster said police are investigating the disappearance but do not have any information regarding her whereabouts. (Committee to Protect Journalists 2007)

KYRGYZSTAN: ALISHER SAIPOV, MURDERED ON 24 OCTOBER 2007

Alisher Saipov, an independent journalist whose reporting criticized human rights abuses in Kyrgyzstan and neighboring Uzbekistan, was shot to death on October 24 in the southern Kyrgyz city of Osh, Human Rights Watch said . . . The Kyrgyz government must ensure a through and impartial investigation into his murder and bring the perpetrators to justice.

On the evening of October 24, the 26-year-old Kyrgyz journalist and a friend were walking not far from the Radio Free Europe/Radio Liberty bureau when an unidentified gunman approached him, shot Saipov once in the leg and twice in the head, killing him, according to reports by local media.

"Saipov's murder is a brutal crime that smacks of retribution for his work," said Holly Cartner, Europe and Central Asia director at Human Rights Watch. "He was a courageous journalist committed to exposing human rights abuses, particularly by the Uzbek government. We extend our heartfelt condolences to his family, friends and colleagues."

Saipov was a regular contributor to news agencies such as Ferghana.ru, Voice of America, and RFE/RL. In May, Saipov began regularly publishing a weekly Uzbek language newspaper *Siosat* [Politics], devoted to covering politics, human rights, and religious persecution in both Kyrgyzstan and Uzbekistan. Saipov distributed *Siosat* widely in southern Kyrgyzstan, where a large number of ethnic Uzbeks live and regularly travel across the Kyrgyz-Uzbek border.

Saipov was one of Central Asia's most outspoken and active critics of the Uzbek government. He was instrumental in reporting about the immediate aftermath of the 2005 uprising and massacre in the Uzbek city of Andijan. Saipov reported on the harassment of Uzbek refugees and asylum seekers, including those who fled Andijan, by Uzbek security agents in southern Kyrgyzstan. In addition, he advocated on their behalf with human rights organizations and other groups.

Over the last few months, articles disparaging Saipov have been published in pro-government news agencies in Uzbekistan. Last month an article in Press-uz. info called Saipov a "traitor's knife in the back of Uzbekistan." It also claimed that he supported religious extremism and terrorism.

Saipov publicly criticized the Kyrgyz government for allowing the Uzbek National Security Service (SNB) to operate freely in Osh to search for Uzbek refugees and asylum-seekers and return them to Uzbekistan. The Kyrgyz government has denied these allegations . . .

"The Kyrgyz government should show its commitment to freedom of speech and rule of law by not tolerating crimes like Saipov's murder," said Cartner.

Kyrgyz President Kurmanbek Bakiev said this morning that he has taken the investigation into Saipov's murder under his personal control.

Saipov faced threats and attacks in the past. In June 2006, he was badly beaten several weeks after publishing an article in which he linked organized crime to politics in his native city of Osh. He was hospitalized for his injuries, which included a broken cheekbone. Saipov told a friend he did not know who was responsible for the attack.

Saipov was also under the scrutiny of Kyrgyz security services. On several occasions, most recently in summer 2007, Kyrgyz security agents questioned Saipov about his work on undocumented migrants. They also inspected his office.

Saipov is survived by his wife and 3-month old daughter. (Human Rights Watch 2007)

The Committee to Protect Journalists is concerned about the Kyrgyzstan authorities' closure of the investigation into the October murder of Alisher Saipov, editor of the independent Uzbek-language weekly *Siyosat* (Politics). This is the second time authorities have officially closed the investigation in as many months.

The Saipov family told CPJ that the local bureau of the Kyrgyz Interior Ministry's Investigative Committee informed them on March 31 that the investigation into their son's murder had been stopped due to "the inability to identify a suspect." The family happened to learn about the closure of the case when they went to the police to inquire about the status of Saipov's seized laptop. Authorities handed them a document dated March 31 that informed them about the end to the case.

Kyrgyz police had opened a murder probe immediately after the killing, and President Kurmanbek Bakiyev had personally pledged his commitment to solving the case . . .

But despite a promising start, there has been no progress in the investigation, and authorities have given confusing information on the case's status. In late January, the Saipovs told CPJ that local police had informed them the probe had been shut down because the allotted one-month investigative period had expired. The Saipovs received an official notice the same day the deadline for appealing the cessation ended.

Shortly after, a police spokesman and the interior minister offered conflicting explanations. On February 4, Kyrgyz Interior Ministry press officer Olzhobai Kazabayev told RFE/RL that the investigation into Saipov's killing had been halted "because the two suspected individuals had not been captured" and no other evidence had emerged. A week later, the newly appointed Interior Minister Moldomusa Kongantiyev gave a different explanation at a local press conference, and told journalists he would be assuming supervision of the newly reopened Saipov case. (Committee to Protect Journalists 2008a)

TURKMENISTAN: SAZAK DURDYMURADOV, ARRESTED 24 JUNE 2008, AND TORTURED

Radio Free Europe contributor Sazak Durdymuradov has been released from the psychiatric hospital to which he was confined against his will after being arrested by secret police on 20 June and tortured.

"We are relieved to learn that Durdymuradov is back at home with his family, which means the mistreatment to which he was being subjected has ended," Reporters Without Borders said. "It is time the authorities realised that the use of such barbaric methods is completely unacceptable and should be abandoned at once."

A history teacher who has been contributing to RFE [Radio Free Europe/Radio Liberty] for several months, Durdymuradov was able to return to his home in Baharden (200 km west of the capital) on 4 July, two weeks after he was arrested there by members of the MNB secret police. His return was confirmed by his family, who thanked all those who spoke out on his behalf.

Durdymuradov was tortured. He was badly beaten and was given electric shocks in an attempt to make him sign a pledge to stop working for RFE. He was then taken to Boinuzin, a psychiatric hospital 700 km east of Ashgabad where dissidents are imprisoned. Former Boinuzin inmates have called it the "Turkmen gulag" and "hell on earth."

Durdymuradov's arrest took place as a European Union delegation and the Turkmen government were holding talks in Ashgabad about human rights. Recent weeks have seen an increase in government harassment of its critics and independent journalists. (Reporters sans Frontieres, 2008).

UZBEKISTAN: SOLIDZHON ABDURAKHMONOV, SENTENCED TO PRISON FOR TEN YEARS, 10 OCTOBER 2008

The Committee to Protect Journalists condemns today's politicized imprisonment of independent journalist Salidzhon Abdurakhmanov and calls for his immediate and unconditional release. A district court in Uzbekistan's autonomous republic of Karakalpakstan gave Abdurakhmanov a 10-year term on fabricated charges of drug possession with intent to sell, according to local news reports and CPJ sources.

Prosecutors had requested a 17-year prison sentence, Rustam Tulyaganov, Abdurakhmanov's defense lawyer, told CPJ. Tulyaganov said he will appeal the verdict in a higher court . . .

Abdurakhmanov, 58, covered economic, human rights, and social issues for the independent news Web site Uznews, and in the past contributed reporting for the U.S.-government funded Radio Free Europe/Radio Liberty (RFE/RL), and the London-based Institute for War and Peace Reporting. On Thursday, CPJ called on Nukus District Court Judge Kadyrbay Dzhamolov, who began hearings in Abdurakhmanov's case last month, to drop the bogus charges [sic] drug charges and acquit the journalist.

Authorities in Nukus arrested Abdurakhmanov on June 7 after traffic police who stopped his car for an ID check claimed to find 4 ounces (114 grams) of marijuana and less than a quarter ounce (5 grams) of opium in his trunk, Uznews reported. Authorities charged the journalist with possession of drugs intended for personal use. Abdurakhmanov protested, saying police had planted the drugs as a means to silence his critical reporting—in one of his last pieces for Uznews the journalist covered corruption in traffic police. In August, investigators acknowledged that the journalist's blood tests found no traces of drugs. They then increased the charge to drug possession with the intent to sell, according to Uznews . . . (Committee to Protect Journalists 2008b).

Conclusions and Implications

As Galima Bukharbaeva's experience in covering the Andijan massacre makes clear, journalists in Central Asia may be subject not only to the trauma of covering danger-filled events but also to longer-term psychological ramifications caused by the pressure of operating under authoritarian regimes. In her own situation, she recalls:

> After slipping out of Uzbekistan, I went with my colleagues to a refugee camp in neighboring Kyrgyzstan to which some 500 Andijan residents had fled. Many of them recognized us from Bobur Square and began weeping and shouting: "They're alive."
>
> A beautiful young girl, Nailya, turned to me with tear-filled eyes and asked: "Do you think we will ever go back home?"
>
> I held her gaze and said: "Of course, we will go back." But I could not say when (2005).

If one principal role of journalism in repressive and post-repressive societies is to build public support for transparent, honest, participatory institutions—especially governmental institutions—individual journalists and their mass media outlets must be free to report on public affairs and controversial issues in a fair, accurate, balanced, ethical, and professional way. As the then-director-general of UNESCO observes: "Every aggression against a journalist is an attack on our most fundamental freedoms. Press freedom and freedom of expression cannot be enjoyed without basic security" (Matsuura 2007, 4). Thus, when freedom of the press is denied in Central Asia, the public should understand that the denial is not merely an abstract theoretical action or policy by governmental or extra-governmental forces. Indeed, the public should know there are individuals who are directly hurt by those restraints as they struggle to carry out their professional responsibilities.

In his book about freedom of speech and of the press in Uzbekistan, the founder of the now-defunct independent newspaper *Hurriyat* explores how censorship, self-censorship, unethical practices, lack of professional and economic resources, and restraints on the media impair both democracy and development. Karim Bakhriev warns that under any authoritarian regime, "face to face, mass media to power is like a lamb before a wolf" (2003, 37). That wolf, hungry to retain power, will do all it can to scare any journalists who might challenge it. And that wolf will attempt to devour those journalists who actually dare challenge its hold on power.

One of the continuing challenges confronting media rights advocates is how to keep the issue of press constraints both fresh and prominent for multiple publics: ordinary citizens and decision makers inside and outside the affected countries, multinational agencies, and foreign NGOs involved in civil society development and democracy building. Official reports are one such method of meeting that challenge, but it is perhaps more effective to disseminate personalized accounts of journalists at risk. A second benefit of publicizing the plight of individual journalists is the possibility it may put pressure on government entities to release imprisoned journalists, punish attackers, rein in abusive officials, or take other measures to ameliorate repressive conditions. In addition, more research is needed into the psychological trauma undergone by journalists under repressive authoritarian regimes such as those of Central Asia. Thus drawing attention to the plight of individuals also draws attention to the need to deepen public and professional understanding of the emotional trauma they undergo and to the importance of providing supportive mental health and counseling services to them.

REFERENCES

Allison, Olivia. 2006. "Selective Enforcement and Irresponsibility: Central Asia's Shrinking Space for Independent Media." *Central Asian Survey* 25(1–2): 93–114.

Bakhriev, Karim. 2003. *A Speech on Freedom of Speech*. Moscow: R. Elinin Publishing House.

Bukharbaeva, Galima. 2005. "Witness to a Massacre." *Dangerous Assignments*. Www.cpj.org/ Briefings/2005/DA_fa1105/galima/galima_DA_fa1105.html.

Committee to Protect Journalists. 2007. "In Kazakhstan, Reporter Disappears after Writing Critical Articles." News Alert. 18 April. Http://cpj.org/news/2007/europe/

kazakh19apro7na.html.

———. 2008a. "Kyrgyzstan: Saipov's Murder Investigation Shut Down Again." Statement. 10 April. Http://cpj.org/news/2008/europe/kyrgyz10apro8na.html.

———. 2008b. "Uzbek Journalist Slammed with 10-Year Prison Term." Statement. 10 October. Http://cpj.org/news/2008/europe/uzbek10octo8na.html.

Eurasianet.org. 2006. "Turkmenistan Takes Terror to New Level." 14 September. Www.eurasianet.org/departments/civilsociety/articles/eav091406a.shtml.

Feinstein, Anthony. 2006. *Journalists under Fire: The Psychological Hazards of Covering War.* Baltimore: Johns Hopkins University Press.

Freedman, Eric, and Richard Shafer. 2003a. "How Media Censorship and Enduring Soviet Press Practices Obstruct Nation-Building in Central Asia." *Journal of Development Communication.*14(2): 57–72.

———. 2003b. "Policing Press Freedom in Post-Soviet Central Asia: The Monitoring Role of Press Rights Activists and Their Web Sites." Paper presented to Association for Education in Journalism and Mass Communication, Kansas City, Mo.

Freedman, Eric. 2002. "Fulbright Scholar Stories." Council for International Exchange of Scholars. Www.cies.org/stories/s_efreedman7.htm.

Hight, Joe, and Frank Smyth. 2003. *Tragedies and Journalists: A Guide for More Effective Coverage.* Seattle: Dart Center for Journalism and Trauma.

Human Rights Watch. 2007. "Kyrgyzstan: Ensure Justice for Murdered Journalist." Statement. 25 October.Http://hrw.org/english/docs/2007/10/25/kyrgyz17171.htm.

Imamova, Navbahor, Freedman, Eric, and Shafer, Richard. 2008. "The Voice of America's Uzbek Service: Political Outreach, Visions of America, or Public Diplomacy?" Paper presented to the Central Eurasian Studies Society, Washington, D.C.

Lupis, Alex. 2005a. "Stress, Anxiety and Trauma Amidst Post-Soviet Repression in Central Asia: Psychological Aspects of Journalism and Human Rights Activism." Paper presented to the Association for the Study of Nationalities, New York.

———. 2005b. "State Repression of the Media in Central Asia: Reflecting on Trauma, Recovery, and NGO Assistance for Journalists." Paper presented to the Central Eurasian Studies Society, Boston.

Matsuura, Koichiro. 2007. "The Safety of Journalists Is an Issue that Affects Us All." In *Press Freedom: Safety of Journalists and Impunity.* United Nations Education, Scientific, and Cultural Organization: 4.

Ognianova, Nina. 2010. "Denied Access, CPJ Manages to Interview Kazakh Prisoner." 21 June. Http://cpj.org/blog/2010/06/denied-access-cpj-manages-to-interview-kazakh-pris.php.

Radio Free Europe/Radio Liberty. 2009. "Kyrgyz Regional Officials Requiring Journalists to File Personal Information," 22 January.

Reporters sans Frontieres. 2008. "RFE Contributor Freed from Notorious Psychiatric Hospital after Being Held for Two Weeks," 26 June.

Simon, Joel. 2007. "Study Shows Journalists Are More Likely to Be Murdered than Killed in War." In *Press Freedom: Safety of Journalists and Impunity.* United Nations Education, Scientific, and Cultural Organization, 72–74.

Stern, David L. 2008. "Inconvenient Truths." *Index on Censorship* 37(1): 16–21.

Stroehlein, Andrew. 2008. "Eyewitness to Absurdity." *Transitions Online,* 16 October.

Volosevich, Aleksey. 2006. "Journalists from Uzbekistan Settle in Sweden and Even Organize Protest Actions." Ferghana.ru. 19 July. Http://enews.ferghana.ru/article.php?id=1515.

Walker, Christopher. 2007. "Muzzling the Media: The Return of Censorship in the Commonwealth of Independent States." Special report. Freedom House. Http://freedomhouse.org/uploads/special_report/54.pdf.

International Broadcasting to Uzbekistan: Does It Still Matter?

Navbahor Imamova

The twentieth century gave the world its first true mass medium. And within a few years of its birth, radio had emerged as a weapon that both powerful and weak governments could use to spread their national ideologies, promote their geopolitical objectives, improve their political and cultural image, gain social influence, and in some cases, cast light into the darkness for those deprived of freedom of speech and expression.

Some governments have traditionally used international broadcasting to persuade foreign audiences of the superiority of their system. The Soviets, for example, maintained a global network to spread the seeds of communism. The United States established the Voice of America (VOA) to convey American perspectives on international affairs and familiarize foreign audiences with its political system and culture (Camaj 2008; Puddington 2000; Heil 2003).. At the same time, post–World War II international broadcasters such as VOA and British Broadcasting Corporation (BBC) encountered what Cull describes as "large-scale Soviet jamming,.. Moscow now regarded Western broadcasting as such a threat that it was prepared to devote millions of rubles to operating powerful transmitters for the sole purpose of broadcasting noise on Western frequencies." In response, those two broadcasters "cooperated to confound the jammers" (2008, 49).

Navbahor Imamova's writing is based on her own study and observations as a media researcher and does not reflect the views of the Voice of America.

The governments in Central Asia—turbulent, oppressed, and in a geopolitically strategic region—have always detested foreign broadcasts such as those from VOA in Washington, Radio Free Europe/Radio Liberty (RFE/RL) in Prague, and the BBC in London, by jamming the airwaves, blocking their Web sites, and harassing local journalists who work for them. While these broadcasters claim to carry the light of truth by delivering news that is unavailable locally, authorities regard them as sources of propaganda and agitation, carriers of banned opposition views, a boundless stage for civil society groups to criticize the ruling regimes, and threats to local culture and values.

The Cold War was the catalyst for international broadcasting to the region when the U.S. government started its Uzbek-language radio programming in the mid-1950s. That initial foray did not last long, however, and ended within a few months. Its reestablishment marked a recognition of the country's strategic importance. This chapter looks at how the audience in Uzbekistan, the most populous country in the region, perceives these services and what the content of these programs is.

Statement of the Problem

Western international broadcasters have always struggled to maintain their audiences in Uzbekistan, one of the former republics of the Soviet Union. Ratings show that the overall average annual reach is less than 4 percent. Meanwhile, even with tight government control, the local media market in Uzbekistan is growing. By 2005 there were at least eight FM stations with varying degrees of popularity in the country. They mostly offer entertainment and generally have stronger broadcast signals than international broadcasters. International broadcasters are on shortwave and are jammed, and they also suffer from limited funding and staff. Their competitive edge is their content—critical analysis of current policies and a window to the outside world (Heil 2005). But how effective and valuable are these programs? What do young Uzbeks, who make up the majority of the population, think about these programs from abroad? This qualitative review draws from the diverse insights of listeners, experts, former government officials, and broadcasters, as well as an analysis of available data. The author conducted an e-mail survey and monitored one week's worth of programming. This chapter also provides background information about each broadcaster and its funding.

Findings

The Broadcasting Board of Governors (BBG), an independent entity since October 1999, is in charge of all U.S.- government-sponsored, nonmilitary, international broadcasting stations. Today it operates the following stations: Alhurra (TV); Radio Sawa, Radio Farda (Persian); Radio Free Asia (RFA); Radio and TV Martí; RFE/RL; and VOA. The International Broadcasting Bureau (IBB) provides engineering support for all of these services. Under the 1998 Foreign Affairs Reform and Restructuring Act (Public Law 105-277), the U.S. Congress appropriates funds for these stations as part of its regular yearly deliberations on the federal budget (Board of Broadcasting Governors 2010).

VOICE OF AMERICA

VOA, founded in 1942, delivers radio, television, and Internet content in forty-five languages. It broadcasts more than one thousand hours of news, information, educational, and cultural programming every week to an estimated worldwide audience of more than 100 million. It operates under a charter enacted in 1976, and its code explicitly states that reporters and broadcasters "must strive for accuracy and objectivity in all their work. They do not speak for the U.S. government . . . VOA professionals strive for excellence and avoid imbalance or bias in their broadcasts . . . VOA is alert to, and rejects, efforts by special interest groups, foreign or domestic, to use its broadcasts as a platform for their own views" (BBG 2010).

Uzbek, the third-most-spoken indigenous tongue in the former Soviet Union, is the only Central Asian language that VOA has ever broadcast in. According to Alan Heil, former deputy director of VOA, "[P]art of the reasoning at the time was that Radio Liberty already was broadcasting in Kazakh, Tajik, Kyrgyz, and Turkmen, so Central Asia was pretty well covered by U.S. international broadcasters." VOA aired its first Uzbek-language broadcasts in February 1956. There is conflicting information about how long this programming lasted before it was closed because of lack of resources (Nasar 2005). VOA Uzbek resumed in 1973 with two subsequent closures, first in the summer of 2001 and then in the summer of 2004. Since the mid-1980s, VOA Uzbek's daily broadcasts have gradually declined from two hours to the present thirty-minute show. The service has provided TV programming to regional affiliates since 2003. The two other principal Western, Uzbek-language international broadcasters are RFE/RL and BBC.

In the summer of 2001, programming was cut from one hour to a half hour and then to only fifteen minutes a day. The events on 11 September 2001 changed that. With the United States preparing to invade Taliban-ruled Afghanistan, most of the previous staff was recalled, and by early 2002 the service broadcast one hour daily. Although listenership numbers remained low and discouraging, VOA Uzbek tried to diversify its programming content, which was mostly centered on human rights and political opposition-type stories. Added to the programming mix were more call-in shows, discussions of the political scene in Uzbekistan, and stories by stringers covering corruption in education and the health care system and internal affairs.

One highlight was an August 2003 investigative series about an ongoing international scandal that involved Gulnora Karimova, President Islam Karimov's daughter, and her former husband, Mansur Maqsudi; their children; and his family's businesses in Uzbekistan, which were then under investigation by the government. Karimov's regime accused the Maqsudis of fraud, tax evasion, and money laundering while the Maqsudis accused the president's family and the Karimov government of corruption and revenge for the divorce of the first daughter of Uzbekistan. VOA Uzbek produced a series of stories that included interviews with the Maqsudi family and Farhod Inagambaev, Gulnora Karimova's former financial advisor. Despite numerous requests, Karimova and Uzbek authorities declined to comment on the issue.

The Uzbek service currently broadcasts a total of three and a half hours on radio and *Exploring America*, a thirty-minute weekly TV program. Radio shows are carried on short wave (SW) and medium wave (MW) in Uzbekistan. Keremet TV, a station based in southern Kyrgyzstan, carries *Exploring America*.

As of 2009 the service maintained reporters in Tashkent, Uzbekistan, and Khojand, Tajikistan. Until October 2007, VOA Uzbek heavily relied on its reporter in Osh, Alisher Saipov, an independent journalist who also founded an Uzbek-language newspaper, ran a media group, and was known for articles criticizing the region's authoritarian governments. Saipov was gunned down by unknown men in front of his office, provoking a sharp response from press rights advocates (Human Rights Watch 2007). The investigation into his assassination produced no arrests, but some evidence points to responsibility of Uzbekistan's secret service. In the midst of growing attacks and harassment of journalists, VOA Uzbek was unable to recruit another reporter in Osh.

In December 2003, VOA initiated the first and, so far, only international television programming in Uzbek. The project began when four local stations agreed to broadcast its daily and weekly programs. Under the agreement, VOA provided them with satellite dishes and other equipment for downloading the broadcast feed. By early 2004 the number of affiliates in Uzbekistan had reached fifteen, including Samarkand TV in Samarkand; Aloqa TV in Gulistan; Bakhtiyor TV in Jizzakh; Koinot TV in Bukhara; Margilan TV in Margilan; Turtkul TV in Karakalpakstan; and Channel 30 in Tashkent.

A December 2003 VOA press release quoted President Karimov as telling the chair of the U.S. Senate Foreign Relations Committee that his people wanted more news and information about America and the West. Then-director David Jackson said in the same release that VOA Uzbek television feeds and radio broadcasts would carry democratic values to the region. "They will reach a broader audience than any other means available to the U.S. government" (Voice of America 2003).

In the summer of 2004, BBG decided to drop the radio broadcasts and focus more on TV production and online content. At the time, VOA Uzbek had six full-time broadcasters and one contractor in Washington, and it maintained six stringers—five in Uzbekistan; one in Osh, Kyrgyzstan; and one in Khojand, Tajikistan. BBG made it clear that it did not want duplicate services since RFE/RL also carried Uzbek-language radio broadcasts. "While VOA has moved to broadcasting in Uzbek on television," said Brian Mabry, a senior advisor with IBB, "its sister broadcaster Radio Free Europe/Radio Liberty continues to reach Uzbekistan, broadcasting by short wave and medium wave radio. RFE/RL broadcasts seven hours of Uzbek-language radio daily" (Institute for War and Peace Reporting 2004). At the time, InterMedia said that VOA had the least number of weekly listeners compared to RFE/RL's 2.4 percent and BBC's 2.3 weekly audience.

The London-based Institute for War and Peace Reporting (IWPR) wrote that the decision of the United States broadcaster to stop beaming radio programs to Uzbekistan had been met with an equal measure of bewilderment and disappointment by its loyal audience. It reported that the closure came at a time of renewed unrest. "The last broadcast went out on the evening of July 31, 2004—the day after suicide bombers attacked the U.S. and Israeli embassies and the Uzbek prosecutor's office in the capital Tashkent," the IWPR article (2004) stated.

Some listeners complained that TV programming about America would not be an adequate substitute for the radio shows' treatment of "unreported issues" inside the country. Amnesty International, Human Rights Watch, and other nongovernmental groups denounced the closure and said the people of Uzbekistan had lost a good source of information. Yuldoshboy Ubaidullaev, a listener from Andijan, told IWPR that "those who closed the Uzbek service of VOA wanted to hide the truth from us . . . I used to tell friends and family in my village about what I'd heard on Voice of America." Martha Brill Olcott of the

Carnegie Foundation for International Peace was also critical of VOA's decision: "It is a demonstration of the confusion that prevails in the [George W.] Bush administration that the U.S. closes down the VOA Uzbek service at the very time that the U.S. Department of State is cutting funds to Uzbekistan because of what it deemed lack of sufficient progress in the area of human rights and in adherence to democratic goals" (IWPR 2004).

With the emergence of television came the problem of how to market it in the region. During the first year of working with local TV stations, VOA Uzbek greatly benefited from cooperation with the country office of Internews Network, a U.S.-based NGO engaged in local media development; the arrangement provided a networking opportunity for VOA and regional broadcasters that seemed interested in airing VOA feeds. But by the end of 2004, the situation had worsened for independent media. Internews was losing its battle with the Uzbek government over trumped-up charges that it had violated the laws governing NGOs.

By then a new association of local broadcasters had emerged. Behind it was Firdavs Abduhaliqov, a former member of the presidential press office and a media owner who had launched Samarkand TV in the mid-1990s and Poytaxt-Inform Radio in Tashkent in the early 2000s. The National Association of Electronic Mass Media of Uzbekistan (NAEMMU), which calls itself a professional union, was formed in 2004 to create a "civilized market for electronic media that provides equal conditions for all broadcasters and their active participation in building civil society" (NAEMMU 2005). Within a year, thirteen stations became members, most of them former Internews partners that had benefited from the NGO's capacity-building activities.

But independent-minded local broadcasters and the international community regarded NAEMMU and its TV network—which sought to control the source of programming for all member stations—as a serious threat to independent electronic media, specifically television. According to Internews, the association's true purpose was to influence broadcasters without overt government control. A special NAEMMU committee determined which programs would be broadcast based on conformity with national and cultural ideologies. Censorship had been officially banned in May 2002, but attempts to control the media continued, and local journalists restrained themselves from covering government-sensitive issues (Shafer and Freedman 2003). In late 2004 and early 2005, four regional TV stations, most of them VOA affiliates, including a local station in Chirchik, found their licenses suspended because, as their owners said, they refused to join the association for fear of losing credibility with their audiences. An assessment of previous and current actions by NAEMMU shows that the organization wants to

TABLE 1. RFE/RL BROADCASTING TO CENTRAL ASIA IN 2005

LANGUAGES	DAILY	FREQUENCY	AFFILIATES	STAFF	STRINGERS	BUREAU	WEB SITE
Kazakh	8 hours	SW, MW, USW, satellite	1	9	29 Kazakhstan 1 Uzbekistan 1 Turkey 1 Egypt	Almaty, Astana	www.azattyq.org
Kyrgyz	5 hours	SW, FM, USW, MW, satellite	3	9	50 Kyrgyzstan 2 Turkey 2 Russia 1 Uzbekistan 1 United States	Bishkek	www.azattyk.kg, www.azattyk.org
Tajik	6 hours	SW, satellite	0	10	18	Dushanbe	www.ozodi.org
Turkmen	6 hours	SW, MW, satellite	0	8	40	None	None (access blocked)
Uzbek	6 hours	SW, MW, satellite	0	9	14 Uzbekistan 1 Russia 2 Tajikistan 1 Turkey 2 Afghanistan 1 Kyrgyzstan 1 United Kingdom	Tashkent	www.ozodlik.org

SOURCE: Radio Free Europe/Radio Liberty 2005.

be the main arbiter and distributor of all content that is seen on local television and to be the sole administrator of all relationships between local broadcasters and international organizations such as VOA and other stations critical of the government.

Another reason to seriously worry about VOA's future in the country was the escalating crackdown on international media, especially after government forces violently suppressed an uprising in Andijan in May 2005. With local media remaining totally subservient to the government and the situation in Uzbekistan volatile, U.S.-based groups, including the United States Commission on International Religious Freedom, called for reinstatement of VOA Uzbek radio broadcasts. Although only cross-border broadcasting appeared viable, VOA resumed daily SW and MW broadcasts on June 12, 2005, airing on prime time in Uzbekistan and Kyrgyzstan.

RADIO FREE EUROPE/RADIO LIBERTY

With its mission "to promote democratic values and institutions by disseminating factual information and ideas" RFE/RL is congressionally funded as a private, nongovernment grantee (2010). Under IRS rules, it is a private, nonprofit Sec. 501(c) 3 corporation. Its programs are broadcast in twenty-seven languages, including all the national languages in Central Asia (see table 1), and its main mission is to promote democratic values and institutions by disseminating factual information and ideas to a large part of Eurasia.

RFE/RL has twenty-three bureaus throughout Europe and the former Soviet Union and more than fourteen hundred freelancers. The station airs nearly one thousand hours of programming a week from its broadcast center in Prague (RFE/RL 2010).

RFE/RL's Kazakh, Kyrgyz, Tajik, Turkmen, and Uzbek services went on the air in 1953. All claim a regular audience among ethnic Central Asians living abroad, as well as inside their respective countries. While VOA offers more American and international news, RFE/RL focuses on domestic developments.

BRITISH BROADCASTING CORPORATION

BBC was founded in 1922 to broadcast experimental radio services; its Uzbek service began in 1994. BBC World Service, its international division, provides news coverage in thirty-two languages, Uzbek and Kyrgyz among them, and broadcast in Kazakh until 2005 (see table 2).

Along with its daily programs to Central Asia covering international and regional events, BBC offers a half-hour special program to Uzbek speakers in Afghanistan. These programs air on FM in Mazar-i-Sharif, Shibirgan, and on MW and SW in Maymana and Kunduz (BBC 2010).

Analysis

Since all three Western international broadcasters deliver Uzbek-language programming, the author employed two studies to find out how listeners perceived their programs. In the first one, carried out in the spring of 2005, ten questions were e-mailed to fifty-six people, ages twenty-one to fifty-nine and most of them living in Uzbekistan. Thirty-three people, or 60 percent of the recipients, responded, among whom seventeen were female. Respondents consisted of students, managers, engineers, doctors, professors, workers, housewives, and

TABLE 2. BBC BROADCASTING TO CENTRAL ASIA IN 2005

BBC CA SERVICES	DAILY BROADCASTS	FREQUENCY	BUREAU	WEB SITE
Kazakh	30 minutes	SW, MW, USW	Almaty Astana	www.bbc.co.uk/kazakh
			Karaganda	
			Saragach	
			Chimkent	
			Kizilorda	
Kyrgyz	1 hour, 30 mins.	LW, FM, USW	Bishkek	www.bbc.co.uk/kyrgyz
Uzbek	1 hour, including 30 minutes special to Afghanistan	SW, MW, FM	Tashkent	www.bbc.co.uk/uzbek

SOURCE: British Broadcasting Corporation, 2005.

journalists. None were affiliated with BBC, RFE/RL, or VOA. The first names and ages of those quoted in this section of the chapter are given; their surnames are omitted to protect their privacy.

Forty-two percent of the respondents reported no access to any of the stations due to jamming, lack of time, or radios not equipped to receive their signals. Most respondents reported listening to international radio stations online. Fifteen percent said they regularly listened to all three stations, while 27 percent preferred BBC coverage. Almost half considered BBC the most objective. Nearly 20 percent gave the same evaluation to RFE/RL, while 10 percent classified VOA as the most accurate, objective, and timely.

Despite the popularity of BBC programs, the station was highly criticized for its language quality. Most respondents perceived BBC Uzbek broadcasters as non-native speakers of Uzbek.

- I'm listening to BBC because I can receive its signals. I like its content, but I have difficulties to catch most of the broadcasters. They do not speak our language. They need to improve their linguistic style. (Kahraman, 56, engineer)
- For me, BBC is the most reliable. But their anchors do not speak good Uzbek. (Dildora, 40, housewife)

Some praised RFE/RL Uzbek for improving its presentation and language quality. Similar credit went to VOA Uzbek broadcasters. Others recommended that VOA Uzbek broadcasters slow down their news-reading speed and diversify the content.

TABLE 3. CONTENT COVERAGE OF BBC, RFE/RL, AND VOA UZBEK FOR SEPT. 6–SEPT. 13, 2005			
STORY CONTENT	BBC UZBEK (1 HR. DAILY)	RFE/RL UZBEK (4 HRS. DAILY)	VOA UZBEK (½ HR. DAILY)
International	12	32	9
Regional	18	27	5
Local	9	91	7
TOTAL	39	150	21

NOTE: International: stories not directly related to Central Asia; regional: Central Asia stories; local: stories specific to the Uzbekistan, including about the opposition in exile, even if stories originated from outside the region.

Most respondents considered RFE/RL an open platform for the Uzbek political opposition, saying the station brought to mind "a very emotional and angry man"; the tone, some said, reflected the mood of some exiled activists. That was seen as the main reason why the station was regarded as less objective and balanced than BBC and VOA.

While BBC's Web site was praised as the most informative and appealing and RFE/RL was lauded for its coverage of internal affairs, most respondents believed that all three stations reflected the policies of their funding countries in some way.

- I think that they present news based from their governments' point of view. (Zulfiya, manager, 23)
- I think that in spite of their openness and objectivity, these services are trying to present and reflect the policies of the country they are located in. (Olimjon, journalist, 24)

The second study, carried out from 6 through 13 September 2005, consisted of monitoring one week's worth of broadcasts of Uzbek-language programming from BBC, RFE/RL, and VOA. The author categorized stories based on whether they were international, regional, or local (see table 3). The study showed that, unsurprisingly, VOA—which has the shortest broadcast—delivered the fewest stories during that period, while RFE/RL, with the longest airtime daily, provided the most coverage.

During the study period, VOA aired five stories about media freedom, human rights, and political opposition; RFE/RL aired twenty-three stories focusing on those topics; and BBC aired five. The most popular story on all the stations was about a court-ordered shutdown of Internews Network's operations in Uzbekistan after ten years of working there to improve the capacity of local media. Another dominant story during the survey week was about the refugee situation resulting from the Andijan uprising in the Ferghana Valley. The most widely covered international story was about Hurricane Katrina in the United States.

For many of its listeners, RFE/RL best fills the gap created by the absence of strong local media outlets that fail to provide local news in a fair, balanced, and timely manner. In this fashion it is also fulfilling its mandate as a surrogate broadcaster. RFE/RL and VOA listeners had specific expectations from these two stations in addition to critical reports. They also wanted to hear more on health and science. Although some of the interviewees think that BBC should localize its presentation style, they commend it for its "soft" features and human interest stories.

For many, VOA represented "an old voice from Washington" and was "an outdated as well as unintelligible voice that had to be replaced by native speakers," said a longtime listener from Tashkent. Research by InterMedia Survey Inc. in 2004 found that a majority of respondents regarded program content as too political, too foreign, and too irrelevant to their lives. Even some avid consumers of world news complained that VOA Uzbek focused too heavily on U.S. interests; they said they were bored by the reports about Saddam Hussein, the war in Iraq, conflict in the Middle East, and the daily activities of President Bush.

Just as in any other media market in the world, many in the region look for good language use supported by a solid broadcast voice and authoritative style on international radio. Young professionals and sophisticated news consumers express deep yet equal interest in both serious and entertainment news. As the research indicates, an average international radio listener in Central Asia prefers more domestic than international news. The majority of people lack access to the Internet, with a penetration rate of only 16.8 percent (Internet World Stats 2010). There are mixed feelings about Russian media among people who struggle to find alternative sources of getting news. Many loyal RFE/RL and VOA listeners perceive Russian-language media with a great degree of suspicion although it is accessible in Uzbekistan. For them, it is merely Russian propaganda.

While many listeners question whether BBC, RFE/RL, and VOA are truly independent from the political powers that fund them, a majority commend the stations' programming. Individual criticisms toward the stations vary, but the general attitude is rather warm to all three international broadcasters.

Conclusion

A major problem facing the people of Central Asia is lack of access to accurate and reliable news, news that is most relevant to their lives, news that can help people make informed decisions of a personal nature and as responsible citizens. Television, which the majority of Central Asians have access to, is tightly controlled by the regimes in all five countries.

In Uzbekistan, people live in an information vacuum. International media in the country can barely move around to report on events, and since the bloody events in Andijan, the government has tightened its grip and even cut off the city from outsiders. BBC, VOA, and RFE/RL still broadcast into the country, but harassment and detention of their reporters has made it increasingly difficult for them and other external news organizations to access information. The local media have been cowed into submission.

There is a growing need in Central Asia for local independent media. Many respondents and interviewees for this study pointed out that the almost complete lack of nongovernmental press and electronic media has been a major barrier to progress in the region. Thus, veteran U.S. international broadcasters to the area, VOA and RFE/RL, as well as the BBC's Central Asian services, have a critical task at hand, because these stations are the main, and sometimes only, sources of uncensored news to the region.

While evidence is there to support the continued existence of these international broadcasters, they are not immune from criticism and, in extreme cases, from calls for their shutdown. Opponents of U.S.-funded international broadcasting characterize RFE/RL and VOA as Cold War relics that have outlived their mission and are no longer necessary. Still, in this post–Cold War era, countries like Uzbekistan and its neighbors exist where access to information remains tightly controlled and individual citizens find it difficult, if not danger-ous, to be informed.

Supporters of termination also argue that shortwave radio used by RFE/RL and VOA limits the audiences and, thus, the effectiveness of U.S. overseas broadcasting. They also maintain that foreigners may distrust the accuracy of broadcasts sponsored by the U.S. government (Congressional Budget Office 2000).

Supporters of international broadcasting in the United States counter that the current level of government-funded services should continue or increase. The process of change in the former Soviet Union needs nurturing, they assert, and RFE/RL and VOA could help in that process. Supporters of these stations also argue that shortwave radio is the best way to reach audiences in closed countries, because few people there own satellite dishes.

The emergence of the Internet has helped international broadcasters enhance their programs and expand their reach. All three international stations are available over the Internet in RealAudio and Windows Media format and are browsed by thousands of language speakers worldwide. For many users with Internet access, BBC, RFE/RL, and VOA Web sites are vital sources of information where mainstream media are weak.

So how effective have BBC, RFE/RL, and VOA been in their outreach? Other than their focus on the least-covered issues in the region, they also help drive the news agenda inside the country. Since most Western-style ethical standards of reporting are ignored, local journalists, editors, and producers both at the state broadcaster and FM stations, record headlines from BBC, RFE/RL, or VOA and use that information to write their international and regional news blocks, usually without credit to the source. Of course, anything critical or perceived to be critical of Uzbekistan is expunged from their stories.

The role international broadcasting plays in the development of civil society should not be underestimated. BBC, RFE/RL, and VOA are venues from which NGOs and the political opposition can have their voices amplified. But it is just as important for civil society development that international broadcasters not become mouthpieces for these groups. While their goals may be laudable, it is not the business of the broadcasters to promote their agendas but, rather, in the spirit of freedom of thought and ideas, to promote a balanced approach to these issues so that listeners and viewers can decide for themselves. At its essence, freedom is first about the freedom to choose. The same standards apply to opposition groups, which tend to be pricklier about not getting covered. This is partly due to their lack of cultural references to an independent press. Unlike international NGOs that promote civil society and are populated with Western ex-patriot activists, opposition groups at times bear a curious resemblance to the governments they wish to overthrow. When their press releases containing yet another gratuitous slap at the power elite are ignored for lack of news value, they gripe about compromised ethics and pro-government bias in reporting by the international broadcasters. Perhaps it is a sign of the success of the international broadcasters that they are castigated with almost equal amounts of venom by the governments they cover and by opposition groups that seek more coverage.

As governments like Uzbekistan's foment anti-Western campaigns by using their own media, one consequence is an increasingly hostile environment for reporters and stringers working for international broadcasters—especially those known for critical coverage of the situation in the country. Domestic media depict international stations' reporters as enemies of the nation and servants of anti-Uzbek organizations and powers. Most of the stringers and correspondents working for international media in Central Asia, specifically in Uzbekistan, work in secret, since it has become increasingly difficult to report from there. VOA journalists continue to face serious constraints. For instance, in September 2010, authorities in Tashkent charged Abdumalik Boboev, a VOA reporter in Uzbekistan, with libel, illegally crossing the border, and publishing information that threatened national security. Boboev has been using a pseudonym because he was not accredited by the government, which has constrained Western broadcasters since 2005 (IWPR 2010).

RFE/RL stringers, for example, have become the most frequent victims of attacks, arrests, and imprisonment on false charges. There were twenty-eight known cases of harassment against its reporters during and in the aftermath of the Andijan uprising. These cases involved beatings, armed attacks, and arrests.

One of the most positive developments in international broadcasting to Central Asia is that the image of the broadcaster is changing. Most first-generation broadcasters at RFE/RL and VOA were not professional journalists or fluent language speakers. They were hired during the Cold War when getting on the air was, at times, more important than what was on the air. Since then they have been replaced by younger specialists, who grew up in their native lands and have a thorough knowledge of the target countries and languages, and whose training included studies abroad.

Finally, international broadcasting is a complex profession with many thorny aspects that need further academic attention. More research should be done to deepen our understanding of its role in transitional environments where, so often, the flow of information is tightly controlled.

REFERENCES

Board of Broadcasting Governors. 2010. Www.bbg.gov.

British Broadcasting Corporation. 2010. "About the Agency." www.bbc.co.uk.

British Broadcasting Corporation Public Affairs Office. 2010. "Contact Us." Http://www.bbc.co.ul.

Camaj, Lindita. 2008. "The New World Order and 'the Voices': International Radio Broadcasters after the Cold War." 25 July. Paper presented at the International Association for Media and Communication Research World Congress, 20–25 July. Stockholm.

Congressional Budget Office. 2000. Function 150: International Affairs. Sec. 150-01. "Eliminate Overseas Broadcasting by the U.S. Government." 1 March. Http://www.cbo.gov/doc.cfm?index=1845&type=0&sequence=5.

Cull, Nicholas J. 2008. *The Cold War and the United States Information Agency: American Propaganda and Public Diplomacy, 1945–1989.* New York: Cambridge University Press.

Heil, Alan L. Jr. 2003. *Voice of America: A History.* New York: Columbia University Press.

———. 2005. Interview with author, June. Washington D.C.

Human Rights Watch. 2007. "Kyrgyzstan: Ensure Justice for Murdered Journalist." Www.hrw.org/en/news/2007/10/24/kyrgyzstan-ensure-justice-for-murdered-journalist.

Imamova, Navbahor, Eric Freedman, and Richard Shafer. 2008. "The Voice of America's Uzbek Service: Political Outreach, Visions of America, or Public Diplomacy?" 20 September. Paper presented at the Central Eurasian Studies Society Annual Conference, Georgetown University, 18–22 September. Washington D.C.

Institute for War and Peace Reporting. 2010. "Voice of America Reporter Charged in Uzbekistan. 19 September. Http://iwpr.net/report-news/voice-america-reporter-charged-uzbekistan.

———. 2004. "Voice of America Goes Quiet in Uzbekistan." RCA No. 307. 13 August. Http://iwpr.net/report-news/voice-america-goes-quiet-uzbekistan.

InterMedia Survey Inc. 2005. "Amerika Ovozi in Uzbekistan, Program Review." 12 October. Washington, D.C.

Internet World Stats. 2010. "Internet Usage in Asia." Www.internetworldstats.com/stats3.htm.

Media Association of Ferghana Valley. 2005. http://enews.ferghana.ru/ http://eng.fergana.org/about/region.

Nasar, Rosi. 2005. Interview with author, 17 July.

National Association of Electronic Mass Media. 2005. http://www.naesmi.uz/en. Puddington, Arch. 2000. *Broadcasting Freedom: Cold War Triumph of Radio Free Europe and Radio Liberty.* Lexington: University of Kentucky Press: ix–x.

Radio Free Europe/Radio Liberty. 2010. "Mission Statement."Http://www.rferl.org/info/mission/169.html.

Reporters sans Frontieres. 2005. "Authorities Foment a Denigration Campaign against Independent Journalists." 14 June. Http://arabia.reporters-sans-frontieres.org/article.php3?id_article=14078.

Shafer, Richard, and Eric Freedman. 2003. "Obstacles to the Professionalization of Mass Media in Post-Soviet Central Asia: A Case Study of Uzbekistan." *Journalism Studies* 4(1): 91–103.

Voice of America. 2003. "VOA Debuts Uzbek-Language Television Reports." 12 December. Http://author.voanews.com/english/About/morereleases.cfm.

———. 2005. "VOA to Resume Radio Broadcasts to Uzbekistan." 10 June. Http://author. voanews.com/english/About/morereleases.cfmwww.voanews.com/english/About/2005-06-10-voa64.cfm.

PART 4

Journalism Education and Professionalism

Journalism Education and Professional Training in Kazakhstan: From the Soviet Era to Independence

Maureen J. Nemecek, Stan Ketterer, Galiya Ibrayeva, and Stanislav Los

Knowing the past helps explain the present and predict the future.

—M. S. Archer (1979)

This chapter traces journalism education in Kazakhstan as reflected in the eyes of some of its teachers. It recounts the legacy of Soviet times, the struggle to find a footing after independence in 1991, and recent developments in higher education—in both the Strategic Plan of Development of Kazakhstan, 2005–10, with goals set by the Ministry of Education and Sciences (MOES), and bottom-up initiatives from teachers at public and private universities (MOES 2006, 6). Kazakhstani and U.S. researchers used in-depth interviews with veteran journalists and teachers, a focus group of administrators, and a survey of teachers in university journalism faculties (colleges or departments) nationwide. The chapter also addresses policy implications for civil society and democratic governance, along with opportunities for media developers and outside donors.

The Legacy of Soviet Times

Kazakhstan's first professional journalists were trained in Alma-Ata in 1934 by the Kazakh Communistic Institute of Journalism, the forerunner of the faculty of journalism at al-Farabi Kazakh State (now National) University (KazSU).[1] In 1940 the Council of People's Commissars of the Kazakhstan Soviet Socialist

Republic (KSSR) closed the institute, and a journalism department was established (officially, in 1949) in the Faculty of Philology of Kazakh State ("Let's See the Road" 1995, 31). The faculty offered majors in the theory and pragmatics of the Bolshevik press and in producing and publishing newspapers and books. After World War II, a major in journalism history was added. Not until 1966 did the journalism department become independent.[2]

The Communist Party's administrative machinery and the KSSR Ministry of Education controlled course content, special courses, and overall curriculum. Russian journalism faculties, especially that of Lomonosov Moscow State University, strongly influenced the ministry. The Directorate of Propaganda and Publicity of the Central Committee of the Communist Party of Kazakhstan controlled the department.

The curriculum was essentially the same as in other Soviet republics. Along with Marxist-Leninist theories, it stressed editing, language stylistics, world literature, and journalism, as well as internships in newspaper, radio, and TV newsrooms. The basic courses were "Parameters of the Development of Democratic and Communist Journalism," "Publishing as a Tool in the Creation of Socialism," and "History of Radio and TV Broadcasting." Professor Baurzhan Jakyp, the dean of the faculty until 2008, said the books used at KazSU and elsewhere in Kazakhstan were mostly published in Moscow. Some of the classics of Kazakh history were written by local journalism professors such as Temirbek Kozhakeyev, Tauma Amandossov, and Kairzhan Bekkhozhin. "Some professors managed to put real facts about Kazakhstan into the books," Jakyp said.[3] However, Jakyp reiterated, "Everyone used the Marxist-Leninist ideology. It was mandatory. Because if you do not reflect Soviet ideology in your textbook, your book will never be published."[4]

Soviet language policies influenced the development of journalism and staffing of journalism teachers. Those policies determined whether students could receive instruction in the Kazakh language and whether media could use it. For a while, editions of newspapers were published in both Russian and Kazakh. In the 1960s, Soviet leader Nikita Khrushchev's language policy emphasized Russian, over Kazakh. During his rule editions of Kazakh newspapers turned into mere translations of Russian versions. Thus, Kazakh-speaking teachers were let go and national journalism weakened because only translators were in demand, not journalists. After Khrushchev's resignation, the policy changed and Kazakh and Russian newspapers became independent of one another (Yegerov 1991).

Along with the cutback in Kazakh-language newspapers, there were fewer Kazakh-language schools. Recalling her childhood, Professor Sharvan Nurgozhina, head of the management and advertising department at KazNU, said that she studied in Russian schools because the only Kazakh schools in her home town Semipalatinsk were mostly in villages.[5] Her story is not unique—many Kazakh educators have not received professional training in their native language. For instance, many Kazakh National University faculty members received their advanced degrees from Moscow State University. They now teach and conduct research in Russian.

After the KazSU department became independent in 1966, it began to emphasize hands-on journalism. According to the minutes of the department's academic council, teachers discussed the launch of a television and broadcasting department along with a photo laboratory. The department also began to hire working journalists to teach special-topic courses. They tried to expand the network of student internships to help students find jobs. The department council diversified the postgraduate curriculum by adding the courses "Theory and Practice of Soviet Journalism," "History of Journalism," "TV and Radio Journalism," and "Journalism Competency and Editing."

Vice Dean Saken Nurbekov, a member of the focus group, said the strong relationship between teaching and Soviet press practice strengthened KazSU's reputation. "Many prominent Soviet journalists worked at the university as teachers. And the mandatory two- or three-year professional experience for students made for a professional workforce."[6] Professor Elena Dudenova said the mass media were "pretty much the same anywhere. There was one universal, unified system: one state, one system, one administration with minor differences. The differences in the Kazakh press were its attention to social problems."[7]

Sagadat Adilbekov, associate professor of journalism at Abay University, described the centralized media. He said two main newspapers existed: the official Russian newspaper, *Kazakhstanskaya Pravda* (*KP*), and its Kazakh-language counterpart, *Socialistic Kazakhstan* (*SK*). For example, *SK* had the same materials as in *Pravda* and *Izvestia*. Reports of Plenums and party positions were simply translations of the originals. The whole Soviet Union had one TV channel, and Kazakh TV broadcast two hours a day on that frequency. From the 1970s, Kazakhstan had its own frequency for its own TV channel. Each district had two or three hours to broadcast local news on that frequency. At the end of the 1970s, a new Orbita satellite broadcast delivery system was established, which was considered a "great step for the development of local television," said Adilbekov.[8]

Because they had prestige, the possibility of wealth and status, great knowledge, and a feeling of solidarity with power, teachers considered it a great honor to teach journalism. "The journalism faculty of the KSU ranked as the third in the Soviet Union," Dean Jakyp said. "Each student received a universal, global education. Soviet journalists were as knowledgeable as the encyclopedia. Journalists had to have knowledge in each sphere of life."[9] Nurbekov agreed: "The status of journalism was very high and it was well-respected by the public and the state. The unofficial title of journalists was 'Helper of the Party.'" [10] And journalism was the fourth power in Kazakhstan. The others were the court, the president and the parliament, he said.

Nurgozhina spoke admiringly of teachers who influenced her early career: "When I was a young teacher, I learned from . . . outstanding people who could perfectly combine communistic ideology in teaching their subjects . . . with a sensible bright, rational, approach for teaching."[11] Teachers were also rewarded financially. Jakyp recalled that his mentor, Amandossov, told him: "If you received a PhD degree, you will be a rich man."[12] Importantly, Adilbekov noted that Bekkhozhin earned more money than a vice minister or governor of an oblast (a governmental entity similar to a U.S. state)."[13]

During this time the "basic principles" of Marxist-Leninist ideology were paramount. According to Jakyp, the Soviet Union was a unified state ruled by the Communist Party. That ideology meant that "we are against the West. We are the world's only superpower. Our information is truthful and trusted. We have to be humanitarian and pacifist. Our work is dedicated to ordinary people."[14] Focus group members said there was great pride in being part of such a system. Nurgozhina recalled that incoming freshmen were welcomed on the first day of classes in the journalism department with the phrase, "We congratulate (you) on entering the ideological school."[15] However, none of the participants of the focus group said they had to join the Communist Party to teach at KazSU.

Some topics were forbidden, Jakyp said, and some professors paid a price for writing about Kazakh national identity. Purges of Kazakh intelligentsia occurred in the 1930s. In the 1950s, he said, some professors were arrested. Yermukhanov Bekmakhanov, a specialist in the history of Kazakhstan, "published the truth about prominent people when it was prohibited to mention their names," said Jakyp.[16] In 1952 he was sentenced to twenty-five years in prison, but he was rehabilitated after serving two. Censorship was so extensive that Kazakhstan had its own censorship body, and all mass media had to submit their materials for approval.

Teaching within the constraints of such a system had another drawback: instruction contained "too much ideology," Adilbekov said. All writing had to conform to tough requirements from the party. "Press Coverage of the Party" was one topic. Adilbekov said his least favorite course was "Problems of Propaganda and Ideology in the Press." Adilbekov laughed and said that he did not understand what the course was supposed to be about and how he could explain it to his students.[17]

One of the system's strengths was its model of professional education. "In Soviet times, teachers were practicing journalists, and the students were as well," said Adilbekov.[18] Not all journalists had a journalism degree. For example, many editors were Soviet military reporters in World War II. Regional newspapers had a difficult time attracting journalism graduates, so they hired and trained local high school graduates. Adilbekov began his career in the Turgay (now Kostanay) region at a time when every applicant needed one or two years of experience in the press before applying to the university. In his region, newspapers were ordered to hire the young and the talented. Those with real talent could go to the university to study; thirty young people from Turgay were sent to KazSU and then returned to work in journalism.[19]

By 1975, the KazSU Faculty of Journalism had toughened entry requirements. Applicants were required to submit three or more published stories, and those with prior experience were favored. They also had to write a creative essay and pass an interview with teachers before they could take the entrance exams.

Moreover, in 1976 the KSSR Education Ministry ordered the reorganization of the Kazakh journalism, Russian journalism, and TV and radio broadcasting departments. Four new departments replaced them: Theory and Practice of Soviet Journalism, History of Journalism, TV and Radio Journalism, and the Art of Writing and Literary Editing. Thus it was until the breakup of the Soviet Union and the birth of an independent nation in 1991.

Finding Their Footing after Independence

The euphoria of independence was soon tempered by the impact of the precipitous decline of the national economy and the out-migration of more than two million people (Anderson, Pomfret, and Usseinova 2004). Inflation was rampant[20] and universities had little money for books and salaries. They were forced to cut programs and classes. New textbooks were out of the question.

Asked what they taught on the "first day back" in January 1992, Nurbekov answered, "We followed the footsteps of a newborn child. We had nothing in the newly created state: no new goals and economic difficulties." "Those were hard times," said Elena Dudenova. "We made about forty dollars a month."[21] The only guide from the president was, 'We shall construct a market economy.'"[22]

Dean Jakyp, who had taught since 1986, described their painful adaptation to new circumstances:

> We knew some topics that had been "forbidden"—and day after day, step by step, we cut Soviet ideology out of the educational process. We want[ed] to give students information about journalism in the world. We spent hours in the library to bring them new, modern, information about foreign states. We were all frightened. How do you shift your mentality to free speech, etc.? There were special lectures at KazSU to explain market economy. After Kazakhstan gained independence I decided to dedicate my life to the freedom of the press.[23]

The financial situation was so dire that some mass-media companies demanded payment from KazSU for students' internships, and the university did not have the funds (Ibrayeva 1995, 25). New career opportunities attracted male students into law and economics from which they could obtain lucrative careers in fields like law enforcement and customs. Fewer stipends were given, meaning students began to pay their own tuition. To attract more students, programs lowered entrance requirements.[24]

Competition in the Marketplace

Educators could look back at the considerable contribution that al-Farati Kazakh State University had made to journalism education. By 1995 more than 85 percent of the staffs of newspapers, publishing houses, and radio and television outlets were KazSU graduates ("Let's See the Road" 1995). However, university journalism education was expanding. Faculties of journalism opened around the country. Among them, Kostanay State University, Almaty State University, Abay University, and Eurasia University. Private universities such as the University of Business, Kazakh-American University, and the Ablay Khan University of Foreign Languages in Almaty were also founded in the 1990s. The prestigious public-private hybrid Kazakhstan Institute of Management, Economics, and Strategic Research (KIMEP) was established in 2002 to train graduate students in business and became "an exemplar of [W]estern-style higher education in practice" (Dixon, Kainazarova, and Krasnikova 2010). A journalism program was added later. Many hard pressed instructors were forced to teach in more than one institution to make ends meet (Organization for Economic Cooperation and Development 2007). Some left the profession to work in business, which led to a shortage of qualified teachers. Consequently, many teachers in newer institutions of higher education are philologists, not journalists, according to Gulnara Assanbayeva, a senior teacher at KIMEP.

A longtime journalist and former department head at Kostanay State University, Assanbayeva recalled that university rectors wanted the prestige of a journalism faculty. As with her former department, rectors got them started but did not invest in the budding programs. She sought external assistance through the United States Information Agency (USIA), the U.S. ambassador, and other funders to launch her department. She moved to KIMEP in 2005.[25]

Support from international donors has been crucial in helping KazSU adjust to the new conditions of teaching. Three USIA grants from 1994 to 2002 allowed ten teachers to take one- to four-month courses at Oklahoma State University's (OSU) School of Journalism and Broadcasting. As part of the exchange, eleven OSU faculty members went several times to KazSU to share their knowledge with undergraduate and graduate students in such areas as media and society, public relations, advertising, TV reporting, freedom of speech, and mass media law.

In Oklahoma, KazSU teachers sat in on classes, studied English, learned to use the university's new technology and library resources, attended faculty and professional meetings, and studied curricula from programs around the United States. The grant also provided computer equipment and software for portable lectures and online publishing. In addition partial funding from the grant and KazSU enabled one OSU master's graduate in mass communications to spend a semester in residence teaching courses in media and society, public relations, and use of new technology.

Important assistance came from Martin Hadlow, UNESCO regional advisor for Asia, and a journalist from Australia. He worked actively in 1996 with then-dean Namazaly Omashev in equipping a seminar room and funding the UNESCO Chair in Mass Media at Kazakh State. One program created through these relationships was the Department of International Journalism at KazSU under Professor Galiya Ibrayeva.

Journalism Education in the Twenty-First Century

Changes in overall ideology have led to significant changes in the journalism curriculum at KazSU. Gone were courses on propaganda, demagoguery, Marxism-Leninism, communistic theory, and other features of Soviet journalism. Attention turned to journalism practice, press freedom, and legal protections for the mass media. Western journalism was studied, including genres of research, essay, and opinion. However, students also had to prepare in macro- and microeconomics, agriculture, international relations, work place issues, social problems, and so forth. The curriculum was reformed to meet the demands of a society moving quickly toward democratic and economic reforms.

Since 2000, foreign universities have continued to render assistance. Cooperation with such institutions as the Center for Politics and Communications at Duke University in the United States, the Southeast Asia Institute for Journalism in Malaysia, and the Foyo Center for the Advancement of Journalism in Sweden have assisted the KazSU faculty in changing course content to meet political and economic challenges.

The country is at a crossroads for higher education, and several factors point to a sound basis for reform. From 2000 to 2008 the economy grew more than eight percent a year, with an estimated GDP per capita income for 2007 in the range of eleven thousand dollars (Central Intelligence Agency 2010). Kazakhstan is projected to be among the top three oil producers in the world by 2015.[26] A study of higher education in Kazakhstan by the Organization for Economic Cooperation and Development (OECD) finds that the students and their parents are willing to sacrifice and save to ensure their children can attend a higher-education institution (2007, 22). And the estimated population of 15,340,000 is more than 98 percent literate (Central Intelligence Agency 2010).

The OECD's snapshot of student demographics in 2004–05 found that about 20 percent—744,200 students—were enrolled in higher-education institutions, 47 percent of those full time. Overall, 46.3 percent attended private institutions (OECD 2007). The ethnically diverse population is comprised of more than one hundred ethnic groups. Slightly more than half of the population (52 percent) is Kazakh, and 31.4 percent are Russian. About half speak Kazakh, the state language, and two-thirds speak Russian, the official language (Kazakh Embassy 2008).

Seventy ethnic groups were represented among the students; about 70 percent Kazakh, 22 percent Russian, and the remaining 8 percent from other groups. Instruction was provided in Russian for nearly 60 percent of the students, and in Kazakh for the rest.

Language issues are increasingly important for journalism students. Mass media have been required to publish or broadcast at least half their material in Kazakh since January 1997, when the law "On languages in the Republic of Kazakhstan" was adopted.[27]

Students are taught in two tracks at KazSU, as well as at Abay University, where 70 percent of its students study in Kazakh. At KIMEP and Kazakh American University, journalism students study in English.

The country has twenty-three faculties (departments or colleges) of journalism, five of them private. Regional universities offer journalism on an as-needed basis; if student demand exists for the program, they offer it. No statistics about journalism teachers or students are available from MOES, but there are an estimated 160 journalism teachers based on phone calls and responses to a 2008 mail survey.

The curriculum of required courses at these programs is nearly identical to the program at the flagship school, the al-Farabi Kazakh National University (KazNU).

They share the cumbersome method of changing or adding to the curriculum. In theory, a way exists to propose new courses through the State Obligatory Standards (SOES) competition. Teachers need permission from their dean and rector to propose one, which will be sent to the MOES. The ministry makes the SOES mandatory for all universities, and syllabi must follow detailed state standards. However, since the SOES covers only 40 percent of disciplines, the majority is de jure in the hands of the dean of each faculty and depends on financial constraints.

KazNU employs about forty-five full-time and part-time teachers, down from sixty in 2008. They are paid according to degrees earned and years of employment. Teachers have eight hundred to nine hundred contact hours, which is high by international standards (OECD 2007, 27). The university sets salaries and curriculum, organization of teaching, and admissions. At KazNU, the trend is to hire practicing journalists to teach skills courses part-time. The pay is competitive. Administrators partner with professional media companies in providing education to aspiring journalists.

The KazNU undergraduate program is modeled after that of the University of North Carolina, Chapel Hill. For master's students, the model is that of Columbia University in New York. Sixty percent of the curriculum is comprised of elective courses. Students can choose what they want according to their "individual educational trajectory," said Dean Ibrayeva. The goal is to create a balance between skills and theoretical disciplines.[28]

In beginning this research, the authors were quite familiar with "systemic barriers to professionalism," that teachers faced in higher education in Central Asia. Issues we investigated included control over curriculum, salary structure, and ways in which the system did not seem to encourage "faculty creativity, innovation, or personalizing of teaching and learning processes" (Caboni, McLendon, and Rumyantseva, 2003).

A Survey of Journalism Educators in Kazakhstan

Based on the history of teaching journalism in Kazakhstan, this study sought answers to two main questions: What do journalism educators think about the curriculum? And what do they think about their teaching?

Thus, the researchers conducted a national survey in Russian, Kazakh, and English. Nearly all educators in Kazakhstan received questionnaires and 53 percent responded. Participants were evenly divided by gender. They were predominantly teachers (81.2 percent) with magister degrees (82.4 percent) in journalism (84.7 percent). Two-thirds were forty-one or older, and nearly the same proportion had eleven or more years of teaching experience. About half had six or more years of journalism experience.

Respondents held strong views about the curriculum. They thought teaching ability has more influence on students than curriculum. But they favored updates to include new media and student internships. Moreover, they supported teaching that focuses on national history and culture, and training students to report the country's accomplishments. They supported, but were less certain, that curriculum should be determined locally instead of nationally.

Asked how to improve the curriculum, several educators said it should emphasize the accomplishments of past Kazakh journalists and writers, as well as the country's traditions. It also should focus more on Kazakh journalism. "Currently, there are no disciplines which prepare students to be adequate citizens of their homeland, to honor national traditions and culture," one wrote. The curriculum focuses too much on Russian disciplines and not enough on Kazakh ones, said another. More practical examples should be available for teachers, especially Kazakh ones, said a third.

The educators held more mixed views about journalism teaching. They most strongly agreed that universities should be free of political influence and that a professional journalism educators' association should be created. Further, they agreed that they teach the difference between news and opinion and that students learn about their rights and ethics. Interestingly, they acknowledged pressure with regard to students' grades and from the media industry. Nearly all agreed they give students the grades they deserved despite pressure from administrators and others and that they feel pressure from employers to teach skills.

Importantly, about half said they plan to leave journalism education because of inadequate salaries. Fewer than one in ten reported they receive a salary based on merit. They also agreed they receive little support and little time for scholarship. Although about half agreed research is important at their university, only 6 percent agreed they keep up with the methods of research and scholarship in Central Asia; the same percent reported receiving some external funding. Only about a third reported reviewing international scholarship for teaching examples.

Not surprisingly, higher salaries, less paperwork, and stronger support for scholarship were the main ideas mentioned in open-ended responses as ways to help teachers do a better job. "A better salary will help teachers to pay more attention to each student, rather than to teach more students with lesser attention for more money's sake," one respondent wrote. "Teachers should be provided with additional time to do scientific work because they are very busy with exercises for students," wrote another. "Teachers should be confident in their future, so they will give all of their capabilities to teach, but not for trying to survive," a third wrote pointedly.

Implications for Civil Society and Democracy

These are troubling results for those engaged in teaching journalism. While educators struggle with the inadequacies of their profession, they must also contend with fundamental changes that the young people they teach have gone through in the years since independence. The authors of "A Social Portrait of Young People in Today's Kazakhstan" say that contemporary students are different from those of the Soviet past. For them, freedom for youth is an "essential condition." Their research finds that students rate positively "the potential opportunities that freedom and democracy promise for their future" (Eshpanova and Nysanbaev 2006). Thus, students demand choices, understand competition, and want a satisfying profession that will present them with good options for a secure future.

President Nursultan Nazarbayev has voiced support for these aspirations and set a goal that the country should aspire to be among the world's top fifty most competitive countries by 2015. His changes include an accreditation system to rank universities according to international standards. In addition, new technology and teaching methods would provide the workforce "for an innovation-based economy" (Lillis 2007). In October 2009 he delivered a lecture on "innovation revolution" from KazNU that was broadcast to all universities in the republic, telling students that "our task is to change the attitudes of the people of Kazakhstan—especially our youth—toward education and intellect.

We need to create a core of national intelligence; we need qualified people who can compete in the international arena" (Kazakhstan News Bulletin 2009). In spite of the 2008 crash of global financial markets and the depreciated price of oil, the national university appears engaged in "innovation revolution." It has completed new classroom buildings and laboratories. In 2009 a free Wi-Fi network was established throughout the university, including dormitories. Other planned measures included its first electronic library, delivery of laptops to all incoming undergraduates, and "interactive boards" in classrooms.

With the support of the new rector appointed by Nazarbayev, changes came swiftly in 2008–09, including a new dean for the Faculty of Journalism. Some teachers were replaced, many by practitioners. Those whose elective courses did not meet students' needs were let go. New courses were introduced in the "applied disciplines"—practical skills-oriented courses in TV, radio, online journalism, and documentary movies. The journalism faculty received 40,000,000 *tenge* (about $250,000) for equipment for new TV and radio laboratories. The number of computer labs grew from one to four. Students started to create their own Web sites and blogs.

Student interest has increased. In the fall of 2008, 115 students were enrolled. By 2010, the numbers had nearly doubled to 221. The cost of education for 2008–09 remained the same as the previous year, about $2,000 a year for undergraduates. The government will pay the faculty more for each student who has won a state scholarship or grant and enrolls there—approximately $5,330 a year. A bachelor's level major in mass-media design was introduced. The master's program will have specialties in international journalism and public relations. Some courses are taught entirely in English.

There is, however, the perception to be overcome that media workplaces do not require a degree in journalism. For example, a young journalist at *Vremya* newspaper said he graduated with a degree in Russian literature.[29] A local television network manager said that no one ever asked him how many degrees he has or where he studied.[30]

In its effort to be internationally competitive, the government has invested heavily in the Bolashak scholarship program, which sends about three thousand students to foreign universities for undergraduate and graduate study, some in journalism (MOES 2006, 37).

The Bolashak program has been extended to faculty. For example, Vice Dean Karlyga Myssayeva spent the fall 2010 semester at the School of Media and Strategic Communications at Oklahoma State University, learning about its master's program in mass communication with an emphasis on media management. She was especially interested in strategic communications, a developing field that merges advertising and public relations.

Further, Kazakhstan has instituted reform within its universities by signing onto the Bologna Agreement, a three-tiered system of preparation—bachelor's degree, master's degree, and doctor of philosophy—based on a system of academic credit hours (Piven and Pak 2006). In response to the agreement, KazNU inaugurated a pilot PhD program in which it invites foreign professors to give intensive seminars to young media researchers and to bring KazNU students to conduct research at their home universities (MOES 2006, 36).

In addition to national programs financed by the MOES, journalism programs in Almaty cooperate with the British Broadcasting Corporation, Radio Free Europe/Radio Liberty, UNESCO, and Internews, as well as the Soros Foundation and International Research and Exchanges Board, which fund international travel for research presentations. The doors have opened to new curricula. Currently, one of the authors has been asked to look at UNESCO's model curriculum (2007) to see how it can be adapted to her program. UNESCO maintains an active presence in Kazakhstan and assists teachers in distance education and other projects.

Reforms and incentives are crucial to help journalism educators improve their qualifications to meet the demands of students in a changing media technology environment. To do so, the administration must provide opportunities, release time, technical support, and financial resources for professional development.

Teachers have also indicated interest in forming an educators association to further their professionalism by providing a network of support for grant opportunities, course syllabi, research ideas, conferences, and academic journals in which to publish their research. The timing looks good for such an association to strengthen journalism education.

Conclusion

Leaving the Soviet mentality behind has not been easy. As Nurgozhina said, "It is a big achievement that now we released communistic ideology from our journalism disciplines in some measure."

Privatization, the marketplace, competition, and new curricula to meet the needs of today's students all pose special challenges to teachers trained in the Soviet system. Higher administration must encourage and recognize personal initiative. In the meantime, teachers must overcome their Soviet past and wrestle with how their teaching can have a positive impact on the changing and challenging environment of journalism and mass media in Kazakhstan. They must figure out ways in which the academic traditions of the country can coexist with what mass media practitioners demand, all the while strengthening their own professional identity through a national association to represent their interests with educational policymaking bodies, with the mass media, and with the public.

NOTES

1. In 2006, Kazakh State University (KazSU) received the title of Kazakh National University (KazNU) from President Nursultan Nazarbayev.
2. Interview. Baurzhan Jakyp, April 16, 2008.
3. Interview, senior administrator Dean B. Jakyp, April 16, 2008.
4. Interview, senior administrator Dean B. Jakyp, April 16, 2008.
5. Focus Group, Sharvan Nurgozhina, April 15, 2008.
6. Focus Group, Saken Nurbekov, April 25, 2008.
7. Focus group, Elena Dudenova, April 15, 2008.
8. Interview, Sagdat Adilbekov, April 16, 2008.
9. Interview, senior administrator Dean B. Jakyp, April 16, 2008.
10. Focus Group, Saken Nurbekov, April 25, 2008.
11. Focus Group, Sharvan Nurgozhina, April 15, 2008.
12. Interview, senior administrator Dean B. Jakyp, April 16, 2008.
13. Interview, Sagdat Adilbekov, April 16, 2008.
14. Interview, senior administrator Dean B. Jakyp, April 16, 2008.
15. Focus Group, Sharvan Nurgozhina, April 15, 2008.
16. Interview, senior administrator Dean B. Jakyp, April 16, 2008.
17. Interview, Sagdat Adilbekov, April 16, 2008.
18. Interview, Sagdat Adilbekov, April 16, 2008.
19. Interview, Sagdat Adilbekov, April 16, 2008.
20. Ambassador of Kazakhstan to the U.S. Yerlan Idrissov, Remarks to the International Club of Annapolis, Maryland, February 4, 2008.
21. Focus group, Elena Dudenova, April 15, 2008.
22. Focus Group, Saken Nurbekov, April 25, 2008.
23. Interview, senior administrator Dean B. Jakyp, April 16, 2008.
24. Interview, Sagdat Adilbekov, April 16, 2008.
25. Interview, Gulnara Assanbayeva, April 18, 2008.
26. Kazakhemb.com, 2008.
27. Akorda.kz, 2008.

28. Statistics are from the Office of the Dean of the Faculty of Journalism.

29. Interview, journalist from *Vremya* newspaper, April 13, 2008.

30. Interview, television journalist, April 30, 2008.

REFERENCES

Anderson, Kathryn H., Richard Pomfret, and Natalya S. Usseinova. 2004. "Education in Central Asia during the Transition to a Market Economy." In *The Challenge of Education in Central Asia*, ed. Stephen P. Heyneman and Alan J. DeYoung, 131–52 . Greenwich, Connecticut: Information Age Publishing.

Archer, M. S. 1979. *The Social Origins of Educational Systems*. London: Sage.

Central Intelligence Agency. 2010. *The World Factbook*. Www.cia.gov/library/publications/the-world-factbook.

Caboni, Timothy C., Michael K. McLendon, and Nataliya Rumyantseva. 2003. "Faculty Professionalization in Kazakh Higher Education: Barriers and Possibilities." Paper presented at the Association for the Study of Higher Education. Portland, Oregon, November 12–16, 2003.

Dixon, John, Mansiya Kainazarova, and Valeriya Krasnikova. 2010. "Applicability of Western-Style Education in Post-Soviet Countries: The Case of Kazakhstan Institute of Management, Economics, and Social Research (KIMEP)." Paper presented at the Central Eurasian Studies Society, Ankara, July 29–30.

Eshpanova, D. E., and A. M. Nysanbaev. 2006. "A Social Portrait of Young People in Today's Kazakhstan." *Russian Education and Society* 48(2): 75–96.

Ibrayeva, Galiya. 1995. "Future Belongs to New Journalism." *Journal of Central Asian Media Studies* 1(1): 24-25.

Kazakh Embassy. 2008. Http://kazakhstan.visahq.com/embassy/United-States.

Kazakhstan News Bulletin. 2009. No 27. Www.kazakhemb.com.

Kazakh State University al-Farabi. 2003 *Zhurnalistiky Fakultety 70*. Journalism Faculty at 70. Astana City.

"Let's See the Road of Our Success." 1995. *Journal of Central Asian Media Studies* 1 (1): 31.

Lillis, Joanna. 2007. "Kazakhstan Plans Education Reform in Drive for Competitiveness." Www.eurasianet.org/departments/insight/articles/eav030707a.shtml.

Ministry of Education and Sciences of the Republic of Kazakhstan (MOES). 2006. *National Report on the State and Development of Education* (summary). Astana City.

Organization for Economic Cooperation and Development and International Bank for Reconstruction and Development / World Bank. 2007. *Higher Education in Kazakhstan: National Policies in Education*. Paris: OECD Publishing.

Piven, G., and Iu Pak. 2006. "Higher Education in Kazakhstan and the Bologna Process." *Russian Education and Society* 48:10, 82–91.

President of the Republic of Kazakhstan. 2008. Www.akorda.kz

UNESCO. *Model Curricula for Journalism Education.* 2007. Http://unesdoc.unesco.org/images/0015/001512/151209e.pdf.

Yegerov, A. I. 1991. *Formirovaniei i razvitie systemy SMI v natsionalnom regione na materiale Kazakhstana,* trans. Sholpan Kozhamkulova (*The formation and development of mass media system on a national scale in the example of Kazakhstan*). Avtoreferat diss.ist. nauk. Moscow: AON.

Professionalism among Journalists in Kyrgyzstan

Gregory Pitts

The crumbling of the Warsaw Pact in the early 1990s, followed by the breakup of the Soviet Union, led to major economic, social, and political reforms across much of Eastern Europe. Foreign aid, business investment, and academic assistance flowed into the region. Among the desired reforms was development of an independent press in much of the region. Meanwhile, the five "stan" countries of Central Asia—Kyrgyzstan, Uzbekistan, Turkmenistan, Tajikistan, and Kazakhstan—declared their independence but retained the same authoritarian leaders. Efforts to foster development of a Western-style press and democratic governance have stumbled badly in Central Asia (Kenny and Gross 2008). As the International Research and Exchanges Board (IREX) noted in 2008, "Central Asia remains the least developed region of Europe and Eurasia in respect to media development."

Among the mix of Central Asia countries, Zviagel'skaia (2005, 75) observes, "Kyrgyzstan has pursued a balanced policy: It was regarded by the West 'as a story of democratic success' (which ensured an influx of assistance), but was always clear to maintain a clear Russian vector in its foreign policy." Strategic relationships in the region changed after the 11 September 2001 attacks in the United States. In preparation for the war in Afghanistan, the United States stationed troops in Uzbekistan, Tajikistan, and Kyrgyzstan (Akbarzadeh 2004). Not unlike the U.S. allegiance with Mobutu Sese Seko in the former Zaire's fight against communism in Africa, the United States has felt compelled to choose between radical Islamists and corrupt dictators. Freedman and Shafer (2003, 9) describe the ruling Central Asia regimes as "run by autocrats, kleptocrats, and neptocrats, regimes marked by wholesale corruption, self-dealing, favoritism, egotism, repression, arbitrary behavior, rigged elections, and stifling of dissent, including the voices of independent news media." Unwilling to relinquish its influence in the region, Russia established an anti-terrorism rapid-action force in Kant, Kyrgyzstan, less than fifty kilometers from the U.S. forces stationed at Manas Air Base (Akbarzadeh 2004). Both the United States and Russia have successfully renewed their base leases; both countries have paid escalating lease fees. China, with similar concerns about U.S. troops at its back door, elevated the status of the Shanghai Cooperation Organization to energize its influence in Central Asia (Hu 2005).

Central Asia is again reminiscent of the political and diplomatic "Great Game" in which Russia and England earlier attempted to delineate spheres of influence (Bensman, 2005). The resumption of the Great Game—now played by China, Russia, and the United States—points to the reason why this small nation of five million people, less richly endowed with mineral wealth than its neighbors, is worth examining as a nation in transition. In its 2010 Freedom House report *Freedom in the World*, a decline from 2009 in political rights and civil liberties led to a categorization change from "partly free" in Kyrgyzstan to a "not free" categorization. The report noted flawed election processes in 2007 parliamentary elections and the 2009 presidential election and that the government has "stepped up pressure on independent journalism in recent years, using licensing rules, criminal libel laws, and various forms of administrative harassment to suppress media scrutiny." Kenny (2008, 36) perceives a situation for the press in a Kyrgyzstan that "now teeters on a slippery-slope of self-censorship and self-doubt." Just as vexing, IREX noted in its 2010 Media Sustainability Index (MSI) that "Kyrgyzstan adhered to the regional pattern of declining media freedom, despite its liberal legislation" asserting freedom of speech, access to information, and the special status of journalists. This chapter will report findings of a survey of journalists' attitudes about their professional orientation.

Adding greater drama to Kyrgyzstan's political dance in the contemporary Great Game have been the limited improvements brought about by 2005's largely nonviolent government change. Following disputed parliamentary elections, Kyrgyzstan made international front-page headlines by ousting President Askar Akayev, who had ruled for fourteen years after the country's independence from the collapsed Soviet Union. Widespread citizen demonstrations were followed by what Western media described as a Tulip Revolution. However, Russian and pro-government media labeled the event a U.S.-backed coup (Kulikova and Perlmutter

2008). The presidential change did little to improve everyday governance; most members of parliament, whose election sparked the social upheaval, retained their mandates. The new leadership inherited the same problems, including growing poverty, corruption, the presence of "criminal elements" in the government, insecure borders, and a perceived gathering threat from Islamic fundamentalist groups (Freedom House 2007). The July 2009 presidential election victory of Kurmanbek Bakiyev led to a more authoritarian regime, including attacks and assassinations on political figures, and crackdowns on civil society groups and independent media (Freedom House 2010). By late-February 2010, with deteriorating economic conditions, corruption, a decaying infrastructure, energy shortages, and a harsh winter, the public exhausted its patience with the regime (Quinn-Judge 2010). By April, protests around the country led to Bakiyev's ouster and the installation of a provisional government. That was soon followed by clashes in the southern cities of Osh and Jalal-Abad between ethnic Uzbeks and ethnic Kyrgyz (Schwirtz 2010; Schwirtz and Barry 2010).

Statement of the Issue

Kyrgyzstan has failed to make full use of the democratic opportunity afforded by the presidential change in 2005. By 2006, the government began a series of efforts to exert control over the country's media environment, a situation that has not yet been reversed even with the ouster of former president Bakiyev. Although Kyrgyz law protects freedom of speech and prohibits censorship, such legal protections are not applied evenly or effectively. The results of departure from the rule of law include a chilled or self-censored journalistic climate where it is sometimes better to fail to report stories that are unflattering to the regime than to report them and face the consequences of intimidation. In the most extreme cases, journalists have been harassed, beaten, and even murdered for reporting stories that raised the ire of the government.

Kulikova and Perlmutter (2007) admirably document the potential of Internet blogs to disseminate information and give life to important stories for readers within and outside of Kyrgyzstan. It is estimated that about 40 percent of the population has Internet access. Access outside major cities is limited, and government action has blocked some independent news and blog sites (Freedom House 2010). During the 2005 Tulip Revolution, the opposition's call for reform of state media led to Bakiyev's pledge to alter the function of the state television and radio company (KTR) by creating a publicly funded public service broadcaster. Once in office and with an eye toward controlling the flow of information, however, his government backed away from such reforms. By mid-2008, the parliament reversed attempts at reform by passing a bill affirming the state's monopoly on national broadcasting. Worse still, the law grants broad authority to state agencies to annul, sever, or revoke media licenses. Article 8.1 of the new law requires that half the programming carried by any television and radio station must be self-produced and in the Kyrgyz language; until then, much, if not most, content had come from rebroadcasts of news service reports, often in Russian and often from beyond the country's borders. The program production burden would overwhelm most private broadcasters in a country where unemployment and economic underperformance will not yet sustain commercial broadcasting. The government took enforcement of the legislation under advisement—thus creating another motive for self-censorship by independent media outlets that knowingly could never achieve the Kyrgyz language broadcast requirements (IREX 2009).

This is the contemporary context in which Kyrgyzstan's journalists and their media owners must function. Journalists who are simply doing their job of covering events, including opposition rallies, have found themselves facing harassment, threats, and violent attacks in reprisal for their reporting. IREX (2008) described the media system in Kyrgyzstan as operating in the space between repression and tolerance. IREX (2009) identified both an increase in the number of cases of violence against journalists and the tendency of independent media to commercialize their content and limit journalistic content to avoid government scrutiny. IREX (2010) describes a society indifferent to freedom of speech violations, where even the NGOs fail to afford protection.

To provide in-depth analyses of the conditions for independent media in seventy-six countries across Africa, Europe, Eurasia, and the Middle East, IREX established a Media Sustainability Index. MSI assesses five contributors to the development of a sustainable media system: free speech, professional journalism, plurality of news sources, business management, and supporting institutions. The sustainability score for Kyrgyzstan declined from 1.97 in 2007 to 1.78 in 2008; it rose to 1.93 in 2009 and declined slightly to 1.92 in 2010. Free speech has hovered above a 2.0 for the last two years; professional journalism practice declined from 1.81 in 2009 to 1.68 in 2010, with professional journalism receiving the lowest score among the five objectives.

Kyrgyzstan and the other countries in Central Asia seldom make the news agenda for most Western readers, viewers, and listeners. Instead, watchdog groups and press advocates such as IREX, the Committee to Protect Journalists, Reporters sans Frontieres (Reporters without Borders), and Freedom House become clearinghouses for information about press freedom there. While little quantitative data has emerged from Kyrgyzstan, the remainder of this chapter will present the results of a survey examining the professional outlook of journalists working there. The legal environment in which journalists practice their craft is important. However, just as important—and often overlooked—is the professional orientation of the journalists who must work within a transitioning media system, particularly a system that has taken as many steps backward and it did forward.

The civil society apparatus of a country, along with the socially compelling nature of media content and its impact on the public, leads most communications researchers to overlook fundamental issues such as reporter career orientation and responsibility. Yet legal reforms and an economically enabling environment are insufficient to ensure the development of a free but responsible press. If the press operates in a slippery-slope environment, one enabling factor is certainly the legal-legislative position advanced and supported by the government, which determines its relationship with media institutions. Another factor is the willingness of journalists to envision a job worth occupying that can promote dissemination of factual information of value to society. Such dissemination is enabled not just by law, but also by professional standards upheld by journalists and the organizations for which they work.

Professionalism—often defined as specialized knowledge, authority over clients, autonomy, and emphasis on public services at the heart of journalists' support for a free press. Even when the legal environment enables the practice of journalism, it is the possession and use of specific journalistic traits by the journalists themselves that enables the practice to exist. Pollard and Johansen (1998, 357) identify professionalism as "an indicator of individual emphasis on societal responsibility and ethical performance, the wielding of thought to action through the application of the highest standards or ideals in the performance of an occupation for the primary benefit of society." Perhaps the most-cited measure of media practitioner professionalism was introduced by McLeod and Hawley (1964). It employed a twenty-four-item professional orientation index that typified "professional" and "semi-pro" newspaper editorial employees with other employees in advertising, business circulation, and clerical positions.

Methodology

A grant from the Open Society Institute provided travel funding for the author to observe press conditions in Kyrgyzstan in November 2007 and March 2008.

Based on previous published research, a four-page questionnaire was created and translated into Russian for journalists to complete. Data were collected between 3 September and 6 October 2008.

Professionalism was operationalized as a Likert scale of twelve four-point items: six measuring professional concerns and six measuring nonprofessional concerns. McLeod-Hawley attitudinal indicators measured professional expertise (initiative and originality, new skill and knowledge development, full use of abilities, and training); employee contribution (the job is valuable to the community, the job makes the organization different because I work there); job benefits (job permanence, income, and variety of the job); enjoyment (enjoy doing the job); opportunity (getting ahead in the organization, contact with important people); and family (job does not disrupt family life and job holds prestige or favor with family and friends). Past research by Nayman (1973), Pollard (1982; 1985; 1995; and 1996), and Pollard and Johansen (1998) successfully used reductions in the McLeod-Hawley index.

Questionnaires were distributed in face-to-face meetings with journalists. As might be expected in an authoritarian country, many journalists declined to participate in the project, either fearing for their safety or unwilling to acknowledge possible problems in their profession. Eventually, surveys were obtained from thirty-one full-time journalists and sixty part-time journalists.

Findings

The average respondent was twenty-two years old (twenty-seven among full-time journalists) and single; most were women (70 percent of full-time journalists and 80.2 percent among the entire respondent pool.) In a tenuous media environment where press freedom may actually be regressing, nearly three-fourths of the respondents (71.8 percent) envision themselves continuing in some aspect of media work in the next five years. Notable, though, is that more than a quarter of the full-time journalists (26.7 percent) are unsure what their future employment may include, while another 13.3 percent expressed a desire to be working somewhere other than in media. Table 1 shows respondent profiles.

Scores on the McLeod-Hawley items were generally high. Respondents indicated the importance of the six professional and six nonprofessional items by rating each item as extremely important, quite important, somewhat important, or not important. Table 2 shows a summary of the McLeod-Hawley mean scores for full-time and part-time journalists.

TABLE 1. PERSONAL AND WORK-RELATED ATTRIBUTES OF KYRGYZ JOURNALISTS

	FULL-TIME	PART-TIME	COMBINED
Respondents	33%	67%	
Married	43.3%	4.9%	17.4%
Single	56.7%	95.1%	81.5%
Mean Age	27	20	22
Mean Years of Media Experience	4.25	0.75	2
Future Desired Employment			
Broadcasting	33.3%	29.6%	30.6%
Print	10%	20.4%	16.5%
Internet	3.3%	14.8%	10.6%
Non–news media job	13.3%	13%	14.1%
Something other than media	13.3%	13%	12.9%
Unsure of future employment	26.7%	9.3%	15.3%

NOTE: $n = 91$

TABLE 2. MEAN RESPONSES TO LEVEL OF PROFESSIONAL ORIENTATION INDEX

HOW IMPORTANT IS . . . ?	FULL-TIME	PART-TIME
Professional Items		
Full use of abilities and training	3.62	3.62
Originality and initiative	3.57	3.57
Learn new skills and knowledge	3.66	3.78
Get ahead professionally	3.66	3.73
Make the place different	3.04	2.95
Essential job to my community	3.07	3.41
Nonprofessional Items		
Job enjoyment	3.66	3.80
Earning a good salary	3.71	3.75
Job security	3.38	3.55
Job with prestige	2.83	3.20
Contact with important people	2.79	3.07
Job does not disrupt family	3.00	3.20

NOTE: Responses ranged from 4 to 1, where 4 meant Extremely Important and 1 meant Not Important.

Perhaps in response to the limited opportunities to express themselves personally or professionally in Kyrgyzstan's recent past, *the opportunity to learn new skills* was the most important professional item. Three-fourths (76.1 percent) rated it as extremely important; 21.6 percent rated it as quite important (97.7 percent combined). The remaining five professional indicators showed similar scores. *Getting ahead in my professional career* was rated as extremely important by 76.7 percent and quite important by 17.8 percent (96.5 percent combined). *A job that provides a chance to make full use of my abilities* was rated as extremely important by 67 percent and quite important by 29.5 percent (96.5 percent combined). *Having an opportunity for originality and initiative* was rated extremely important by 62.1 percent and quite important by 33.35 percent (95.4 percent combined). The two remaining professional measures, *a job essential to my community* and *a job where I can make my workplace different because I work there,* were both rated as extremely important by fewer than half of respondents (44.9 percent and 30.7 percent), with combined scores of 85.3 percent and 73.9 percent.

Nearly all respondents enthusiastically supported three of the six nonprofessional items:

- A measure of personal security, *earning a salary that's a good living* was rated as extremely important by 75.6 percent and quite important by 23.3 percent (98.9 percent combined).
- *Having enjoyment of what the job is* was rated as extremely important by 82.2 percent and quite important by 12.2 percent (94.4 percent combined).
- *Having job security* was the third most highly rated nonprofessional measure. Fewer than two-thirds of respondents (61.1 percent) rated it as extremely important and 28.9 percent as quite important (90 percent combined).

Fewer than half rated the three remaining nonprofessional items as extremely important:

- Although most respondents were unmarried, *having a job that does not disrupt family life* was extremely important to 47.2 percent and quite important to 27 percent (74.2 percent combined).
- *Having a job with prestige* was extremely important to 38.2 percent and quite important to 34.8 percent (73 percent combined).
- *Having a job that brings me in contact with important people* was extremely important to 34.1 percent and quite important to 36.3 percent (70.4 percent combined).

TABLE 3. MEAN RESPONSES TO JOURNALISTIC EXPECTATIONS		
	FULL-TIME	**PART-TIME**
Journalists should go to jail to protect sources	2.79	2.88
It is okay to accept promotional trips	3.46	3.37
Journalists should take periodic refresher courses	3.97	4.07
Journalists need an organization to police the profession	3.64	3.93
Certification is needed for journalists	3.69	4.16

NOTE: Responses ranged from 5 to 1, where 5 meant Strongly Agree and 1 meant Strongly Disagree.

Journalists also rated their agreement to a series of statements about expectations in the practice of journalism on a scale from strongly agree to strongly disagree, with the middle point described as neither agree or disagree. Table 3 shows a summary of the means scores of the items measuring journalistic expectations.

In the United States, the concept of source protection is an often-cited journalistic standard. In Kyrgyzstan, when asked whether *journalists should go to jail to protect their sources,* responses fit into three distinct groups. The largest group (41.1 percent) disagreed or strongly disagreed. Thirty percent neither agreed nor disagreed, and only 28.9 percent agreed or strongly agreed.

A second question asked journalists whether *accepting a trip from a business or government agency was acceptable if there were not story-specific coverage requirement.* More than half (55.8 percent) agreed or strongly agreed. An equal number (22.1 percent) indicated neither agreement nor disagreement, and 22.1 percent indicated disagreement or strong disagreement.

A third question asked *whether journalist should be certified by his or her profession as to qualification, training, and competence.* Nearly three-fourths agreed or strongly agreed (71.6 percent) while only 8 percent disagreed or strongly disagreed and 20.5 percent neither agreed nor disagreed.

Conclusions and Discussion

As experience with many governments around the world shows, the taste of authority may quickly shift from advocating for the press to squelching it. Add to the press conundrum a history of Soviet-domination where the press system was a tool of the state along with a decaying economy and the likelihood of legitimate and sustainable press reform is grim. Rose and Shin (2001, 344) write that "a civil society requires trusted political institutions as well as interpersonal trust." Kyrgyzstan has no such trust, not from the legacy of the communist regime nor from the presidencies of Askar Akayev or Kurmanbek Bakiyev. Citizens who are socialized in an undemocratic regime have little reason to trust the press, nor does the press have reason to trust its institutional roots—roots anchored in a political system that fosters self-censorship.

Survey results suggest that journalists value "correct" professional practices, such as using their training and learning new skills. But escalating government violence against journalists and failing economic conditions have bisected the population into a cadre with access to wealth and a much broader impoverished population. Somewhere in the middle are journalists who, like all citizens, aspire to thrive personally and professionally but there is little expectation that circumstances will improve in the near term. Until they can report without fear of violence against them, they will see limited prospects to achieve professional aspirations. Put simply, journalists cannot be professional until their citizens and government value such conduct.

REFERENCES

Akbarzadeh, Shahram. 2004. "Keeping Central Asia stable." *Third World Quarterly* 25(4): 689–705.

Bensmann, Marcus. 2005. "Return to the Great Game." *Index on Censorship* 34(1): 131–34.

Freedman, Eric, and Richard Shafer. 2003. "Policing press freedom in post-Soviet Central Asia: The monitoring role of press rights activists and their web sites." Paper presented to the Association for Education in Journalism and Mass Communication, Kansas City, Missouri, 4 August 2003.

Freedom House. 2007. "Freedom of the Press: Kyrgyzstan." Http://freedomhouse.org/template.cfm?page=251&year=2007.

Freedom House. 2010. *Freedom of the Press: Kyrgyzstan*. Http://freedomhouse.org/template.cfm?page=251&year=2010.

Henningham, John P. 1984. "Comparisons between three versions of the professional orientation index." *Journalism Quarterly* 61: 302–09.

Hu, Richard W. X. 2005. "China's Central Asia policy: Making sense of the Shanghai Cooperation Organization." In Boris Z. Rumer, ed. *Central Asia at the End of the Transition*. Armonk, NY: M. E. Sharpe.

International Research and Exchanges Board. 2008. "Media Sustainability Index—Europe and

Eurasia: Kyrgyzstan." Www.irex.org/print/resource/kyrgyzstan-media-sustainability-index-msi.

———. 2009. "Media Sustainability Index—Europe and Eurasia: Kyrgyzstan." Www.irex. org/print/resource/kyrgyzstan-media-sustainability-index-msi.

———. 2010. "Media Sustainability Index—Europe and Eurasia: Kyrgyzstan." Www.irex. org/print/resource/kyrgyzstan-media-sustainability-index-msi.

Kenny, Timothy. 2008. "Once-bright future of Central Asia now fading." *Quill* 96: 36.

Kenny, Timothy, and Peter Gross. 2008. "Journalism in Central Asia: A victim of politics, economics, and widespread self-censorship." *International Journal of Press/Politics* 13: 515–26.

Kulikova, Svetlana V., and David D. Perlmutter. 2007. "Blogging down the dictator? The Kyrgyz Revolution and the *Samizdat* websites." *International Communication Gazette* 69: 29–50.

McLeod, Jack M., and Searle E. Hawley, Jr. 1964. "Professionalization among newsmen." *Journalism Quarterly* 41: 529–38, 577.

Nayman, Oguz B. 1973. "Professional orientations of journalists." *Gazette* 34: 195–212.

Pollard, George. 1982. "Radio communicators." *Canadian Journal of Communication* 9: 31–50.

———. 1985. "Professionalism among Canadian newsworkers: A cross-media analysis." *Gazette* 36: 21–38.

———. 1994. "Social attributes and job satisfaction among newsworkers." *Gazette* 52: 193–208.

———. 1995. "Job satisfaction among newsworkers." *Journalism Quarterly* 72: 682–97.

———. 1996. "A comparison of measures of job satisfaction used in studies of social communicators." *Gazette* 57: 111–19.

Pollard, George, and Peter Johansen. 1998. "Professionalism among Canadian newsworkers: The impact of organizational control and social attributes." *Journal of Broadcasting and Electronic Media* 42: 356–70.

Quinn-Judge, Paul. 2010. "When patience runs out." *New York Times.* 12 April. Www.nytimes. com/2010/04/12/opinion/12iht-edquinjudge.html?ref=kyrgyzstan.

Rose, Richard, and Doh Chull Shin. 2001. "Democratization backwards: The problem of third-wave Democracies." *British Journal of Political Science* 31(2): 331–54.

Schwirtz, Michael 2010. "Kyrgyzstan president is offered passage from country." *New York Times.* 9 April. Www.nytimes.com/2010/04/10/world/europe/10kyrgyz.html?scp=6& sq=kyrgyzstan&st=cse.

Schwirtz, Michael and Ellen Barry. 2010. "Russia weighs please to step in as Uzbeks flee Kyrgyzstan." *New York Times.* June 14. Www.nytimes.com/2010/06/15/world/ asia/15kyrgyz.html?scp=8&sq=kyrgyzstan&st=cse.

Zviagel'skaia, Irina 2005. "Russia and Central Asia: Problems of Security." In Boris Z. Rumer, ed. *Central Asia at the End of the Transition,* 71–92. Armonk, NY: M. E. Sharpe.

PART 5

New Media, New Frontiers

Internet Libel Law and Freedom of Expression in Tajikistan

Kristine Kohlmeier and Navruz Nekbakhtshoev

O n July 30, 2007, Tajikistan president Emomali Rakhmonov signed amendments to the country's criminal code to extend the application of existing libel laws to the Internet. Article 135, for example, was amended to say: "Defamation, contained in public presentations, mass media, or *Internet sites,* is punished by obligatory labor from 180 to 240 hours or by fines from 500 to 1000 times the minimum yearly salary, or imprisonment up to two years" (emphasis added). The national assembly (Majlisi Oli) enacted the legislation limiting the right of freedom of expression online despite Tajikistan's minuscule number of Internet users. Although the government estimates that as many as one in twelve citizens use the Internet, most estimates are around one in a thousand; Internet World Stats (2010) put the penetration rate at 9.3 percent. Tajikistan is one of the poorest republics of the former Soviet Union, and Internet costs, currently averaging $0.75 to $1.20 an hour, are beyond most people's means. Furthermore, landlines are decayed and electricity outages are common, especially in winter. Nevertheless, the government determined that Internet regulation is a national priority.

For many countries with highly controlled presses, the Internet remains a last refuge for freedom of expression. It also offers the benefits of limited anonymity and a worldwide audience. The lengths the government will go to stifle freedom of expression online reflects the need to examine the country's Internet laws. Although few citizens now go online, that does not make the Internet irrelevant; regulations on use and access affect many groups connected with Tajikistan, including citizens, the Tajikistani diasporas, and scholars of the country and Central Asia.

Research Questions

Why would the government enact the Internet libel amendments, given that the masses lack Internet access? How will media, and Internet content in particular, change as a result of the amendments?

The chapter first argues that the government uses the libel amendments as part of a broader so-called information security campaign against opposition elites with Internet access as a weapon to deter online scrutiny into government incompetence and abuse. In effect, the law is intended to curtail the freedom of a few active opposition members, whether at home or abroad. Second, it hypothesizes that the amendments will produce a chilling effect on online media within the Commonwealth of Independent States (CIS) and will encourage online contributors to set up Web sites from countries outside the CIS. Furthermore, the law will target nongovernmental organizations (NGOs).

Thus this chapter discusses and evaluates the development of the Internet libel amendments and anticipates their adverse effects on Internet use and freedom of the press. First, it conceptualizes and examines libel, both generally and specifically, in Tajikistan. Second, it argues that libel laws are used as a means of de facto censorship. Third, it discusses the likely effects of criminal libel laws and anticipates their implications for the Internet and media in Tajikistan.

Conceptualizing Defamation

Defamation is making false statements to harm another's reputation. Slander and libel are both forms of defamation: slander is generally spoken and libel is recorded, most often in print, broadcast media, or on the Internet (Garner 2004). What constitutes libel depends on a country's legal system. For example, some countries recognize the truth of a statement as a defense. Other reasons, such as public comment and journalistic relevance, may also serve as defenses to libel. Libel can be against a single person or a group, but generally, the larger the group, the less likely a libel case is to succeed (Sadler 2005, 174). Some countries impose criminal liability for seditious libel, which is libel specifically against the government and its representatives, regardless of a statement's truth or falsity.

In addition to libel laws, many countries have "insult laws" that shield elected officials from public criticism and can, in effect, penalize the truth. Having both libel and insult laws puts great strain on freedom of expression. In countries with only libel laws, opinions and value judgments are generally protected speech. With the addition of insult laws, almost any negative opinion faces scrutiny.

Libel can be prosecuted in civil courts (where individuals and groups sue for legal or equitable remedies, such as monetary damages and injunctions against dissemination of allegedly defamatory material) or criminal courts (where the government prosecutes and convicts defendants and imposes fines or jail sentences). Criminal libel laws exist throughout the world, including in many European countries and some states in the United States. However, most Western countries do not criminally prosecute under such laws (Article 19: Global Campaign for Free Expression 2006).[1] Miklos Haraszti, the former Organization for Security and Cooperation in Europe (OSCE) representative on freedom of the media, called criminal libel laws "inadequate, even detrimental, to a modern democracy where freedom of the press and uninhibited discussion of public issues could be diminished by a general chilling effect of a criminal libel sentence used against journalists for their work" (OSCE 2004). Additionally, other organizations cite Article 19 of the Universal Declaration of Human Rights, which recognizes freedom of expression and opinion.

Most international media rights and human rights organizations prefer libel claims be settled in civil rather than criminal courts, but costly lawsuits can be as damaging to defendants as jail time. Governments can use both civil and criminal libel laws to counter criticism. In the United States, following the Supreme Court's opinion in *New York Times v. Sullivan* and subsequent cases, public figures, such as elected officials and well-known people, must meet a heightened standard of proof to win a libel case.[2] They must prove that the information was not true, that the publisher knew of its falsity or acted with "reckless disregard for the truth" but still published it, and that the publication damaged the plaintiff. The justification for that heightened standard is that public figures have better access to the media and can more easily combat libel than ordinary citizens. In contrast, many countries take the opposite approach by adopting seditious libel laws so that public figures, particularly elected officials, need to meet only a *lower* standard of proof. Seditious libel laws greatly increase both an official's chances of winning a civil suit and a government's chances of obtaining a conviction. Says free speech scholar Harry Kalven Jr., "[A]ny society in which seditious libel is a crime is, no matter what its other features, not a free society" (qtd. in Gillmor 1992, 4).

Libel Law in the Soviet Union and the Post-Soviet Union Sphere

During the Soviet era, self-censorship was a honed skill (Loersch and Grigorian 2000, 13). Defaming the Soviet authority was a criminal offense, with a possible seven-year prison sentence. Libel laws were relaxed during glasnost, and after the breakup of the Soviet Union, some Eastern European countries abolished, or at least relaxed, their criminal libel laws (save Belarus). But in some Central Asian states the situation is worse today than during the last years of the Soviet era (Yanchukova 2003, 883).

Legal Provisions in Tajikistan

Article 30 of the Constitution of Tajikistan guarantees freedom of speech and publishing and forbids state censorship and prosecution for criticism.[3] Among other laws, Article 2 of Tajikistan's law "On the press and other media" gives citizens the right to free expression in the media, without censorship.

Laws in the Tajikistan Criminal Code. Article 135 defines *libel* as distribution of knowingly false information through public presentations, media, and Internet that defames a person's honor, dignity, or reputation. Punishments escalate for publicizing such information in speeches or mass media, making defamatory statements in tandem with another crime, and having base motives.[4] *Insult* is defined in Article 136 as abasement of honor and dignity, expressed in an indecent way, through public presentations, media, and Internet, and punishment is increased if the insult relates to the victims' discharge of their public duty.[5] The seditious libel provisions provide up to five years in prison for insulting the president in the media (Article 137) and up to two years for insulting a public official (Article 330). Articles 137 and 330 contain provisions extending them to Internet content.

Relatively few court cases in Tajikistan have focused on media law, let alone Internet law, so the laws are primarily interpreted as written (Loersch and Grigorian 2000, 3).

Tajikistan Media Law in Perspective

Tajikistan became an independent republic after the breakup of the Soviet Union in September 1991. Immediately before and after independence, it adopted laws promoting openness and freedom of expression during a period of "democratic romanticism."[6] By mid-1992 the country was immersed in what would become a five-year civil war. The public blamed the media for instigating the war because there were "too many outlets" spread among the government and opposition parties. The government banned opposition parties and opposition media from 1993 to 1999. During the war the death toll of journalists was "one of the highest . . . ever documented," according to the Committee to Protect Journalists (CPJ). As a result, most competent journalists had left the country by 1994 (Loersch and Grigorian 2000, 6).

The civil war remains a pretext for the government's restraints on free expression (Article 19: Global Campaign for Free Expression 2007, 4). After the war, opposition media was allowed to reopen their outlets and opposition parties entered the government, but significant democratic progress failed to materialize. Independent media organizations still face frequent inspections, denials of licenses, and financial difficulties.[7] The Media Sustainability Index 2010, published by the International Research and Exchanges Board (IREX), rated Tajikistan as having an "unsustainable mixed system," reflecting limited progress in professionalism, free press advocacy, and media business (IREX, 254). In general, the media exercises self-restraint for fear of violating the law, and lack of media law specialists and judicial interpretations of media laws have ensured that journalists err on the side of caution or over-caution. For example, the law "On television and radio" includes a clause limiting authorities' ability to interfere in the creative activity of television and radio organizations and prohibits state action against criticism. Some analysts claim that law limits freedom of expression because the direct reference to "creative activities" suggests that only creativity will not be questioned, but all else is open to prosecution (Loersch and Grigorian 2000, 8). The absence of definitive legal rulings means that the first and second clauses of the statute remain open to interpretation.

Presently, entertainment-oriented newspapers and broadcast media remain popular. The government dominates broadcasting by supplying most outlets and controlling who can enter the media market. Between 2004 and 2006 the government shut down three newspapers, two television stations, and British Broadcasting Corporation radio. One television station regained its license in 2007 (CPJ 2007). In 2003, 2005, and 2006 the government ordered Web sites closed. The October 2006 temporary shutdown of five sites came before the November 2006 presidential election, which Rakhmonov won with 79 percent of the vote (Article 19: Global Campaign for Free Expression 2007, 5–6, 16). The professed rationale for closing Web sites was that they "undermined the state's policies"

(U.S. Department of State 2009). Even so, in general, filtering and blocking sites is not an official policy because restraining freedom of expression jeopardizes the government's ability to obtain foreign aid; however, the government "maintain[s] firm control over the distribution of information, particularly before elections" (OpenNet Initiative 2007).

Individual Internet service providers (ISPs) have also been accused of blocking Web sites. The Web site Toptj.com reported being blocked by the popular ISP Babilon-t during the energy crisis of 2008 (Ariana.su 2008).

Libel Laws as an Institution to Constrain Internet and Media in Tajikistan

The government proffers several rationales for its criminal libel laws. One is "information security." Information security is similar to, but wider than, provisions guarding state secrets. For example, limiting distribution of information about pornography, violence, ethnic and religious hostility, and information that intends to "discredit the honor and dignity of the state and the president" are considered aspects of information security (OpenNet Initiative 2007). According to National Association of Independent Media of Tajikistan (NANSMIT) program coordinator Abdufatoh Vohidov, by denying licenses to local radio and television programs under the pretext of information security, the government actually undermines national security. This happens because in the absence of local programming, people listen to and watch programs with allegedly anti-Tajikistan agendas that are broadcast from neighboring countries. For example, Tajikistani television, for lack of airwaves, does not operate properly in the northern Soghd region, so residents there watch Uzbekistani television programming. He holds that "the emphasis on information security serves as a convenient tool to intimidate and repress independent media."[8] Additionally, analysts suggested that information security was the reason for the government's blocking of sites in anticipation of the November 2006 presidential election (Ghufronov 2007).

Another reason the government presents for the existence of criminal libel laws is to respect individuals' dignity, including the dignity of public servants. In the constitution, the honor and dignity of the individual is sacred (Article 5). In other former Soviet states, seditious libel laws are often defended under a "defense of democracy" theory (Yanchukova 2003, 870). However, human rights groups counter that legislation against slandering politicians restricts political debate.

Enhancing the professionalism of journalists is a third reason the government offers for maintaining criminal libel laws. As a spokesperson for the cultural ministry said, there need to be "instruments to make people think about the consequences of their actions before they do anything" (CPJ 2007). Overall, journalistic professionalism is low. Media organizations attribute that to financial difficulties, lack of training in proper journalistic methods, and the exodus and murders of competent journalists during the civil war (Loersch and Grigorian 2000, 14). As NANSMIT program coordinator Vohidov says: "The media has chief editors whose job is to ensure that no material containing defamation gets published. Therefore, to suggest that the Internet libel law was adopted to improve the quality of journalism is misleading. If anything, this law forces media to self-censor and this undermines all that is good about journalism."[9]

Although self-censorship has prevented many actual convictions, there have been prosecutions. In one, the government charged an editor of *Ovoza* and two journalists after a pop singer complained about their negative concert review. The government charged the journalists under the criminal libel and insult laws, meaning a possibility of time in jail. The newspaper's editor said: "We are being persecuted for expressing a critical opinion, and this is a violation of Article 30 of the Constitution" (International Freedom of Expression eXchange 2007). In another case, a city court fined a woman the equivalent of fifteen hundred dollars after two judges claimed insult to their "honor, dignity and business reputation" as a result of a letter she wrote to the president about a decision she found unfair (Human Rights Watch 2008). The organization Article 19: Global Campaign for Free Expression reported on nine civil cases dealing with the honor and dignity of officials in 1999–2004 and six cases in 2006. It also cited three criminal libel cases during the same period. One defendant received a five-year sentence for insult and defamation of the president; another man was sentenced to one year of forced labor for accusing a professor of corruption (Article 19: Global Campaign for Free Expression 2007, 4). A third case involved Dodozhon Atovulleov, founder of the newspaper *Charoghi Ruz* (Light of Day), which was shut down in 1992 and then published from Moscow with grant money from the National Endowment for Democracy (Loersch and Grigorian 2000, 6).[10] At Tajikistan's request, Moscow police arrested Atovulleov and threatened him with extradition for the crime of insulting the president and defamation, among other charges. The prosecutor general characterized him as an "information terrorist" (Committee to Protect Journalists 2009). The case was later dismissed in Russia, but it shows how a journalist can be prosecuted for libel, no matter where the allegedly libelous statement is printed or spoken (Article 19: Global Campaign for Free Expression 2007, 13–14).

Several civil lawsuits against media outlets were litigated in the run-up to the February 28, 2010, parliamentary elections. In October 2009, Tajikstandart, a state corporation, sued the newsweekly *Paykon* for libel over an open letter from a group of businesspeople to the president concerning corruption by the corporation. The guilty verdict, a fine of $40,000 to be paid to Tajikstandart, was upheld in January 2010 (Radio Free Europe/Radio Liberty 2010). A similar lawsuit was filed against the newsweekly *Millat* for criticizing the agricultural ministry. In another lawsuit in late January 2010, judges sued *Ozodagon, Farazh*, and *Asia-Plus* for 1.2 million dollars in damages over allegations of judicial corruption. The judges also asked the court to cease publication of the popular news sources. "The fact that the plaintiffs in this case are powerful judges sends a chilling message to the independent press," said Nina Ognianova, the CPJ Europe and Central Asia Program coordinator. (CPJ 2010). In fall 2010, the authors contacted a former Radio Free Europe/ Radio Free Liberty reporter for updates on the cases; neither he nor any other editors he contacted could find information about the cases. A criminal libel prosecution was reported in IREX's Media and Sustainability Index 2010 (2546) in which a journalist was ordered to do 200 hours of community service as punishment for an allegedly libelous article about corruption.

It is important to recognize that aggressive use of libel laws is just part of the government's anti-press arsenal. As a U.S. Department of State (2009) human rights overview noted:

> The government subjected the media to different means of control and intimidation; media outlets regularly practiced self-censorship out of fear of government reprisal. Credible media sources observed that certain topics were considered off limits including derogatory information about the president or his family members, or questions about financial impropriety by those close to the president. Government authorities occasionally subjected individual journalists to harassment and intimidation . . . Journalists reported that government officials limited their access to information or provided advice on what news should not be covered . . . Other common types of harassment included prosecutions to intimidate journalists, warnings made by telephone and in person at a prosecutor's office or during visits to editorial offices, and selective tax inspections.

Tajikistan's Internet Libel Laws

On July 19, 2007, the Majlisi Oli, Tajikistan's pro-presidential People's Democratic Party–dominated parliament, passed a series of amendments that extended defamation and sedition laws to online content (CPJ 2007). Rakhmonov signed the amendments on July 30, and they were printed on August 7 in the state-run journal *Sadoi Mardum*. The process of amending the criminal code "went off too hurriedly, without discussions with journalists," said Qironsho Sharifzoda, head of an association of journalists in Tajikistan (Ghufronov 2007). There is consensus among analysts whom we interviewed concerning the factors that led to adoption of these amendments. According to one OSCE senior media analyst in Tajikistan, the amendments were instigated by the government's discovery of critical discussions on online forums such as Ariana.su and Ferghana.ru, in particular comments about Amirsho Miraliev, the former chairman of the Khatlon region and now head of the presidential administration, who allegedly acquired key assets through illegal means.[11] NANSMIT program coordinator Vohidov asserts that "it was a string of compromising reports against the president's administration malfeasance and incompetence rather than one single incident which led the government to adopt the [Internet libel] amendment to curtail the discretionary power of several websites." He described how Ariana.su published materials criticizing the president's daughter Tahmina Rakhmonova for monopolizing business in Tajikistan and illegally acquiring her rivals' assets. Additionally, Vohidov said a clear indication of the libel laws' repressive effects on local media was illustrated by news about the death of Hasan Sadulloev, head of Orion Bank, who was allegedly shot by the president's son for outcompeting the president's daughter in business transactions. In-depth commentary and conspiracy theories about Sadulloev's death were notably lacking on Web sites ending with the country code *.tj*.[12] One site, Uzmetronom.com, claimed that Rakhmonov sought to punish any source that published information about such a conspiracy (Najibullah 2008). According to Vohidov, little doubt remains that the primary motive for the libel amendments was to prevent investigations into the president, his family, and his associates' malfeasance.

The July 30, 2007, amendments applied to criminal code Articles 135 (libel), 136 (insult), 137 (defaming or insulting the president), 144 (violating one's privacy), 307–307.1 (calling for an overthrow of the government and extremism), 330 (insulting a public official), and 396 (calling for war). The crimes and punishments remain the same as for print and broadcast libel, with the potential for heavy fines and jail time.

The judiciary has devoted little exploration to concepts such as defamation and insult, and many analysts worry that broadening the libel laws will only make understanding libel as it applies in Tajikistan more difficult. One consideration is the language of the laws themselves. Miklos Haraszti, the then-OSCE media representative, said words such as "Internet," "information," and "distribution" are too vague and governments could interpret them too broadly. Further, "[d]istribution could mean sharing, debating, or just obtaining information through any Internet-based media, from e-mails to personal websites, from online diaries to news portals" (Hamroboyeva 2007).

Dissemination through the Internet is difficult to track because messages can be forwarded, reposted, translated; sent via blogs, e-mail, chat rooms, listservs, social networking sites, and discussion groups; and posted on servers hosted in multiple countries. Additionally, the relative anonymity of the Internet enables people to post in someone else's name, creating the risk of wrongful prosecution. For example, the government in Azerbaijan convicted Eynulla Fatullayev, the editor of that country's largest independent newspaper, of criminal libel and insult against the community of Azerbaijanis living in the village of Khojali in the contested territory of Nagorno-Karabakh. To win a conviction, the government used statements attributed to him on a Web site, based on an article he had previously written. That conviction suggests that in Tajikistan, an online article or book review also could be subject to libel laws (Human Rights Watch 2007).

Multiple prosecutions for the same or similar online postings may be possible. In Belarus, which has defamation laws comparable to Tajikistan's, the publication of a single article triggered two successive criminal prosecutions. The first time, the government fined the editor; the second time, the government closed the publication (Article 19: Global Campaign for Free Expression 2006). Retraction of articles on the Internet can be impossible. Certain types of sites aggregate online postings to increase the amount of traffic they receive (and therefore advertising revenue), and removing a post from a "spam" Web site or "splog" is next to impossible.

Questions about where to prosecute libel remain unanswered. Earlier this chapter noted the case of Dodozhon Atovulleov, who was arrested in Russia for defamation of the president of Tajikistan. Russian authorities did not extradite him, but other countries may agree to extradite journalists as part of their plans for regional information security. The government may find several ways to establish jurisdiction: if the person who posts (or accesses) information online is in Tajikistan; if the ISP and Internet Protocol (IP) are in Tajikistan; if the person is outside Tajikistan but writing on a Web site hosted in Tajikistan (.tj); or if the person is a citizen but is outside the country and is posting on a site hosted outside Tajikistan.

Conclusion: Implications of the Internet Libel Amendments

FOR INTERNET JOURNALISM

Tajikistani journalists already self-censor, so the amount of hard-hitting news and editorials will remain low. The common wisdom is "when in doubt, leave it out," and with an unclear, rarely interpreted legal code, much doubt remains. Government officials tend to interpret criticism as libel and sue their critics, says the director of the Tajikistan press freedom group Foundation for the Commemoration and Protection of Journalists (CPJ 2007).

Civil lawsuits against print newsweeklies increased in 2010, but no prosecutions based on Internet content have occurred. Nurali Davlatov, editor-in-chief of *Farazh*, states that bloggers in Tajikistan, few in number, remain relatively safe because the government is not well versed on blogging (IREX, 257). Nonetheless, some analysts predict that the chilling effect of the government's treatment of journalists will become more pronounced and self-censorship will rise. Vohidov of NANSMIT says the "Internet libel law is used as an instrument to intimidate journalists."[13] Nuriddin Qarshiboyev, who heads NANSMIT, predicted that journalists will increase self-censorship (Ghufronov 2007). Journalist Marat Mamadshoev went further, stating that the amendments were a "reactionary step" against the Internet, a "sphere of maximum freedom" (Institute for War and Peace Reporting 2007). CPJ predicted in July 2007 that popular sites would reduce their criticism. In winter 2007 through summer of 2008, the authors examined the Web sites mentioned in the CPJ article and found that (1) Ferghana.ru and Centrasia.ru did not significantly change over the past few years; (2) Tajikistantimes.ru was online in February 2008 without any Tajikistan-related content and was offline in March 2008; (3) Charogiruz.ru was not updated since February 2007; and (4) Asiaplus.tj, the only site mentioned by CPJ that is hosted in Tajikistan, was still editorializing, but its articles are less critical than they once were.[14] On the other hand, Ariana.su ran critical content. In fall of 2010, the authors reexamined the Web sites and found that Ferghana.ru and Centrasia.ru remained consistent, Asiaplus.tj ran more neutral articles Ariana.su has only one update in the previous six months. The other sites no longer carried news. New sites that featured news and critical commentary about Tajikistan had appeared in 2010, such as Tjknews. com, hosted from the United States.

FOR THE REGION

Libel laws throughout the world are not heading in a uniform direction, even in the same regions. In Eastern Europe, for example, some countries have abolished criminal libel and restrained civil libel; other countries have advanced and regressed in their libel laws. The countries of former Soviet Central Asia, despite infighting, share many structural features, including similar legal systems that developed from Soviet legal codes. Now that Tajikistan has implemented online defamation laws, it is more likely that other Central Asian countries will enact and enforce similar laws. However, like Eastern Europe, these countries do not move in lock-step, but the overall trend among the region's authoritarian regimes is to continue prosecutions under criminal libel laws. Expanding libel to the Internet, therefore, appears likely.

Tajikistan keeps close ties with regional powers Russia and China. Given that most critical Web sites are hosted outside the country and do not use a .tj domain name, it remains to be seen whether Russia and China will help the country enforce the Internet libel amendments. At the Shanghai Cooperation Organization summit in Bishkek on August 17, 2007, President Rakhmonov called on member states to work out a concrete information security plan. That plan does not appear to be jointly created or enforced, and therefore countries will have to decide to what extent they will cooperate with Tajikistan's and other national information security plans. Russia's rejection of the government's extradition request for an arrested editor, Atovulleov, suggests Russia will cooperate—but only so far—so Tajikistan will have only limited say in what could be seen as Russia's internal affairs. Further, if Russia tries to regain favor with Europe, it will be less likely to take part in investigations that involve potential human rights abuses. China is well known for its censorship of the Internet, as well as all other forms of media, and is carrying out many infrastructure projects in Tajikistan, especially roadwork. In the future, China may also share Internet technology so that online posts can be tracked to individual computers and use can be monitored, especially if Tajikistan is convinced that such monitoring is necessary.

FOR DEMOCRATIZATION AND CIVIL SOCIETY

The Internet libel amendments are detrimental to democratization because they prevent journalists and lay commentators from openly writing and speaking about internal affairs. The government monopolizes the system of communications in

Tajikistan, where the Internet has the potential to create new venues for self-expression, by both individuals and traditional mass media outlets, and tougher Internet libel laws stifle communication.

The amendments create yet another way for civil society groups and NGOs to be closed down by the police or sued out of existence. If an NGO loses its yearly budget through civil fines or must spend most of its time defending lawsuits in civil court, the NGO will be less capable of doing its mission. Civil lawsuits by government officials stemming from potential Internet libel are more likely because the government can avoid responsibility for harming a civil group. If the NGO or civil society group tries to blame the government for its lost resources due to libel suits, the government can shift the blame to nongovernmental groups or individuals suing in their individual capacities. This way, even if governmental officials are the plaintiffs, they are not suing as government entities per se, but as private citizens, and the government can technically remain an outsider to the proceedings.

NGOs and civil society groups in Tajikistan and Central Asia as a whole feel pressure from the government to self-censor, and that pressure has increased since passage of the Internet libel amendments. Even if the amendments are never enforced, they have still damaged democratization and civil society.

NOTES

1. Article 10 of the European Convention on Human Rights (ECHR) protects freedom of speech and has discouraged criminal libel prosecutions.
2. *New York Times v. Sullivan*, 376 U.S. 254 (1964).
3. Legal documents are cited come from the following Web sites: The Constitution of Tajikistan, www.legislationline.org/upload/legislations/c9/94/5f95858dea5e2a62de8 4f0c7f650.pdf (includes post-war amendments); law "On the press and other media," www.nfoic.org/tajikistan-media-law?s=tajikistan%20media%20olaw; the Criminal Code of Tajikistan was privately sent from the Bureau on Human Rights and Rule of Law and is updated through July 30, 2007; law and "On television and radio," www.medialaw.ru/exussrlaw/l/tg/broadcast.htm.
4. Article 135: Defamation reads: (1) Defamation, that is, the spread of false information defaming the honor and dignity of another person or tarnishing his reputation, is punished by obligatory labor from 120 to 180 hours or by fines from 500 times the minimum yearly salary, or corrective labor for up to two years. (2) Defamation, contained in public presentations, mass media, or Internet sites, is punished by

obligatory labor from 180 to 240 hours or by fines from 500 to 1000 times the minimum yearly salary, or imprisonment up to two years. (3) Defamation, associated with accusing a person of a serious crime, is punished by imprisonment from three to five years.

5. Article 136: Insult reads: (1) Insult, that is, the humiliation of someone's honor and dignity, expressed in an inappropriate form, is punished by obligatory labor from 60 to 120 hours or by fines from 200 times the minimum yearly salary, or corrective labor for up to two years. (2) Insult: (a) contained in public presentations, mass media, or Internet sites (b) is punished by obligatory labor from 120 to 180 hours or by fines from 200 to 500 times the minimum yearly salary, or corrective labor for up to two years.

6. The law "On the press and other media" is such an example.

7. Media outlets must officially register and be licensed, according to the law "On the press and other media."

8. Author's interview, Dushanbe, Tajikistan. July 29, 2008.

9. Ibid.

10. Atovulleov has most recently been called an "information terrorist" by Tajikistan's general prosecutor, Bobodjon Bobokhonov (Ferghana.ru 2008).

11. The suffix .su is the country code top-level domain for the Soviet Union, and .ru is hosted from Russia.

12. The following spellings were searched on Google.com on August 16, 2008, to find relevant articles about the alleged death. The results for postings were in English: Sadullaev (7), Sadulloev (35), Asadullozoda (6), Saduloev (11) (no Sadulaev); in Russian/Tajik language: Sadullaev (8), Sadulloev (4), Asadullozoda (27), Saduloev (4); and on .tj sites written in Russian/Tajik language: Sadullaev (1), Asadullozoda (6), Saduloev, Sadulloev (0).

13. Author's interview, Dushanbe, Tajikistan. July 29, 2008.

14. Www.minirank.com/tld/tj/ lists the most popular Web sites in Tajikistan by domain name. At the time of writing, Asiaplus.tj ranked as third most popular .tj site.

REFERENCES

Ariana.su. 2008. "Babilon tsenzura" (Babilon censorship). August 13. Www.ariana. su/?S=5.0802131923.

Article 19: Global Campaign for Free Expression. 2006. "Defamation law and practice in Belarus, Moldova, and Ukraine." June. Www.article19.org/pdfs/publications/ the-right-to-criticise.pdf.

———. 2007. "The policy of control: The state of freedom of expression in Tajikistan." July. Www.article19.org/pdfs/publications/tajikistan-policy-of-control.pdf.

Committee to Protect Journalists. 2007. "CPJ calls on Tajik president to veto Internet criminal defamation bill." July 26. Www.cpj.org/news/2007/asia/tajik26july07na.html.

———. 2009. "Attacks on the press in 2008." February 24. Www.cpj.org/2009/02/attacks-on-the-press-in-2008.php.

———. 2010. "Tajik judges seek millions from weeklies in civil libel case" February 3. Www.cpj.org/2010/02/tajik-judges-seek-millions-from-weeklies-in-civil.php#more.

Ferghana.ru. 2008. "Tajikistan: General prosecutor accuses dissident of 'informational terrorism.'" July 11. Http://enews.ferghana.ru/news.php?id=495&mode=snews&PHPSESSID=8b ocfd9b8e3c7f9de1b9660f2c6a9a8a.

Garner, Bryan A., ed. 2004. *Black's Law Dictionary.* St. Paul, MN: Thomson West.

Ghufronov, Daler. 2007. "Tajik journalists say Internet libel law to have negative consequences." Asia Plus. August 24. Www.asiaplus.tj/en/news/41/21366.html.

Gillmor, Donald M. 1992. *Power, Publicity, and the Abuse of Libel Law.* New York: Oxford University Press.

Hamroboyeva, Nargis. 2007. "OSCE media freedom representative calls on Tajikistan to protect free flow of information on Internet." Asia Plus. September 25. Www.asiaplus.tj/en/news/19/22618.html.

Human Rights Watch. 2007. "Azerbaijan: opposition editor sentenced to prison." April 25. Www.hrw.org/english/docs/2007/04/26/azerba15790.htm.

———. 2008. "World report: Tajikistan: Events of 2007." Http://hrw.org/englishwr2k8/docs/2008/01/31/tajiki17748.htm.

Institute for War and Peace Reporting. 2007. "Tajiks face jail for Internet libel." July 24. Http://iwpr.net/report-news/tajiks-face-jail-internet-libel.

International Freedom of Expression eXchange. 2007. "Alert: Editor, two journalists face criminal libel charges over concert review."October 15. Www.ifex.org/en/content/view/full/86995.

International Research and Exchanges Board. 2010. "Media and sustainability index 2010." Www.irex.org/system/files/Europe%20MSI%202010_Full%20Version.pdf.

Internet World Stats. 2010. Www.internetworldstats.com.

Loersch, André, and Mark Grigorian. 2000. "Report on the media situation in Tajikistan." CIMERA (Civic Development, Media Support, Research and Analysis). October. Www.cimera.org/files/reports/Media_Report_Tajik2000.pdf.

Najibullah, Farangis. 2008. "Tajikistan. 'Disappearance' of president's brother-in-law sparks rumors." Radio Free Europe/Radio Free Liberty. May 15. Www.rferl.org/content/article/1117487.html.

OpenNet Initiative. 2007. "Tajikistan." May 19. Http://opennet.net/research/profiles/tajikistan.

Organization for Security and Cooperation in Europe. 2004. "Successes and continued concerns over libel." July 29. Www.osce.org/item/204.html. Radio Free Europe/ Radio Free Liberty. 2010. "Tajik court upholds verdict against independent weekly" January 29. Www.rferl.org/content/Tajik_Court_Upholds_Verdict_Against_Indepen- dent_Weekly/1941643.html.

Sadler, Roger L. 2005. *Electronic Media Law.* Thousand Oaks, CA: Sage.

U.S. Department of State. 2009. "Tajikistan." *2008 Country Reports on Human Rights Practices.* February 25.

Yanchukova, Elena. 2003. "Criminal defamation and insult laws: An infringement on the freedom of expression in European and post-communist jurisdictions." *Columbia Journal of Transnational Law* 41: 861–94.

Blogging Down the Dictator? The Kyrgyz Revolution and Samizdat Web Sites

Svetlana V. Kulikova and David D. Perlmutter

Kyrgyzstan, a small Central Asian country of five million people, made the front pages of print and Web newspapers and the broadcast leads of the world media on March 24, 2005. On that day, President Askar Akayev, who had ruled the former Soviet republic for fourteen years, fled the country after a series of large public protests, including one in which demonstrators seized the government building in the capital of Bishkek. As in many such events, narrative and causality were in the eye of the beholder. Western media, drawing parallels with earlier uprisings in the Republic of Georgia and Ukraine, initially described the events as a Tulip Revolution (referring to the flower held up by protesters as a symbol of spring renewal) enacted via "people power" (*Christian Science Monitor* 2005; *Herald Sun* 2005; *Houston Chronicle* 2005). Other characterizations abounded. The fall of the Kyrgyz leader was deemed a "garden-variety" coup (Smith 2005; Burkett 2005), a "scary democratic rebellion" (Sullivan 2005), and even a CIA black-op (Spencer 2005; Laughland 2005).

Russian pro-government media labeled the events in Kyrgyzstan a U.S.-backed coup, "sandpaper revolution"(Yuferova 2005), and unconstitutional ouster of Askar Akayev, creator of "the most liberal regime in Central Asia" (Leontiev 2005). Russian independent media portrayed the leader's departure as a case of "democratic barbarianism against civilized authoritarianism" (Panfilova, Sas, and Gordienko, 2005). The media in the neighboring Central Asian republics of Kazakhstan and Uzbekistan—ruled by similar oppressive regimes—either ignored the fall of the long-term ruler or condemned it, putting the main emphasis on the night of looting following the revolution. The message delivered to their populations was: "Don't try this here!"[1] Most of the domestic media in Kyrgyzstan were in a difficult position when reporting the events of March 24, as no one knew where President Akayev was. State-controlled media, confused as to who was in charge, produced unreliable and erroneous accounts, which forced many people to search for alternative sources of information, often Internet-based.[2]

The motivations behind the downfall of the president, who styled himself a "true democrat," will probably not be sorted out for years. After gaining independence in 1991, Kyrgyzstan faced a number of historical challenges to becoming anything approximating a democracy: a weak tradition of free elections and civil society; a population long reared in either Soviet totalitarianism or tribal paternalism; regional divisions and unrest; a possible Islamic insurgency that reflects more frustrations with secular political alternatives than any true turn to fundamentalism; huge gaps between the super wealthy (often members of a few families like the Akayevs) and the impoverished multitudes; and a growing division between a rising urban middle class and a countryside still dominated by clans and populated by peasants.

Among many challenges, the ruling elite largely controlled Kyrgyzstan's mass media. Anti-government voices could be found in only two opposition newspapers, *Moya Stolitsa-Novosti* and *Res Publica.* It was widely suspected that these tribunes of anti-Akayev sentiment were allowed to exist so that the regime could point them out to Westerners as examples of press "freedom." The other avenue of opposition expression—until the street protests—was the Internet. Those with Web access could obtain information from the oppositional sites at newspapers *MSN* (www.msn.kg), *Res Publica* (www.respublica.kg), and those of NGOs and political movements, such as the Coalition of NGOs for Democracy and Civil Society and the youth movement Birge, the popular online newspaper Gazeta.kg (www.gazeta.kg), and the Web site Kyrgyz.us (www.kyrgyz.us), targeted Kyrgyzstanis abroad. However, after the controversial parliamentary elections in February 2005, a team of hackers hired by pro-government interests regularly blocked access to and hacked into the content of these sites (Kyrgyzinfo 2005).

In a land where almost all information is controlled by the government or its allies, sources such as Gazeta.kg and Kyrgyz.us present a sort of virtual *samizdat*, the name given to the Soviet-era unofficial, self-published opposition writings. The term is comprised of two Russian words—*sam* (meaning "self") and *izdat* ("publishing"), and Western audiences perhaps know it best for the contribution of samizdat dissident literature to the Polish Solidarnost movement in the 1970s–80s. Then, however, samizdat spread via mimeograph machines and briefcases. Today oppositional literature is largely an incarnation of the Internet, a venue where dissent can be open and clear or camouflaged in metaphors and allusions, depending on the effectiveness of online censorship (Zha and Perlmutter 2008). The "how" and "why" and "with what effect" of such a phenomenon is of great interest. As Barber, Mattson, and Peterson argue, the convergence of democracy and technology is the most important question facing society (1997, 17). It is also an applied question: how we as individuals, students of neither the political order nor of new media, can understand what people are actually doing with technology to push political transformation. The issue is complicated because repressive governments are quite aware of bloggers: they employ their own technology (filters, hacking) as well as old-fashioned strong-arm tactics to silence blogs. China, for example, is increasingly sophisticated in blocking and filtering objectionable content, often with the assistance of Western software providers (Fallows 2008; Open Initiative 2005; Perlmutter and Hamilton 2007; Chinese Human Rights Defenders 2007; Zha and Perlmutter 2008).

This chapter evaluates the impact and significance of Akaevu.net (www. akaevu.net), an advocacy blog created by the author of Gazeta.kg and Kyrgyz.us as a temporary solution to deliver information to people who could not access the blocked and hacked sites.[3] It addresses these questions:

- To what extent do samizdat blogs serve as legitimate sources for oppositional information for citizens and international observers?
- What content in samizdat blogs differentiates them from oral, written, or other sources of unofficial information?
- What content in samizdat blogs differentiates them from what readers may learn from traditional outsider media, such as international newspapers or television news?
- What evidence is available to evaluate the effects of samizdat blogs on the political events, in this case the revolution itself?
- To what extent can samizdat blogs serve to incite or sustain democratization in Third World countries? If so, must the democracy model follow Western patterns?

At first glance, the weblog would seem to be the loneliest form of opposition in a country where computer access and Internet use can be counted in the single digits among a poor rural population (Dimitrova and Beilock 2005). But in revolutions, sheer numbers are not the main guarantor of success or failure. A few thousand Bolsheviks, for example, seized Russia in 1917, while millions of protesters could not move the Chinese government in 1989 (Zha and Perlmutter 2008). Indeed, only about a thousand demonstrators in Kyrgyzstan actually took over the government building and sent the president packing (British Broadcasting Corporation 2005).

While no direct link exists between blogs and the fall of authoritarianism, this study explores the Akaevu.net blog's role in the Kyrgyz opposition and, more specifically, in covering the revolution itself. It argues that Third World blogs can be a significant producer, collector, sifter, distributor, and exhibitor of information. In addition, for fast-moving events occurring in a world news economy that increasingly precludes staffing correspondents in "out-of-the-way" nations, the blog can also "scoop" international media, because the "citizen journalist" is literally on the scene with cell-phone camera and laptop (Perlmutter and Hamilton 2007; Perlmutter 2008).

Can Democracy Be Transferred—by Blog?

This section speculates on whether the blog may serve as a training ground or mechanism in creating alternative communities of opposition. Blogs may be online journals, but in terms of participative association they are equivalent to tavern meeting groups of pre-revolutionary America and reading clubs and salons of prerevolutionary France. Individuals who tend to participate in revolutions, ranging from students to technicians to intellectuals, not only can communicate with and mobilize one another but also get to a vast realm of information outside official content. In numbers, the rise of blogs is impressive: there are now hundreds of millions of bloggers, who post reports and opinions on subjects as wide-ranging as pets to plumbing and food to politics (Perlmutter 2008). Many international nongovernmental organizations have tried to raise the profile of the voices of the developing world. Harvard's Global Voices Project, for example surveys blogs around the world.[4]

In nations where blogs are actively politically repressed, they can constitute a political factor. Farsi (Persian), for example, is the third most represented language among blogs. Many blogs reflect deep antipathy to the mullah and conservative regime, and they were invaluable, along with updates on Twitter, in uncovering the truth about the flawed 2009 presidential election in Iran. In response, the Iranian government has hacked, blocked, and filtered many blogs and arrested a number of prominent bloggers.

What role do blogs play in struggles over democratic transformation? The status of the blog, whatever its origin or purpose as an expression individuality, is significant. As Oravec noted, "The weblog is a malleable and fluid medium through which individuals can develop an individualized voice that can reflect facets of their personal style and idiosyncratic intellectual approaches" (2002, 614). But do ordinary people in developing (or undeveloping) countries have time for idiosyncratic intellectuality and its expression? International surveys of bloggers find that they almost always come from middle and educated classes, so, as a rule, "peasants don't blog" (Perlmutter 2008). As Hurwitz argued, "The Internet's diffusion has increased the opportunities for political action among those who are already the most politically active and informed" (1999, 656). Does this cohort, however, constitute a potential source of oppositional leadership and the development of collective associations of democracy building? Blogs are for people with something to say to the world *and* the means to say it through a new medium. In countries like Kyrgyzstan, only a few thousand people make up such a "guild"—but that was enough for a revolution.

Background: "Whatsistan?"

Kyrgyzstan gained independence in 1991 as a result of the breakdown of the Warsaw Pact and collapse of the Soviet Union. Similar to the other Central and Eastern European countries and former Soviet republics, Kyrgyzstan declared democracy as its final goal in development by defining itself as "a sovereign, unitary, democratic republic constructed on the basis of a legal secular state."[5] Outcomes for these new nations, however, have been quite different. According to a *Nations in Transit* report about countries in transition (Freedom House 2008), only the three Baltic states among the fifteen former Soviet republics achieved that goal and joined the European Union. Others lag considerably behind, either recovering from having shaken off newer authoritarian regimes (the Ukraine and Georgia) or sliding deeper into autocracy (Azerbaijan, Russia), if not already there (Belarus, Uzbekistan, Turkmenistan).

To evaluate the state of freedom in these countries, Freedom House uses a typology ranging from a consolidated democracy to a consolidated authoritarian regime (see figure 1). Country assessments are based on the state of political rights and civil liberties during the year assessed. Most countries in transit fall into the big "partly free" zone that encompasses semi-consolidated democracies, hybrid regimes, and semi-consolidated autocracies, all of which combine the elements of both democratic and authoritarian forms of governance at varying degrees

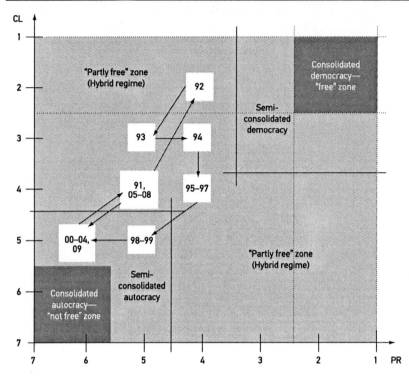

Independent since 1991, Kyrgyzstan started with the score of 5 for political rights and 4 for civil liberties. In 1992, it shot to 4 and 2, the closest to the "free zone" the country has ever reached. Starting from 1993, the movement reversed. In the following three years, Kyrgyzstan improved in political rights, but it worsened again in 1998–99 with rigged parliamentary and presidential elections. In 2000 the country was downgraded to 6 on political rights and 5 on civil liberties and remained there until 2005. After the 2005 uprising, Kyrgyzstan gained 1 point on each dimension and returned to the degree of political rights and civil liberties where it started in 1991. In 2009 the country moved deeper into the semi-consolidated autocracy zone again, similar to the 2000–04 period.

NOTE: CL = civil liberties; PR = political rights
SOURCE: Freedom House, 1992–2010, *Freedom in the World: The Annual Survey of Political Rights and Civil Liberties.* Graph design by Svetlana Kulikova.

and levels. The ideal movement is toward a consolidated democracy, which Linz and Stepan define as having attitudinal, behavioral, and constitutional aspects of governance and requiring at least three prerequisites: (1) "*stateness*," that is, a strong, confident government resting on the majority's support and rule of law; (2) a "*completed democratic transition*" that has produced fair and contested elections and efficient and separated executive, judicial, and legislative powers;

and (3) a "*culture of democratic governance*" where rulers observe the constitution and rights of individuals and minorities, respect the legislature, and tolerate criticism and pluralism of opinions (2001, 94–95).

Before the March 2005 revolution, Kyrgyzstan was still considered to be in transition, although the pattern of the previous five years showed the country sliding toward a consolidated authoritarian regime, the exact opposite of a consolidated democracy. In 2000, *Freedom in the World* categorized Kyrgyzstan in the "not free" zone (Freedom House 2001). This downgraded assessment was based on several important events and processes: (1) highly controversial 1999 parliamentary elections, in which numerous frauds were reported; (2) the presidential election of 2000, when Akayev ran for an unconstitutional third term after having the Constitutional Court invalidate his first term of 1990–95 because he had been appointed by the parliament and approved by a national referendum instead of elected by a popular vote; (3) a highly manipulated 2003 national referendum that approved constitutional amendments to provide immunity to the president and his family and a new parliamentary reform (Organization for Security and Cooperation in Europe 2003); (4) high rate of corruption at all levels of government described in the special Freedom House report "Countries at the Crossroads" (2004); and (5) the Akayevs' successful acquisition of most media assets between 1991 and 2004. By some estimates, the family owned or controlled up to 80 percent of all media outlets and production facilities such as printing houses and distribution services (Kulikova and Ibraeva 2002, 15–17).

In short, Kyrgyzstan's political leadership adopted the philosophy of *managed democracy*. Managed democracy can be described as a regime with formal democratic institutions such as regular contested elections and other forms of popular participation like referenda, diverse and private press, and developed civil liberties such as freedom to travel. At the same time, this type of regime is authoritarian in essence, as it allows limited autonomy for democratic institutions (Pribylovsky 2005). Akayev's government embraced the concept after it was revived by Russia with Putin's rise to power in the early 2000s. One of the main ideologists of the managed (later rebranded as "sovereign") democracy in Russia and chair of Effective Politics Foundation Gleb Pavlovsky, labeled the March 2005 events in Kyrgyzstan "a grave political catastrophe" that threatened the "entire architecture of security in the region" (Interfax 2005).

Kyrgyzstan in the latter years of Akayev's presidency typified the managed democracy model: elections were regular and contested but manipulated so skillfully that even outside observers could not confirm fraud; political parties existed but had little influence on the actual legislative process, because candidates preferred to run on an individual ticket rather than a party list; more than 500 media outlets were registered with the Ministry of Justice, but only about 150–180 operated at any given point; and there were more than three thousand registered NGOs, many of them quasi-NGOs created by pro-government circles to channel grant money. At the same time, citizens were free in their consciousness (religion), thinking, expression, and travel in and outside the country.

According to classical democratic theory, such an obvious discrepancy between abridged political rights and what is allowed to individual citizens in terms of civil liberties should inevitably result in a tension between the two (Dahl 1971). To establish balance the government can either loosen up political rights or put more controls on civil liberties. The Akayev government cherished Kyrgyzstan's image as the most democratic society in Central Asia and could not afford to curtail civil liberties, the only true and tangible features of democracy in the country. However, the worsening economic situation and Akayev's low popularity widened the gap. The disparity became even more pronounced when the government devised an elaborate scheme of maintaining power within the family based on the 2003 constitutional amendments that called for a new one-chamber parliament. The plan included:

1. creating a new broad-based party, Alga, Kyrgyzstan! (Go forward, Kyrgyzstan!) to provide the base for loyal nominees to the 2005 parliament;
2. electing a new one-chamber parliament in February 2005 that would include Alga, Kyrgyzstan! members and other family-trusted people, including the president's son, Aidar Akayev, and daughter and party leader, Bermet Akayeva;
3. collecting three hundred thousand citizens' signatures for "the people's legislative initiative," a national referendum to extend Akayev's term until at least 2008;
4. conducting the referendum, manipulating its results if necessary, and
5. prolonging the president's term by parliamentary validation of the referendum "decision."

The plan was followed through only to the second step. When Alga, Kyrgyzstan! was being formed, oppositional media reported on the aggressive methods of recruiting, including bribery and threats against potential constituents. At the second step, however, this became even more obvious, and numerous violations in the registration process for parliamentary candidates could not be ignored. Prior to the elections, citizens in the northern region of Naryn and southern regions of Jalal-Abad and Osh organized protests against the rejection of registration of candidates whom they wanted in the parliament. However, the government insisted that the rejections were justified.

After the first round of elections on February 27, 2005, opposition parties and election-monitoring organizations such as Interbilim and the Coalition of NGOs reported numerous violations and fraud. In several contested constituencies it was decided to conduct the repeated elections at the time of runoffs, March 13, 2005. When the repeated elections revealed the same fraud and pressure on voters, people in the most impoverished areas of the Osh region organized protests and demonstrations. Government attempts to suppress the protests inflamed them into popular uprisings and what is referred to as "exercising the people power"—ousting local state administrations and exercising direct decision making through people's councils while involving more citizens in the opposition movement.

By March 21 the opposition controlled the southern regions of Osh and Jalal-Abad and a substantial part of Naryn in the north, with some organized protests in other northern regions, excluding Bishkek (Kimmage 2005). Opposition demands soon included not only invalidation of the parliamentary elections but also Akayev's resignation. Organized groups started to move from Osh and Jalal-Abad to Bishkek, and on March 23 the capital saw its first large protest. The government used police forces against the demonstrators, and about five hundred participants were taken to jail, including activists of the Kel-Kel and Birge youth movements, journalists, and political leaders. The next day, a larger peaceful demonstration of about ten thousand people gathered in Bishkek's central square. The protest culminated in the government building takeover and Akayev fleeing to Moscow. He ultimately resigned on April 4, 2005, and a revolution leader, Kurmanbek Bakiyev, was elected the new president on July 10, 2005.

Analyzing the causes of Kyrgyzstan's revolution, Kimmage (2005) points to the following:"a widespread perception that the Akayev government was massively corrupt, that the distribution of whatever economic benefits had accrued to Kyrgyzstan in the post-Soviet period was grossly inequitable, that the Akayev-led ruling elite was actively manipulating the mechanisms of democracy in order to prolong its rule, and that the state-controlled media were distorting the real situation in the country." State-controlled media's distortion of events was a particularly important development, because a key feature of managed democracy is control over information. In Kyrgyzstan the president's family tightly controlled ownership of mainstream media and production facilities. The first breakthrough happened when the Media Support Center, sponsored by the U.S. and Norwegian governments, opened a printing house in November 2003 to print opposition newspapers. By March 2004 the center was printing more than ninety papers, about thirty of them in opposition to the government. Earlier such periodicals either did not exist or had been printed at the state printing house, Uchkun, which could and often did refuse services under various pretexts (for examples, see Kulikova and Ibraeva 2002). After independent newspapers acquired this new venue of production, their circulation shot up, as did their influence. In the aftermath, Akayev made a direct connection between the printing house and the coup. Western media also assessed the printing house and independent newspapers as instrumental for the revolution (Associated Press 2005; Spencer 2005).

Although newspapers presented a challenge for the family-run political regime, the Internet posed an even greater danger. Akayev, a trained scientist, always pointed out the importance of quality education and modern information technologies, which resulted in a mushrooming of universities and a quickly developing Internet. Indeed, Kyrgyzstan led other Central Asian republics in development of the Internet, which lagged tremendously behind the Eastern European countries (Dimitrova and Beilock 2005, 175–76). According to the UN International Telecommunications Union data, the number of users in the other four Central Asian republics in 2005 varied from a low of 0.3 percent of the population in Tajikistan to a high of 3.3 percent in Uzbekistan, while in Kyrgyzstan it was 10.53 percent.[6] Most users in Kyrgyzstan were state and private company employees or students with Internet access at work or school, which explains why the number of visits to popular Web sites dropped on weekends.

Despite official statements on the necessity to develop the Internet as a way to achieve openness and prosperity, the government attempted to control it, especially during the 2005 parliamentary elections. Understanding that Internet content cannot be restricted, the government tried to control access by blocking or hacking opposition sites, such as the newspapers *Moya Stolitsa-Novosti, Res Publica,* and the online newspaper Gazeta.kg, all hosted by AsiaInfo (Kyrgyzinfo 2005). The administrators of Gazeta.kg, in 2005 the second-most popular site in Kyrgyzstan after the commercial news agency Akipress (www.akipress.org), developed a creative way to solve that problem: starting the advocacy blog Akaevu.net (Introweb 2005).

Akaevu.net as an Advocacy Blog

Akaevu.net was created as a temporary stopgap to fill in for the blocked sites Gazeta.kg and Kyrgyz.us. Its name reflected the blog's advocacy character—"Akaevu net" in Russian means "Down with Akayev"—and explicitly stated its mission in a passionate and aggressive opening editorial by its author, Ulan Melisbek, a Kyrgyz citizen who was then residing in the United States:

> As a result of the foul order by the Akayev-Toigonbaev gang, the most popular sites of Kyrgyzstan, Gazeta.kg and Kyrgyz.us, have been blocked. Access is also blocked to the popular regional resource Centrasia.ru, which is also covering the events in our country. Our response to Chamberlains-Akayevs will be the creation of innumerable sites on various servers, so that they shake up the financial position of Toigonbaev [Akayev's son-in-law]. Hackers are people who value their time and skills, and sooner or later Toigonbaev will become weary of paying for blockage of numerous sites.

Akaevu.net was hosted in and administered from the United States. However, since content was mostly in Russian, it targeted users of the Russian segment of the Internet. The placement proved to be in the blog's favor for two reasons: (1) in terms of audiences, the Russian Internet is much smaller than that of the United States or European countries, which allowed the blog to quickly occupy the highest-ranking positions among political sites in Russian cyberspace; and (2) hosting in the United States significantly reduced opportunities to hack the blog from Kyrgyzstan.

Akaevu.net started to operate on March 23, just one day before the revolution. From the outset it positioned itself as "a trumpet of the Kyrgyz revolution," whose mission was to provide up-to-the-minute information on the current political situation.

CONTENT AND VISIBILITY

On its first day the blog carried three stories: advocacy materials generated by the bloggers and news on protests organized by Kyrgyzstanis in other countries. Starting from the day of the revolution, the blog reoriented itself to carrying stories from other mainstream media and Web sites, often just as they had been published or with a short comment by the bloggers. To understand the nature of the posts and readers' comments, a simple content analysis was done

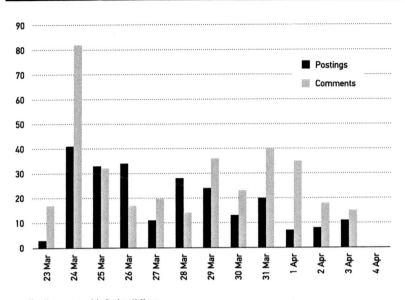

FIGURE 2. NUMBER OF POSTINGS AND COMMENTS ON AKAEVU.NET, MARCH 23–APRIL 4, 2005

SOURCE: Blog Akaevu.net, graph by Svetlana Kulikova.

for the period March 23 to April 4, 2005 (the date of the official announcement of Akayev's resignation). The number of stories in the period shows that they generally declined from the highest of forty-one on the day of the revolution, March 24, to zero on April 4, when the blog announced that its mission had been accomplished (see figure2).

As figure 2 illustrates, there is no direct correlation between the number of posts and the number of comments to the posts. In fact, on some dates the total number of comments was two to three times higher than the number of posts; the reverse was true on other dates. The number of comments per post varied from zero to twenty-two, with no distinguishable pattern. The only predictable indicator of the number of comments per post seems to be whether the post focused on Akayev or his family. Such posts generally provoked heated reader discussions. For example, the post of March 31, which provided Bermet Akayeva's interview to the Russian newspaper *Komsomolskaya Pravda* titled "I left Bishkek in what I was wearing—jeans and sweater," had the highest number of comments (twenty-two) for the study period. All of the comments were highly negative about Akayeva and her attempts to present her father and her family as victims. Another example was Askar Akayev's interview with Russian radio Ekho Moskvy on March 30, which provoked one neutral and eleven highly negative comments.

Most stories in the sample are materials from other media and Web sites. Some appeared within thirty minutes after being published by the original source, which suggests that several bloggers were monitoring the net at the same time and immediately posted what they could find. The bloggers must have had direct access to one of Akayev's longest-standing political opponents, Felix Kulov, who had been in jail before the revolution for five years. On March 24, when Kulov was released, Akaevu.net was the only site that carried an exclusive thirty-minute advance announcement about his first appearance on television. This resulted in a higher visibility of the site, as the announcement was picked up and carried further by other major domestic and Russian media and Web sites that cited Akaevu.net as a source.

Another factor that increased the blog's visibility on the net was an erroneous March 24 report on Akayev's resignation attributed to Euronews TV. That one-line announcement, which read, "Euronews has just reported that Akayev resigned," was picked up by so many sites and online media in Russia and near abroad (e.g., news sites Utro.ru, Polit.ru, Sistema.ru, Russian newspaper *Novye Izvestiya*, Ukrainian newspaper *Tribuna*) that Euronews had to officially retract the information. The story was repeated almost identically on April 2, however, when Akayev indeed resigned and Euronews reported on it. This interaction with the mainstream media is in line with the phenomenon that Fortunati (2005) calls "mediatization of the Internet and internetization of the media"—mutual sharing of information among traditional media and their online versions and other Internet sites, and popular blogs in particular.

The original source determined characterization of stories. When placing posts, bloggers categorized and labeled them in four groups:

1. *Foreign media* covering Kyrgyzstan (e.g., CNN, BBC, Reuters). Most stories in this category were in English or in both English and Russian.
2. *Kyrgyz media* covering local events and providing local experts' analysis. Posts in this category were drawn from both mainstream and oppositional newspapers, *Moya Stolitsa-Novosti* and *Res Publica* in particular, and major news agencies Akipress, Kabar, and Kyrgyzinfo.
3. *Russian media* carrying stories on the revolution and its implications for Russian politics and policies in the region. The spectrum of media in this category is impressive: news agencies ITAR-TASS, Interfax, RIA-Novosti and online Lenta.ru; newspapers *Kommersant, Novaya Gazeta, Komsomolskaya Pravda, Moskovsky Komsomolets, Rossiyskaya Gazeta, Vremya Novostei;* Moscow-based radio station Ekho Moskvy; and news and political analysis

sites such as Polit.ru, Utro.ru, Kreml.ru, Dni.ru, Ferghana.ru, Strana.ru, and Gazeta.ru.

4. *Proprietary materials*—posts generated by the advocacy group itself, mostly petitions or analysis and alternative interpretations of other media stories.

A clear evidence of the blog's anti-Akayev stance is that of all 143 posts in the sample mentioning Akayev and his family, almost half—60—are negative, 66 have a neutral tone, 8 are mixed, and only 9 are positive. Moreover, the 9 posts that tried to present Akayev positively were either interviews with him and his daughter, Bermet, or stories written by their political consultants and by Russian or Uzbek political analysts who claimed Akayev to be democratic. Bloggers provided many of these posts with a sarcastic subhead, such as "Akayev wants to return home clean and rosy" or "Akayev is searching for scapegoats to blame." Most such "positive" stories also provoked a high number of comments, between nine and twenty-two, of a highly negative tone, and sometimes direct threats.

On April 4 the only post was the message announcing that the blog's advocacy goals had been fulfilled:

> www.akaevu.net has accomplished its mission. Today we can say with certainty that there is no more place for Akayev in the political life of Kyrgyzstan. We are happy that we were able to deliver for you the needed, interesting and updated information at the most difficult times for all of us. We are glad that we made our contribution into the coverage of events in Kyrgyzstan during these days. We were carrying out our civic duty. Stay tuned! [Signed] Kyrgyz.us, Gazeta.kg, Kyrgyzcha. org—team of Akaevu.net.

On April 5 the blog resumed placement of posts, but their number never reached the same level. The total number of stories between April 6 and 15 was twenty-one, and on April 12–14 and April 16–24 no new posts were placed in the "news" section, although visitors still could participate in the interactive poll and leave comments on old posts. On April 25 the blog was redirected to Gazeta.kg, marking the end of the Akaevu.net era in the blogosphere.

DESIGN AND NAVIGATION

When the blog first appeared, it received praise for its design innovation, collection of photos and interactive polls. The site was indeed easy to navigate, well-organized, and provided numerous opportunities for feedback. The home page carried a selection of key stories starting March 23, 2005. The rest of the stories were catalogued by date and could be accessed through the archive calendar in the upper-right corner of the screen. The blog had a counter of visitors and counter of hits for each story. Some stories were complemented with downloadable video and audio materials.

These opportunities for feedback and involvement were available to the site visitors:

- *Comments on stories.* Each story had a window for comment with the default identification as "guest" and default subject matter as the story title. That made commenting easier for those who wanted to do so without disclosing their identity. This feature later sparked a debate on the blog about whether people should be allowed to comment without identification, because many commentators abused their anonymity and resorted to rough language and sometimes direct threats to authors and other commentators. However, no general agreement was reached on the identity issue among those who participated in this debate.
- *Comments on the blog.* A separate section for general comments on the entire blog, titled "Testimonials of our visitors" was listed in the left-bar menu of the home page.
- *Forum participation or observation.* The forum had three main sections: "News," "Politics," and "Looting," with several subcategories in each. The forum did not require those who wanted to leave comments to register or provide their identity. This option, again, resulted in numerous anonymous and "guest" comments, which sparked controversy among forum participants even though it made participation easier and safer.
- *Voting in the blog's public opinion poll.* There were four interactive polls: "Should Akayev be impeached or given the status of First President with all privileges?" "Who should be the next president of the Kyrgyz Republic?" "What should we do with the Akayevs?" and "Should force be used to calm down Osh and Jalal-Abad?" Visitors could vote and view the results, with statistics and graphs immediately displayed on the site. The second poll was the most popular, collecting almost 1,000 votes and more than 250 comments.
- *Subscription to the Listserv that provided alerts on newly released stories.* According to the blog, the Listserv had more than four thousand subscribers.
- *Viewing, contribution to, and evaluation of photographs of events.* Albums were labeled Bishkek, Osh, Looting, and Occasional. The gallery had a meter for the most frequently viewed photographs and a star rating system for their evaluation.

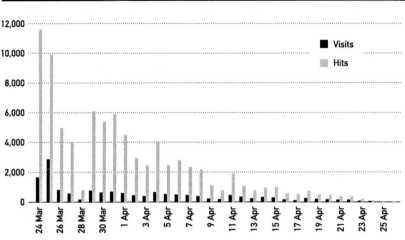

FIGURE 3. NUMBER OF VISITS AND HITS ON AKAEVU.NET, MARCH 24–APRIL 26, 2005

SOURCE: Russian Internet rating service http://top.mail.ru, graph by Svetlana Kulikova.

- *E-mail contact* for contribution of stories, photographs, comments, signing petitions, and providing suggestions. The e-mail address was indicated on the home page.
- *Searching additional information* from the recommended sites: *Moya Stolitsa-Novosti, Res Publica,* political party Ar-Namys, youth movement Kel-Kel, Birge's Citizen Campaign, Youth Movement for Democracy, and Kyrgyz.us.

AUDIENCES AND IMPACT

From the rating tables and visit dynamic analysis available through www.top.mail.ru when the blog was active, some patterns could be derived and accurate assumptions made about its audiences. First, figure 3 presents the dynamic of visits and hits for the life of the blog.

As the graph shows, the largest number of hits—more than 11,500—fell on the day of the revolution, when the blog also had the largest number of posts. During the revolution, cell phones in Kyrgyzstan experienced transmission problems, and many young people used the Internet to send messages to friends and to exchange news. They spontaneously formed three forums that posted the most current information: one on Diesel, a forum platform of the second-biggest Internet provider, Elcat; one on Akaevu.net; and one on the Birge youth movement site. Akaevu.net had a clear advantage of being hosted in the United States when the overload occurred and sites in Kyrgyzstan were inaccessible.

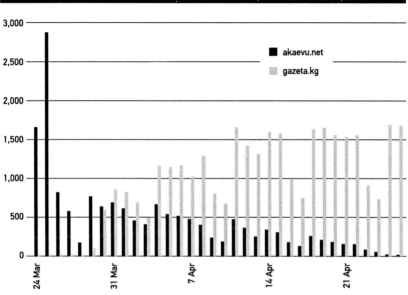

FIGURE 4. COMPARISON OF VISITS TO AKAEVU.NET AND GAZETA.KG, MARCH 24–APRIL 26, 2005

SOURCE: Russian Internet rating service http://top.mail.ru, graph by Svetlana Kulikova.

The high number of visits and hits on March 24–25 can be explained by several factors: (1) novelty of the blog and the news about its appearance on major Russian news sources; (2) a catchy Web address that created interest; (3) links from other major sites that picked up the Euronews-attributed erroneous story on Akayev's resignation and provided the link or the name of the blog as a reference; (4) interaction with the other two forums, Diesel and Birge; (5) absence of coverage of the night of looting, when the only way to find out what was going on was to follow one of the three forums. The extreme popularity of the blog and demand for its information propelled it to the thirty-first, eighteenth and fourth place among the most popular political blogs on the Russian Internet on the first day, first night (looting), and second day, respectively, of its existence.

However, after the first two days, interest in events in Kyrgyzstan decreased and a significant part of the audience, especially from Russia and other neighboring countries, stopped visiting the site. The number of visitors dropped continuously after April 5, when news of Akayev's resignation became universally known. Some visitors may have switched to Gazeta.kg and Kyrgyz.us after the April 4 "mission accomplished" announcement, which explains the slight increase of visits on Gazeta.kg during the week of April 4 and on April 25, when the remaining fifty faithful visitors on Akaevu.net were redirected to Gazeta.kg (figure4).

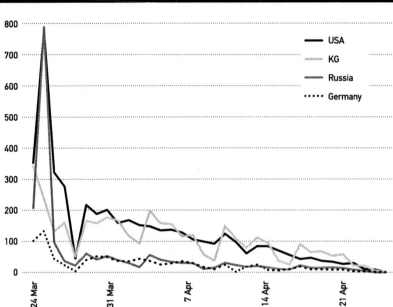

FIGURE 5. VISITS TO AKAEVU.NET BY COUNTRY, MARCH 24–APRIL 25, 2005

SOURCE: Russian Internet rating service http://top.mail.ru, graph by Svetlana Kulikova.

Figure 5 demonstrates the geographic dynamic of visits. Only four countries were selected, because they represent the highest concentrated numbers. The other twenty-eight countries on the list represented a handful, sometimes only one visitor; they include Great Britain, Kazakhstan, Turkey, China, Belgium, Uzbekistan, Tajikistan, Italy, Australia, Ukraine, Georgia, Iran, Belarus, South Korea, Norway, Spain, and Japan (see table 1 for data from March 25).

Both the array and the number of visitors suggest that the site was highly popular among Kyrgyzstanis abroad, especially students. This conclusion is also supported by the comments identification; whenever the comments were signed, the name indicated either a "student" or "graduate student."

The second-largest category consisted of media professionals, political scientists, and other experts who expected to find the most up-to-date information from the original source. The multiplication of the exclusive announcement on Kulov's television interview and the hoax about Akayev's resignation attributed to Euronews supports this idea. Finally, there were a number of comments on anti-Akayev stories in particular, suggesting that they were planted to disseminate disdainful comments on the revolution, looting, Kyrgyzstan without Akayev, and

TABLE 1. NUMBER OF VISITS ON AKAEVU.NET BY COUNTRY, MARCH 25, 2005		
Russia .788	South Korea 14	Belarus .14
Ukraine 127	Europe. 314	Lithuania. 12
Canada. 25	Turkey 43	Germany 133
Uzbekistan 20	France 21	Hungary. 31
Italy 14	Norway .15	Japan. .20
United States 777	Finland. 13	Georgia 14
Kazakhstan. 79	Kyrgyzstan 239	Others .20
Poland .22	Great Britain 41	
Latvia. .17	United Arab Emirates 20	

SOURCE: Russian Internet rating service http://top.mail.ru/.

other issues. The nature and style of these comments suggest that they were the work of a large group of people rather than one or two activists.

The bilingual setup of the blog also allows some inferences about the audiences. The total number of posts in English (52) and the total number of comments to them (27)—significantly lower than for the stories in Russian—suggests that the blog attracted mainly a Russian-speaking audience. This assumption is also supported by the fact that the highest number of hits for a story in English is 167, compared to 483 in the Russian-language sample, as well as by several irritated comments to English posts asking why they were in English; most of the comments to English posts were in Russian.

Along with the obvious measurements of visits, hits, and comments as well as geographic locations of the visitors, the blog's impact can be evaluated with these indicators:

- *Cross-referencing among blogs of a similar theme.* Several stories from Akaevu. net appeared at other blogs relating to Central Asia, such as Registan.net and the blog by Ben Paarman, Thinking-East, at http://www.thinking-east.net.
- *References and stories in the Internet-based media.* A Rambler.ru search on April 29, 2005, yielded eighteen stories in which Akaevu.net was presented as a new blog, "the trumpet of the Kyrgyz revolution," by online newspapers and news agencies in Russia and Ukraine.
- *Advertising and exchange of banners with other information resources.* During the process of this research, the Akaevu.net banner was spotted on eleven major Kyrgyz media and NGO sites.

- *Mentioning in traditional print media.* Tatiana Orlova (2005) of *Moya Stolitsa-Novosti* referred to Akaevu.net in the context of Internet discussions of the Kyrgyz revolution.
- *Regular contributors* such as Tengis Gudava, a Georgian-American political analyst specializing in the Caucasus and Central Asia.
- *Feedback* from first-time visitors praising the site for the amount and quality of information.
- *Hate mail and threats to the bloggers.* One message, allegedly from "Kyrgyzstanis abroad supporting Akayev," was placed in the comments section for three postings. It used obscene language and threats of "getting to" Ulan Melisbek, the blog creator, for "filtering information and suppressing freedom of expression" on the site.

Conclusion

At present, it is still difficult to assess whether any of the "stans" of the former Soviet Union will become a successful democracy in the foreseeable future. The 2005 Kyrgyz revolution raised hopes that democratic developments could be brought into the region, but after Uzbekistan president Islam Karimov used deadly force against demonstrators in Andijan in May 2005, such hopes were put to rest. In Kyrgyzstan, President Bakiyev, who came to power on the 2005 revolutionary wave, led the country into even a deeper economic crisis with higher levels of poverty and corruption and lower levels of political rights and civil liberties, according to such human rights reports as *Freedom in the World* (Freedom House 2010). On April 7, 2010, Bakiyev was ousted by a second wave of people power and fled into exile. Disillusioned with the presidential model of democracy that had turned into an untamed rule of the first family and clan, the citizens voted to establish a parliamentary republic in a June 2010 constitutional referendum. It is yet to be seen whether the parliamentary elections under the new structure of governance will indeed bring meaningful change and return Kyrgyzstan onto a path to democracy.

A more hopeful question is whether new technology might bring about *a more prosperous information environment* in countries like Kyrgyzstan. In this light, Akaevu.net demonstrated several features of illicit, informal, unofficial literature—that is, the samizdat, which sustained dissidence in a previous era. First, there was little original content; most content was generated by other sources, such as more traditional media, outside reports from NGOs, and expatriates. The material was republished on the blog, making it more accessible for users, who otherwise would have to visit twenty to thirty sources, many physically outside the nation, to collect all the information. In addition, the content circulated among a limited group of users who understood the goal and advocacy character of the data. In turn, the content recirculated on other sites, with multiple references and hyperlinks in other sources. Content was also highly partisan, burning with fierce opposition to the ruling regime. And in a parallel to the hunting down of samizdat creators in the Soviet Union, the Web site was constantly hacked, allegedly by government agents.

At this point the similarity ends between past and present. In technical terms, Internet interactivity and pervasiveness added two additional features to blogs that were not available for printed samizdat: physical security for bloggers, who cannot be reached (and are almost impossible to trace) by the government to be put in jail; and dialogue with users through the comments section that allows the bloggers to know exactly what their readers say about the content and the situation it covers. In political terms, as one of the authors of this chapter can attest from personal experience with the circulation of samizdat in Russia of the 1980s, the KGB was much more efficient and frightening in its anti-subversion efforts than the worst of the Akayev regime. Likewise, it was (and is) much easier to be an oppositional blogger in Kyrgyzstan than, say, in today's Iran or People's Republic of China.

From this analysis, then, it is possible to conclude that the blog Akaevu.net, although existing for only one month, contributed meaningfully to coverage of the Tulip Revolution on the Internet. Thus it fulfilled its mission as a temporary solution to the attempt by pro-government forces to quash the flow of information from opposition sites. Such a case suggests that managed democracy may be unable to control the only truly free medium—the Internet, at least with available means. If a weakest link exists in antidemocratic tightening of controls over the public sphere and freedom of speech, it is the Internet. And when that link breaks, the information flow is impossible to stop.

Depending on which course postrevolutionary governments decide to take, the role of such blogs may be that of the constructive criticism facilitating public debate or that of a lonely opposition voice cornered on the Internet for several thousand readers. The world does not yet have an example, to paraphrase Joe Trippi's (2004) famous metaphor, of a "revolution [that] will be blogged," but in revolutions to come, blogs will play some role, even if the role is restricted to the enrichment of an information-poor environment.

NOTES

An earlier version of this article appeared in February 2007 issue of *The International Communication Gazette* 69(1): 29–50.

1. President Karimov of Uzbekistan delivered on this threat when he ordered the use of firearms on a peaceful demonstration in Andijan in May 2005.
2. For example, during the day the national news agency Kabar reported or cited other sources that Akayev was in the country at his residence, then later allegedly went to Kazakhstan, then to Russia, and finally admitted not knowing the president's whereabouts.
3. The blog was available for viewing but inactive until April 2008 and currently is inaccessible. Cached April 5, 2005, issue can be found through the Internet archive Wayback Machine at Http://web.archive.org/web/20050405014137/http://akaevu.net.
4. For more on the Global Voices Project, see Http://globalvoicesonline.org.
5. Constitution of the Kyrgyz Republic (adopted in 1993, last amended in 2010), Art. 1(1).
6. All Central Asian countries, except Turkmenistan, significantly increased their Internet penetration rates by 2010, but Kyrgyzstan is still in the lead with 40 percent of the population having access, Kazakhstan at 34 percent (from 2.96 percent in 2005); Uzbekistan at 17 percent (from 3.3 percent in 2005); Tajikistan at 10 percent (from 0.3 percent in 2005); and Turkmenistan at 1.5 percent (from 1.0 percent in 2005). Key Internet usage and penetration statistics from ITU are available at Www.itu.int/ITU-D/icteye/Indicators/Indicators.aspx#.

REFERENCES

Associated Press. 2005. "US programs aided Kyrgyz opposition." April 1.

Barber, Benjamin R., Kevin Mattson, and John Peterson. 1997. *The state of "electronically enhanced democracy": A survey of the Internet.* New Brunswick, NJ: Walt Whitman Center of the Culture and Politics of Democracy.

British Broadcasting Corporation. 2005. "Protestors oust Kyrgyz government." March 24. Http://news.bbc.co.uk/1/hi/world/asia-pacific/4379441.stm.

Burkett, Elinor. 2005. "Democracy falls on barren ground." *New York Times*, March 29.

Chinese Human Rights Defenders. 2007. "China: Journey to the heart of Internet censorship." October. Http://chrdnet.org/2007/10/26/china-internet-censorship.

Christian Science Monitor. 2005. "Central Asia's Tulip Revolution," March 25, 8.

Dahl, Robert A. 1971. *Polyarchy: Participation and opposition.* New Haven, CT: Yale University.

Dimitrova, Daniela, and Richard Beilock. 2005. "Where freedom matters: Internet adoption among the former Socialist countries."n*Gazette: The International Journal for Communication Studies* 67(2): 173–87.

Fallows, Deborah. 2008. "Few in China complain about Internet controls." Pew Research. March 27. Http://pewresearch.org/pubs/776/china-internet.

Fortunati, Leopoldina. 2005. "Mediatization of the Net and internetization of the mass media." *Gazette: The International Journal for Communication Studies* 67 (1):27–44.

Freedom House. 2001–2010. *Freedom in the world: The annual survey of political rights and civil liberties.* New York: Rowman and Littlefield Publishers. Http://freedomhouse. org/template.cfm?page=15.

Freedom House. 2004. *Countries at the crossroads: A survey of democratic governance. Country report on Kyrgyzstan.* New York: Rowman and Littlefield Publishers. Http://freedomhouse. org/template.cfm?page=47&nit=336&year=2004.

Freedom House. 2004–2009. *Nations in Transit: Democratization in East Central Europe and Eurasia.* New York: Rowman and Littlefield Publishers. Http://freedomhouse.org/ template.cfm?page=17.

Herald Sun 2005. "People power strikes." March 26, 25.

Houston Chronicle. 2005."Bravo for Bishkek: More good news from an outpost of the former Soviet Union as another despot hits the road." 2005. March 26, 10.

Hurwitz, Roger. 1999. "Who needs politics? Who needs people? The ironies of democracy in cyberspace." *Contemporary Sociology* 28(6): 655–61.

Interfax. 2005. "Gleb Pavlovsky schitaet sobytiya v Kirgizii katastrofoi dlya kirgizsckogo obschestva" (Gleb Pavlovsky believes the events in Kyrgyzstan are a catastrophe for the Kyrgyz society), March 29, http://www.gazeta.kg/view.php?i=12388.

Introweb. 2005. "Kirgizskaya oppozitsiya otkryla sait Akaevu.net" (Kyrgyz opposition opened site Akaevu.net), March 24, http://introweb.ru/inews/news4270. php?day=24&mout=03&year=2005.

Kimmage, Daniel. 2005. "Kyrgyzstan: The failure of managed democracy." Radio Free Europe/Radio Liberty. April 12. Http://www.rferl.org/content/article/1058399.html.

Kulikova, Svetlana, and Gulnara Ibraeva. 2002. *Historical development and current situation of mass media in Kyrgyzstan.* Geneva: CIMERA. Http://www.cimera.ch/en/publications/ ind_publications.htm.

Kyrgyzinfo, 2005. "Obnaruzheno mestopolozhenie hakerov, atakovavshih Kyrgyzskie web-saity vo vremya parlamentskih vyborov" (The hackers who attacked the Kyrgyz Web sites during the parliamentary elections located), April 26, www.gazeta.kg/ print.php?i=12369.

Laughland, John. 2005. "The mythology of people power." *Guardian,* April 1, 22.

Leontiev, Mikhail. 2005. "Kirgizskiy zvonok dlya Rossii" (Kyrgyzstan rings the bell for Russia), *Komsomolskaya Pravda,* March 28, 8.

Linz, Juan J., and Alfred Stepan. 2001. "Toward consolidated democracies." In *The global divergence of democracies,* ed. L. Diamond and M. F. Plattner. Baltimore: Johns Hopkins University Press.

Open Initiative.2005. "Internet filtering in China in 2004–2005: A country study." April 14. Http://cryptome.org/cn/cn-filter.pdf.

Oravec, Jo Ann. 2002. "Bookmarking the world: Weblog applications in education." *Journal of Adolescent and Adult Literacy* 45 (7): 616–22.

Organization for Security and Cooperation in Europe. 2003. "Kyrgyz Republic: Constitutional referendum, 2 February." Political assessment report. Warsaw: Office for Democratic Institutions and Human Rights. Http://www.osce.org/documents/odihr/2003/03/1381_en.pdf.

Orlova, Tatiana. 2005. "Bratiya, my vas v obidu ne dadim" (Brothers, we will let no one hurt you), *Moya Stolitsa-Novosty,* April 13.

Panfilova, Viktoria, Ivan Sas, and Anatoliy Gordienko. 2005. "Revolyutsiya tolpy" (Revolution of the crowd), *Nezavisimaya Gazeta,* March 22, 4.

Perlmutter, David D. 2008. *Blogwars: The new political battleground.* New York: Oxford University Press.

Perlmutter, David D., and John M. Hamilton, eds. 2007. *From pigeons to news portals: Foreign reporting and the challenge of new technology.* Baton Rouge: Louisiana State University Press.

Pribylovsky, Vladimir. 2005. "Chto takoe 'upravlyaemaya demokratiya'" (What is "managed democracy"),. *Democracy under Siege,* March 17, http://osada.sova-center.ru/discussion/4E7884B/526B722.

Smith, Craig S. 2005. "Kyrgyzstan's shining hour ticks away and turns out to be a plain, old coup." *New York Times,* April 3, 6.

Spencer, Richard. 2005. "American helped plant tulip uprising." *Ottawa Citizen,* April 2, A14.

Sullivan, Elizabeth. 2005. "A scary democratic rebellion in Kyrgyzstan." [*Cleveland*] *Plain Dealer,* March 27, H3.

Trippi, Joe. 2004. *The revolution will not be televised: Democracy, the Internet and the overthrow of everything.* New York: Regan Books.

Yuferova, Yadviga. 2005. "Kirgizskiy perevorot" (The Kyrgyz coup), *Rossiyskaya Gazeta,* March 30, 2.

Zha, Wei, and David D. Perlmutter. 2008. "Blogs as stealth dissent? 'Eighteen touch dog newspaper' and the tactics, ambiguity and limits of Internet resistance in China." In *International Media Communication in a Global Age,* ed. by T. Johnston, W. Wanta, and G. Golan. New York: Routledge.

Through the Crystal Ball

Richard Shafer

T he end of the Cold War represented an apparent victory for by NATO, capitalism, free enterprise, and democracy over Marxism-Leninist communism, the Warsaw Pact, and the Russian-Soviet empire. With that watershed event, the five newly independent states of Central Asia emerged from the wreckage of the Soviet Union as potentially committed to free enterprise economic systems and democratic governance. At least that was the hope of Western democracies and human rights advocates. Unfortunately, we have documented a long list of obstacles to the development of functional and effective Central Asian press systems that could serve as public advocates and independent analysts while sufficiently profitable to maintain their economic and political autonomy from governments, political parties, and powerful policy shapers.

This book presents detailed evidence that the obstacles to the establishment and sustainability of free and effective press systems in Central Asia are complex, diverse, and profound. As our introductory chapter observes, "constitutional promises of democracy, including an independent press—a keystone for civil society—remain unfulfilled," and "nowhere is the stillborn nature of democracy building in Central Asia clearer than in the state of press constraints." It is a grim portrait that offers little reasonable grounds to expect substantive, meaningful improvements in the near future. Even the façade of autonomy within journalism distorts reality and provides grotesque caricatures of independence, professional ethics, and professional standards.

As a foundation to our examination of the state of the press in post-Soviet authoritarian Central Asia, Richard Shafer reviews the lasting impact of seven decades of an imposed Soviet journalism philosophy and practices that formed the foundation for the contemporary Central Asian journalism professional ideology. Adherence to Marxism-Leninism and its economic model of state ownership created imposing barriers to any significant movement toward establishing and sustaining independent mass media.

For the region's older journalists, their former commitment to furthering Marxism-Leninism has been replaced with an enforced dedication to newly engineered nationalist ideologies, he writes in "Soviet Foundations of the Post-Independence Press in Central Asia." To varying degrees, elements of the Soviet system remain, although now clothed in the garb of statehood, including a heavy emphasis on centralized controls, interpretation of news and information based on an established ideology, and the governments' operating assumption that journalists are primarily servants of each regime's agenda.

Although Shafer finds some positive aspects of the Soviet press system, particularly with regard to its successes at integrating diverse ethnic groups, and stimulating national development and modernization, it is obvious that the legacy of professional journalistic habits, conventions, ideology, and remnant socialist economics continue to obstruct the transfer of a functional form of Western models that are hallmarked by independent journalism and advocate for a different form of social responsibility to readers, viewers, and listeners.

Research Findings

Our authors' research illuminates how complex and interwoven factors such as economics, politics, nationalism, cultural and religious identity, foreign relations, energy and natural resources, and history contribute to shaping Central Asia's contemporarymass media development.

In "Oligarchs and Ownership: The Role of Financial-Industrial Groups in Controlling Kazakhstan's 'Independent' Media," Barbara Junisbai recasts Josef Stalin's comment that the press "is the sharpest and the strongest weapon of our party" in examining how corporate-government interests, rather than political parties, use media ownership as a potent weapon to gain and maintain wealth and power. Junisbai documents how financial-industrial groups tied to President Nursultan Nazarbaev gained control over much of the country's print and electronic media and used their holdings as weapons against rivals as they attempted to mold public opinion in their favor. Press coverage of politically sensitive issues and events appears driven in large part by conflict within Kazakhstan's elite competing for preferential access to lucrative political and economic goods.

Luca Anceschi's "Reinforcing Authoritarianism through Media Control: The Case of Post-Soviet Turkmenistan" spotlights a media system without any pretense of independence in a country where media policy has significantly contributed to the strengthening authoritarianism before and after the 2006 death of President-for-Life Saparmurat Niyazov. Anceschi's analysis traces the development of two main media policy prongs: repression and propaganda. The former helped maximize control over political life by silencing dissent and obliterating independent voices. The latter left an indelible mark on the political behavior of the population by promoting a window-dressing ideology designed to legitimize the regime.

The threat of terrorism, real or hyped, can shape media coverage, as Irina Wolf explains in "Hizb ut-Tahrir in Kyrgyzstan as Presented in *Vecherniy Bishkek:* A Radical Islamist Political Organization through the Eyes of Kyrgyz Journalists." For ordinary citizens, she writes, knowledge about radical clandestine organizations usually comes from the mass media rather than from direct interaction. Thus, it is enlightening to see how a major media player—the largest-circulation newspaper in Kyrgyzstan—covered Hizb ut-Tahrir and how that coverage changed between 2001, withf the World Trade Center terrorist attacks in the United States, and 2005, the year of Kyrgyzstan's Tulip Revolution. She also demonstrates the extent to which journalists' use of certain terms and information about Hizb ut-Tahrir reflected their personal or editorial attitudes, as well as state policies regarding control of such religious groups.

In "The Future of Internet Media in Uzbekistan: Transformation from State Censorship to Monitoring of Information Space since Independence," Zhanna Hördegen explains that although connectivity has improved and the regime has pursued infrastructure development, Internet wide-spread access and use remain underdeveloped due to state control. The Uzbekistan government maintains the most extensive and pervasive state-mandated filtering system in Central Asia, filtering and blocking Web sites of international and domestic human rights organizations and opposition-in-exile parties. Meanwhile, the country's regulatory framework no longer distinguishes between Internet and traditional print forms of content distribution, requiring Web sites to officially register as mass media. In so doing, that framework resembles the Soviet-era perspective that regarded every computer or word processor connected to a printer as a prospective printing press.

Peter Gross and Timothy Kenny turn to journalists themselves as sources to delve into the impact of self-censorship by outlining the disturbing practice of deliberately failing to report news for fear of retaliation from aggrieved parties or their agents. Their survey-based "Journalistic Self-Censorship and the Tajik Press in the Context of Central Asia" emphasizes how the government of President Emomali Rakhmonov has been loath to end censorship of print, broadcast, and Internet media, while politicians are more than happy to capitalize on traditions and extant cultures that quash initiative and foster self-censorship. Here the political system and a quasi-feudal financial system mesh with a culture that puts a premium on familial ties, friendships, and personal contacts to sustain self-censorship and let journalism appear to work, while simultaneously avoiding the pursuit of gathering potentially controversial news and information.

In "Loyalty in the New Authoritarian Model: Journalistic Rights and Duties in Central Asian Media Law," Olivia Allison evaluates how media statutes remain influenced by the juxtaposition of "rights" and "duties." The chapter addresses whether the principle of loyalty remains central in media law and its enforcement. Referring to Kazakhstan, Kyrgyzstan, Tajikistan, and Uzbekistan, she identifies the most important categories for assessing the role loyalty plays in government restrictions on press freedom, while faulting journalists for remaining uncommitted to, or equivocal about, professional ethics and a commitment to using the press to deter corrupt business practices.

Olivier Ferrando's "Ethnic Minorities and the Media in Central Asia" begins with an overview of Central Asia's multiethnic and multilingual mosaic and proceeds to the assumption that its public sphere is experiencing a fragmentation of media audiences along language lines. In this case study, minority media in the Ferghana Valley of Uzbekistan, Kyrgyzstan, and Tajikistan navigate between specific aims such as community-based expectations and universal appeals, market imperatives, and systems of patronage. They may serve the purpose of pursuing a survival strategy, Ferrando writes, through empowerment of targeted ethnic groups threatened by cultural domination by majority groups.

Beyond laws and governmental regulations, there is a human aspect of journalism when professionals seek to practice it in Central Asia. That is the theme of Eric Freedman's chapter, "Journalists at Risk: The Human Impact of Press Constraints," focusing on high-profile incidents of assassination, assault, disappearance, self-exile, and arrest. In addition, it raises the challenging question of how human rights advocates can keep the issue of press constraints fresh and prominent for multiple publics: ordinary citizens and decision makers inside and outside Central Asia, multinational agencies, and foreign NGOs involved in civil society development and democracy building.

Navbahor Imamova inquires into the role and impact of foreign broadcasting systems—Voice of America, British Broadcasting Service, and Radio Free Europe/Radio Liberty—in her chapter: "International Broadcasting to Uzbekistan: Does It Still Matter?" Using audience survey data, she reports that only a small percentage of the public listens to such services in Uzbek and found that listener access remains a problem because of jamming, lack of listeners' time, and radios not equipped to receive foreign broadcast signals. In addition to her discussion of broadcast content, Imamova observes that many listeners in the country now get access through the Internet rather than the radio, and she argues that international broadcasters help shape the news agenda for domestic media outlets.

In "Journalism Education and Professional Training in Kazakhstan: From the Soviet Era to Independence," Maureen Nemecek, Stan Ketterer, Galiya Ibrayeva, and Stanislav Los offer an overview of journalism education in the context of the history of the country's press. Not only does the legacy of Soviet journalism ideology and practice remain, but privatization, the marketplace, competition, and creation of new curricula challenge media educators striving to prepare a new generation of professionals that might succeed at furthering r a media system that best serves the public in an emerging democracy.

Gregory Pitts relies on interviews in "Professionalism among Journalists in Kyrgyzstan" to conclude that failing economic conditions have bisected the Kyrgyz population into a cadre of government supporters with access to wealth, and a much broader impoverished population. Meanwhile, a separate class—journalists—aspire to thrive personally and professionally in a field that offers only limited prospects. The study also shows how these journalists value "correct" professional practices. In "Internet Libel Law and Freedom of Expression in Tajikistan," Kristine M. Kohlmeier and Navruz Nekbakhtshoev describe the huge disparity between government claims concerning Internet development in that country and the actual availability of service and access. Their chapter also documents the draconian libel laws that force Tajik Internet contributors to work from outside the region for fear of punishment.

The potential impact of the Internet on political events is the topic of "Blogging Down the Dictator? The Kyrgyz Revolution and Samizdat Web Sites" by Svetlana V. Kulikova and David Perlmutter. They critique the Akaevu.net advocacy blog in the run-up to Kyrgyzstan's Tulip Revolution as an interim technique for delivering information to the public regarding the political situation in the country. In providing insight into the use of new technologies that can perhaps lessen press controls and governmental information management in Central Asia, they argue that such Third World blogs can be significant producers, collectors, distillers, distributors, and exhibitors of information and can serve as either constructive critics facilitating public debate, or as lonely opposition voices "cornered" on the Internet to communicate with a relatively small audience.

Conclusions

Examined collectively, these chapters explore a past and present that help us envision the future in Central Asia. The touchstones of that past and present are:

- strict governmental and extra-governmental restraints on the press regardless of the type of medium—print, broadcast, or Internet;
- inadequate professional training, leadership, resources, financial incentives, and ethical standards for journalists and would-be journalists;
- limitations on the ability of domestic and international press and human rights defenders to compel changes in policies and laws;
- absence of sufficient market resources to create and sustain independent news organizations; and
- a resulting, lack of credibility and trust in the press among the public.

Several important lessons that are directly relevant to the future of the press in Central Asia emerge from these studies. First, the virtually complete absence of independent media is a significant barrier to the establishment and maintenance of democratic institutions, transparency, human rights protection, and participatory governance. Press freedom is not an end to itself, but a cornerstone of civil society and the rule of law.

Many scholars also consider it essential to move postcommunist countries from authoritarian-socialist to democratic-capitalist economic systems. Their operative assumption has been that promotion of democracy, press freedom, free markets, and civil society helps establish the primary prerequisites for free and prosperous nations. Like other development models and ideologies fostered by Western governments over the past half century, the results have fallen short of expectations.

A second lesson is that foreign models informing press systems and journalism education and training cannot serve as templates for Central Asia. The structure of mass media organizations, their operations, and their regulation in any country—developed or lesser-developed, authoritarian or post-authoritarian—must reflect that country's traditions, cultural values, societal standards, and political and economic realities. They cannot simply be imported and transplanted. That said, there are widely accepted expectations for the press, especially in our increasingly globalized and information-driven world: a commitment to accuracy, fairness, balance, and ethical professional practices.

And a third lesson is that any substantial movement toward open, independent, and market-sustainable media systems in Central Asia will take many years, possibly decades, to come to fruition. That is largely due to the lingering legacy of Soviet press practices, the near-uninterrupted continuation of repressive press practices, the lack of any pre-Soviet ethos of or experience with independent media, pervasive public distrust of the press and lack of financial resources to build independent media. There is also a widespread belief among journalists that the press is obligated to further the development of national identity and a sense of statehood among the ethnically diverse populations of their young nations.

Even so, our authors find some reasons for optimism, including a commitment from some journalists to improving their ethics and professional skills and standards. There is also evidence of a willingness of foreign governments, multinational and nongovernmental organizations, and journalism educators and professionals, to provide training, advice, equipment, and collaborative opportunities for Central Asian journalism. Finally, technological advances, such as increased Internet and satellite access and availability may raise public demands for a more diverse universe of news, information, and opinion.

Contributors

Olivia Allison is a senior analyst at Stirling Assynt, a global intelligence firm, and specializes in international law, security, counterterrorism, political risk, media, and politics. A former research assistant at Rice University and the British American Security Information Council, she earned her master's degree at King's College, London. She is coauthor of *Understanding and Addressing Suicide Attacks.*

Luca Anceschi is lecturer in international relations at La Trobe University in Melbourne, Australia, and research associate at the university's Centre for Dialogue. He is a graduate of the University of Naples L'Orientale and La Trobe University. His principal areas of research are the politics and international relations of post-Soviet Central Asia. His recent publications include *Turkmenistan's Foreign Policy: Positive Neutrality and the Consolidation of the Turkmen Regime.*

Olivier Ferrando earned his doctorate at the Institute of Political Sciences "Sciences Po" in Paris where he teaches courses on international relations and the sociology of Central Asia and the Caucasus. He worked and lived three years in Central Asia, mostly in the Ferghana Valley. His research focuses on nationalism and ethnic minorities in Central Asia.

Eric Freedman is associate professor of journalism and associate dean of International Studies and Programs at Michigan State University, where he

is affiliated with the Center for European and Russian/Eurasian Studies, Asian Studies Center, and Muslim Studies Program. He was a Fulbright senior scholar at World Languages University in Tashkent, Uzbekistan. His research interests include journalism practices, press constraints, and journalism education in Central Asia. He also has directed study-abroad programs in Australia, the United Kingdom, and Ireland.

Peter Gross is director and professor at the University of Tennessee's School of Journalism and Electronic Media in Knoxville and has written widely on postcommunist media evolutions in Eastern Europe. He wishes to thank the International Research and Exchanges Board for the generous grant that made his research in Central Asia possible.

Zhanna Hördegen earned her doctorate in law at the University of Basel, Switzerland; a master's degree in international and European protection of human rights from the University of Utrecht, Netherlands; and a law degree from Kazakh State Law University. She has worked at the International Centre for Asset Recovery in Switzerland and the United Nations Development Fund for Women (UNIFEM) Regional Office for the Commonwealth of Independent States in Almaty.

Galiya Ibrayeva is professor and dean of the Faculty of Journalism at Kazakh National University, where she opened the Department of International Journalism. She is the author of *Regional Conflicts in Mass Media*.

Navbahor Imamova is senior editor with the Voice of America Uzbek Service in Washington, D.C., where she hosts radio and television programs and reports on U.S. policy about Central Asian countries. She is the primary producer and anchor of the weekly news show *Exploring America*. She began her career as a Uzbek state broadcaster, hosting youth programs, and later became a political reporter. She earned her bachelor's degree at Maharaja's College at the University of Mysore, India, and her master's degree in journalism at Ball State University.

Barbara Junisbai is a visiting assistant professor at Pitzer College and earned her doctorate at Indiana University. She is working on a book about political opposition movements in the Soviet successor states. Her research has been supported by the Kennan Institute, Fulbright-Hays Doctoral Dissertation Research Abroad program, Smith Richardson Foundation, U.S. State Department Title VIII

grant program, Political Science Department at Indiana University, and Indiana University's Russian and East European Institute.

Timothy Kenny is associate professor of journalism at the University of Connecticut. He is a former *USA Today* foreign editor, nonprofit foundation executive, and Fulbright scholar at the University of Bucharest. Kenny traveled widely in Central and Eastern Europe from 1989 to 1993, reporting from Russia and throughout the region, including Bosnia and Croatia, during the early stages of conflict in the 1990s. He worked in Kosovo from 2002 to 2003 and has reported from Kazakhstan, Kyrgyzstan Uzbekistan and Afghanistan. He was selected as an international scholar in journalism by the Open Society Institute for 2010–11, working with faculty at the American University of Central Asia in Bishkek.

Stan Ketterer is associate professor and director of graduate studies at the School of Journalism and Broadcasting at Oklahoma State University. Ketterer is also the writing coach at the *Oklahoman,* the state's largest newspaper. He teaches computer-assisted reporting and quantitative analysis.

Kristine Kohlmeier earned her law degree at Indiana University Maurer School of Law and her bachelor's degree in international studies and political science at the University of Nebraska. She was a Peace Corps volunteer teaching in Uzbekistan and has received fellowships and grants from the Social Science Research Council and International Research and Exchanges Board.

Svetlana V. Kulikova is assistant professor of international communication at the Department of Communication at Georgia State University. Prior to entering the doctoral program at Louisiana State University, she taught media and public relations courses at American University in Central Asia. She is coauthor of *The Historical Development and Current Situation of the Mass Media in Kyrgyzstan.*

Stanislav Los received a doctorate in political communication at al-Farabi Kazakh National University in 2010. Los is a mid-level manager at the KTK TV company in Kazakhstan. His dissertation examined Internet regulation in Kazakhstan.

Navruz Nekbakhtshoev is a doctoral student in political science at Indiana University and earned his master's degree in social and public policy at Duquesne University. He has been a researcher for the Organization for Security and Cooperation in Europe, a research assistant for the Social Science Research Council

Eurasia Project, an Aga Khan Foundation International Fellow, an Edmund S. Muskie Graduate Fellow, and has written for Radio Free Europe/Radio Liberty.

Maureen J. Nemecek is associate professor emerita of the School of Media and Strategic Communications and founding director of graduate programs in international studies at Oklahoma State University. She has worked with students and instructors at Kazakh National University through the U.S. Information Agency, Department of State, and Ministry of Education and Science programs since 1995. She consults from Annapolis, Maryland.

David D. Perlmutter is director of the School of Journalism and Mass Communication and a professor and Starch Faculty Fellow at the University of Iowa. He is the author or editor of seven books on political communication and persuasion, including *Blogwars: The New Political Battleground; Picturing China in the American Press: The Visual Portrayal of Sino-American Relations in Time Magazine, 1949–1973;* and *From Pigeons to News Portals: Foreign Reporting and the Challenge of New Technology.* He has written several dozen research articles for academic journals as well as more than two hundred essays for U.S. and international newspapers and magazines.

Gregory Pitts is chair of the Department of Communications at the University of North Alabama and former associate professor at Bradley University. He earned his doctorate in communications at the University of Tennessee–Knoxville and has been a Fulbright fellow at the University of Montenegro and University of Zambia. His research interests include international broadcasting and press freedom.

Richard Shafer is professor of journalism in the University of North Dakota Department of English, where he teaches graduate and undergraduate courses. His doctoral dissertation at the University of Missouri focused on the role of the press in social change and development. He was a newspaper journalist and taught journalism courses and seminars in more than twenty countries, under sponsorship of funding agencies such as the Fulbright program, the Soros Foundation, IREX, the International Center for Journalists, and the U.S. State Department.

Irina Wolf is a staff member of the Peace Research Group, Department of Psychology, at the University of Constance, Germany, where she is completing her

doctoral dissertation on coverage of Hizb ut-Tahrir in German, British, and Kyrgyz newspapers. She earned her bachelor's degree in international and comparative politics from the American University in Central Asia and her master's degree in political science from the OSCE Academy, Bishkek. Her research interests include constructive conflict coverage, conflict resolution, and media content analysis.